UP from the CELLAR

Lini de Vries

UP from the CELLAR

Vanilla Press
Minneapolis

All persons, places, and events in this book are real. The names of some persons, however, have been changed to protect their privacy.

Copyright © 1979 Lini de Vries

All rights reserved.
No part of this book may be reproduced or transmitted for any reason, by any means, without permission in writing from the publisher.

Minneapolis, MN: Vanilla Press

Library of Congress Catalog Card No.: 78-66429

Library of Congress Cataloging in Publication Data
de Vries, Lini.
   Up from the cellar.

   1. de Vries, Lini. 2. Mexico — Biography.
3. United States — Biography. I. Title.
CT558.D48A38   362.1′092′4 [B]   78-66429
ISBN 0-917266-17-X
ISBN 0-917266-18-8 pbk.

Printed in the United States of America

To Mary Lee and Toby Irene

The author gratefully acknowledges the invaluable assistance of many friends and associates in the preparation of this book. A special thanks goes to Alice Rossin and Harriet Kimbro.

The majority of the photos used herein were obtained from the author and the Schlesinger Library of Radcliffe College, and are reprinted with their express permission. For graciously facilitating photos obtained through the Schlesinger Library, we are indebted to Elizabeth Shenton. Photos of the Thompson and Caraza families are by Cliff Thompson, and are printed with express permission. Photos of the Papaloapan River and the dam at Temezcal are by Walter Reuter, and are printed with due permission. Photos of the Lincoln Battalion are courtesy of members of the Medical Unit of the Battalion, especially the author and Fredericka Martin, and are reprinted with their express permission. The author is deeply grateful to all who supplied photographs or assistance in obtaining them. Photo section compiled by Jean-Marie Fisher.

*He preaches well that lives well, . . .
that's all the divinity I understand.*

— Sancho Panza

UP from the CELLAR

New Jersey, 1907-1925
The Cellar 1

"Get to the cellar, you damned child," my mother yelled. Almost frozen with fright, I slowly walked down the stairs to the coal cellar and closed the door behind me. Quietly whimpering, I stared back at the beady black eyes of the rats. Fright left as hate filled me. How I hated my mother! She raved, she ranted, she hit, and worst of all she sent me to the coal cellar. I would sit and plan to run away from home. Often I did run away, but the police knew me by now and always brought the crying four-year-old child back to her mother. The police could not speak Dutch, and I could not speak English. At those times I hated the police and my mother.

When a few days passed and I was not put away in the dark, rat-filled coal cellar, I suspected that we were going to Dobbs Ferry to see the Man. Mother would tell Papa that we were going for the day to visit friends in the country and would be home late in the evening. I knew better. She dressed me pretty. She wanted me to look nice for the Man. She gave me candy as we rode in the streetcar. She told me if I said anything to my father about where we had been, she would lock me in the cellar for the whole night. To be sure, I never told Papa. Every time I was in the coal cellar, I was scared that I'd never see daylight again. I much preferred lies to rats.

I liked those trips to see the Man. When we got off the streetcar from Paterson, we took a ferry boat across a wide, wonderful river called the Hudson. From there we took a trolley to the 125th Street Railroad Station in New York City. Waiting for the train was fun, watching the strange people and not understanding a word they were saying. The train followed the wide, deep river, noisy with boats. I was secure and knew I would not be slapped.

But I did not like the Man. He patted me on the head as he gave me a candy bar, but I still didn't like him. It was always the same. "Play in the garden for awhile until we call you to come in," they said. I would peek in the house to see what they were doing, but all I saw was white sheet-covered furniture. I supposed they were upstairs in the bedroom. Wandering around the garden, I made the candy bar last until I would be called in for coffee, bread and cold meat. At last I was allowed in the house. The Man had a butcher shop, so the cold meat was always good, and I could eat all I wanted to, not like in our house. I did not know why, but Mother was almost like a mother to me after she had been alone with him awhile. She was nice to me; she even put her arm on my shoulders in a nice way. She was different when she was with him. I wondered why.

Going home again, she would remind me not to tell my father, and believe me, I never did.

My father was tall and dark. His hair was black, and his skin was blackened by coal dust. As long as I remember, he shoveled coal into furnaces which made gas.

As usual, he stood near our shiny black coal stove, which he polished daily. He sipped coffee he had made. We both listened to my mother as she said, "I don't trust these foreign American doctors. I am sure that if I go to Amsterdam, the doctors there can cure me of my deafness so that I can hear again."

I watched my mother read my father's lips as I heard him saying, "Why don't you go with Lientjie? We have enough money saved for the trip." Less and less I got sent to the coal cellar as more and more they talked of Holland.

In no time, it seemed, we were on the boat. If there were coal cellars on the boat, I did not see them. My mother sat on the deck and chatted. I was allowed to run around the boat. Quickly I made friends with the ship's cook and his workers. They gave me fruits and cakes that I had never seen or tasted before. Leaning against the ship's railing I would blissfully eat the cream-filled cakes and watch the huge ocean slip by. The ocean stretched big and wide around us, and even my hatred for my mother seemed to be slipping away. I felt safer here than at home. The foreigners on the boat, who spoke no Dutch, were nice to me, but I preferred being with the workers on the boat. They spoke my language. The boat became home to me.

I was sorry when we sighted land. Land and water seemed blended with one another as we sailed up a wide river, the Maas. The boat seemed topheavy as we towered over the landscape. At Rotterdam we got off the boat. Our next destination was Viana, Netherlands, where my grandparents lived. We took a train to a nearby station.

With my nose and eyes glued to the windows, we passed land and water bathed in a shimmering golden light. Wide-sailed boats skimmed the surfaces of canals. Children wearing wooden shoes pedalled their bicycles on the tops of the canals. Mother seemed happier than I had seen her in a long time. She seemed glad to be going to her home in Viana. If I were not being hit or slapped or shouted at, then she must be okay.

When we got off the train, Mother rented a horse and buggy to take us to Viana. Over the flat land we rode until we came to another wide river. This river was called the Lek and was part of the Rhine River, my mother told me. There was the queerest bridge over it that I had ever seen. It was made up of boats. The surface of the boats formed the road. But we were waiting, since part of the bridge had sailed out to let other boats go through. The missing part of the bridge sailed back into line, and we clippity-clopped over the bridge. In front of us loomed a high wall which completely encircled the small village.

Mother directed the driver of the horse and buggy where to take us. You could see she was excited. Here she had been born, and here she had played as a child. From Viana, it was a long way to Paterson, New Jersey.

Mother led me right to the kitchen. The many who sat there drinking coffee jumped up and embraced us both. As the greetings simmered down a bit, I began trying to separate my relatives. My grandfather wore a small black skullcap on his head. My grandmother was a little woman who danced around serving more and more coffee. I counted thirteen aunts and uncles and innumerable small cousins. The uncle who intrigued me most of all was Uncle Simon. He was six years old, and I was not quite five!

Uncle Simon asked me if I would like to see the pictures on the walls of the kitchen. He had seen me looking at them. I could not take my eyes off them. From the floor to halfway up the wall and all around the room were blue and white tiles with pictures. Shiny brass pots hung on the upper wall. Red and white checked curtains fluttered at the windows. My Uncle Simon could not read, but he knew the Bible stories the tiles told. He explained the stories they told from the Old Testament. We must have been chattering too loudly, since Uncle Simon was told to take me to play outside.

Uncle Simon took me to the tall watchtower that dominated the village. As we climbed up the round stairs, the arms of the windmills cast shadows through the occasional window. Finally we got to the top and were glad to sit down. We counted boats going up the Rhine to Germany and ships going down the Rhine to Amsterdam. Then we counted windmills. When we tired of this we went to the market and counted sheep — white sheep, black sheep, all kinds of animals that were being bought and sold. Many a good morning we spent in the watchtower above the moat that surrounded Viana.

My grandmother and grandfather (*oma* and *ompa* in Dutch) made a great fuss over me, and the more they showed affection and love for me the meaner my mother became. Once when I asked Mother, "Why does Ompa wear a black cap in the house?" I got my first slap in Holland. As she bickered more and more with her parents, the slaps increased. I learned that it was usually when we were alone. I tried to stay near the sheltering arms of my Oma. I also managed to be outside as much as possible with Uncle Simon. He told me that all his brothers and sisters wished my mother would leave, as she was "making trouble." They said she had always made trouble. They called her "mean Betty." I was afraid that before long we would be leaving Viana.

One night my mother took me to my grandparents' room. She flung me alongside my grandfather's bed. "Repeat the Lord's Prayer," she said. I was on my knees where she had flung me. I lifted my hands and began the Lord's Prayer.

Ompa gave a queer cry. His mouth twisted, and froth appeared. One hand fell over the side of the bed and weighed helplessly heavy on me. I began to weep with shock and fright.

My grandmother yelled at my mother, "Look what you have done with your gentile religion! Get out of this house with your child, and never come back again!"

Cowering, words flying around me, I understood nothing. My mother's hands pulled me up and out of the room. "We are going to Amsterdam. Help me pack," she ordered. I helped, but I didn't want to leave. I wished she would go, and let me stay in Viana with my grandparents. She was mad. I had never seen her quite so mad. I kept out of reach of her hands. When I asked permission to go to the kitchen for a glass of water, she said, "Go, and tell me what they are saying."

As I slowly sipped the water, the doctor came into the

kitchen with my grandmother. I heard him say, "Your husband has had a stroke. He may be crippled for life."

Uncle Simon whispered to me, "Ompa can't walk or talk, and it's your fault."

When I told my mother, she said, "Good, good, that's fine."

Less than a month after our arrival in Viana, we were on our way to Amsterdam.

Although Mother had brothers and sisters living in Amsterdam, we did not stay with any of them. We went to the house of Mevrow Workum, who seemed to be an old friend of Mother's. Her little son, who was my age, introduced me to the sights one could see from the third-story window. Funny, the things I recall that happened when I was all of five years old. From the back window we saw the canal, with its slowly moving barges. The back of the house was right on the canal. In front, first there was sidewalk, then road, and then a big canal. Again I was counting boats, but on these canals there were more barges than small boats.

At noon the doorbell would ring. I loved to pull the cord that opened the door three floors below. Up would come the bread man carrying hot rolls. They tasted so good!

At bedtime it was cozy to pull the door almost shut as I cuddled on a feather bed, under a feather spread, in a closet bed placed in the wall.

Mornings we walked along the canal to go to the doctor's office. She would not go alone since she could not read everyone's lips as well as she read mine. I watched her having test after test. Finally I had to tell her, "The doctor says there is no hope for you. You will never hear again. Nothing can be done." I felt sorry for her as I watched her reading my lips.

"You lie! The doctor lies!" she shouted. Her face got red with anger. Lord help me now! I thought. My feeling of pity passed quickly as I got ready to protect myself from her ill-humor.

Now Mother wanted to go back to America. I wished she would stay in Holland.

We crossed the Channel for England. There we took the English boat, the *St. Paul*, for the United States. I missed the Dutch boat. Here no one spoke Dutch, and no one slipped me good things to eat. We were ordered off the deck because of stormy weather. I still remember the huge waves that seemed to engulf the ship. It took us almost two weeks to get to America. Mother was in an awful mood. I almost began longing for the coal cellar, where at least her voice and her slaps couldn't follow me.

Up the Hudson River we sailed. My father was on the dock waiting for us. I was sorry to come back to the United States, but I was glad to see Father. Before the day was over I was back in the coal cellar with the beady, black eyes of the rats staring at me. It was as if I had never been away.

My father said I had to go to school. I was five years old. Mother could not make up her mind whether to send me to the private Dutch Reformed School for the good of my soul or to send me to the public school which was free. She decided it was a waste of money to send me to a religious school. Unless it was spent for her, Mother was very careful with the all-important dollar. I was delighted. I much preferred going to the public school where one had to learn English.

We lived on North Seventh Street and the school was on North Ninth Street. I soon found little companions to walk to school with me. I did not feel too alone, since the majority of my classmates were learning English just as I was. Not that Mother would let me speak English at home. She would say, *"Dit is een Hollands huishouden, and hier wort Hollands gesproken."* But when her back was turned my father and I spoke English. When she was out of the house, he and I worked on reading and writing lessons. My father spoke English but could barely read and write it.

Through our working together I learned more of my father. He told me that he had had twelve brothers and sisters, but that they had all died of tuberculosis. They had lived crowded together on a small freighter which had sailed up the Rhine from Overflakke. When he was nine years old he had come to America with his parents. He had never gone to school, not in Holland or in America.

Although my father could not read or write, he spoke like a book about his youth on the boat, and of Holland. He had never been back to Holland, and he longed to return. His father had not been able to get work other than as a janitor in a saloon. He died when I was two or three years old. I vaguely recalled him. My grandmother did housework for others. I saw her once in awhile when my father sneaked over to see her. My mother did not like my Grandmother Moerkerk.

Helping my father helped me in school. Unfortunately, I was skipped a grade. This meant I would finish school quicker, and I loved school. Teachers were kind. Work was fun, and it meant less time spent listening to my mother shout. Now I only spent Saturdays and Sundays in fear of being sent to the coal cellar, which still frightened me. Father would come down to the cellar to stoke the furnace or to pull some turnips out of the sand-filled boxes. He would come over to the coal bin and say, "Don't be afraid. The rats won't hurt you. Jump a bit; that will scare them." They filled me with loathing. At times I became hysterical and could not distinguish between the face of a rat and that of my mother.

We went less and less to Dobbs Ferry to see the Man as my mother's belly got bigger and bigger. My beatings and trips to the coal cellar increased. On December 26, 1913, my sister was born. Her name was to be Elizabeth like my mother's name.

She was a cute baby with her black, curly hair and her blue eyes. I wanted to touch her, to hold her. Every time I tried, my mother would shout, "Get away from her, you *lellabel*, you whore, you thing of sin!"

Mother was being nicer to Father. He, too, shut me out. If

he had had a tail, he would have wagged it, he was so grateful for her kindness to him. Now I could not trust him either. I wondered what a whore was. What were those things she called me?

Time went on, and when my sister was old enough to talk she soon learned the trick of how to get more candy from Mother. All she had to say was that I had hit her. She had the candy, the cookies, and I had the rats. At those times I hated her. When Mother went to the market, I liked the little sister with her black curls. But when Mother came home and accused me of mistreating little Betty, I hated them both. And Father no longer tried to protect me at all.

When I was about nine years old, we moved down the hill from Prospect Park to Paterson, New Jersey. Now I went to a public school in Paterson. No longer were all my companions Dutch, but Irish, Italian, Syrian, Armenian, Polish — all kinds of children whom I had never met before. In anger, in fights, each group was called its own special name — "Wops" for Italians, "Spics" for Mexicans and all Latins, "Hunkies" for Poles, and my group was called "Cheeseheads." I resented this name-calling, which reminded me of Mother and her name-calling.

Often when I came home from school, I found Mother entertaining a man in our home. More and more I disliked him. He was always trying to touch me. He was a missionary. He had a Bible school for children. Mother said that he had been a Jew and now was converted to Christianity. Both he and she decided that I needed special lessons in religion. When he left, I begged my mother not to send me to him. I promised to go to the Dutch Reformed Church three times every Sunday, if needed, if only she would not make me go with that man. I didn't know why I was afraid of him, but I was. He gave me the same feeling of loathing that the rats in the cellar gave me.

And in this house, which Mother owned, the coal cellar had more rats. We lived over a combination meat and grocery store on North Main Street. Foods were stored in the basement, and the rats were better fed.

Mother made me go to Bible school. Slowly I walked down the street to the address she had given me. It had been a store. Dark, shabby green curtains stretched in front of the store window. Why had he said, "I'll give special lessons to you"? If I did not go in, he would tell Mother. She would beat me or put me in the cellar, or both. I dreaded to enter the somber green cave and feel his fat, oily hands on me. Fearing my mother's hands more, I entered.

His fat, moist hands led me to the back room. He locked the door. He sat down and pulled me on his lap. With one arm embracing me, he began telling me about Christ and his teachings. I noticed that with his other hand he was opening his pants. He pulled out a long, hard thing that looked like the end of a broomstick. He began rubbing the thing on my privates. I struggled to get away. He held me tight. Numb with shock and horror, I pleaded with him to let me go. He kept on talking of brotherly love. The thing wet me. I broke away. He made me promise not to tell Mother and to come back for another lesson after school in two days. Filled with anger, shame and guilt, I walked home with wet pants.

I controlled my wish to scream and to weep all the way home, but once home I broke down. Mother demanded to know why I was crying after a Bible lesson. I spoke slowly so that she could read my lips as I told her the contents of the lesson. She frightened the tears away as she shouted, "You whore, you slut, your belly will swell! You led him on! I'll put you away!"

A few days later, I was swinging on the street gate when two well-dressed ladies asked me if Mrs. Moerkerk lived here. They looked surprised when I told them she was my mother. I escorted them upstairs and translated what they said into Dutch. "We are from the Florence Crittendon Home for Unwed Mothers," they said.

The ladies asked my mother what the complaint was. I translated my mother's answers into English. "My daughter is bad. She has been with a man. Her belly will swell. I want you to take her to your house for bad girls." My mother watched my lips as I told them what she had said. But she could not read lips in English.

I told them what the man had done to me. Feeling the guilt and shame again, I began crying. In between the sobs and tears I begged them to take me with them. I said, "I would rather live in a home for bad girls with nice ladies like you than live with my mother."

The ladies said, "Tell your mother that the experience has been a shocking one for you. Tell her that our home is for much older girls, unwed mothers, not for nine-year-olds." I didn't understand very well as I translated, but Mother did. She became furious. She showed them the door and asked them to leave.

For weeks I felt my belly to see if it were swelling. Why it should swell I didn't know. Swelling of stomach and badness were the same, my mother told me. I did not feel like a bad girl; my belly did not swell. This proved to me that I was not bad.

But she never sent me to Bible school again. The man never again came for a cup of coffee.

June 1917 — I was almost twelve years old. I graduated from grammar school. We were again living in Prospect Park with all the Hollanders. We all had to have white dresses for the graduation ceremony. I recall Mother making me a white dress and trimming it with the fringe from old curtains. I just hoped no one would notice the curtain fringe. Certainly I was not graceful; I was fat and dumpy, as wide as I was tall. My hair hung in tight ringlets, since I had wound them in rags and left them that way all night and day. I was sorry to finish school. Now I wanted to go to high school.

Finally I realized that it was no use to coax her. She would not let me go to high school. She said, "I have fed you long enough. You don't need book learning. You will go out and work." She had to lie about my age to get my working papers, but she got them. She even got me my first job in a silk mill. The mill was on the same street where we lived, a few blocks down.

Very early in life I had learned not to expose my fright to anyone. It was useless. Yet I really was scared that first day in the mill. Machines roared. Belts whirled. Workers shouted at one another over the noise of the clacking looms. The spools that I carried got heavier and heavier as the day dragged on.

The winder kept the skeins twirling. When a thread broke she would run to tie it. The warpers demanded filled bobbins to make the warp. I was the link between them, the bobbin girl. Bobbins bright with silk thread to the warpers and empty bobbins back to the winders. All day long, ten hours a day, six days a week, I carried bobbins, bobbins, bobbins. I could not see why I had to give every cent I earned to my mother. It was *my* back that felt as if it were breaking. I demanded part of my earnings. I got blows, but also the promise of five cents on every dollar I earned. This gave me thirty-five cents a week, which was all mine.

However, life was easier. I was home only evenings and Sundays. I much preferred the good-natured shouting and teasing of my co-workers to the angry yells of Mother. Such a mixed-up child I was. I wanted to go to high school. I could not give up the dream. I was ashamed of being a "mill dolly" and despised myself for being ashamed. I did not know how, but I knew that someday I would get back to school again.

Gradually I was accepted into the workers' ranks. I heard "union talk." The union delegates had been trying to get the boss to give us a shorter day without a cut in wages. They had no luck; instead, they got insults. Now they were talking "strike, strike!"

The words "strike" and "union" were not new to me. My father approved of them. Whenever "Big Bill" Haywood came, my father took me along to listen to the big union meetings in Haledon. Since he was not allowed to have meetings in Paterson, Haywood spoke in a suburb called Haledon, which was right near Prospect Park where we lived. I did not need a Big Bill Haywood or my father to explain unions to me now. By way of my aching back, I was learning the value of unions.

One of the few times I heard my father talk back to my mother was when she said, "Lini will not strike; she will work. Socialists, that's what the workers are and their unions."

My father replied, "She will not scab; she will strike like the others. She will not be a strikebreaker."

I did not care what either one said. I knew I wanted an eight-hour day instead of a ten-hour day. Unions, socialists, scabs, strikers were only words which did not make my back ache less. When the workers walked out, I walked right out with them. Pigtails flying in the breeze, I picketed. We picketed the mill for days.

Mother came and stood near the line shouting, "Dirty socialists!" She encouraged the scabs trying to get by us. I was ashamed for her.

At home in the evening, the yelling went on, "A war is being fought! Strikers are traitors! They are dangerous!" Suddenly she was a patriotic American. I did not understand her, but my back knew the difference between eight and ten hours a day.

WE WON THE STRIKE!

Having been part of a strike, I found I had strength to refuse to go to the rat-filled coal cellar. I was as big as my mother, and she could not make me go. I had always fought back at her with words, with silence or by running away. Now I was openly defying her. I refused to be sent to the coal cellar. My biggest problem now was to duck as the flying frying pan or dirty dishrag was hurled at me. But her dislike for me, the words she shouted at me bothered me. There were times when I wished I would just die. I wanted — what did I want? Love, understanding, a high school education — what did I want? Then I would say to myself, "DON'T LET HER DESTROY

YOU. DON'T LET *ANYTHING* DESTROY YOU!" Neither curses, nor shouts, nor backbreaking days could destroy me as the words surged up in me, "I WON'T BE DESTROYED. I WILL LIVE. I WILL GROW, AND I WILL LEARN."

The Dutch Reformed Church, my mother's church, wore me down. I say "Mother's church," since my father refused to go to any church. He said, "Church is for hypocrites."

In the church I listened: "Dancing is a sin. Playing cards is a sin. Movies are sinful." You shall not do this or that. It seemed that living itself was sinful. Church in the morning, church in the afternoon, and church at night — one chewed strong peppermint candies to keep awake. The long pole tapped one on the shoulders for the collection and tapped harder if one dozed.

All one heard in heavy, drowsy Dutch on Sunday was hate and more hate — wars in the past and wars in the present. What sort of God was this who hated all who were not Dutch Reformed? How could there be room in hell for all who were not God-fearing Dutch Reformed?

One Sunday after church services, I sat on the back step singing. I don't remember whether it was "Shiek of Araby" or "Margie." Our upstairs tenant came rushing down and into our kitchen. She told Mother, "She is singing sacrilegious songs on Sunday."

Mother came out yelling, "You will burn in hell! You have no respect for the Holy Day, you whore!"

When I could stand no more, I shouted back, "You are cruel! Your God is cruel! Your religion is hate and more hate! I will never go to the Dutch Reformed Church again. I'll look for a church that lets me sing!" I continued, "If I can earn the food that I eat, then I can sing when and where I want to." With Mother slapping my face, I tried to keep on singing. I was too mad to cry. I never entered the Dutch Reformed Church again.

One of the winders had told me of the First Baptist Church Junior Choir. Choir practice was held on Friday nights. Defiantly I told my mother I was going to try to join the choir. I hoped I would be accepted even though I could not read a note of music. The choirmaster tested my voice, and I was accepted, since I had a good contralto voice. I picked up a song quickly by listening. Despite what mother said, I kept on going to choir practice and sang every Sunday morning and evening with the group.

When I watched the immersions from the choir stall, I thought it was silly to get all wet. What on earth did a ducking in water have to do with God? I did not ask, and I did not say anything of my thoughts. I was too happy to be singing.

When Billy Sunday, the Sawdust Trail religious leader, was in town, I would frequently go up to the tabernacle where he preached, after the Sunday services in the First Baptist Church. Here I could sing rousing hymns all over again. It was fascinating to watch and yet embarrassing as I watched people go into a frenzy and "hit the sawdust trail" to be "saved." He talked of the future in the sky; I was more interested in the present future.

My choir companions had told me that the First Baptist Church had a branch Sunday school called the Bethany Baptist Sunday School. It was in the vicinity where I lived. Many of the mill dollies went there. The main thing that intrigued me was that they said it had a good library. I enrolled in the Bethany Baptist Sunday School and attended their services every Sunday afternoon. Again I was in church three times a day on Sunday, but with such a difference. I sang my way through the Holy Day.

Just as soon as I could after services, I dashed into the library room. There were so many books to read — Elsie Dinsmore, Horatio Alger, Louisa Alcott, Zane Grey, and many more. After I had read all the books in their small library, the Sunday school librarian suggested that I begin going to the public library in Paterson.

Since the public library was open only during the hours I worked in the mill, I had to figure out a way to go without my mother or the boss knowing it. Early I had learned to lie in order to live. I told the boss that I had a dental appointment every Wednesday, and I told my mother that our salary had been cut. The take-home pay would be less — something about taxes to win the war. Since the "War against the Huns" was to her way of thinking a Holy War, she did not question me at all.

Without guidance I took books and more books. I was allowed four at a time. I took four. I read every chance I got, far into the night, at times with a flashlight. All lights had to be out at nine to save money on the electric bill. I read Zola, Balzac, Victor Hugo — these are the authors I recall. My sister and I shared the same bed. She was five years old. She would tell Mother that I read at night. I denied it. Lies, lies — one should not lie, the church said. My mother said the same, but one had to lie to live. Often I wondered why I wanted to live with my miserable home life, but gropingly I knew I had to live, to feel, to see, to hear, to learn. More than anything, I knew I had to survive these years for the unknown future. More than anything, I read as a defense against my mother's trying to destroy me. Reading was a way to live and a defense against an emptiness, a lack of love.

An exciting idea was being discussed after Sunday school sessions. Eva Venema, one of the girls in our class, had heard about Girl Scouts. We knew about Boy Scouts, since our Sunday school had a troop, but there was no Girl Scouts in Paterson. Eva offered to go to New York City to Girl Scout headquarters to inquire about organizing a troop. Since she was the only one of us who did not work in the mills, she could go. Although her parents were Dutch, they seemed less strict than ours.

With the information Eva brought back from headquarters, we organized Girl Scout Troop #1 of the Bethany Baptist Sunday School. We elected Eva Captain. I was fourteen years old when I was made First Lieutenant. Now I was working for merit badges. I wanted to be a Golden Eaglet. It was a struggle to pay for the merit badge after I had earned it. It was more of a struggle to pay for my uniform and other scouting equipment. I saved my precious allowance for scouting.

Chills ran up and down my spine as I pledged allegiance to the flag at troop meetings. I studied the scout laws. I tried to live by them. Scouting was the most important thing that had happened to me. I began feeling that maybe I was an American after all and not one of those "damned foreigners" as we were called in the mills. Saturday afternoons and holidays we went to swimming holes. Head high with joy, I sang as we marched. Our uniforms made us look like any other American girls. Life was better, more interesting, but it was worse at home.

Mother forbade me to be a girl scout. She said it would lead me astray. I kept on going and paid no attention to her. Tuesday nights were the worst of all. Our troop met that night. The boy scouts met on Thursday nights, but on Tuesday evenings there were always a few boy scouts waiting outside of Sunday school where we met. Each would pick a girl scout to walk home. We had real competition among ourselves as to by whom and how many times we were walked home. I kept track with pencil marks behind the door on the bedroom wall. The scout who walked me home was Jan van der Schaik.

My mother would be waiting on the front porch in the dark. As she saw us approaching under the street lights on the corner of North Eighth Street, her shouts began, "Is your belly full? I'll not help you when it gets fatter, you whore!"

Since Jan understood Dutch, I was ashamed, but he said, "Don't worry, we all know that your mother is crazy." And if Jan had tried to kiss me I would have run. I was afraid of physical contact with boys — and with almost anyone. I had read the word "love." I did not believe in it. The church said, "Love thy parents; love thy neighbors." Love? I had to see it.

Yet about this time, when I was sure that love and affection were mythical words, I met a soft, gentle girl in our troop. She was quiet, reserved; our friendship developed gradually. She invited me to come to her home some Saturday after work.

I called on her the next Saturday afternoon. There were two teenaged boys and two teenaged girls. Their mother was Dutch, and their father was German. They spoke only English in their home. This was the first time I had been in a home where only English was spoken. They did not shout at one another. They seemed to like one another. Not that they kissed or embraced, but their voices were filled with teasing warmth and affection when they spoke. How could this be? I was suspicious.

Their life together drew me like a magnet. Every chance I got I climbed the stairs to the fifth floor tenement in which they lived. I never spoke to them about my home life, of the quarreling, of the shouts, of the blows. I was ashamed of my home life and more ashamed that I was ashamed of my parents. One was supposed to love one's parents. These four children did; I didn't. I hated my mother and had contempt for my father. What was wrong with me?

Through the Bauer family I learned that there were families who loved and respected one another. More and more I was accepted by them as part of the family unit as they went on Sunday trips to Bear Mountain, Walden Lake, and other places. There were six of them who had to fit in the old open Ford. Somehow they found room for the seventh — me. Through Girl Scout Troop #1 and the Bauer family, I got my first glimmer that life did not have to be misery and hate, but could be love and fun.

Why was I ashamed of being a mill worker? Not only I, but all of us lied when anyone asked us what we did. We would be surest to lie if a boy asked us. First I used to say, "I go to Central High School," but I soon stopped that. I got caught once too often in that lie. I had no idea of the high school subjects when they pumped me. I changed my answer to, "I am an office worker."

Stubbornly I continued begging my mother to let me quit the factories and to go to high school. Her answer had very little variation, "A whore needs no high school education." She went on, "You keep on working, and bring home money for the food you eat." Her words and the scorn the high school kids had for us began searing me. The high school kids called us "Cheeseheads," "Spics," "Wops," "Hunkies," "Squareheads," as we piled out of the factory doors.

True, we were first-generation Americans. Our parents did not speak English. In grammar school I learned that I was an American. Or was this not true? When I was at scout meetings, I wanted to be, and felt I was, an American. But when I was with the high school boys and girls at choir practice, I felt like a foreigner. If one went to high school, if one's parents spoke English, then one was an American. Therefore, since none of that was true for me, I was a foreigner.

What a miserable way to grow up — hating, feeling rebellious, frustrated — and why? What I did know was that I would not stand being snubbed by the high school crowd. I figured the only way to prevent that was to get out of the mills. The first step was to learn new skills within the mills. Earning more money would please Mother. If I could climb up within the mills, maybe I could climb right out of them. I didn't know how, but I was determined that I would.

I watched the hands of the winder as she tied the knots when the threads broke. I watched her shake out the skeins as she put them on the reels. I watched the quill winder as she helped the silk run from the bobbin to the small, pointed quill that the weavers used. One of the girls taught me the secret of tying the square knot. Another one showed me how to shake out the smelly silk skein that came from Japan. The smell of raw silk was never like cherry blossoms. I was learning.

Quill winding seemed the easiest to learn. It was less backbreaking. I quit my job as bobbin girl. I was scared. I had to bring home money to Mother. Five days I found jobs as a quill winder. Five times I was fired for being inept, but the sixth job I kept. I was a quill winder. More money for Mother and more for me on the basis of five cents on every dollar. This meant more money for scouting.

In this mill it was easy to see why I had not been fired. It was a cotton mill. The threads were humid and sticky. They smelled worse than raw silk. Cotton dust was all around us. When I blew my nose, gobs of black-tinged mucus came out.

Soon I discovered that the girl at the next machine was Dutch too. She lived near me, and we walked back and forth to work together. The factory, called Cedar Knolls, was in Haledon, New Jersey, the suburb next to Prospect Park where we lived. It was too far to go home, so we took our lunch. My work companion's name was Carrie Niekerk. Every member of her family was working to get enough money to return to Holland. They came from the same island as my father did.

Carrie and I chatted like any teenagers the world over, I suppose, but mainly we talked of our co-workers. We had never met so many different kinds of people. There were Syrians, Armenians, Italians, Poles, Irish — all sorts of nationalities and mostly Catholic. We had never known Catholics. My mother had forbade me to associate with other than Dutch people, and even then they had to be of the Dutch Reformed Church.

But Mother's fussing became increasingly unimportant. I liked most of the Dutch I knew less than my co-workers. Mother said they were foreigners. What was I but a foreigner also? They were not afraid of emotions. They expressed their likes and dislikes in broken English, but they expressed themselves. They were kind and good. I felt at home with them.

I could now quill wind in my sleep. More and more I tried to learn winding. I knew winding cotton skeins was easier than silk, but I was learning winding. When I felt I had learned enough to try to find a job as a winder, I quit. I hoped that I would never see a cotton mill again. Silk had a funny smell, but at least it did not fill my lungs with dust. This time I was fired only three times, and the fourth time I had a job as a silk winder.

Skeins of brightly colored silk glowed against the bodies of young girls like myself as we shook them into proper shapes to place on the reels. The dark, gloomy sweatshop needed this color. The mill was on lower Market Street in Paterson. It was across the street from the car barns and close to the Passaic Falls where the river dropped. We worked between the roar of the falls, the whir of the streetcar wheels and the clanking of the looms.

I had learned in grammar school that Alexander Hamilton had pointed out the value of the Passaic Falls as a source for water power. With the boldness of the water rats that dashed around our feet, I wished he had never discovered the falls. We were low on the river bank; water seeped in, and rats ran in. Our feet got wet. Our eyes hurt from the poor light. Many wished they could quit, but jobs were getting more scarce. The war was over. We stopped asking for planks to stand on and guards around the belts of the machines. A depression was beginning, my co-workers said.

Who could complain? Most of the workers had whole families to support. I had only a mother I was afraid of. Mills were laying off workers, and the union was helpless.

I will never forget this rat-infested, wet, hole-in-the-wall sweatshop. I wish I could. When I recall this mill, I hear shrieks, I smell death, and I see calla lillies. I have forgotten her name but not her pale face.

Her hair was long and red-gold, like mine. It hung in two pigtails that day. She was my working partner. We worked back to back at the winding machines. We talked and sang over the noise as we worked. We even enjoyed a bit of fun to see who could slide down the wet floor the fastest when a thread broke. We were kids.

Between songs, I heard a shriek. As I turned, she was being pulled up from the floor by her hair, caught in the belt of the

the machine. She was being scalped before my eyes. Screaming, I ran to turn off the power.

They cut her hair from the machine. They laid her down and said she was dead. Could that have killed her? It did.

Numbly I walked out of the factory, up Market, down Main, down North Main, up Haledon Avenue to my home. I told my mother what had happened. I said, "You go for my pay. I won't go back no matter what you say or do to me."

At the funeral three days later, from a bed of calla lilies her pale face reproached me for having been afraid to fight the boss for a protector on the machine belt. I had said, "There is no use now. Too many people want our jobs." Guilt lay heavy on me. I had been afraid of my mother. My friend lay among the flowers. Now her coffin was closed, and dirt would be thrown on it. I felt it was my fault that she was being buried. I vowed then never to be afraid again to ask for what was just and right.

Finally I found another job. This one was in Johnson's Ribbon Mill, which perched on the banks of the Passaic River about two miles down from the falls. From where I worked on the second floor, I could see the dye-streaked, refuse-filled river. At the falls it was still clean, but here it was plain dirty. I dreamed of how the river must have looked when the Indians lived on its banks.

When I applied, my first thought was that I would like to work here. Ribbons gleamed like jewels. The sun's rays played mischievously with their colors. We had clean machines, clean restrooms and a clean place to eat. There was a nurse and an infirmary. I felt less ashamed of being a mill dolly. I just hoped that the boss would be different also.

The mill and its machines were kept clean to protect the ribbons. We were kept clean for the same reason. I wanted warmth and humanness. I got cleanliness and efficiency experts. The efficiency expert hovered over us. He timed us as we tied knots in the silk thread. My fingers got clumsy as he timed me tying the knot. He timed us when we went to the toilet. It was annoying to sit on the toilet knowing that he was timing us. But he took his newspaper when he went to the toilet. We timed him. His plumbing system must have been different from that of the workers.

In a starched white uniform, a perky cap sitting on her head, the nurse would rustle by us. I admired her, this person from another world. I was warned by my co-workers not to trust her. We learned not to report sick except for dire need. In her best high school English she pumped us as to which workers were complaining. We said "goils," "youse," and "ain't," but we were not stupid. The girl in white thought she could make informers out of us for an aspirin or two. To the contrary, we went in with faked, planned headaches on occasion to find out through her questioning what the boss wanted to know. I no longer admired her. I, too, said, "Cheese it, here comes the stool pigeon!"

In this clean factory we wanted to like our work, to be joyful in it. But the efficiency expert and the stool-pigeon nurse made us feel like getting even with them. We stole little — only a skein of silk here and there for embroidery. Clean factories, dirty mills, protection from machines or no protection, what was the difference? None at all when one could not be prideful of oneself and one's craft. The preacher, Billy Sunday, said that we had souls; but the bosses denied this with their actions. Yet when Depression layoffs increased, I was sorry to be one of the twenty workers laid off. I was sorry to leave this bright, clean factory. I hated to go jobhunting again. I had to have a job. Life was hell with Mother, and without a pay envelope she was worse.

The preachers like Billy Sunday wanted my soul. My mother wanted my money. In the mill where I next tried to get a job as a picker, it seemed that the three sons of the boss wanted my body.

The youngest son showed me the picking machine which stood in the office. This was strange, as usually machines were in the factory and not in the office. The silk crepe de chine went from one roll to another. One moved the roll by hand after one had picked out the flaws, which were loose threads. It had to be done most carefully to keep from tearing the delicate silk. As the young, foul-smelling, pimply faced lad explained this to me, I said, "I know, I know." I wanted to get to work and not have his hands touching my breasts as he showed me the workings of the machine. He nauseated me — his looks, his smell, his roving hands, and especially the expression in his eyes.

Those three sons of the boss seemed to take turns touching my body as they leaned over me and the machine to check my work. Both my hands were busy, one rolling the bolt of cloth and the other picking out the loose threads. I was afraid to slap their hands, afraid to tear the cloth, and afraid to lose my job.

One lunchtime I complained to the workers in the mill. I should have done this sooner. When I told them how the sons bothered me, they sent a committee to the boss. I don't know how they managed it, but that day the machine was moved by the workers to the mill behind the office. I merrily picked away, singing with the workers. What a relief to have the boss's sons' hands in their own pockets and not on me!

At home Mother always talked against "those foreigners" although she herself was one. She spoke no English. To her all were foreign who were not Dutch and of the Dutch Reformed Church. Yet how can I ever thank "those foreigners" who worked in the mills and helped protect me from roving hands? Was it my person, my virginity, that was important? I don't think so. I think it was the concept of the right to be one's self, to give or not to give by choice and not as a means of holding a job.

Mother could no longer influence me against race, color or creed. At lunchtime I was apt to share Polish sausage, Italian spaghetti, filled flaky Syrian pastry or stuffed grape leaves, in exchange for some Dutch cheese filled with *comino* seeds. My ears and mouth were open as I listened to stories in various forms about weddings, baptisms, and so forth. It was fun to listen to the many differences as I ate my lunch. Our cultural differences were great, but the most important thing I learned in the mills was our similarity as humans.

I wondered why anyone should be ashamed of being a foreigner or of being a child of foreigners. We mill dollies, first generation, had this feeling of shame. We tried to avoid admitting that our parents spoke no English. I was not as bad off as some of the others, since my parents were Hollanders and were higher on the immigrant scale. (The darker the skin, the lower one was on the scale.) Eastside society, mainly made up of our employers and the high school kids from the area, didn't see us. We were nothing; we were foreigners, mill workers. God, I was confused! I wanted to be and live like the Eastside, and yet my loyalty went to my co-workers.

In the early spring of 1921, I was laid off with many other workers. Factories were closing all over town. I did not understand why, but I knew that I'd better find a job fast to still my mother's lashing tongue.

Shivering as the cold, damp wind hit my neck, my feet wet from walking in the slushy snow, I jobhunted. My throat hurt, and I was sneezing, but I walked on. I could not sit near the kitchen stove for warmth. Mother had sent me out to get a job. Where there were mills I walked. All had signs, "Not hiring." Almost weeping, I began the long walk to Prospect Park. Across the street from Quackenbush's department store, I saw a sign which said, "Clerk wanted." I inquired at the entrance desk of the office building. The elevator took me up to the fifth floor. The lettering on the office door said, "Private Investigators." Without the vaguest idea what the sign meant, I entered the dimly lit office.

Two men interviewed me. They asked, "Can you type? Can you keep accounts? Can you take messages accurately?"

To all questions I answered, "Yes, but I am not an expert." To my surprise I was hired.

I was scared to death. I knew nothing about typing or accounting. The only thing I was sure of was that I could take messages. Since I had learned quill winding and picking by bluffing, stumbling, practicing, I said to myself, "You can do the same here." The wage was very low. The important thing to me was that I was finally out of the mills. Mother would be furious. She wanted me in the mills, since she knew I wanted out. As far as I was concerned, I would never go back. I was almost sixteen years of age. I hoped I could say honestly now, "I am an office worker."

The detectives were not busy. I had time to study the books I had borrowed from the library on writing and typing. Accounts were just good arithmetic, I noticed. Most of the job consisted of waiting for the phone to ring and making believe that the detectives were very busy. Obviously both the employers and the employee were bluffing. I enjoyed this learning job situation, working with detectives. And then I pulled a real boner. I told my mother I was working in a detective office.

The pot with the shelled peas flew at me. I ducked fast so that only the peas hit me. "So you are using your whoring to break up homes!" she hollered. I did not know what she meant, but then I rarely did. I was on the floor, picking up the peas I had just finished shelling, when I heard her say, "You get out of that detective office and back to the mills where you belong."

I shouted back, "I won't leave this job!"

"Then I'll get you fired," she replied. I wondered what she would do.

A few days later, my mother's lawyer, whom I hated, walked in the door. He demanded to see the detectives. I said, "They are not in." I hoped they would stay in the back office and continue playing cards, but just then they walked out. The lawyer introduced himself and told them that my mother did not want me working there, that my morals might be corrupted, and that I was a minor. The detectives appeared not to want problems with irate mothers. They fired me.

Mother was determined that I should look for a mill job. I was just as determined that I would not. The Depression helped me. Even she could not find me a mill job. I must have had at least fifteen odd jobs in those early months of 1921, from passing out advertisements to demonstrator jobs in the five-and-dime. Things were worse than ever at home. I was not supplying Mother with the money she wanted.

About this time my girl scout friend, Mary Bauer, told me that she had been accepted for a job as a telephone operator. She told me of the wonderful conditions at work, the good wages, and how well the workers were treated. This was it. I wanted a job as a telephone operator. I asked her how to apply. I was nearly sixteen, which was the age requirement; maybe they would make an exception. I wanted this job so badly I was trembling with fear of rejection when I applied. I was interviewed and given written tests. I was accepted for the in-service training course on a trial basis!

There had been few full, rich, happy days in my life up to then. My first day of learning to be a telephone operator was one of them, and it stands out like a song. In fact, I sang under my breath. I sang on my way home as I tried singing the numbers nine and five ("ny-on" and "fi-ov"). Then every day I was waking up full of joy. Sometimes I had to think quickly, "Why?" — and the answer was that I was commuting to Newark to the school for telephone operators. I was learning to put plugs into their proper places, to say with a questioning song in my voice, "Number, please?" I could sense the teacher's approval of the rapidity with which I was learning. I had a glimmer, which I was afraid to admit, that I was not stupid. Maybe I could learn other things, many things. This was an amazing thought, a wonderful one for a mill dolly!

At the end of a month's training, I was assigned to the Lambert-A Board, a manual switchboard. I pushed in a plug when a light flashed and sang, "Number, please?" My work hours were five in the afternoon until eleven at night. These were the unwanted hours which new employees had to take. At that time, I preferred them to the split hours or the day hours. I was away from home in the evenings. Afternoons I could go swimming or go to the library. My mother could rave and rant, but I surrounded myself with a world of books. Their contents built a wall against her voice.

After a short while on the A switchboard, I was transferred to a more responsible job as an information clerk. This was like playing detective searching for the unknown number, or like a bacteriologist searching for the unknown germ. I enjoyed helping the client. When I had to locate a number in another state, I was taking an imaginary voyage. The recognition that I could not get at home, I began to get for service to the clients. Their "Thank you, operator" became a substitute for family warmth.

Can you imagine my surprise and fright when I saw my mother walk into the chief operator's office one morning? I was on my fifteen-minute relief period. From where I sat in the restroom I could see the chief operator's door. Shortly afterward I saw a Dutch-speaking girl go in the same door. I was sick with sorrow. I knew my mother's vile tongue only too well.

My rest period ended, and I forced myself to go back to the information board. I answered the signals, saying, "This is information; can I help you?" while I held back tears. I could not confide in anyone. My companions liked their mothers. They would not understand, and I would have lost face. They would have thought there was something wrong with me if I had told them my mother was cruel, mean, and even frightening at times.

That hour of repeating "Information" was one of the longest in my short life. The supervisor came over to relieve me at my position and told me to go to the chief operator's office. The girls looked at me curiously. This usually meant a serious offense, most often ending in being fired. I trembled with fear as I walked toward the door. I opened it slowly, and the chief operator's face appeared in my line of vision. What a contrast between my mother's red, angry face and gentle Miss Paul's face — soft, gentle, rounded but firm, light sparkling on her white hair. My heart is full of thanks to her as I write this.

"Sit down, Miss Moerkerk," she said. Then she asked me, "Where do you go on your alternate nights off, Tuesdays and Sundays?"

Mother began shouting. Miss Paul showed her to the door. Words tumbled helter-skelter from my mouth. "Please don't believe whatever my mother told you. She has always hated me. I don't know why, but she has always tried to destroy me, and she hates me so."

Again Miss Paul asked me, "But where do you go on your nights off?"

I replied, "On Tuesday I go to girl scout meetings and on alternate Sunday nights I sing in the First Baptist Church Junior Choir. Afternoons I either go swimming or to the public library." Words and tears still tumbled out of my mouth as I begged her to listen to me. Gently she questioned me until she dug the story of my life from where I had tried to keep it buried. This was the second time in my life that I had told all. The other time was when I was nine years old and had told the social workers from the Florence Crittendon Home for Unwed Mothers.

I am grateful to Miss Paul. I will always be grateful to the many "Miss Pauls" in my life who believed me and in me. She told me to take the rest of the day off. I asked her if I was fired. "Absolutely not," she replied. "Go to the movies until you are more relaxed," she said. I didn't tell her that I had no money for movies. I had all I could do to scrape the money together to buy the merit badges I was earning in scouting.

Late that afternoon and evening I walked up Broadway as far as the river and back again. Unhappy, unloved, unwanted — how deep could my depression go? I felt physically sick with depression. Back to the Passaic River I walked again. Was death, drowning, the only way out? Suddenly the anger welled in me, anger against my mother. I stopped thinking of death and began thinking of how one could survive living with her. I walked home.

I didn't speak to my mother when I entered the house. I didn't answer her when she shouted at me, "Now, my fine lady, you can go back to the mills where the likes of you belong!" She grabbed me by the arm and turned me toward her so that I had to look at her ugly, angry face. She spit at me, "I told your boss that you are a slut, a whore. I told her that you are with boy scouts on Tuesday nights and maybe Sundays too. I told her that your belly would swell, and you would bring disgrace on the phone company. I told her!"

Ignoring her, I struggled to break loose and to leave the room. She grabbed me again and yelled, "I am your mother! I am your boss! How dare you think that you can run your own life, work where you please, go where you want to and read what you care to? I fixed you," she said with glee.

I wanted to kill her. How strong was the feeling to see her dead at my feet, this shouting, ugly, fat woman who called herself my mother! My hand reached for the kitchen knife lying on the table. I wanted to put it through her, when, strangely, Miss Paul's face came before me and stopped me. It was her gentle, strong face before my eyes that held the knife back.

Shocked and frightened at so wishing her dead that I was actually ready to kill her, I decided then and there that I must leave her and home. What would I do if I got angry like that again? To protect myself I had to leave. The neighbors upstairs were knocking on the floor and yelling, "It's midnight! Tell your mother to keep quiet!" I just left the room, which I knew would quiet her. I pushed my sister over to make room in bed for me. I wondered how I could get my clothing out of the house. Where should I go? My sister wanted to know what it was all about this time. I told her to go back to sleep. Finally I had it worked out. Up on Broadway there was a YWCA Boarding Home for Working Girls. I would go there and apply for room and board. I relaxed and went to sleep.

I pretended to be asleep next morning until my mother had gone to market, my father to work, and my sister to school. Then I could not move fast enough. I tied my clothes together with some kitchen string. Without regret I began the long walk to the YWCA. The house stood next to the new Masonic Temple on a small hill. I walked up the steps, rang the bell, and asked for the lady who ran the house.

The room where I waited was sunny and uncluttered. I savored the calm of it while I waited for "the lady." When she came she asked me who I was, how old I was, and why I wanted to leave home. I was embarrassed and ashamed. I could not bring myself to tell her of my mother and of the home I had left. She did not want to believe that I was sixteen years old. She did not want to give me a room. In desperation I asked her to phone Miss Paul, the chief operator at the telephone company. She did, and her attitude changed. She rented a room to me.

Will any room ever again look as wonderful as that room, my room looked to me that day? It represented freedom from tongue-lashings, slaps and humiliations, from compulsions to self-destruction and desires to see my mother dead. Unpacking my few belongings — my scout uniform, my few skirts and blouses — I heard a symphony of birds. The trees were thick outside my window, not a factory in sight. This was the Eastside. I had arrived on the other side of the river, or "tracks." Factories, sweatshops and Mother were all tied together in my mind on the other side of the tracks. I was out of them all.

This side, the Eastside, meant tennis courts, children who could go to high school and college, bosses' sons who thought we of the other side could be "made." I knew the Eastside would not accept me. That didn't matter too much as long as I could see the fresh white curtains gently moving in the window, hear the birds sing, not see smokestacks of the mills, and feel free of filthy words heaped on my head. Life seemed new and washed clean.

Walking down Broadway in late afternoon on my way to work, I began worrying what the girls would say. I was sure the Dutch girl who had interpreted for my mother had told some of the story or all. I decided to face it and to tell the truth, that my mother was a problem, and I had left home, period! A little verse came to my mind, "Gossip shall not cramp my life. Boldly through this world I'll walk. I'd rather far be talked about than one of those who merely talk." Dorothy Parker wrote it. It still serves me.

Meals at the Home were a bit of a nightmare to me the first week. It was pleasant not having the meals thrown at me, but I dreaded the lady's words, "Keep your mouth closed when you eat. Don't stuff your mouth so. Break your bread in small pieces. Don't make noise when you eat soup. A lady eats this way; watch me," she said. On the other hand, no one shouted at me or threw the dirty, wet dishrag in my face. I don't think I ever learned anything so fast in my life again as table manners acceptable to others. Not that I objected. I was anxious to learn these things.

Life had never been so good before. In the mornings I often swam, up above the Passaic Falls. Rainy days I spent in the public library. I had books to read and books to think about. I loved my job, and to top it all, on alternate nights off I had choir singing or girl scout meetings. Life was good.

One afternoon about a month after I had run away from home, I saw my father climbing the stairs leading to the front porch. I saw his tall, thin, elongated body bending over the number of the house, but my legs could not move to run down the stairs and let him in. My heart turned. I knew that the good life would be over. I just knew. My father, my poor father, grimy with coal dust that stuck to him all the time from the gas he made in the gas factory. I wanted to love him. I liked him, yet I despised him at those times when my mother made him cower and squeal. In my thoughts I could hear her shouting at him, "I married beneath my class. You were a sickly bum, a drunk. I made a man out of you, a respectable man. Now you have a suit and a tie, but you are a thief. You steal from me."

The latter was true. My father often told me with great glee how much small change he had been able to steal from Mother in a week. I understood. She gave him fifty cents a week spending money. That was not enough for his cigarettes. He had to steal. Every payday she met him at the pay office. Not that she cared for him, but she did about the dollars that would be in the pay envelope. One could always count on her keeping her fangs covered until the envelope was in her big black leather bag.

Once I asked Father, "Why do you stay with her? Why are you afraid? Why don't you leave Mother?"

"I stay because of you and Elizabeth," he replied.

Often I would say to him, "Let's go, you and I, and leave Mother with her pet Elizabeth." Even I with my young eyes could see that he loved his wife and enjoyed the verbal beatings he took from her. At least she was giving him recognition. It was worse when she didn't speak to him. Then he really fawned and cowered before her. He was such a decent man. I learned this as I helped him laboriously read the newspaper. She gloated with the scandal sheet and the Hearst Press; he read the labor papers.

The maid knocked at the door and told me my father was waiting to take me home. I had to face it. I walked down the stairs to where he was waiting. He greeted me with the words, "Please come home. Your mother is crying for you, and I miss you."

With bitterness in my voice I answered, "I am sure she is crying, not for me but for my pay envelope which she wants. What has she ever done for me except hit me, tongue-lash me, and humiliate me?"

"But she is threatening to make a court case of you. She

says you are only sixteen years old, a minor. If you want to keep your job, you had better come home," said Father. Afraid of my mother but more afraid of losing my job, I quickly decided that I had better go home. I was not so important to the phone company that they would want the scandal my mother threatened.

This was not an easy choice. I loved the peaceful life, the swims, the library. I even liked learning to speak English properly and to use correct table manners. Having my own pay to do with as I pleased had been a pleasure. I had some money saved that I would not tell Mother about. I didn't tell Father what I was thinking, since in order to curry favor with her he would squeal on me. This I knew from long experience.

"All right, tell Mother that I'll be home by the end of the week. My room and board is paid up till then," I told Father. I knew she would understand my staying if room and board were paid. She understood anything that related to the almighty dollar. I planned to use my saved money for scouting equipment and come home penniless. Before my father left I said, "Tell Mother that from now on I want ten cents on every dollar I earn, and if she yells too much I'll leave home and go far away so that you can't find me." Having left home I felt strong enough to say that. I felt I could cope with her with less fear. After all, the age of eighteen was only two years away.

When I entered the house at the end of the week, my mother met me with a smile. With that smile on her face instead of a clout to my face, I knew I had won the first round. I did not think she would ever be sure of her control over me again. Before I sat down I told her, "I am sixteen years old. I earn a good sum of money which you want, but since I am the one working for it, I want at least ten cents of every dollar that I bring home." She began opening her mouth. "Wait," I said, "I am not finished. I will spend my money as I see fit. I will go where I want to go on my night off, and I will not stay home on my day off to polish brass or to scrub the kitchen floor." She closed her mouth.

I had never seen my mother do a lick of work. Father did it all, and I helped. He did the cleaning and the scrubbing before and after his own job in the gas factory. She marketed and cooked, true, but that was all.

With yells and shrieks she supervised the housework. Father washed and ironed; he scrubbed; he did the dishes; he had done it all alone while I was gone. Now I would be helping him again, but I was damned if I would spend my whole day off doing housework. As we scoured, her fat — spreading layer of fat upon fat over chairs and beds wherever she sat — quivered with her yells. Smelly of unwashed fat, sweet-smelling of diabetes, fat that shrieked in a hard, sharp voice that was hard to escape. She was round, but her voice was narrow. She ate like a glutton with manners that now made me nauseated. She begrudged us seconds in food unless it was something she had cooked too much of, and then she forced it on us till it was finished.

"Je zal eeten wat de pot scept" (You will eat what the pot brings forth), and we did as she ordered. I still can't bear the sight of cooked carrots. Once I refused to eat carrots, and she served the same dish to me for two days, three meals a day, until I ate them and then vomited them. All things that were costly, sweet, or that she liked were doled out to us. The Dutch butter almond cookies were kept under lock, and only she had the key. But Father had become adept at picking locks, and we ate the cookies. Locks were changed frequently. Father always stole for me before holidays so that I could have some cookies in my lunch.

Holidays — why did one steal cookies and save money for holidays? One was supposed to go someplace, be happy, have fun. I'd save dimes and nickels. The girl scouts would plan, talk, discuss the merits of Palisades Amusement Park versus taking the boat up the Hudson River to Bear Mountain Park. The planning was lots of fun — what to wear, what to take to eat, would we meet The Boy? We were all growing up with the Cinderella myth: Meet The Man and live happily ever after. I didn't hope for much. I was too fat and dumpy for a prince, but maybe I might get one of his noblemen. I wanted to look like Mary Pickford did in the movies. One glance in the mirror told me I might be fair-haired, but I was no Mary Pickford.

The day of days came — July 4th, Independence Day. It was fun riding in the trolley car through the marshes and swaying cattails up toward Palisades Park on the Hudson River. The view of the broad river was almost all I needed. I felt I should stay here to gaze on the river, busy with big and little boats, but my friends hurried me to go into the amusement park.

Tingling with anticipation, I bought my ticket to enter the park. In time with the music, up and down, up and down went the horses on the merry-go-round. The loop-the-loop was filled with shrieking people. The ferris wheel majestically moved high over the park and the Hudson. I yelled and shrieked in the loop-the-loop. I tried to pull the rings in the merry-go-round. I hovered over the Hudson in the cage on the ferris wheel. I tried to be happy; I felt blue, depressed.

I'd saved money for weeks. My father had robbed the closet for goodies for my lunch. I'd happily planned with the group, and now in the midst of a crowd I felt alone and unhappy. I could not explain it to my friends. They would think that I was queer. Was I queer? What was wrong with me? Like a flash, the reason for my depression came to me. Everyone was working, struggling so hard to have fun, that the shrieks sounded false, their smiles were strained. All of us seemed to be running away from our lives on the steeplechase. Was I ever happy?

Swimming in the river, skating on the ice, marching with our girl scout troop — these actions had contained moments of happiness. But fat me, looking sideways at the boys, acting brave on the loop-the-loop, making believe I was having fun and all the while thinking of home and the mother to whom I had to return — I was nothing more than a miserable, fat adolescent.

Night came. In a dark corner I pulled my girdle down and smoothed my hips trying to brush my fat away. With my girlfriends I bought a ticket to enter the dance hall. Trying to blend in with the wall, I became a wallflower. After what seemed a long while, a young man asked me to dance with him. I didn't dance very well, but he danced every dance with me. He lived in Paterson on the Eastside. His father was a mill owner.

On the one hand, I was thrilled that a boy of the Eastside had asked me to dance with him and was dancing every number with me. At the same time I was recalling the many times I had heard a mill owner's son say to his pal, "Let's go to Palisades Park and pick up a mill dolly; they're easy to lay." They talked like that in front of us as if we had no ears but were parts of the machines with which we worked. I had not told this boy that I had been a mill dolly. I had said that I worked at the information desk of the phone company.

As we danced he held me rather close. I didn't like that. On the other hand, the girls with whom I had come could see that I was dancing with a man. This in itself was an achievement and worth the money I had saved. I was more scared than happy when he asked to take me home. On the long trolley ride home, he only held my hand. I began feeling a bit more secure. Yet when I suggested that he get off on the Eastside where he lived and let me continue to the end of the line where I would change for the Ridgewood Trolley, he insisted that he would take me all the way home. Now I had a problem!

If I got off at the foot of Haledon Avenue, walked up the hill and then down North Eighth Street, my mother could see us coming under the corner street lamp. She would begin shouting, and that would shame me. If he heard my mother shout, he might not ask me for a date. Not that he understood Dutch, but her yells had such a nasty quality that it was enough to frighten a strange lad. However, if we got off the trolley much nearer to my home, at the foot of the hill where we lived near the Passaic River, then we would have to walk through unlit fields. Would he behave?

Halfway up the dark hill, he pulled me down on the grass and began fondling me. I resisted. Why? My mother was sure that I would become an unwed mother. I couldn't give her this satisfaction. Only this made me resist, I am sure. I wanted a boyfriend badly. I wanted to be kissed and fondled. Other girls had boyfriends; why not me? I couldn't explain this to Harry, but I did get it across that I wouldn't. He gave up trying. I was not angry at him. I had taken him up through the dark fields. I might just as well have taken him down brightly lit North Eighth Street and let him have a dose of Mother's shouting. He didn't ask me for a date. He told me that telephone operators did; in me he met one who didn't. So ended my holiday and my first dance with a young man.

About this time when I was hungering for a boyfriend, a "kind" neighbor, who delighted in making people miserable with her sweet barbed tongue, told me that my mother was a Jew who had been converted to the Dutch Reformed Church. I couldn't believe it. I didn't want to believe it. I was shocked. My mother was cruel, I knew, but being a Jew was worse. How could a fanatic, religious Protestant be a Jew? No wonder my grandfather had had a stroke when Mother made me say the Christian Lord's Prayer at his bedside in Holland in 1910 when I was five years old! I was seventeen, nearly eighteen, and I longed for male attention. Now I knew my case was hopeless if the boys found out my mother was a Jew. What boy would want to marry the daughter of a Jewess? Being fat was bad enough, but being Jewish also was worse. My mother had filled me with stories against Jews; now those stories had come home to roost.

Black clouds belched out of the huge smokestacks of the gas factory where my father worked. Walking alongside the factory wall, swinging the lunch pail, I was talking to my father when I noticed the words scrawled on the wall, "Dirty Jew." I had never taken much note of the "four-letter" words before. Now they branded me.

Gingerly holding onto the hot iron rail of the spiral staircase, I climbed up to where Father was standing as he shoveled coal into the furnace. Over the noise of the furnace I asked him, "Is it true that Mother is a Jew? Why did you marry her?"

My father, grimy with coal dust, looked at me. He saw the hurt and anger in my eyes. He replied, "There are many things wrong with your mother, but being a Jew is not one of them." He continued, "What does it matter what religion one has? What matters is how one lives with one's fellow man."

"But why did you marry a woman who does not love you and who is a Jew?" I asked.

"I married her because I loved her and still do," he replied.

"But, Papa, you know how she always talks of the Jews as if they are the scum of the earth. Everyone I know hates Jews. Now I'll never have a boyfriend or a husband if they find out my mother is a Jew. Isn't life hard enough for me?" I kept on muttering.

"Do you know any Jews?" asked Father.

"No, I don't," I replied.

"Then don't be like your mother and hate for hate's sake," said Papa.

That checked me. I did not want to be like my mother in any way. I thought, "He is right. My mother was a Jew; now she is a Protestant. So what? If they (meaning the boys) didn't like it, they could lump it."

Walking home, the empty lunch pail clattered with cutlery as if it were speaking to me, "You are a Jew. Your mother is a Jew. You are living a lie. You sing in the First Baptist Choir. You are a girl scout in the Bethany Baptist Sunday School of the First Baptist Church. You were christened Dutch Reformed, but once a Jew, always a Jew, they say. Keep quiet about this; don't tell anyone," the pail said. Or was it me?

I began looking at people with different eyes. I wondered, "Is she a Jew? Is he a Jew? Wasn't Christ a Jew? What makes a Jew?" Some of the mill owners were Jews, some Catholics, some Protestants. Had there been any difference in their treatment of us? No. Why this insane feeling against Jews? Why my disgust at being the daughter of a Jewess? Why? Was The Man whom we used to go and see in Dobbs Ferry a Jew? What about those wonderful aunts and uncles and cousins in Holland; were they not all Jews? They loved me and I them, when I was a little girl of five.

By the time I had walked the long way home, I decided that I would keep quiet about Mother's being a Jew. Someday I would try to find out more about what makes a Jew and why there was this fear of being one. Was I a Jew? I was afraid of my mother; I was embarrassed by my father; and now I was ashamed of myself for being ashamed of the word "Jew."

To escape this knowledge, this worm that gnawed at me, I threw myself more intensely into girl scout work. Every badge I earned became a symbol of Americanism. The sleeve of my girl scout uniform gradually became dotted with bright-colored badges. I lacked one to become a Golden Eaglet scout, the home nursing badge. I could not work for it, since I would have to attend classes held in the Red Cross. They were held at night, and I worked the night shift.

Because of the telephone company's seniority system, which was most fair, I'd be an old lady before I got on the day shift. Few operators left the company by the time they got on the day shift. If they married, they remained at work. I began looking at newspaper advertisements which said, "Switchboard operator wanted," although I loved working in the phone company. I felt indebted to Miss Paul, the chief operator, yet more and more I began to think of leaving for a day job.

The decision was taken out of my hands. When I came home from girl scout meeting one evening, the words that my mother shouted penetrated my wall against her. "And you are coming with me. If I leave you in America, I'll come home to find you with a big belly. You will go with me to Holland and learn to be a respectable Dutch girl, not like this American *drek*!"

Obviously my mother was planning a trip to Holland. She wanted to see the doctors again about her deafness. She did not trust American doctors. She did not want to spend the money on my fare, but she needed me as her ears in Holland and as her voice in England. I didn't want to go. I did not look forward to having my face slapped across the Atlantic Ocean and back again. She was always worse when I didn't bring home a pay envelope. I suggested that she use my ten-year-old sister as interpreter and leave me home, to save money. I brought up the fact that if she left me home, I could keep on earning money for her. But she said, "And then I'll come home to find you pregnant; you are coming with me."

Passage was booked for the newly renovated *S.S. Leviathan*, the largest passenger boat in the world at that time. It had been used as a troop transport in World War I and now was ready for her first trip as a passenger boat again. Mother said that we would go over third class and come back second class. She told me that she had heard that third class going over to Europe was fine, since the passengers were mainly students and Americans. But coming back we would come second class to avoid the foreigners — Slavs, Italians, and the like. To her they were all still foreigners — except the Dutch — but she accepted Americans.

I hated to go. I hated to leave my job and my girl scout troop. Yet I did want to see Holland again. I thought to myself, "Here is your chance to find out something about Jews from Mother's family."

With my sister and mother I sailed in May, 1923. Why talk about the voyage? If I stayed in the cabin with my seasick sister, I had quivers in my abdomen. If I stayed on deck, I was not nauseous but was humiliated by Mother's shrieks and the slaps she directed at me. The voyage was a nightmare.

I don't remember if we docked in Southhampton or Liverpool, but I do remember the beauty of the English countryside as we sped by train to London. Fields of red poppies — red poppies even growing out of thatched roofs — kept my mind off Mother's complaints. She couldn't read lips in English and had no one to listen to. I could hear, yet I had trouble understanding the English spoken. London, to me, was a cheap, hot, bedbug-filled hotel with horrible food. What a relief it was to get on the clean, Dutch channel boat and have good, hot vegetable soup with meatballs! When I came up on deck in the morning, we were passing the Hoek van Holland and entering the Maas River.

Holland, the Netherlands, the Lowlands — this was the country to which I felt I belonged. Tulips and hyacinths, a patchwork quilt of colors, waved me on to Amsterdam. The train went much too fast. Wide-skirted petticoats sailed up and down the canals below the land, their colored sails dancing across the landscape. I had never thought of boats as dancers till then. Windmills slowly turned their wings as if saluting the sailboats. A mellow, soft, golden light diffused over us. To whom could I say, "How beautiful!"? I hugged the beauty all to myself.

Getting off the train at Amsterdam, my mother waved and called to one of the homeliest redheaded men I had ever seen. When she called "Sara" to the little woman with him, I realized that this must be my Uncle David, since I recalled my Aunt Sara. With them were two youngsters, my cousins Gerrit and Dina, who were about my age. They all kissed us. When my uncle embraced and kissed me, I was suspicious. He was a man. What did he want from me?

Living with them I noted that they kissed and hugged one another hello, goodbye, good night, and at every excuse they had. It looked phony to me. Once I had seen a family who liked one another, the Bauers, but they did not show their emotions openly. Gradually it dawned on me that this family, my relatives, really loved one another and expressed it. I stopped waiting for my Ome David to make a pass at me.

Tante Sara said Mother was up to her old tricks, trying to make trouble between the members of the family. As she became more objectionable, Tante Sara, a wise little woman, suggested that Mother go to see a relative in another part of Holland or Belgium. Since Mother was one of thirteen sisters and brothers (survivors of 26 siblings), she had relatives all over the Low Countries. Off she would go with my sister, and I would stay, blissful in the shelter of the David de Vries family.

Drying the dishes with the traditionally proper towel, I would ask, "What is kosher? Why kosher? Why is Mother so different from the rest of the family? Why can't she be like them?" The questions poured out, and Tante Sara avoided answering most of them, except to explain what "kosher" was and why.

As we worked in the kitchen, we could hear Ome David singing as he cobbled the family shoes. We always knew when he had a new part to practice in the Amsterdam Men's Choir, since he would go around the rooms looking for shoes that needed repairs. His hammer squeaked with the high notes and banged with the low notes. Tante Sara teased him, but he said, "The song is easier to learn when cobbling shoes."

I no longer thought of him as homely or ugly. His hair was flaming red. His eyes were small and deepset, his face fat and his cheeks freckled over their ruddiness. My Ome David was not handsome, but he was a good man, such a good man. He worked as a streetcar conductor, and he loved his work, since he could meet and talk to many people. Evenings he would regale us with the happenings of the day on his trolley. With the gusty laughter and a Rabelaisian touch — not vulgar, but earthy — he held forth. With what joy he sang, worked and cobbled shoes!

One night Ome David turned to me and said, "Yesterday you rode on the trolley with my friend Van der Horst, and you did not say good morning, or thank you, or goodbye. Is that the way one behaves in America?"

Then my aunt chimed in, "I sent Lientjie for cheese this morning, and Mijnheer van Praag told me that she did not say please, or good morning, or thank you."

"What a barbaric country that must be where you come from!" they both said in unison.

This was confusing. They were not Americans; they were foreigners. They were Jews. They always thought of one another and of others. They had the virtues one learned about in scouting, and at the church which froze out Jews. In Holland I was the foreigner, the barbarian, crude and uneducated, but LOVED!

My aunt and uncle were proud of being descendents of the Sephardic Jews who had fled from Spain to Holland. They wanted me to know that one of my ancestors had been the famous biologist Hugo de Vries and that one had been Spinoza. But they took the greatest pride of all in the fact that they were Hollanders. As far as they were concerned, I must learn about my ancestors, my Dutch, Sephardic Jewish ancestors. Yet they had humility, and they lived humbly. Their apartment was five flights up, near the Amstel Railroad Station, and looked over the Amstel Canal. It was a railroad flat in the poorer section of town.

In this humble flat, Friday nights were beautiful. With the lighting of the candles, peace would enter like a dove. The family ate and, later, various members of the clan would drop in for tea and discussion. They sat around the table drinking tea, eating chocolate and shelling peanuts. I sat quietly absorbing an education on music, art and socialism. Sometimes singing would begin, invariably led by Ome David, as the women cleared the table for more tea and cookies, peanuts and chocolates. We had to be careful to wash the dishes in the proper pan for the "milk dishes." My aunt was not "religious"; she was a socialist, but she kept the Laws of Moses "because it is clean and healthy." Practically all of the family were ardent socialists, excited with the coming anniversary of Queen Wilhelmina's twenty-five years on the throne. They loved the Queen. With inward shame I used to wish my mother would drop dead so that I could stay with Tante Sara and Ome David forever.

I expected my cousins to be jealous of me, since Tante and Ome were always thoughtful of me. They were not. I got plenty of scoldings from them, but in the same voice they used for their own children. The scoldings were mainly for lack of good manners according to their cultural standards. My aunt would also get annoyed when Dina and I spoke English together. She had such great curiosity that she could not stand being left out. She felt she might miss something when we spoke in English. Besides, it was bad manners, she told us. So Dina and I spoke English on the street away from home. Dientjie was in high school and spoke English, French, German and her native language.

Sometimes I could not avoid going places with my mother. I preferred being with my uncle and aunt and my cousins, but when Mother would come back to Amsterdam I had to make some visits with her.

One of those visits I had to make I will always remember. She said, "We are going to call on Mrs. Pollock, who is the mother of the gentleman we used to see in Dobbs Ferry." She told me not to say anything of our visits to him when I was a little girl.

As I sat in the small garden behind her home, I looked at her with a strange shock. I saw an older edition of myself. I remember thinking and asking myself, "Is my father my real father, or is that Man in Dobbs Ferry my real father? Is she my grandmother?" It was such a weird thought that I brushed it away.

The next day when Mother was out of the house, I told my aunt of my queer thinking. I asked her what my mother's relationship had been with the Pollock family. My aunt told me that Mother had nursed old Mr. Pollock before he died, and had been in love with the oldest son, who was the one who lived in America. Mother had followed him to America and was engaged to him. Suddenly they heard that she had married an illiterate man from the south of Holland, a gentile. This had been a shock to the family, since she had been the first one in the family to marry a gentile. In the family they married Sephardic Jews.

"Is that why my grandfather had a stroke when I said the Lord's Prayer at his bedside?" I asked my aunt.

"We think so, and he died shortly after that," my aunt replied. "I am surprised that you remember it. You should not be disturbed; it was not your fault," she assured me. My aunt continued, "You know Bernard, who could have been your father, don't you?"

I answered, "Yes, I know him. We used to go to his home often before Elizabeth was born. Those were the only times that she was decent to me. She used to bribe me with candy to keep quiet and not say anything to my father about where we had been. They stayed hours in the house, and I amused myself in the garden. It is no wonder that I remember those visits so well. The most boring were when she would meet him in a New York hotel, and I waited in the lobby."

Tante Sara looked at me strangely as I continued, "I wish she had married him. Maybe she would have been happier, and me, too. His daughters go to high school. They studied violin and piano. One will study medicine and the other law, and I was not allowed to go to high school."

Tante asked, "How do you know these things?"

"Oh, his sister comes from Bridgeport, Connecticut, to visit us, and I hear Mother questioning her about Bernard. And you know, Tante, it is thought-provoking to me that she looks enough like me to be an older sister," I said.

With a very curious look at me, she said, "Take the *gember koek* out of the oven." That tart — crispy, buttery, rich with whole pieces of ginger in it — made me forget to question my aunt further. I loved the symphony of smells in Tante's kitchen, especially on Friday. The best dishes were cooked for Sabbath Eve.

After one of those wonderful Friday nights, my uncle and aunt insisted that I was a barbarian without culture. I knew nothing of Rembrandt, Hals, Steen, Brueghel, and if it were possible, I knew less of Bach or Beethoven. We had visitors too, involved in the discussion. A relative of Ome David's had just returned from many years in Java, where he had been editor of a newspaper. He agreed with them that I needed culture. Sitting at the table sipping my tea, I listened to them planning an educational program for me which ranged from painting to Dutch history and music. While listening, I stole glances at the other visitor, David Schaap, the son of the newspaper editor. He had just returned from a trip around the world. He volunteered to take me to some of the concerts at Mengelberg's Concertgebouw. His family had a box for Thursday and Sunday nights.

The culture they had been talking about didn't interest me as much as the chance to get to know this young man better. I asked Dina in a whisper, "How old is Cousin David?"

"Twenty-six," she answered.

It was one month before my eighteenth birthday. Twenty-six and eighteen — not too bad, I thought. From the point of view of an Arrow shirt advertisement, he would not be considered handsome, but I responded to him. I liked his deepset dark eyes, the tenderness in them, and his thoughtfulness in his relations with the family. His tallness seemed to shelter me as he sat next to me. I liked him; yes, I liked him. I hoped he would like me. He had this culture they talked about. Maybe I'd better get some to have David Schaap become interested in me. All I could talk about was mills, the telephone company and girl scouts.

I told my Tante Sara that I was worried what Mother would say if she found me going out to concerts with David and to museums with others, plus theater, as this was all part of the broad plan. Tante said, "You leave your mother to me. She is hardly here, and when she is she can't object to your going out with members of the family. Young David is family on Ome David's side. Why, you can even go with young David without a chaperone," she continued. This is wonderful, I said to myself. I could think of nothing more exciting than to be with young David Schaap.

Whenever I hear the music of Bach, I think of the first concert I attended — sitting next to David, the music swelling and rising in my body as my heart pounded with his nearness. Thursdays and Sundays, twice a week I went, and always with David. How different Bach, Brahms, Chopin sounded from "Yes, We Have No Bananas," to which I was accustomed. I understood little of this music intellectually, but my emotions responded to it.

Mijnheer Groen, an old friend of the family, was going to take me to the museums. He was the art expert in our family and circle of friends. He was a diamond broker, and one day on our way to the Rijks Museum he took me to the Diamond Exchange. On the street in front of it, the herring stalls did an active business. Fresh, pickled, smoked, whole fish, pieces of fish, herring and more herring was being eaten by pompous, fat-bellied diamond brokers. I found this amusing and told Mijnheer Groen. His answer first was to order two pickled herring. We held the pickled herring by their tails so that the juice would drop in our mouths and not on our clothes. "Herring and diamonds — how funny!" I said.

Mijnheer Groen said, "Young lady, a fine city and a fine culture were built on herring bones. Amsterdam rests on piles of wood and piles of herring bones, a much finer culture than your United States is building on hot dogs." I said no more about the lowly, tasty herring as we entered the diamond *bourse*. Mr. Groen took me to the huge safe where he showed me diamonds, cut and uncut, rough and polished.

From there we went to the Rijks Museum. I had never been in a museum, and I expected to be bored. How can one be bored when suddenly confronted with the "Night Watch" of Rembrandt? How exciting it was to see in paints my mother's constant phrase, *"Dit is het husihowden van Jan Steen"* (This is the household of Jan Steen). She always shouted that if the house was disorderly, and here it was on the wall. I said to Mr. Groen, "Why, painting is life splashed on canvas with warm and vivid colors!"

Mijnheer Groen was pleased with my reaction, and he said, "There is hope for you yet, young barbarian."

Soon Ome David and Mr. Groen decided that it was time for me to know the works of Frans Hals, and I was to go to Haarlem. This was no problem, since we had relatives all over Holland and Belgium. Young David, who was more interested in music, insisted that I must go to the Oudekerk on Thursday mornings to listen to the Bach organ concerts. Mijnheer Groen said, "You must sit in the room with Hals' work and absorb it." To all of them I promised that I would keep on reading Motley's *Rise of the Dutch Republic*. With these admonitions I was put on the train for Haarlem.

The Haarlem branch of the family lived in a lovely, restful home. Most of their living was done in the inner courtyard, or patio. The house was built Moorish style many centuries ago when Spain was in power and controlled the Lowland Countries. Out on the street away from the inner courtyard life, the canals were brilliant with barges carrying tulips and hyacinths toward Amsterdam. The Oudekerk loomed huge over Haarlem. Inside the church the walls were cool and whitewashed, with the music of Bach flooding the building.

The Hals Museum was alive with robust color and the joy of life on canvas. These characters of Hals were hearty, earthy people. One felt like laughing with the "Fisherwoman" and joining in the joke. This was the Haarlem of the Sea Beggars, the people who ate rats rather than surrender to the Spaniards. *The Rise of the Dutch Republic* came alive to me as I walked and strolled through the streets of Haarlem.

I could not stay longer than a week. I had to go back to Amsterdam, as my mother would be returning from her trip to Freisland in the north of Holland. I did not dread seeing her as much as before, as I knew Tante Sara and Ome David were there to protect me. I had family. Then, too, I was anxious to see young David. He would listen to me with a quiet, tender smile on his face as he squeezed my hand under the table. This worried me. What would my mother say about David and me and our budding romance?

There was another relaxing thing about being in Amsterdam with the family. I did not go around with a feeling of inner shame because of my dislike for my mother. Since the family had agreed for many years on their pity and dislike for my mother, everyone understood how I felt, so I disliked her less. My aunt said, "Lientjie is different. She is more like us." They seemed to pity Mother more than to dislike her, although they called her "mean Betjie."

I used to ask my aunt, "Why did you hate her when you were younger, and yet now you feel sorry for her?"

She would not tell me, but would say, "What is past is past, and let it be forgotten." All I could get were glimpses of meanness by my mother to her younger brothers and sisters. My aunt would say, "And besides, it probably was not all your mother's fault. She had been the oldest of twenty-six children and the oldest of the living thirteen. She did not have an easy time of it either."

I didn't question any more, since I got hesitant answers or no answers. I only said, "Tante, I wish I could live with you the rest of my life and never have to go back to America. I have never had it so good or been so happy."

Finally Mother gave me permission to go to Oudorp on the island of Overflakke, where my father had been born. My friend, Carrie Niekerk, had returned to this island with her parents and brother. The last time I had seen her was when we worked side by side in Cedar Knolls Cotton Mill in Haledon, New Jersey, where we had been quill winders together. I was curious to see how she liked being in Holland again. I assumed it was a Holland quite different from the big cities I knew such as Amsterdam, Rotterdam or Haarlem.

Father had told me to look for anyone who remembered the Moerkerk family. He doubted that I would find anyone, since the family had left in the late nineteenth century. He was about nine years old when they left for America, the youngest of thirteen brothers and sisters, all of whom, except himself, died of tuberculosis, he had told me. Father himself was an arrested tuberculosis case. He told me that they had all lived crowded together like packed sardines on the small freighter which my grandfather owned and on which they sailed up the Rhine and among the many islands of Holland.

The flat countryside lay bathed in a shimmer of golden light as the train sped toward the south of Holland. Pancakes of yellow-green earth, the Netherlands reflected the golden light as we crossed the canals. I got off the train at the last stop on the mainland. Now I would have to take a boat.

Slowly we sailed in this little freighter-passenger boat to Overflakke. As I stood on deck, another rail-leaner pointed out to me the islands of Zeeland and where one could see Belgium. At Overflakke, a small bus waited for the boat's passengers. On the tops of dikes we traveled past windmills — the silent workers of Holland, high above the fields with their grazing, healthy cows. We rode higher than the ocean and the farm fields and finally arrived at the village of Oudorp, a fishing port which defiantly stuck its nose out into the North Sea.

Among the people awaiting the bus passengers, it was easy to pick out Carrie Niekerk. She was the only young girl without a tight bodice, a full skirt, wooden clogs and a blue lace cap on her head. When I stepped off the bus, there were now two girls dressed in city clothes. This was the Holland of the storybooks. Unmarried girls had blue lace caps on their heads, while the married girls had starched white caps. Clogs clumped on cobblestones, waded through mud, and pedaled bicycles. And here was I with the taste and style of a mill dolly. I have the photo of Carrie and me that day. My dress was blue crepe de chine, bunches of grapes embroidered on it with steel-cut beads that glistened in the sun, and a three-inch fringe of beads that dangled down toward my city shoes. Carrie looked at me, and I, at her; then she said, "Let's get out of these city clothes. I'll dress you like an Oudorp young maiden."

"Do you have clothes like everyone else wears here?" I asked Carrie.

"Of course. I only wore city clothes to make you feel more comfortable when you got off the bus. And if I were you, I would take off those shoes and silk stockings on the last stretch, as it is all mud. It rained last night," she said.

"When does it not rain in Holland?" I asked in reply.

Bead fringes jangling and dangling, shoes and stockings in my hands, bare toes swishing in the mud, I entered Carrie's backyard. Her parents laughed affectionately as they saw the two of us in our city finery with our legs and feet plastered with mud. We washed our feet out-of-doors. Mrs. Niekerk gave us woolen booties to wear in the house. No one wore shoes, or rather their wooden clogs, in the house: They were left in a row outside of the door where the new clogs given to me joined the row.

From Carrie's attic room we could look out on the sea, which was peaceful and calm that moment. First there was an expanse of meadowland of about a mile, and then there was a big dike. Then came another expanse of meadowland and the *groote*, or main dike. The dikes were made of large stones mortared with clay and planted with grass. The ocean seemed to tower over us even when calm, I remarked to Carrie. "Wait till it storms, and then you really will see something. Look, the storm warnings are up now," Carrie said.

The roaring of the waves slamming at the dike and the assault of the rain on the roof awakened me that night. No finger in the hole could hold that dike, I thought. Carrie had said that they were strong. With a delicious sense of danger, yet feeling safe in the security of the two dikes, I went back to sleep.

In the mornings we were fortified with a breakfast of sliced homemade bread cut from a round loaf at least a foot across. This we dipped in bacon grease flavored with sugar and ate big, solid pieces of fried bacon. My aunt with her kosher household would be shocked if she saw this, I thought. But it was very tasty. After breakfast, Carrie and I would walk on top of the dike when the tides ran high. When they were low, we went below the dikes to search for mussels, which I had learned to eat in Oudorp. From the top of the dike we could not see as far as distant Belgium, but we could see the shrimp boats come in and unload.

When heavy loads came in, Carrie and I would earn a bit of extra money helping to sort and to salt the shrimp for export. I could hear my socialist Ome David saying "child labor." But what fun this was compared to child labor in the mills in Paterson! Carrie and I knew the difference; we had both worked in the dirty, sticky cotton mill. An old man sat and told stories while we sorted shrimp. He spoke of their ancestors who had fled from Scotland as Catholics to this part of Holland. They had been supporters of the Scots' Queen Mary. I asked about my father's people. The old man remembered them, but there were no more left there. He told me that they had come from the village of Muirkirk in Scotland.

Calvinism versus Lutherism was discussed as nimble fingers separated shrimp, and parts of the Bible were read. The town was deeply religious. It was a way of life and rang true here in Oudorp, Overflakke, as it never had in Paterson, New Jersey. Somewhere in the transition from Scotland to the south of Holland, they had become Calvinists. I expected them to ask me about America, but they didn't. Their town was sufficient for them. Maybe this was provincial. I don't know, but they all seemed to have their place in the sun, and the town lacked the tensions of a town in America.

All too soon it was time for me to return to Amsterdam. My eighteenth birthday was approaching, and Tante Sara had planned a party, the first party ever given for me. I also missed David and was anxious to see him. I didn't know if this were love, but I thought of him all the time. I wanted to be near him; I felt complete when I was with him. Yet with real sorrow

I said good-bye to the Niekerks and the village of Oudorp, Overflakke.

When I was waiting in the railroad station in Rotterdam for a train to Amsterdam, whom should I see but my Uncle Simon. He took great pleasure in introducing me to his school companions as his niece. He was only one year older than me. They were on their way to Amsterdam for the twenty-fifth anniversary of the coronation of Queen Wilhelmina.

Simon said, "Come along with us in our car." He had a first class ticket and I had a third class, which I really preferred. The people were friendlier, and the time passed quickly as I listened to them.

As I was thinking of this, I asked Uncle Simon, "But what will the family say if I ride with four young men?"

Simon replied, "Have you forgotten that I am your uncle and family?"

"Yes, I know you are my uncle, and such a young, naughty one," I answered. We bantered a bit as I thought what fun it would be to ride with four young men, even though one of them was my uncle. I felt a bit guilty wondering what David would say, but the temptation was great to flirt a bit with Uncle's university pals. I had never had the chance to do this before. After all, I had my mother's youngest brother, my uncle, as a chaperone.

Nearby, a uniformed woman stood observing us intently. When I mentioned this to Uncle Simon, he said, "Oh, she probably thinks we are white slavers." I made believe I understood this, but I wondered what on earth white slavers were. Thinking nothing more of the woman, I entered the train with my uncle and his pals, and we chatted our way to Amsterdam.

I was saying goodbye to my Uncle Simon and his friends when I felt a touch on my arm. I turned, and there stood two policemen who said, "Come with us."

"Why?" I asked.

They replied, "We want to see your papers and to know why you are travelling alone with four young men."

A crowd was gathering as I explained, "But this one young man is my Uncle Simon de Vries." The police smiled unbelievingly.

I don't know what Uncle Simon was thinking when he said to the policemen, "Don't I look pretty young to be her uncle?" He probably thought it was a big joke. He continued, "I am nineteen years old, and she told me that she would be eighteen years old tomorrow." With that each policeman took one of my arms, and off we went as Uncle Simon gave a parting, mocking wave saying, "I'll see you tomorrow night at your birthday party."

I yelled at him, "The least you can do is to phone Tante Sara and tell her where I am and ask her to come and rescue me!"

Protesting bitterly, I explained to the police that he really was my uncle. I explained that I was in Holland with my mother and my younger sister. Then they asked me for my passport. "But I don't have one. I am on the same passport with my mother and sister."

"Where is your mother?" they asked. I told them I assumed she was en route from Groningen to Amsterdam.

A woman was interviewing me now: "No foreigner ever spoke Dutch like you do, like a born Amsterdamer at that."

"It is my first language. I spoke Dutch before I spoke English. We never speak English at home, only Dutch," I explained. I insisted that they get in touch with my Ome David and Tante Sara, and they did.

All Amsterdam was festive, ready to celebrate the Queen's birthday. My own birthday was the next day, and here I sat in a police station with policemen who would not believe me and who were protecting me from white slavers. The woman who had seen us in Rotterdam had reported me, and they had been waiting for me.

I was weeping with anger. I was hungry and thirsty, but I would not accept their food or water. Furiously I said, "How dare you do this! I am an American citizen. How dare you hold me and treat me like this!"

"Where is your proof of American citizenship?" they asked in reply.

They were just about ready to take me to a Home for Unprotected Girls when my Ome David and Tante Sara rushed in. Petite, gentle Tante Sara had the police backed up to the wall as she roundly scolded them for not believing me and for wasting taxpayers' money on a young girl. My Ome David was trying to calm his wife as she kept on poking the point of the umbrella at them to emphasize her words.

"Now, now, Sara, they were doing their duty. Stop scolding the police, and scold your brother Simon instead," said my uncle.

I was released in the custody of my aunt and uncle. Tante dried my tears as she continued muttering at police in general.

Passports and papers — it was a queer feeling. I was not a Hollander, yet I felt and spoke like one even though I was an American by birth. I did not feel strongly at all like an American. I didn't even want to return to America. Riding in the streetcar through streets hung with orange, songs pouring out of the coffee shops and Dutch flags everywhere — this thrilled me. I decided I preferred being a Hollander even though I was born an American. Passports and papers, so what?

It was July 27, 1923, and I was eighteen years old. The clan had really gathered to help me celebrate my birthday. There were eleven aunts, twelve uncles and about twenty cousins. Young David, his father Uncle David Schaap, and his mother were the only ones present who were not actually de Vries. But my beloved Ome David de Vries was a nephew of Uncle David Schaap, so they were family also. Songs, talk and laughter filled the air. Ome David and Tante Sara led the folk songs. Then my young David told of his trip around the world. I had never felt as wanted and loved as this before. Even my mother was too overwhelmed by the family's fussing over me to fuss at me herself.

How they talked! I had never heard such talk in America, where one was afraid to mention the word "Bolshevik" except with a sneer for fear that one might be called one. Not that I knew what a Bolshevik was, though my uncles did. Uncle Anton leaned toward Lenin and thought that the revolution in Russia was justified. Ome David agreed that it was justified but thought that the communists were too extreme; he leaned toward socialism. My young Uncle Simon was the most radical of all, but that was expected of youth, they said. Yet every one of them idolized the Queen. I understood little of the discussion. What was important to me was David holding my hand.

Gifts surrounded me. The only two that I still have are a photo of Ome David and Tante Sara and a copper plate with a rustic Dutch scene. No matter where I have been these two things have gone with me, and I always place them so I can see them. I want to recall my eighteenth birthday in Amsterdam as long as I can. We ended that evening promising to meet the next day in Rembrandt's Plein to join in the festivities for the Queen's birthday.

David was already waiting for me when we arrived at Rembrandt's Plein the next morning. We stood on the street together waiting for Queen Wilhelmina and Princess Juliana to pass by. The sun shone bright on the faces of the people of Amsterdam. Orange bunting hung on trees and on street lights, and orange ribbons hung on us. I was thrilled as the Queen passed, but I identified myself with Princess Juliana, since the family said I looked like her.

My cousins Dina and Gerrit said, "Wait till you see the fireworks tonight. I'll bet America has nothing like it."

I told them that on July 4th America did have big fireworks. But they were right; I had never seen anything like this in the United States. Using fireworks, scenes were displayed and stories were told. Canals were filled with boats whose orange-colored lighting twinkled. Orange, the color of the House of Orange, was everywhere. People walked and danced and sang in the streets. Herring stands did a whopping business.

Amsterdam was getting another layer of herring bones. I am sure a hot dog stand would have been less messy, but I didn't dare tell the family that.

Ome David must have thought I had had enough of fun and needed some culture again. He began suggesting that I go to The Hague. In The Hague we had a wealthy branch of the family, the van Niekerks, with whom I could stay. Ome David had arranged that. He wanted me to see the museums, the historical sites and the Peace Palace. Less and less did I want to leave Amsterdam, since David whom I loved lived there. I wished that David could go to The Hague also, but he was not feeling too well. He had diabetes. This did not frighten me, since my mother was ornery and active despite her diabetes. David's diagnosis had been recent, and he was on a strict diet regime.

"You Americans take the word 'freedom' too lightly. It must be cherished jealously," Ome David said to me. "I want you to go and see where leaders of ours like Jan de Witt were tortured by the Spaniards rather than give up religious freedom. I want you to go to the Peace Palace and to think of the importance of peace to this world," he continued. My serious, jolly, red-headed Ome David — why had I considered him ugly when I first saw him? Laughingly he said, "And don't come back with those den Haag pretensions."

"What do you mean?" I asked.

He explained, "When a family from den Haag has no fruit or a baked ham they put wooden, painted fruit or meat on the table, and so it is called the city of wooden hams."

With thoughts of torture, peace and wooden foods mixed up in my mind, I left for The Hague. The Hague branch of the family did not have wooden hams or wooden fruits on the table. They were considered rich. Mr. van Niekerk had a flourishing meat market. He could not understand that Ome David was a socialist and thought him more than queer to want me to see such sights. My two cousins, Saima and Aronda, had never been to those places. Uncle advised us to go to the tea dance at Wassenar, to go swimming at Scheveningen. We did what he suggested with pleasure. But I also took the protesting cousins to see the Peace Palace, to the museums, and last of all to Gravenhaag where Jan de Witt had been tortured. I can never forget the fantastic instruments of torture I saw which the Spaniards had used against the Dutch in the 16th century.

After I had been in den Haag almost a week, I was ready to go back to Amsterdam. I agreed with Ome David and Tante Sara that The Hague was pretentious. I got tired of hearing, "Take your gloves," "Take your hat," and "What will people say?". I far preferred my beloved Amsterdam, a city without pretensions, an earthy city nourished by the lowly herring of the North Sea.

It wasn't that I didn't like the branch of the family in The Hague. They were very kind to me, but here I was in what was the equivalent of the Eastside in Paterson, and I felt as though I were trapped in a stuffy room. The train could not take me fast enough back to Amsterdam, my uncle, my aunt, my cousins, and David.

Home again in Amsterdam, my life revolved more and more around David. I used to dream and stumble as I walked, thinking, "How can he love me, a simple, gauche, uneducated girl of eighteen?" David was my teacher, my mentor, my guide. His lips touched my forehead gently as he said good night. For this I was grateful, as Mother had frightened me with the dirtiness of sex. His love was a gentle one, a controlled one. Often I was bewildered with the desires and emotions that arose in me when he embraced me.

Our arms entwined, we would walk down to the cafe, planning where we would live after we married. I could stay with Tante Sara until then. He was sure he could handle Mother, but I was not sure. She would do anything to defeat my happiness. She needed me to vent her anger. In a situation where she was with people, she could be polite and charming. Later anything that had bothered her would come out on me with a shout or a clout. I was miserably afraid of her. As the time approached for Betjie and my mother to return to Amsterdam, I became increasingly fearful.

Mother and my sister had visited almost all of the relatives we had in Holland. Mother, as usual, had left squabbles and quarrels behind her. The family called her "the troublemaker." She had a knack of locating a person's weak spot, twisting it, and torturing the person with it. Obviously she was no longer welcome, and she began to look at sailing notices. David and I enlisted the aid of Ome David and Tante Sara.

My aunt and uncle invited my mother and David's parents to dinner. Tante cooked special dishes for Mother. That night they admired the diamond ring that she had bought, her ability to bargain. They paid special attention to her all evening until she seemed mellow. Since Mother liked my Tante Sara better than her other sisters, Sara had been delegated to ask the questions. When it seemed an appropriate moment, Tante asked her if I could stay with them in Amsterdam to be engaged to David and to marry him. As Mother read my aunt's lips, I could see her expression change. She became like a wild animal.

She shouted at me, "What have you done, you slut? You are probably fat with baby! You are underage! You will come back to America. You will work in the factories where you belong, and earn the money to pay me for raising and clothing you!" No tears, no pleading on the part of anyone availed. Although she gloried in being the center of attention, she would listen to no one. She finally pulled the trick I knew well. Suddenly she could not read my lips, or anyone else's. I knew she could. I had no idea of disobeying my mother. In 1923 one didn't.

In October 1923 we sailed for Hoboken, New Jersey. Unhappiness may only be a moment in time. One does forget, I know. But I'll never forget the depth of unhappiness and longing that I had on that boat for David and the family. I wrote to

David daily, pleading with him to wait for me until I was twenty-one. I urged him to come to the United States, and I promised to run away with him.

North Eighth Street, Prospect Park, Paterson, New Jersey — was this home? At times the six months of belonging and being loved in Holland seemed like a dream. "Number, please?" said a voice. It was my voice. Over and over again my voice said the same phrases. At the same time a quiet voice that only I heard was saying, "Maybe there will be a letter from David when you get home. Pray that Mother is out, since if she gets there first, you will never see the letter." I did not know where to have the letters sent. She boasted that she opened them, read them and then burned them. She had always opened my mail, but now I had to have his letters. I asked at the factory where I was running the switchboard whether I could have my mail sent there. The answer was yes.

With his letters coming to the factory, I began feeling alive again. Mother could not understand what had happened to the flow of mail she had been reading. I did not tell her that I was receiving them at work, or she would have gone there or to the post office. I considered her capable of doing anything to thwart me.

David was coming! He was coming to marry me, to kidnap me if necessary. He would take me back to Amsterdam — home, Holland, Amsterdam, the family, Tante Sara, Ome David, my cousins, my wonderful, friendly, loving, quibbling family! My dark, tall, gentle, strong, beloved David was coming. Regardless of my fear for Mother, I knew that I would go with David in some way or other, even if I had to stow away on the ship. I was eighteen, and my love poured out to him in letters as I waited for him.

Two weeks later a black-bordered envelope fell out of the mailbox at home. The return address said "Schaap, A'dam, Netherlands." I was afraid to open it. In a way I wished my mother had been home to get it first. For a long time I stood with the black-bordered envelope in my hand. Finally I opened it. David was dead. David had been buried. He had died suddenly of diabetes. His parents asked me to come live with them, to be a daughter to them. David had been their only child.

Even Mother was subdued by the letter when I showed it to her. She left me alone with my thoughts. If only I had been with him a short time, any time; if only I had been strong enough to defy my mother and had not returned to the United States. I wished, at least, that I were his widow, with a child of his in my womb. Wishes, desires, tears — but my David was dead. What was the use? What could I do? I pleaded with Mother to let me go to Holland. I told her, "You know you hate me. Why don't you let me out of your sight? Let me live in Holland with the family. Let me go to David's grave with his parents."

She laughed and said, "I'll do all I can with the police to not let you go."

I was numb. Nothing mattered.

Home became even more intolerable. I had to escape in some way. I had to get out. How?

"Number, please?" "Your party does not answer." "The line is busy." I repeated them over and over again, weeks, months, a year. I went on hikes, went to scout meetings, sang in the choir, but all the while I was thinking, "How can I escape?"

I began to think of applying to enter a nursing school. I don't think I was altruistic. To me it was a way of getting away from my mother and home, a way of climbing out of Paterson filled with its memories of rat-filled cellars, dirty mills, and my mother.

Soon I found out that most schools of nursing demanded that the applicant have at least two years of high school, and others demanded that one be a high school graduate. I had neither the diploma nor the minimum years required. What next? I looked at advertisements in magazines. One night I read one asking for applications for the New Rochelle Hospital School of Nursing. "High school is not required, but advisable," it said.

My pen flew as I wrote to ask for application blanks. When they arrived, I lovingly, anxiously filled them out. To my surprise, Mother did not fuss much. And more to my surprise, I was accepted to enter as a probationer for September 1925!

Mother wanted to go with me to the hospital on entrance day. I still don't know how I convinced her not to come with me. I was worried enough about my own propensity to make mistakes without adding her and the uncertainties of her behavior. How lucky that I had the influence of the YWCA Home for Working Girls, where I had learned to use table manners. I was also grateful to my family in Holland, who had helped open my eyes to painting, my ears to music, and my heart to philosophies of other peoples.

My acquaintances from the mills, the phone company, the scouts, and the choir thought I was crazy to want to study to be a nurse. It was dirty, hard work. One got the feeling that to be a graduate nurse was most respectable and fine, but that the process of becoming one was disreputable. Undaunted and as happy as could be, I took the trolley one morning bound for New Rochelle, New York.

New Jersey, 1925-1928
Coming out of the Cellar 2

The wheels talked as they clacked, "You will be a registered nurse." They clicked, "You are leaving home forever." I had ridden the Hudson River Trolley many times. With the girl scouts, I had gone to Palisades Amusement Park and had crossed the Hudson River to New York City. With my mother, I had come up this same route to see her favorite man. This time I was riding the trolley with a new purpose, desire and excitement. The future was mine, I felt. Failure did not worry me. I had survived my own urge to self-destruction and the urge to destroy my mother. The words "failure" and "impossible" were not in my dictionary. I wanted to shout to the world and to the passengers as we crossed the river on the ferry boat, "I am going to be a nurse!" But my fellow passengers were deeply immersed in their own problems and interests.

Ungainly, fat, unsure, a gawky and gauche young woman twenty years old, I stood looking at the shores of New York City. That I would be a nurse I was sure, but of myself I was unsure. As we crossed 125th Street I kept asking the conductor for the railroad station; I was afraid I might miss it. I am sure he was glad when I got off the trolley.

As I rode through Westchester County in September 1925, to me it was the most beautiful countryside I'd ever seen. The train could not go fast enough to take me to New Rochelle. Yet the nearer we came, the more my bravado started slipping, like a petticoat with a loose elastic at the waist. I was frightened, but I dared not admit it, even to myself.

When I got off at the New Rochelle station, I just sat until I got up enough courage to proceed to the hospital. Slowly I walked; a suitcase in each hand contained all my possessions, including my beloved girl scout uniform, which still lacked the home nursing badge which would have enabled me to be a Golden Eaglet scout.

Here was the nurses' home, a three-story, red brick building right next to the hospital. White-capped and with white aprons over their blue dresses, girls flitted in and out of the doors. Everyone seemed to be hurrying. I walked up the short stairs and entered what appeared to be a living room or reception room. One girl asked me, "Are you a new probie?"

I countered, "And what is a probie?"

"Are you a new student?" she continued.

"That I am," I answered. She told me where to sit and wait for the other probationers.

Soon, a lovely, white-haired woman came out of a small room. She reminded me of Miss Paul at the phone company. Her starched white uniform rustled as she walked toward me and asked my name. I told her, "I am Lini Moerkerk from Paterson, New Jersey."

She told me that she was Miss Harriet Wilday, Directress of Nursing, and said, "Sit back in the chair. Don't be frightened; relax. Soon the other probationers will be here with Miss Wilbur, the Instructress of Nursing Arts. She will show you your room, assign you a roommate, and take you to supper. Don't worry."

I had not known my worry was so obvious.

Shortly, seven girls walked in. The room was not large enough to keep us apart. We began asking one another questions. The others were from Bangor, Maine, and had all been friends since grammar and high school days. High school — had a mistake been made? Miss Wilday had accepted my application. She knew I had not had high school. I was sure they would be much smarter than me, since they had had high school. I kept quiet, and determined then and there that I'd catch up by studying hard. One girl was missing, the only other probie who was not from Bangor.

A stern, unsmiling woman walked toward us. The stiffness of her back and of her uniform awed us. We stopped giggling and chatting, and the smiles dropped from our faces as phony curtains of respect rose in our eyes. In my mind flashed the thought, "Cheese it! Here comes the stool pigeon!"

"I am Miss Wilbur, your nursing arts instructor," she said. In a clipped voice, she told us don't do this and don't do that if you want to pass your probationary period. With the don'ts ringing in our ears, we followed her like little, chastened, quiet lambs to the dining room. Fortunately, she ate in the supervisors' dining room, and we, in the student nurses' dining room. With giggles and friendly smiles, we began again exploring one another.

Now we waited for Miss Wilbur to show us to our rooms. My corset was pinching me, and my bra left me little room to breathe. (Corset by Spirella, brassiere by Spirella, ordered by Mother.) If only I could take these off, I'd feel free. Mother had insisted on tight, binding corseting so that I would have no curves but be straight up and down. I could not wait to take off the spiral steel garments.

Our rooms were on the third, or top, floor, the hottest in the summer and the coldest in the winter. As our status changed, we would move down a flight. By the time we were ready to graduate, we would be on the first floor. The Bangor girls had doubled up. My roommate was the missing Katherine Calderwood. Closing the door, I looked about the corner room. One window looked out on the street and onto the changing autumn leaves. The side window looked into the new wing of the hospital.

Taking off my tight corset and bra, I heaved a sigh of relief and carefully tucked them under a pillow. I had been raised with the attitude that underwear was unmentionable, that the body was a dirty thing, and one kept it squeezed in and covered. We had been told always to bathe when we came off duty. Obviously, no one tried to save on water bills here. I decided to take a shower right away.

Returning from my shower, bathrobe primly wrapped around me, I stepped into our room. A slim, well-groomed girl faced me. With a Scotch burr in her voice she said, "Corsets and bras should be hung on chairs and not tucked under pillows. Why do you wear the damned things anyway?" she asked. "Besides, I want this bed; you take the other," she continued. I was speechless listening to her. Her voice, her diction, her choice of words were worlds apart from the factories, from the phone company, from anything I had ever heard. I liked it. As she told me how recently she had come from Scotland after her parents' deaths, she took out a cigarette. "Want one?" she asked.

"Oh, no thanks, it is against the rules, and I don't smoke," I replied.

"Such a silly rule! You stand near the door and lean against it to prevent someone from walking in," she told me. She moved near the open window, and the smoke drifted out. For the next two and a half years, I leaned against the door while Scottie had her bedtime smoke.

Although worlds apart, fortunately we liked one another. In no time, she was known as Scottie, and I, as Dutchy. She helped me to be accepted as part of the group. Scottie was the dominant one in our relationship. She would tell me, "Dutchy, the word is 'girls' and not 'goils.' We say 'going to' and not 'gonna.' Don't say 'ain't'; it hurts my ears. Stop murdering the king's English! The only words you pronounce correctly are those you learned in the telephone company." Believe me, I listened to her and tried to speak as she did. My English improved and picked up a bit of a Scotch accent, much to Scottie's amusement. Now it was clothes. She wanted me to throw out my frilly clothes and get tailored clothes. "Fine, but with what money?" I answered.

One night when Scottie had fallen asleep, I lay in bed wondering, "What am I? Part of me is Ome David and Tante Sara. Another part was taught by David. Now I am absorbing all that Scottie is giving me. What is *me*?" From 1925 through 1928, Scottie from Kilmaroneck, Ayershire, Scotland, became a part of me, and she still remains a part of me.

Even Miss Wilbur became a part of me. Almost every morning for four months we listened to her. "Your uniforms must always be thirteen inches from the floor, no more and no less. Don't wear rings or earrings — in other words, no jewelry on duty. Don't come on duty without a hairnet." On and on she went. One day she walked into my room and began scolding me, "What do you mean standing there before a window combing your hair?" She emphasized her words with a strong pull on the shade. She turned to me and said, "Why did you faint this morning when you saw blood being drawn out of an arm? *You want to be a nurse*, yet you think only of yourself. That is why you fainted."

"I am sorry," I said.

"You spoiled young girls; I don't know how you will ever become nurses," she muttered as she walked out.

Scottie walked in, and when I told her what had happened she said, "Bend your head low next time you feel like fainting. Don't let Old Horseface get you down." Nothing seemed to faze Scottie. She was secure. Scottie knew of my insecurities and helped me. Miss Wilbur also sensed them and ragged me like a terrier.

Miss Wilbur gave us our classes in the nursing arts, with emphasis on the care of the patient in the 24-hour day. She was tough, and she was strict. Thanks to her, we really learned bedside nursing. Theory we received from the doctors. I asked many questions and made many a faux pas, like the time I asked, "And who is Hoyle?" I filled pages with notes in all classes. Scottie did not bother, since she knew that I would have them.

In the evening our room would be full of chattering classmates. When they made up their minds, off they would go to a movie or a party or a date while I remained to study. My constant questioning and studying gave me the best marks, which sometimes became annoying to my classmates. Most of them crammed the night before exams in our room, as I filled the role of the teacher. Forgive me, classmates. I was no brighter and no dumber than any of you. You were high school graduates, and I was not. I had to get through training school. It meant my liberation, my freedom; my growth depended on it. It was a way to escape my mother, a way to be me, whatever was me, or to become me. How could I tell you of my home or my parents? I was ashamed of my parents and of my background. You all casually talked of your homes, your parents, and took for granted the love they gave you. If I had told you that I hated and feared my mother, you would have thought me even more queer.

Gradually, as the months passed, we were allowed to work in the hospital itself, under supervision.

I took TPRs (temperature, pulse and respiration) the first afternoon that I was assigned to the women's ward as a probationer. One patient who lay there unconscious had the queerest breathing I had ever seen or heard. Her pulse was rapid and hardly perceptible. The thermometer that I took from under her arm read 107°! With the thermometers tinkling perilously on the tray, I ran down the ward to the office of the Assistant Directress. "What shall I do?" I asked anxiously.

Coolly she replied, "Call the graduate nurse, and assist her in getting the patient ready for the morgue."

"But she is alive!" I exclaimed.

"She won't be much longer. Go back and finish the TPRs."

Under the graduate's supervision, I tied up the woman's chin and did all the other things we had been instructed to do in practical nursing. I wheeled her to the morgue. Is she dead, or isn't she dead? I wondered. The doctor had pronounced her dead. Was all done that could have been done? When I put her body in the icebox, would I be killing her? I went nearly crazy inside, thinking, questioning. I stood there, one hand on her pulse and one on the locker door. I could not bring myself to open the door and shove her in.

Then I came to life as the graduate, who had been sent down to see what had happened to me, said, "My God, Moerkerk, this is a hell of a place and time to daydream. Jesus, trays have to be served, and you stand here holding hands with a corpse. These probies!" she finished, muttering. She shoved the cadaver in and closed the door for eternity.

Following her, emotionally torn by self-questioning — "Was the woman really dead?" — I went back upstairs to serve the living their supper.

My classmates, the Bangor girls, were always out on dates. At 10 p.m. they would be under the covers for the bed count, but in their clothes. Only their shoes stood in front of their beds. After Miss Wilbur had made her rounds, they would sneak out; but I was afraid. I did not have the nerve; besides, I wanted to finish training. I did not want to be expelled, and since I didn't want them expelled either, I would sneak down and leave the latch off the door. At all hours, they came back.

They decided that I should have a date. I was thrilled, but insisted that I would not go out after 10. I showered and dressed and borrowed frilly clothes from Murphy. Scottie was not there to say, "Go tailored." I was going with Biddle and Florence. Three men called for us. I could hardly see the face of my escort in the car. I blushed in the darkness as they told risqué jokes, and made myself laugh. My escort's arm was now on my breast. I was miserable, but I had a date, didn't I?

The car stopped in a dark park, and necking began. My lips were forced open, and a tongue rolled over mine. A hand was going up my thigh. I asked the girls to take me home. I felt sick, nauseous. As they drove me back to the nurses' home, I felt guilty for spoiling their fun. Upstairs, I showered again and washed my teeth and mouth thoroughly. I felt dirty. Crawling into bed, I began to cry. What was wrong with me? Why could I not enjoy a date like they could? Yet I had had many, many dates with David and had never felt dirty.

Scottie walked in and asked, "What is the matter, Dutchy?" As I explained what had happened, she listened and said, "There is nothing wrong with you, Dutchy. Wait for another David. Your English is bad, but your values are good. There is nothing wrong when you dislike cheapness; to the contrary. Don't worry. I'll take you ice skating with my brother Jock and me next week."

The way Jock treated me reminded me of David. I wished he would like me more, but he treated me like a kid sister. I still wondered underneath why I should be disturbed when a man tried to neck with me. Was something wrong with me? Was I queer? One of the girls in the senior class only necked with girls. She just preferred girls. Once on a dare she went out with a man, and he repulsed her. Unfortunately, the one time she went out with the man she became pregnant and was expelled. Was I queer like her? When I talked about these things to Scottie, she would laugh and tell me, "Don't worry. You like men too much to be queer."

Scottie and I did most of our talking as we scrubbed the endless white basins (that already were shining) before we went on the wards to give P.M. care. I did not mind the chore of scrubbing bedpans in the intimacy of the small utility room as long as I could listen to Scottie. I learned much from her and never could hear enough. How fortunate I was to have her as a roommate!

Scottie went to women's ward, and I went on to men's ward to give P.M. care. I actually enjoyed giving this care, rubbing a back till the kinks were out, helping a man wash his face and hands, straightening the bed and scolding the men for mussing them so. My problem was remembering not to sing as I worked. Even the sickest in men's ward enjoyed my singing, but it was against the rules, and I would hear myself and stop.

The men would say, "Keep on singing. We feel better. It makes us forget our hurts for a moment."

"This is a hospital. Neither you nor I are supposed to sing," I replied.

A husky truck driver, with his fractured leg up in traction, said, "Well, I am paying my bills, and this is a free country. You sing, and I'll sing."

Invariably I would compromise with the rules and with them, and we all sang. "Softly, don't let the supervisor hear us down the hall," I would say. Softly we would sing. The combination of good nursing care and a bit of singing did wonders for men's ward in the late day, when backs were hot and itchy from rubber sheets, tempers were short, and temperatures higher.

Good nursing is a challenge. In those days we had no antibiotics. It was a battle to the finish between the host and the invader, the microbes. Nursing care came to the aid of the host. The doctor worked with his baton and said, "A little more of this, and a little less of that."

But as the days passed in December 1925, I felt less like singing and more like getting into bed beside the patient. My head throbbed. The pain radiated from a molar to my whole head, and I was hot with fever.

Scottie said, "Tell Miss Wilbur that you don't feel well."

"I don't dare. We have final exams this month, and if I pass, I'll be capped. No, I am afraid to tell her. She might send me home," I replied.

Soon afterward Miss Wilbur came to see me. "What are you complaining about?" she asked. "You are here to take care of the sick and not to baby yourselves," she continued.

"Who told you?" I asked.

"Your roommate told me that you had a toothache. Go see a dentist," she said and walked out of the room.

The very next morning, in the supply room where I was supposed to make cotton balls, I sat holding my head instead. Our ear, nose and throat doctor-teacher walked in. "What is the matter, Miss Moerkerk?" he asked.

"I really don't know, but I am sure it is more than a toothache. I can hardly stand the pain," I answered.

He stepped out of the room and asked a passing nurse to call Miss Wilbur. She came and looked daggers at me, but she said nothing. After all, a well-trained nurse did not speak unless she was spoken to by a doctor.

Dr. Stevenson, with great gentleness, began tapping my cheek. When I regained consciousness, I found myself on the floor. This was the second time I had fainted in front of Miss Wilbur. I looked at her pleadingly and hoped she was not thinking of having me expelled from the nurses' training school.

Dr. Stevenson ordered Miss Wilbur to have me admitted as a bed patient, and he asked for a wheelchair. It felt strange to be rolled in a wheelchair to a four-bed, semi-private room. Routine admission services began, such as blood for testing, urine for urinalysis, and so forth. I felt so sick I didn't much care what they were doing to me. However, when a nurse appeared with a tray set up for an antrum puncture, I did ask, "Will it hurt?"

"And how it will hurt!" she replied. Patients are rarely told the truth, but the nurse did not consider me a patient. That, too, was coming.

When the doctor appeared, he explained that he would have to pass a bone-crushing instrument through my nostril and break the bone to my antrum (sinus) to allow the pus to drain. My sinus was heavy with pus, and the tooth directly below it would have to be pulled later. It seemed to be draining pus into my antrum, he told me. He tried to give me local anesthesia, but it had no effect. With a push and a shove, I felt the bone crunch. The pus squirted over the bed and into the basin I was holding. Within no time, my head felt like a flat tire but less painful.

My classmates began dropping in as soon as they heard that I was a bed patient. They consoled me but said, "You have to get well fast, Dutchy; exams are next week. Then comes capping if we pass. Best of all comes Christmas!"

"Oh, I'll be out of here in a few days," I replied.

Scottie said, "You'd better be! Who else can help us cram for exams?"

One week passed. Instead of being out of bed, I was worse. I was desperate. My right arm was swollen. I could not move my left leg, or my back. I could not hold a book. Even Miss Wilbur was gentle with me. I told her of my worries about exams. I could not get out of bed to take them. Miss Wilbur told me that she would speak to Miss Wilday, the Directress of Nurses, about the problem.

In the meantime, my classmates spent evenings at my bedside as I verbally helped them to cram. One would rub my arm and another my leg with oil of wintergreen. My arms and legs were packed in warm cotton and bandaged, and last of all my back was rubbed.

I dreaded the signal for lights out when they had to leave, and I was left alone with pain and fright. As the room cooled off, the pain got worse. I slept fitfully. In between catnaps I worried about exams and about me. "Acute rheumatic fever" was the diagnosis of both the doctor and me. I had seen patients die from the heart damage, and I had seen people who would be invalids all their lives for the same reason. I was not frightened of death but of disability. If my heart developed a murmur, I would be sent home. What home? Was that home in Paterson? I would rather die than go back there.

The day I was to have my tonsils out under local anesthesia, Miss Wilbur brought me the good news. The decision had been made that I would not have to take the exams, since I had had 95 or better in every exam up to my illness. It was considered that I had passed the exams, and they gave me a grade of 90. This knowledge comforted me while my tonsils were being taken out. If only my mother had permitted them to take my tonsils out when I was younger, when I had complained of frequent sore throats. She had told the doctor she could not afford to spend the money. I sensed that the houses she bought and sold should have made her financially secure, but I would not have considered protesting.

Salt-free, sugar-free, meat-free diet — antrum washed daily — tooth out — parts of my body swollen — joints stiff — and now I had a postoperative sore throat, too. As miserable as I was, I was grateful that I was a patient in the New Rochelle Hospital and not at home in the hands of my mother. I was treated with affection and gentleness by the nurses, the doctors, the Directress of Nursing, and even by Miss Wilbur, who now appeared in a different light.

Mother had been up to see me after she had been notified of my illness. She could not understand how I could live in an environment where there was no Dutch spoken. This shocked her, and it bothered her that I was happy although in pain. I suppose she could not resist saying, with a knowing smile on her face, "You will be an invalid. You will have to come home. You will not be able to finish training, but there are some jobs you will be able to do in the factory."

"I would rather die," I replied.

"You may at that," she answered.

Shortly after my mother's visit, a classmate said, "There is a man here, a Mr. Pollock from Dobbs Ferry. He wants to see you."

Hysterically I replied, "I don't want to see him! Tell him that I am very sick and can see only members of the family. Tell him anything you want, but keep him out!"

"Don't get upset, Dutchy; he told us that he was family," she continued.

"Not to my knowledge," I affirmed. "I don't want to see him!"

Less than a week later Mr. Pollock's sister came down from Bridgeport to see me. I liked her, and I liked their family in

Holland. I had an unreasonable dislike for her brother. I certainly did not enjoy the memories I had of our visits to him in Dobbs Ferry and the threats my mother made of what would happen to me if I told my father where we had been. I still remember the long, cold waiting in the back yard while they were warmly ensconced in the house.

"Why won't you see my brother?" Flora asked.

"I really don't know, except that I dislike him. It upsets me to think of him," I answered. "Why should he want to see me?" I asked.

"The family — your family and my family in Holland — know, and I thought you knew," she replied.

"Know what?" I asked. I was quite sure what she was going to tell me. Ever since I had spent most of my eighteenth year in Holland, I had suspected what she would tell me. "Don't tell me; I don't want to know," I begged.

"Then you do feel and suspect that my brother is really your father?" she asked. She continued, "He has a right to see you. He is your father."

"What makes a father — the fact that his sperm and my mother's ova united and made me? Does that make him my father? Or is my father the man who worked to feed me, who loves me, who cares for me, and who suffers living with my mother for my sake, as he once told me? No, I refuse to recognize your brother as my father even though he may be my biological father. I hope the man I call Father never learns what you have just told me," I said emphatically. "I am a bastard," I muttered to myself.

"Don't say that! You are a love child," answered Flora.

"The only love I have ever known was given to me by Tante Sara and Ome David, and by David Schaap and his family," I replied with bitterness. "Yes, and inasmuch as he is able to, my nonbiological father loves me; but he is afraid of my mother. Because of my mother's passion for your brother, she has wrecked a home. She has made her husband miserable, and me. She married a Protestant and became a convert. She is anti-Semitic; she thrives on hate. Does she know that you have told me?" I asked.

"No, and don't tell her," answered my visitor.

"Will you see my brother?" she asked.

"No, I'll stick to the man I call Father. As you and Mother say, he may be lower class than your family or her family; but he is good. He is my father! I'll not see your brother," I said. I began to put two and two together. I understood the bitterness in my mother when she had said, "Bernard came to this country to marry me, and he married another woman for her dowry."

"I am really burned up when I think of my stepsisters, for that is what they are. I don't know them; I know of them. They are sheltered and protected. They went to high school. One plays the piano; the other, the violin. One is studying to be a doctor, and the other, a lawyer. They never had to work in a dirty mill. I am sure they were never called whores by their mother. I never want to hear my mother tell me about them again. Does my mother treat me as a love child or as a child of sin?" I asked my visitor.

I could not seem to stop talking. "The only time Mother sees your brother now is when he gets in touch with her to borrow money. She complains, but always loans it to him. Is this what I worked in the sweatshops for? If Mother had had my tonsils out when I complained of sore throats as a child, I would probably not be in bed with rheumatic fever now. She could not afford to spend one of her carefully hoarded dollars on me, but she could lose them to your brother."

Flora interrupted, "Remember, he is your father!"

I replied, "Not to me. Love child? For years, all my life, she has tried to put her guilt feelings onto me. She calls me a whore. Well, I won't feel guilty for her or for him. I'll live despite you all. I want nothing from you or your family or my mother. Forget that I exist. But I will exist," I said.

Flora said, "You should not hate your mother."

"I don't hate her," I replied. "But now I understand. She always said that she married my father to spite another man.

She really married him because she was pregnant with me by your brother. Clever of her, no? No, I don't hate her. It is worse; I loathe her. Her malice and envy contaminates everyone she comes in contact with. In a way, I am glad that you told me this," I said. "Now I know that I owe her nothing. I can free myself of her. I can try to become a whole person. Now please go," I said with less anger. "I want to be alone."

My misery was great, and so my pains seemed less by comparison. My heart was one big sore spot in my chest. I could not tell anyone what I had heard, not even Scottie. If only Tante Sara could get to me, or I to her. She would help. She could help. I was a bastard, a Jew, unwanted, unloved, sick and miserable in bone, muscle and spirit. This was one of the lowest spots in my life. It was cold outside, and it was colder in my heart. I could not turn or move without help. I did not want to call a nurse. I wanted no one to ask me, "What is the matter, Dutchy?"

As the snow fell slowly outside, each jewelled flake struck and chilled my spirit more. My back was one big aching throb. My knee was swollen to twice the normal size, and my right arm and hand were immovable unless someone else moved them. I watched the snowflakes melt to nothing, and I wanted to melt to nothingness like a flake of snow. Long night after long night of pain I had managed to keep up my spirit. With what Flora had told me, something had happened.

Mother would come, and she made it worse. Gloatingly, her sharp tongue would say, "Who will feed you? Who will take care of you, my fine young lady? Your sins have come home to you. This is your punishment for being rebellious to me. Now you can't become a nurse. You will have to be sent home to me. You have no one except me. How do you like that?"

How true this was! I had no one. How could I die? I couldn't walk to get to the drug cabinet. There was never a knife on my tray. I was being fed. I could not hold a fork or knife. How could I pass into oblivion?

My classmates dropped in to see me less and less as I lost my spunk and my smile. Who wants to be with a morbid person? They had enough of that in their daily work. The nurses got so that they hated to brush and comb my long, thick hair and wanted to cut it. One day I said, "Go ahead, cut my hair; maggots don't eat hair." With that they knew that my spirits were at a low ebb. I had always been proud of my long, thick, bronze-colored hair. No matter how fat and ugly I might think I was, my hair gave me satisfaction. With that comment, though, the doctor must have decided that I had been alone too long. I was moved to a semiprivate room.

One night a young, unconscious girl was brought into the room where I lay. Broken in body — pelvis, leg and arm — she looked like a dying flower. Work went on all night to keep her alive. When the nurse had to leave the room, she would put the call bell in the hand that I could use. The nurse put me to work to help save the life of another. Listening to her breathing, watching her color, made me forget my miserable self. Life began in me again.

Days and weeks went by as Madeline and I shared one another's miseries. I shared her company and her flowers. I enjoyed her visitors. One evening her brother Howard came down with a friend of his from Port Chester, New York. I was introduced to his friend, whose name was Wilbur Fuhr. He did not talk much, but he listened with a smile of shared enjoyment. He reminded me somewhat of David Schaap. Certainly he did not look like my memories of David, but his mannerisms were similar.

One night after the boys had left, I asked Madeline, "Is Wilbur your boyfriend?"

"Goodness, no. He is like a brother to me. I like them tall, dark and handsome. Wilbur is short, blond and not handsome. Besides, he is much too serious for me," she answered. "Why, do you like him, Lini?" she asked.

"Well, I do, but I'm sure I would not stand a chance," I replied.

"Don't be unsure of yourself. Of course you stand a chance. Why does he drive down so often from Port Chester to New Rochelle? I am sure it is not to see me; it is to see you," she answered. I had been wondering about that myself, but was afraid to admit it. Now that Madeline had said it, I was quite sure that Wilbur came to see me.

Now I became a nuisance to the nurses. I wanted my hair combed various ways. I wanted a mirror. I wanted bright ribbons to grace the ends of my braids. I begged my classmates to loan me silk nightgowns or bedjackets for visiting hours. They were both amused and annoyed. Since my arm and hand were still useless, this meant that they had to wait on me. Teasingly they would say, "You were less trouble when you wanted to die, Dutchy."

Buds were bursting on the trees. Spring was around the corner, and it was entering me. I began to forget the long three months of misery. I was in bed, but I wanted to live. I was falling in love from New Rochelle Hospital.

The pains and swelling were leaving my arms, my back, my bones. I could move one finger, then another. Then I could pull my leg up. Now my back ached less, and I could turn in bed without help. It was wonderful to be able to slowly use my body again. No one would tell me if my heart was damaged or not, and I tried not to think of it. I wanted to be completely well. I wanted to finish nurses' training, and I did not want to be sent home. I wanted to see more of Wilbur, and I hoped he would continue coming to see me.

Four months had passed, and it was now April. I was able to get up in a wheelchair for a few minutes, later for a half-hour. Soon I would be walking again. When the nurse was not around, I would dangle and swing my legs on the side of the bed. Now I was walking a bit, but conflicts began. I wanted to hide how well I was feeling. I was afraid I would be sent back to Paterson for my convalescence period. New Rochelle Hospital was home to me. Madeline would have to be in bed for another month. She did not want to lose me as a roommate, and I did not want to be dismissed from the hospital. I hid the fact that I was walking with ease. Yet I wanted to get outside. I wanted to walk the streets again toward Long Island Sound and to watch the waves lap the shore. I wanted to touch the bark of a budding tree.

Early in May 1926, I was discharged as a hospital patient. I was told to go to my room, to take it easy. I could go across to the dining room for my meals, but I was to rest. I was to await the decision of the cardiologist and the ear, nose and throat doctor. I waited with dread for their decision as to my fate.

Within a few days, I was called into the nursing office. The doctors and Miss Wilday were present. Gently they explained to me that I could not finish my nurses' training. The acute rheumatic fever I had had left me with a heart murmur. The cardiologist cheerfully explained that I could live longer than most people, since I had had enough preparation in knowing the body. He said, "You will know the importance of taking care of yourself. You will know not to swim, not to walk fast, not to climb stairs, to go to bed early, and so forth."

Certainly I could not tell them that I absolutely would not live that way! Could I tell them that death was preferable to life with Mother? They had already written to Mother, and she was coming for me, they told me. I had to accept what they said, and superficially I did. I thanked them for the splendid care they had given me, saying the thank-yous politely while inside I was asking, "Why didn't I die?"

Scottie found me weeping in my room. My classmates came when they heard the bad news. I went over to the hospital to say good-bye to Madeline. As I gave her my address in New Jersey I said, "Give it to Wilbur if he asks for it."

When my mother came, I left the Nurses' Home, New Rochelle Hospital Training School for Nurses, and my future behind me.

With sorrow I retraced the path I had taken with so much pleasure nine months before. Whistles were blowing when we entered Paterson. It was closing time, and workers were going home. They were going home with fast steps, but I was going home — to what? I kept thinking: If I can't walk fast, if I can't live whole, then why live? I began planning: The first chance I get, I'll go to Jackson's Quarry swimming hole and let myself drown.

Mother's gloating, biting remarks barely registered. She tried to get me to fight back, to talk back as I had always done. I did not care enough to fight back. I was thinking of Wilbur. I was sure he would not want to see me if I had a heart murmur. He would not want to be my friend. The only friend I had was Death.

Stumbling, fumbling along in life, somehow or other I had always been able to face problems and survive. Now I was numb. My twenty-first birthday was approaching. I recalled the happy one I had had at eighteen in Holland with Tante Sara, Ome David and young David. What had I now? The fight to live despite all had left me. I sat on the front step and listened to the rumble of my mother's voice. I heard her shriek at my father. I watched my sister come and go to school. I sat numbly, not knowing what to do: to end it all, or to try to survive in this house. The latter seemed impossible; escape seemed the best.

Sitting on the front porch day after day, I began seeing Prospect Park. I had never been aware of the strangeness of it before. Having lived for ten months in another city, some of it in bed, I had met many people but no Hollanders. In this little suburb of Paterson lived five thousand Hollanders with seven Dutch Reformed Churches to serve their spiritual needs — van den Kampens, Hulzebos, de Vries, two-story houses, carpenters, masons, buy nothing on credit, vote Republican, read the *American Journal* and the Hearst Press, strikebreakers — all living on what was called Scab Hill. What had happened to them in the New World? They were different from the

Hollanders in Holland; they had changed. This was not a bit of Holland, and it was not America either. It was nothing yet, like me. I woke up as I heard Mother yell, "Don't sit there with your hands idle! String the beans. Earn the food you eat. Answer me!" she commanded. I took the beans and began stringing them.

Often the phrase lay on the tip of my tongue to answer her, "I know who my real father is," but I couldn't say it. I did not want to hurt the man I called Father. I did not want to take from him any self-respect he had. His life was hard enough with her shouting at him. I tried to understand my mother, to dislike her less; but she made it impossible. I peeled potatoes, shined copper, washed silver, and kept quiet.

As I became stronger, I went for walks. One day I walked as far as Jackson's Quarry. Many a hot day I had rested here in my girl scout days. The water falling from the cliff caught the unseen jewels in the air and brought them to life in a rainbow. The foliage was a deep green, and the water, a darker, more somber green. I took off my clothes and folded them carefully. I stood naked in the silence, caught in the problem between life and death. I dived in. Swimming had been forbidden. Tingling with life from the shock of the cold water, my thoughts were on death.

While I was trying to get up enough courage to dive down to the bottom, I thought of Heaven and Hell. White, fleecy clouds floated above me and gave no answer. Who went to this Heaven and this Hell that Mother spoke of? According to her, the Dutch Reformed went to Heaven, and the rest went to Hell. Well, then I preferred Hell. Stalling for time to live, I played with thoughts of the hereafter. With one last look at the beauty around me, I surface-dived as deep as I could and tried to stay under water. I swallowed water and tried to drown myself. Life was stronger, and I rose to the surface gasping for air. Again I tried, and again I could not kill myself. Finally, gasping for air, I dragged myself to the bank where I wept for the death that I could not achieve. I could not conquer life or death. I felt weak. Rationalizing, I thought, "I'll come here frequently until I further damage my leaking heart valve. Maybe in that way I can die."

But I got stronger instead of weaker. Maybe my heart had stopped murmuring. Was there hope for me to finish my nurse's training? Perhaps the doctors had made a mistake. Every day I walked to Jackson's Quarry and took a swim in the cold water. Hope came. I did not know when, but I was going to ask to be checked and readmitted to the New Rochelle Hospital Training School for Nurses.

One day I was ambling down North Eighth Street, in no hurry to arrive home, when a car pulled up alongside me. It was Wilbur. I was so happy to see him that I stuttered with delight and confusion.

"Hop in. I am just as glad to see you," he said. "First, I want to apologize for not coming before. I had meant to come the next week after your discharge from the hospital. Madeline had misplaced your address; my brother got sick, and I had to be on the job day and night at the dairy; and four weeks just slipped by," Wilbur said.

"Why didn't you write?" I asked.

"Because every week I was sure I'd get down from Port Chester to Paterson and see you. I wanted to surprise you," he continued. "What have you been doing? You look much better," he said.

"First I wanted to die. I tried to die, and then I found the will to live was much stronger," I answered. It was wonderful to have someone with whom I could talk and feel at ease. I had not had this since I returned from Holland.

"Listen, Lini, I have a heart murmur also. I had rheumatic fever ten years ago. I pay no attention to my murmur," he boasted. I looked at him with amazement. I had not known that.

"How silly to want to kill yourself! I want you alive, not dead. I don't want a memory; I want you to live. You are part of my life," he said. I wondered whether he was proposing. He put his hand on the brake to release it as he said, "Let's go to your house."

"Just a minute, Wilbur. Let me explain some things to you before you meet my mother. Let me tell you why I wanted to die," I said, as I took his hand off the brake. I did not want him to meet my shouting mother without some sort of explanation.

I told him that Mother was a bitter, unhappy, strange woman. I told him that she did not speak English and might hurl insults at him and me in Dutch. "Please don't let her disturb you," I said. I was afraid that I might not see him again as I tried to explain my mother and why I had not wanted to live with her. It was as if I were talking to David; it was easy to pour it out.

After he had listened he said, "I came to see you and not your mother. I'll get you away from all this someday."

We drove to my home. I think that Mother was so surprised that she forgot to shout as I explained in Dutch who Wilbur was. After dinner we spent the afternoon sitting on the front porch, talking and talking. Mother sat with us and looked as if she did not know what it was all about. She didn't. When Wilbur left, with a promise of a return the next week, I felt very much better.

In the following weeks, seeing Wilbur and feeling wanted helped me regain my strength. He encouraged me to think in terms of re-entering training. One day he drove down from Port Chester to Paterson to pick me up, and then we turned around and drove back to New Rochelle. I had been writing to Miss Wilday begging for a medical examination, begging her to reconsider me on the basis of the doctor's findings. This was the day I was to be examined.

On the two-hour drive Wilbur encouraged me. I could not get to New Rochelle fast enough, yet I dreaded disappointment.

Before I knew it we were there. The doctors were called and arrived to examine me. It was discovered that most of my heart murmur had been toxic. There was slight, very slight damage to my heart. I sat speechless with joy as the voices talked around me. "There is no reason why she can't come back," said one doctor. Another one said, "But she will have to take it easy for awhile." They were saying I could come back! I looked pleadingly at Miss Wilday, who would have the final decision. Her eyes gave me a gentle look. She conceded that I could re-enter the nurses' training school.

How fortunate for me that at the times when it counted most there had been people in my life like Tante Sara, Miss Paul of the telephone company, and now Miss Wilday. I worshipped her; we all did. She was tall, white-haired, dignified, unbending in her stiffly starched white uniform; but her love and warmth for people seeped through the starch.

September 1926, one day after Labor Day and exactly one year from the date I had first entered training, I returned to the nurses' home. I had left the hospital without being capped. Officially I had not finished my probationary period. In a simple ceremony, Miss Wilday placed the cap on my head. I was now a student nurse again. I had to make up the eight lost months before I could graduate. "So what?" I thought.

Scottie had been sure that Dutchy would be back. She had resisted another person's being put in our room, so we were now back together again. I was impressed with my classmates who knew so many things. They talked knowingly about diseases, doctors, treatments, and so forth. The tables were turned, and now they helped me catch up. Miss Wilday placed me in the supply room, where I sat making cotton balls and gauze squares. I often wondered how she patched up my work record. The time she had me in women's ward I sat making cotton balls. I felt like a teacher's pet and wanted some action, some work. I wanted to get on the floors and wards.

After a thorough checkup, I was assigned to the emergency room. In between the emergencies I was to continue making cotton balls. I loved working in the emergency room. If one worked fast enough, it meant the difference between life and death. When the intern said, after a particularly gory case, "Moerkerk, you will make a good operating room nurse," I felt satisfied. The height of my ambition was to be a good operating room nurse.

Men's ward was next, with its mixture of cops and robbers, truck drivers and carpenters, broken bones and burns, typhoid and emphysema, old wooden splintery floors, chipped bedpans and chipped dishes, black tea, songs and curses, bravado and kindness mixed in the languages of Europe and accentuated by the curses of a Brooklyn truck driver who had smashed his truck on the Boston Post Road. Men's ward frightened most of the young student nurses, but not me. I felt at home with them.

Their trades and skills were different from the ones I had learned in the mills, but our vocabulary was much the same. The boss, eight-hour days, the scab, the stool pigeon, the union and the union organizer were all old words to me. This talk whirled around my ears in men's ward as I bathed them, rubbed their backs, and gave them their medicines. The little boss carpenter could not see why one should be "union." When the supervisor was not around, I joined in talking "union." When a new man was brought in on a stretcher, he would be told quickly by the men, "This nurse is okay. She was union in the factories." I suffered and sang with them, depending on their moods. If a man wanted to give up, I would sit by him, hold his hand, and tell him about Jackson's Quarry, where I, too, had wanted to die.

I am sure Miss Wilbur, our nursing arts supervisor, often wondered what "sex madness" went on between me and the men on men's ward. Reports on me always said, "Rapport extraordinary."

My classmates would ask me, "Dutchy, how do you do it?

When any of us are on men's ward, it is as if there were a wall between us and the patients. They never swear at you or Scottie. They curse us and insult us. How do you do it, Dutchy?"

I would try to explain to my classmates that these men, regardless of their trades or their misuse of the English language, were humans. I said, "Try treating them as human beings, with the same desires for living and the good things in life as you have, and note the difference in their relationships with you." They could not. They had grown up as bosses' daughters, and held factory workers and truck drivers in contempt. The workmen in men's ward sensed this and reacted accordingly. They had limited cultural backgrounds for understanding; I had even less, but I had worked in the mills. However, Scottie, with her rich cultural background, got on fine in men's ward. She often sneaked a cigarette to them and sometimes had a puff with them.

I was bothered. I was an ex-mill dolly entering the professional world. I wanted to pull the various factions together, but I could not separate myself from worker or professional. We were all the same basically. How could we get together?

On my afternoon off, I would share with Wilbur the discussion we had on men's ward. He would say, "Forget it. You are studying to be a professional. Forget that union talk. Don't be friendly with those truck drivers and workers."

"But Wilbur, I don't want to forget it. You always say that one should be objective and scientific. You had a scientific education. I am having one, but in a different field. Life is a science also. Mills and shops are getting larger. These workers can't go up to a boss and say, 'We need a raise.' No longer is the boss one of the guys who works with them. Now he is part of a group, an unknown group. He might even be on a yacht in the Mediterranean. They need organization. They want organization and union representation. It is the butter on their bread, the dresses for their little girls. This union talk, as you call it, is their very security for life!" I explained, fumbling for words to express myself.

"But, Lini, don't you know that unions are led by Bolsheviks?" he asked.

"What on earth is a Bolshevik?" I asked in return.

"They are communists, who want to share all with all, no rich, no poor; they would kill people like us," he answered.

"Oh, nuts! In any mill I ever worked in we never heard such talk. The union organizer was one of us, and our wants were simple. First, we wanted to be treated like human beings, not like cattle. We wanted an eight-hour day, decent conditions to work in, and wages equivalent to comparable work elsewhere. That's Americanism. That's not foreign, or communism," I concluded. "You know, Wilbur, it is funny that I talk this way to you. You are the other side of the tracks," I said.

Invariably Wilbur would reply, "What you should do is forget all these things, marry me, keep house, and raise my family."

I always answered with one part of my thinking hidden and one part spoken, "I'll marry when I finish training and not before. I must finish what I set out to do." Unspoken, I would wonder, "Dare I marry? Dare I have children? Suppose my children hate me the way I hate my mother? I might be like her." Yet I loved Wilbur. I hoped in time he would understand a little more about my side of the tracks.

I was in love with Wilbur, with my work, and with the world. Most of the time I went about in an aura of well-being, but sometimes I would feel out of things. I could not get up enough courage to do things forbidden to a student nurse, such as stay out all night or smoke. I thought it silly to break the rules. Maybe I didn't have enough courage. Whatever it was, the girls knew I would not tell on them. Despite the fact that "Dutchy was different" I was gradually admitted to the inner circle of the first year nursing students. We borrowed one another's clothes. We stole food for the gang from the private floors. We protected one another from second and third year students and from supervisors. We browbeat the new probationers as once we had been treated. Life was good.

As much as I could, I buried my knowledge of my illegitimacy, of my former life at home and of the mills. I didn't want to talk about it or to think about it. The present was fine; there was no point in thinking of the past. I certainly could not tell Wilbur about everything. He was different from his family. He might understand, but I was taking no chances. I had confessed the fact that my mother was a converted Jew. He had seen that my mother was difficult. Wilbur's mother looked at me with enough suspicion as it was. He was close to her and might tell her. Wilbur had always been her favorite. He could always be counted on to take her to church or to Long Island to visit her relatives. Wilbur had taken the place of her husband. And now here was this stranger, a foreigner whose family hardly spoke English, and, worst of all, who were not Methodists. I was sure that Wilbur's mother and younger sister would never understand, so I'd better keep quiet.

I did not know many families, so the Fuhr family was difficult for me to judge. They did not shout at one another, but there was no affection. Mother Fuhr ran her children and the dairy business. They all vied for her approval. Three of her children were married, two were not. They came running to their mother with tales. I could not understand them. In a way, I preferred the open shouting and expressed dislikes. I felt uncomfortable with the undercurrents in the Fuhr home. All were, or appeared to be, deeply religious, but none practiced the warmth of Christianity.

As we became more intimate, Wilbur pleaded that I give up my nurse's training and marry him. I, too, wanted to marry, but I always replied that I owed it to myself and to the hospital to finish training. They had been exceedingly good to me when I was ill, and now I must do my part. Not that I was not tempted at times to give it up, especially when I was on night duty in the nursery.

What a trial the night shift in the nursery on maternity ward was! I could not get away from the cries of babies. I heard them when I tried to sleep in the day and in between classes — babies and more babies, babies that never seemed to stop crying. When the lights in the nursery were turned on, there was silence. As soon as the door closed, twenty mouths opened and yelled. Twenty babies to be bathed before morning. Twenty babies to be taken to their mothers. Twenty babies to be given supplementary feedings. Twenty little bottoms to be diapered.

God, those long nights — burning eyes so hungry for sleep that the stretcher looked like a Simmons mattress! If I got caught napping, I might be expelled. Sometimes I would sit on the stretcher and hope that the night supervisor would not catch me with my cap askew. The babies would not let me doze, but I didn't like the nights when I was not fighting sleep, as that meant we were fighting for the life of some baby. As much as I felt like spanking their little bottoms, I never would have. At times each baby was as important to me as to its parents.

Nevertheless, this was my favorite floor in the hospital. Women came in and labored to bring forth their babies. Fathers waited and then rejoiced. The smell of disease was not in the air, and death rarely hung over us. I looked forward to the time when I would be advanced enough to return to this floor as scrub nurse in the delivery room.

Now I was on the private floor. Frankly, I preferred the wards. Here we veiled our eyes and "played dumb." It was only glorified maid service. When they rang their bells, a starched nurse doll stepped in and asked, "What can I do for you?" Yachts in the harbor, long weekend drunks and colonic irrigations to be given in flower-filled rooms. Invariably, Monday brought in patients whose standing orders read, "No liquor, give sedation and daily colonic irrigations."

On this floor I began to distinguish between the "new rich" without much culture, whose demands were unlimited, and the cultured people with whom one took off one's mask. I assure you that the latter got much better nursing care. A patient cannot buy skilled, gentle, comforting nursing care with money or with demands. It must be given as a loving gift. I found pleasure in giving good care where it was needed and appreciated.

Vacation time was around the corner. One of the senior student nurses, Christine Smith, asked me if I would like to go to her home in Vermont. I accepted with pleasure. Certainly I was not going to spend two weeks in Paterson, New Jersey. Chris, as we called her, was a sensitive girl. I don't know how she knew that I had no place to go for my vacation, but I was grateful to her, and still am, for the chance to know a Vermont family like hers.

Wilbur drove the two of us up to Vermont. On the way back, he planned to call on the farmers in Connecticut from whom the dairy bought milk. I was able to see a sample of America that I had only seen in magazines. The photos had looked posed and unreal, but these little towns were not unreal. Their white, steepled churches shone against the emerald green countryside, and I wondered about the people who lived in such tranquil surroundings. Occasionally we came to a river town with its dirty face, its smoking factories, and its pinched workers' faces. I wanted to close my eyes as we drove through these towns. I did not want to remember my factory days.

At Christine's house we were greeted by the matriarch of the family, her mother. Their father was dead. The big rambling house shone with the waxed mellowness of old furniture. Golden nasturtiums spilled over the sides of milk glass vases and reflected in the gleaming, satiny woods. Mellowness and gentleness permeated the home and its inhabitants.

Gentle voices asked questions of me. I would not tell them of my home, but I began telling them of Tante Sara and Ome David in Amsterdam. Before long they forgot to ask me about my family in the United States, as I brought the streets of Amsterdam to life in Vermont.

The Smiths lived on one side of the White River in Vermont; on the other side of the river was New Hampshire. I asked questions and learned about Vermont and New Hampshire through the stories of the Lovelands, the Hapgoods and the Smiths who, it seemed, were all related. I had never dreamed that America was also this great contrast to the silk mills on the riversides in Paterson. This America I admired and liked. The Revolutionary War was only a scant 150 years old in this home in Vermont. The ideals of democracy were alive, and I felt at home here the way I had in Amsterdam.

The two weeks passed all too quickly. Then I was back in New Rochelle, doing my stint of service on the maternity ward and in the delivery room.

In those days the delivery room was painted a gleaming white. The silvery instruments reflected in the glass of the shining headlights. A woman lay strapped on the table, begging for anesthesia. Then her doctor arrived and ordered a whiff of anesthesia to be given with each pain. How puny I felt as I watched with awe the struggle going on before my eyes! A baby was demanding birth, and a uterus was forcing it out. The mother was sweating and half-conscious. I wiped the sweat off her brow and murmured words of encouragement. I felt my own uterus contracting with hers, and wished I could stop identifying myself with the patient.

The "dirty nurse" was trying to keep the doctor's sweat from dropping on the sterile field. With the sweat of many people a baby is born. We all sweat the moment when the head is carefully eased up and over the pubic arch to prevent a tear in the mother's flesh. We relax as the shoulders ease through, and the rest of the body comes slithering out. Then comes the anxious moment when the mother is almost forgotten as we wait for the baby's first breath. The baby cries! Another life has begun in this world. While the mother rests, the baby is getting its first rough treatment after its nine months of tranquil life in the womb.

The baby yells some more as I force open his eyelids and place drops of silver nitrate solution on each eyeball. I place the blue beads, strung beforehand, on the baby's neck, and then weigh little Jennie. I check her cord stump again to be sure that it is not bleeding and wrap her warmly. By now she is yelling so much that her personality is felt in the delivery room. "May I see my baby?" the mother asks. With weak hands she gently touches the baby's face as the doctor tells her, "You have a fine girl."

We all wait — doctor, mother, Jennie, and the nurses — for the afterbirth to be born. The placenta through which life flowed to Jennie is no longer needed, and in about fifteen minutes the mother's body casts it out. All is well, and mother and baby are put on the stretcher to be taken to the maternity floor where Jennie will join other babies in the nursery, and mother will be transferred to a bed in her room, where her husband is waiting.

The average person's concept is that deliveries are messy, but I never could see this. Blood is a river, carrying fighters, food, and occasional enemies. Precious blood is spilled so that a new life can be. Precious blood has to be scrubbed off the instruments and the floors, and the sheets have to be soaked. Usually, as I scrubbed the floor, I relived the wonder of birth. Then I would wonder about the logic of hospital rules which denied the father the right to be present. I wished the father could be allowed to participate in the wonder and struggle of his son's or daughter's birth. Not that I felt a father should be present in order to feel guilty for his wife's pains. I did not agree with that type of thinking — or lack of thinking. Rather, I wished he could be a part of the whole. His part was not only the introduction of the sperm with which life began, but the tensing of his muscles with those of his mate as their child clamored to be born.

Seeing babies born was the most exciting thing that had happened to me. I began thinking more of my mother with pity. What a tragedy was our dislike for one another! She also had sweated to give birth to me. With each delivery I felt less dislike for Mother and more sorrow for our lost relationship as mother and daughter.

After I had helped in thirty deliveries, I was transferred to another section of the hospital. I was sorry. This was the most normal place to work in the whole building.

Another September came, September 1927. My classmates would finish their training in another four months, but I had time to make up and would finish later. Two and three at a time were leaving for Philadelphia to do their stint in pediatrics. We heard the same thing from all of them: Children's Hospital of Philadelphia offered excellent training in pediatrics, but the food was horrible and living conditions were worse. They wrote of the "Black Cloud" who was none other than the Directress of Nursing. She wore a black uniform instead of the traditional white, and they wrote that her disposition matched her uniform. My turn to go to Philadelphia would come in the first three months in 1928.

In the meantime, I was in the operating room. In the beginning I was scared stiff that I would hand a doctor the wrong instrument. Some of the doctors were notorious for having excellent aim when they threw an instrument back because of its being the wrong one. Of course, a nurse new to the operating room began with the simple operations, such as tonsillectomies, circumcisions, helping in the setting of a broken bone, and so forth. These were called the "dirty operations," since the field of operation could not be sterilized completely. For example, a mouth is full of germs, and regardless of the amount of cleansing, it remains full of germs throughout an operation. Nevertheless, all instruments had to be thoroughly boiled, even for a tonsillectomy.

I had been "dirty nurse" for awhile, which means picking up after people, wiping sweat off brows, carrying things, washing linens, making up packs for the sterilizer, running errands, and observing everything you can. Finally, I was considered ready for "scrub" or "clean nurse," to assist the doctor in an operation. I will never forget that first operation, since I really pulled a boner.

My hands had been scrubbed the required twenty minutes. A mask covered my mouth and nose. A sterile cap was pulled tightly over my head. Clasping my sterile-gloved hands in front of me, I waited for the patient to be rolled in on the stretcher. Once he was well under anesthesia, I carefully covered him with a sterile sheet and began to attach cotton balls to the sponge sticks. I laid them in a row on the patient's abdomen, in order to hand them rapidly to the doctor to swab bleeding. In my nervousness as scrub nurse assisting in my first operation, I kept on trying to smooth down a bump which was rising under the sterile sheet. As a sponge stick rolled off the bump, I would push the bump down with another sterile sponge stick. Suddenly I heard the doctor say, "Stop playing with the man's penis. Just place the instruments higher on his abdomen." He laughed, the intern laughed, and I blushed. This story made the rounds of the hospital, much to my embarrassmment.

Time flew by in the operating room. I was on night call for emergencies and worked all day. We worked a ten-hour day, from seven in the morning to seven at night, but with two hours off when the operating room was quiet. I was now a senior nurse and very proud that I was kept longer in the operating room than my stint demanded. I enjoyed beating the doctor to his spoken word and handing him the correct instrument. I enjoyed the organizational aspects of the operating room. A person's life depended on the nurse's ability to have her instruments laid out for an emergency that might arise during the operation. A patient with an emergency could not wait for twenty minutes while the instruments boiled. I began thinking that if I ever worked again, after marriage, I would do operating room work.

All too soon January came and I was on a train bound for Philadelphia. It was New Year's Day. The station was gloomy, and the sky was overcast. Instead of trees, tall buildings covered with soot loomed out of the smog. My entrance into the City of Brotherly Love was depressing. With my companions from New Rochelle, I took a cab to the Children's Hospital of Philadelphia in a crowded, all-black section of the city. We were told to go to the nurses' barracks and wait for the nursing directress.

This nurses' home certainly was not like the one we had been accustomed to in New Rochelle. These horrible, thin-walled, cold, temporary barracks would house us for three months, although we had heard that a new nurses' home was to be built. Waiting in the nurses' home, I was reminded of the day when I first entered training, feeling insecure, not knowing anyone, and sneaking looks at my future companions. At least now we were three from New Rochelle, and we chatted together animatedly to hide our nervousness. About fifty other girls, divided into small groups, did the same. Many hospitals from the Eastern seaboard sent their students to Children's Hospital at Philadelphia for their pediatric training.

The door opened, and a gust of cold air entered with an apparition of a woman. She was tall, stern, unsmiling, bucktoothed, and garbed in black. You could hear a pin drop. Obviously all fifty girls, silently cowering, had been warned about the Black Cloud. Behind her stood a meekly bent, stiffly starched, pale nurse. Without further ado the Black Cloud began, "I am your directress of nursing for the next three months. Unless you conform and obey the rules that I have laid down, you will be sent home. You cannot graduate from your school without these three months of pediatrics, so I advise you to conform." I did not know that there could be so many rules and regulations. She reminded me of my mother. I did not like her.

Her closing remarks were, "This is a very bad neighborhood. It is all black. You may never walk the streets alone.

Only go out in groups, or you might be raped or robbed."

I was shocked at this kind of an introduction to a pediatric nursing course. I resented it, and felt like raising my hand and questioning her statement on blacks. From years of experience I knew that student nurses were seen and not heard, so I kept quiet. It was not that I knew any blacks, although I had taken care of a few in New Rochelle Hospital, but it was her assumption I resented — that, per se, blacks were rapists and robbers. On the operating room table, once the skin was opened and laid back, there was no difference between white and black. I muttered under my breath, and she was almost shouting, "Don't wear earrings or rings. Don't use rouge or lipstick. Don't let me see you without a hairnet on." I wondered what made her mad and at whom.

She stalked out, and her mouselike follower, the nursing arts supervisor, said, "Come, girls, I'll show you to your rooms."

Our rooms were a fright. The supper was worse. I offered to go with my companions to buy salami and cheese, but they were afraid to go out in the street after what the Black Cloud had said. I didn't dare go out alone and break a rule the first night I was there, so I sat down and wrote to Wilbur, pouring it all out. I asked him to bring delicacies every time he came, which would be once a month. I asked him especially to bring one of his mother's wonderful cakes.

There was no book by Dr. Benjamin Spock on baby and child care in those days, and every bit of attention was given rigidly by a time clock. I felt that babies needed much less rigidity in schedule and lots more love and affection, but what could I do? I had to sneak the extra love and attention to the children according to their needs while following the time schedule on the chart, since I had no Dr. Spock to back me up. Regardless of their medical or surgical problems, these little children wanted recognition and love. Children with rickets whose legs had to be broken and reset because of lack of vitamin D in their diets, little ones with bellies swollen from celiac disease, others with feeding problems were to me little people wanting love.

Every time I got a glimpse of the Black Cloud I attempted to make myself scarce. I felt in my bones that it would be better for me if I remained only a name on the roll to her. One day I was sitting holding on my lap a two-year-child who was the size of a one-year-old. His black skin was lustrous and pale, while mine was rosy. I was talking to him, playing with him, trying to get him to eat his noon meal, when suddenly I heard the Black Cloud say, "Take that rouge off your face! How dare you appear on duty with rouge on your face?"

I looked up at her in amazement as I answered, "That is not rouge. It is my natural coloring."

"Don't be insolent! Put that baby in the crib, and wash the rouge off your face!" she said.

As I put the little boy in his bed I said, "Watch; here is a clean, white washcloth; here is water and soap. I'll show you that the cloth will remain white." I scrubbed my face and showed her the clean washcloth.

"Such impertinence!" she muttered. "What is your name? What school are you from?" she asked.

I told her. I was no longer an unknown name on the roll.

As I look back, I can see that the Black Cloud became the symbol of my dislike for Philadelphia, its miserable winter climate, its dirty streets, and its unreasonably strict hospital routine. Possibly the Black Cloud was a splendid person. Perhaps having to face groups like us every three months drove her mad. However, early in 1928 she was the clotheshanger on which I hung my hates. Nevertheless, the sum total of the three months of training was excellent. I learned a great deal more than I could have in our own small pediatric ward in New Rochelle, but it was a relief to finish and to be able to leave for New Rochelle again.

On my return I found out that I had been assigned to the operating room as senior nurse. My classmates had finished their training and were in white, while I was still in blue. In a few months more I, too, could wear the white uniform. In the meantime I sat in front of the hospital at night in Wilbur's car hoping that I would not be called for an emergency. On evenings that he could not come down, we studied for the state board examinations. Regardless of the years that we had studied, if we did not pass these examinations we could not be registered nurses. My retentive memory came in handy in these jam sessions in Scottie's and my room. We all piled on beds and studied.

Here I was studying for state boards, seeing my fiancé, working in the service that I liked best, and happily planning marriage after my graduation. Personally, I was ready to get married by a judge in Greenwich, Connecticut, and tell the folks later; but Wilbur thought that his folks would think it most queer if we were not married from my home in New Jersey. We drove over, and I mentioned it to my mother. To my great surprise, she seemed pleased to arrange the marriage with a Dutch Reformed minister of her choice. I felt mellower toward her in those days, and I feared her less. Wilbur and I gratefully left the arrangements in her hands. I had to pass the State Boards, and I had to graduate. Driving back to New Rochelle, we talked of the many things we wanted in our lives — children, home, and so forth. I had never felt so secure and wanted.

The first Friday in June of 1928, I proudly walked up the aisle to the stage to sit with my classmates, all awaiting our diplomas. For once our caps stood completely straight on our heads. Not a hair was out of place, not a speck on our white uniforms or shoes. After three years, after illness and problems, I was graduating. I could hardly believe it. When the awards were presented, I discovered that I had had the highest marks in theory all through the three years. I shook with pleasure as they pinned the medal on me. My trembling really came with the thoughts inside of me as I said to myself, "Thank God you couldn't kill yourself when you tried!"

The following day Wilbur drove me down to Paterson where

we were to be married the following Tuesday. It had been with mixed pain and pleasure that I had removed my belongings from the room that I had shared with Scottie for three years, as I said goodbye to my classmates, and as I looked forward to marriage with Wilbur.

We had already bought our furniture. Our little attic home over the garage, where the Fuhr Dairy milk trucks were kept, was waiting for our return. Wilbur's mother lived in the big house in front of the garage. I would have preferred living further away from Wilbur's mother and his sister Lily. However, his mother felt that he should be near the dairy (which was around the corner) and near the phone in the big house. The rent was high, I thought: thirty-five dollars for four of the tiniest rooms I had ever seen. Two tiny bedrooms were on the top floor; downstairs were the kitchen and living room; and underneath us were the dairy trucks. Since Wilbur and his brother Ernie were buying the dairy from their mother, we would have to scrimp. We hoped when they had bought the business from Widow Fuhr that we would have enough money someday to buy a piece of land on which to build our own home. In the meantime, we were to be married June 5th.

Port Chester, New York, 1928-1933
The Wedding Chalice 3

Late in the morning on June 5, 1928, the Fuhrs arrived from Port Chester, New York. We all drove over to the house of the Dutch Reformed minister who was going to marry us. I can see myself standing there holding Wilbur's hand while we were being married. I wanted his family to like me, but I knew we were worlds apart. The ceremony was in Dutch. I nudged Wilbur when he had to say, "I do." Now I was Mrs. Wilbur Fuhr.

We returned to North Eighth Street to share the wedding dinner which I had helped to prepare. As I helped serve, I translated back and forth from Dutch to English and English to Dutch. I prayed that my mother would not blow up and that my father would not tell them risqué stories of his co-workers in the gas factory. The guests were so interested in the strangeness of one another and their language that the wedding dinner went off peacefully. Finally Wilbur and I escaped to head north through the New England states to Niagara Falls.

The days were lovely as together we discovered the White Mountains and the Green Mountains. Niagara Falls was everything two honeymooners wanted. Yet our nights were tense, because Wilbur labored under the idea that too much sex led to insanity and that sex was mainly for propagation, not for pleasure. Since he did not want to become insane, he tried to control his sex drive. I knew that his idea was unnatural; his idea was insane, not sex. I made him promise that when we got back to Port Chester he would go to a doctor friend of his and talk about his thinking on the subject of sex. I was a flame that needed quenching. I had a husband who would not quench it. I began to feel guilty.

Fortunately, when we got back to Port Chester the doctor assured Wilbur of the normalcy of sexual relations. Now we began living like man and wife with easier adjustments. Now marriage was what I had dreamed of, the warmth and closeness of relationships, the quiet talks in bed at night, the sharing of breakfast in the morning, seeing your man off to work, puttering in the kitchen, cleaning the house, and drives in the evening along Long Island Sound. Marriage was good.

In our little attic home, life was easy. Out of the home, it was more difficult. I wanted Mother Fuhr and her unmarried daughter to like me, to accept me. I wanted them to keep on talking when I entered the room. Maybe if I joined the Methodist Church, Mrs. Fuhr, Sr., would be pleased. I did that and felt like a hypocrite.

Since Mother Fuhr was a member of the Ladies' Aid Society of the YMCA, I also joined. There was no YWCA in town, but we had Ladies' Nights at the YMCA. We cooked and served the dinners when the various men's clubs met there, such as the Lions, the Rotarians, and the Forty-Forty Club. We had cake sales to help raise money for the YMCA. I also joined the volleyball team of the young matrons. I learned bridge so that I could play with our set of young married couples.

God, I was bored — with them, with cards, with the church, with the Ladies' Aid Society, and mainly with myself. I could not figure myself out. I should be happy. I had a husband whom I loved. At times I wondered what love was. Why was I bored? Books — no one read. There was talk, talk and talk. It said nothing but was destructive to neighbors and friends, and I could not join in that kind of talk. I felt a vacuum all around me.

What was this drive in me which would not let me be in peace? I would try to explain to Wilbur, but he didn't understand. Neither did I understand myself. I thought if I did some home study to make up the missed high school, it might eliminate my boredom, so I registered for an extension course from Columbia University.

Basically I realized that I still had a deep-seated inferiority complex because I had not had a high school education. I hoped by home study to be a high school graduate. Beginning with English, as suggested by the extension services of Columbia, I haunted the libraries, wrote compositions, and patiently waited for my corrected work to be returned to me. Rather, I waited impatiently. I wanted to discuss and share my excitement with Wilbur. I wanted him to help me, but when he came home from the dairy he did not want to discuss books. He wanted to rest or to take a drive along the Sound or, preferably, to play bridge.

Besides studying, I baked cakes, all kinds of cakes. I took most of them down to New Rochelle and gave them to classmates, who were now supervisors. Each still retained her sweet tooth. My body got fatter and more sluggish from all the rich foods I ate. Wilbur brought home unlimited amounts of cream, cheeses, butter, eggs and milk. The cakes were good. I ate and ate, but I could not seem to dull my mind as I did my body.

I did not have to fight anyone here in order to survive, as I had fought my mother. I was fighting myself. What was the matter with me? Why could I not be like others? Why could I not adjust and be happy? What was happiness, I wondered. Wilbur and I never quarreled. But to whom could I toss my questions that tumbled helter-skelter in my mind? Who could answer me, rebuff, argue and interest me? No one, it seemed.

Everyone I knew talked about this one or that one. No one talked of ideas or problems. The scapegoats in this community were the Italians. Thousands of them lived in Port Chester, and they worked in a nut-and-bolt factory. I didn't know them socially, but I saw them on the streets. They were "not our class," I was told. Ranking lower than the Italians were the Jews. Once, at a bridge party, I felt like saying, "My mother is a Jew; my biological father is a Jew; and I am a bastard to boot. Does that make me untouchable?" But I refrained. This white-skinned, fair-haired, blue-eyed culture was beginning to get me down. Their superiority complex was not helping my inferiority complex a bit!

Later I would sputter at Wilbur. He would laugh and tell me not to take myself so seriously. These were his friends from school days. They had gone to the same Sunday School, to the same high school, and were nourished in identical cultures. These were the respected citizens of Port Chester, New York. Would I ever be one of them?

The few times that Wilbur and I drove up to Vermont to see Christina's family, I would feel cleansed of this slimy environment and its backbiting, frosted over by religion. Not that the Smiths' conversation was sprightly, but it was of the earth and what comes from it. For me this had logic and excitement.

Late in 1928 I was pregnant. I chose a doctor from New Rochelle whom I respected as an obstetrician. After he examined me and told me everything was fine, I felt that now life had more meaning. Wilbur and I were thrilled to be having a child. Booties and bonnets that I made began piling up, even though I was only ten weeks pregnant — pink ones if the baby was a girl and blue if a boy. Wonderful!

One night, when I was nearly three months pregnant, I woke up with pains and felt my life hemorrhaging away. My pulse was thready and weak. I woke Wilbur and said, "Don't question me. Just get the ambulance from Port Chester Hospital. Tell them I am aborting and bleeding to death."

Wilbur phoned his doctor, and the ambulance came. I knew that if I were not operated on immediately I would soon be dead. I didn't think of the ethics of my doctor's being in New Rochelle. Life was more important to me than ethics at that moment.

As the men carried me down the twisting, narrow stairs, I lay on the stretcher and hoped this would not be the end of my fretting at myself and my dissatisfaction. Even as I slipped away under the anesthesia, I said to myself, "You can't die. This is not the end for you yet."

The bleeding placenta was removed. I stopped bleeding. In no time, I felt fine. I now knew the cause of the abortion. My uterus was tipped, retroverted. At twelve weeks, it would not lift itself up, and the baby had broken away from the placenta. I was angry at the doctor in New Rochelle for not suspecting this.

After my near escape from death, I thought I would lose my feeling of living in a vacuum, but I didn't. How can one explain the emptiness of middle-class life in a small town in the United States in 1929? If I had never lived in Holland with Tante Sara and Ome David, I might not have known that another world existed, a world in which people talked about ideas, problems, plays, music, literature — a world in which I was interested and learned. In that world I did not feel inferior. Except for the actual sex contact, my life lacked taste and flavor. I made up my mind that I would try to adjust to Wilbur's set of friends and the community.

A new element now entered into conversations around the bridge tables: Bolshevism. Factories were slowing down; some were closing. Workers in the mills were protesting. All Italians were anarchists and Bolsheviks, I was told. I worried along with my bridge-playing set that May 1 would bring trouble. The workers planned to parade that day. When May 1 passed and no bombs were thrown, I felt relieved. At that time Bolshevism and bombs were synonymous to me. I had heard about socialists, and my uncle was one. I had heard about communists, since my uncle didn't like them, and I didn't either. Obviously Bolsheviks and communists were the same, but this was the first time I began hearing about them in the United States.

Finally we had a "hate" we could discuss and agree on!

One day I read some publicity about the Port Chester Visiting Nurses Association. It spoke of their service to the community and asked for volunteers. This interested me. When I had been a student nurse, I had had two weeks of intensive in-service training with the New Rochelle Visiting Nurses Association, and loved it. The approach and education of the nurse — to keep people well, to teach home nursing, to share one's knowledge with the people, to try to make everyone a health teacher — had been an eye opener for me. This was the nursing at the roots. This helped people keep well and helped to prevent disease.

I lifted the phone and called Miss Duffy, the Directress of the VNA. I asked how I could help, and she invited me to come to the office to discuss my offer with her. I met her the same day, and found another "Miss Wilday" or "Miss Paul," another of the whole people in life to influence me. She needed a chauffeur to take women and babies to clinics, someone she could depend on. I volunteered.

Wilbur did not mind at all, since it made me more content to have other interests. He even told me to put us down for a monthly contribution to the VNA. However, he and our friends did ask, "Why do you want to fill your car with dirty Italian children and their mothers?"

It was true that the children were dirty. Money went for

food, not soap. The only major industry in town had closed down. The majority of the Italians were out of work, had been out of work, and it seemed would stay out of work. A baby on her lap and another on the way was the rule and not the exception. I had great sympathy for these poor women trying to keep their homes together. They were hungry, and their children were hungry. I tried to get the various organizations interested in helping with food. Not that I wanted to be Lady Bountiful; I didn't. I preferred that the men would have work again, but there was no work to be had.

My pleas fell on deaf ears. To our social set the Italians were riffraff. One did not associate with Jews. One looked at Catholics as a strange breed of idol worshippers. Only Methodists or closely allied Protestant groups counted. I knew they were wrong. I could not penetrate them, or they, me. Here I was supposed to live the rest of my life. I dreamed of hungry Italian children's faces. Months went by, and I became more and more immersed in volunteer work with the VNA and the problems of the unemployed.

But I was pregnant again. I had to stop driving people to clinics and doctors and take care of my own pregnancy. I spent most of the first three months resting so I would not lose this baby. I breathed a sigh of relief when I was well into the fourth month and knew that the danger of the three-months' abortion was past.

Early in 1930 I was awakened one night by Wilbur's coming home injured. It had been his night to relieve one of the milk truck drivers. He complained of his shoulder hurting, and so I drove him to the doctor. The X rays showed a slight fracture of the clavicle bone, which was not too serious, I knew. What worried me was the doctor's concern with Wilbur's heart. As Wilbur stepped into the dressing room, the doctor told me that Wilbur had had quite a lot of damage to his heart from the rheumatic fever he had had in his youth. Since his mother believed only in chiropractors, he had not had the bed rest he should have had. To the contrary, she had not prevented him from participating in foot races or even marathon races. I tried my best to see to it that he had adequate rest. I knew his diet was good.

We expected our baby in early May. In the evenings we would take short drives along the Sound, which seemed to relax both him and our kicking, intrauterine baby. I had felt gloriously well throughout the pregnancy, but now that I was approaching term, I was uncomfortable. As I got bigger, Wilbur got thinner. He refused to go back to the doctor, always insisting, "But I feel fine. I have always been thin." I wanted to believe this, but I worried.

May 15, 1930, I woke up with gnawing pains in the small of my back. I tried to ignore them and go back to sleep. I did not want to disturb my husband, who needed his sleep. But they would not let me sleep. Waking up my husband, I said, "This is it, I am sure."

Driving down the Hutchinson River Parkway toward New Rochelle, I said to Wilbur, "Hurry, these contractions are strong and coming every five minutes." I knew first babies usually take twelve to eighteen hours to be born, but I was sure this one wouldn't.

At midnight I was admitted to the maternity floor. My former classmates who were on duty came to see me. They all said the same, "We came to hear you yell." I was determined I would not yell. My husband was in the downstairs waiting room. I wished he could be with me, but that was inconceivable in 1930.

The pains gave me no rest; they came too fast. I had only been in labor two hours when I was taken to the delivery room. I practically grabbed the ether mask out of the nurse's hand and put it over my nose. I wanted an out from those pains. When I came out of the anesthesia, they showed me a 10-pound baby girl with a golden curl on top of her head and big violet eyes which said hello. Now I was to go under anesthesia again so that the doctor could sew up what had been torn by the rapid delivery of a 10-pound baby.

Back in the room I insisted on seeing my baby. I wanted to count her toes, her fingers, see the beads on her neck which said "Fuhr." I wanted Wilbur to touch her before she was shut in the nursery for two weeks, when he could only see her through the glass windows. It was no wonder I had been so huge and uncomfortable. Our baby, an hour old, looked a month old.

How can any mother describe the feeling of accomplishment and well-being after she has given birth to a child? I can't. I felt fine. I could see no sense in being in bed two weeks, but this was the rule. I wanted to be up, to take care of my own baby. I knew the nurses would be leaving bottles in her mouth. I knew they would spoil her for breast feeding. I remembered all the things I had done myself when I was a student nurse. I could see no logic in the rigid four-hour schedule. I wanted to feed her by demand, but in 1930 this was considered wrong. Another reason I wanted to get back home to Port Chester was that Wilbur was getting thinner and thinner. He didn't look well at all, and I didn't want him using his strength to drive down once a day to New Rochelle.

Finally, not a day earlier than two weeks, I was released. It was good driving back up the Parkway. The trees were in blossom. Flowers bloomed, and our baby was in my arms. Slowly I climbed the long, steep stairs to our attic apartment. I was weak from the enforced bed rest.

Wilbur and I were closer than ever with our firstborn. She absorbed my interest and time. These were tranquil days except for my occasional gnawing fear of Wilbur's appearance. He was thinner, and he was always tired. He rested without my asking him. When Mary Lee was one month old, I really saw how bad my husband looked, and I began insisting that he go to a doctor for a checkup. He would go for a chiropractic adjustment instead.

I nagged him so that he finally went to see a doctor. When he told me this, I asked, "And what did the doctor say?"

He replied, "He said that I was run down. He also said that

you should drop by and see him in a few days when he has the results of some tests he took."

I asked, "What kind of tests?"

"Oh, he just took some blood from a vein," he answered.

I had a strange sense of doom, since the doctor had told Wilbur nothing at all but had said that he wanted to see me. I hoped that he would tell me that nothing was wrong which rest and diet could not cure.

The forty-eight hours of insecurity and worry ended. I went to see Dr. Kennedy. He looked serious and upset as I asked him, "What is it?" He seemed at a loss how to answer me, or as if he dreaded telling me. "You know that I am a nurse. You must tell me so that I can combat whatever is wrong," I insisted.

He replied, "It is not good."

"Tell me. I must know. He is thin. He has little pep. He looks almost transparent, as if his red cells were disappearing in front of my eyes. I am going mad with worry. Please tell me the truth," I said.

The doctor replied, "Unwittingly you have diagnosed the problem. Your husband has a streptococcus infection in his bloodstream. The germ is rapidly destroying his red blood cells. One valve of his heart is badly damaged from the rheumatic fever which he had as a child, and perhaps the accident stirred up things. He is seriously ill."

"What can I do? Is it fatal?" I asked.

Dr. Kennedy replied, "All you can do is try to keep him as comfortable as possible. We have no medications that can cure a hemolytic infection in the bloodstream. You know that yourself."

"How sure are you that it is a strep hemolytic organism? Have you seen it under the lens of the microscope? Did you test it in a guinea pig? Are you sure?" I insisted.

"Yes, Mrs. Fuhr, all of this has been done. You must prepare yourself to accept the fact that the disease is fatal. You must prepare yourself for a long siege of nursing care. Transfusions may keep him alive a while longer, but I doubt if he will live more than two or three months. You must decide whether you want your husband to know this or not," Dr. Kennedy gravely answered.

"I cannot accept this. I don't believe it. There must be something. We are happy. We have a baby girl two months old. Our life is ahead of us. It is only beginning. I can't believe it. I refuse to believe it," I answered, weeping.

"You know it is true, Mrs. Fuhr. You have studied nursing. Do you want him to go to the hospital, or do you want him at home? In time he will have to go to bed. He may have strokes, since blood clots form in the bloodstream. He may be helpless before he dies. Prepare yourself," he said.

I knew what he said was true. I had to face it.

I hardly remember leaving the doctor's office as I drove into the country, trying to compose myself. I wanted to be able to face Wilbur without tear-stained cheeks and red eyes. One moment I refused to believe what I had heard; yet I knew it was true that Wilbur's disease was fatal. Before I turned the wheels toward home, I decided that I would not tell Wilbur. He was a happy man of 25 who loved his wife and his child. He liked his work, and he had many friends. No, I would not tell him, nor would I allow anyone else to tell him. No, if it killed me, he would never know from my face or actions that he was dying. I felt like a stone. I knew that I must act out a lie for the last months of his life.

Driving home, I hardly believed that this was happening to us. It must be a nightmare. Certainly it was not true. I would not allow him to die. I would feed him red meat and liver. I would love him, cherish him, care for him. He would be the exception in medicine. Had we not been taught of these exceptions?

As I began climbing the stairs to our attic home, I heard Mary Lee's wails. I had almost forgotten her. I had only thought of Wilbur, and this shocked me. Soon I would be a widow, alone with a baby in my arms. I walked more slowly. I must compose myself. How would I answer Wilbur? What could I say to him? What lie should I give?

My husband stood waiting at the top of the stairs. I hugged him and held him tight as he asked me, "What took you so long? The baby is yelling. It is past time for her feeding, and no amount of boiled water will please her. She wants milk. What did the doctor say?"

I opened my blouse and gave Mary Lee my breast. I kept my head bowed and fumbled with my breast as if the baby were having trouble holding the nipple of a full breast in her mouth. I was fighting for time, but finally I answered, "Dr. Kennedy said that you have a low red count, that you are run-down and need lots of rest, red meat and liver. I had to wait in the doctor's office, which is what took me so long."

Then Wilbur said, "You see what a waste of my time and yours it was to see a doctor. I am sick and tired of the liver you have been feeding me for the past few weeks. I am going to a chiropractor to get some adjustments. That will fix me up." I looked up at him with pain in my eyes.

"What is the matter? Don't you feel well, Lini? You look as if something hurts you."

"It is nothing. The baby just bit my nipple," I answered. This gave me a jolt. I had to be more careful of the expressions on my face. I said to myself, "Be careful; hide your thoughts. Don't let him know what you are thinking. There will be months of this."

What torture and agony it was to see Wilbur getting weaker and weaker. Finally he went to bed. I moved the bed into the living room and fixed a cot to sleep alongside of him at night. The baby's crib stood in the other corner. Several times every day he asked the same question, "Should I make a will?"

Invariably I answered the same, "Don't be foolish! You have years to think of that. You will be better soon."

He looked at me intently when I answered. He wanted assurance. He did not want to die.

I talked about the kind of a house we hoped to build someday. I talked about world news. Now I was reading newspapers, which I had hardly ever done before. I read to him and did anything to keep his mind off his own illness. I didn't even fuss when he asked to have the chiropractor come in to give him adjustments. What did it matter, if it helped him think he would get well? I did not want him to know that he was dying a little every day. What did wills mean to me? What did anything mean to me except to keep him unaware of his inevitable death. After all, over and over I'd say, there is always a possibility of a new drug being discovered which will keep him alive for us.

Now we tried some transfusions. I rode the ambulance with Wilbur. After the transfusion, his color was improved. He felt better for about twenty-four hours, and then he felt worse. His red count was going down: fifty, forty, thirty. I was numb and tired.

Day and night I dragged my weary body about: making beds, washing diapers, making formulas (my milk had dried up during the seige), bathing Wilbur, rubbing his back to prevent bedsores, all the while keeping my face a mask. God, how I wanted to weep, to let my tired, lying, facial muscles relax in sorrow! Instead, with a forced smile I teased my husband, telling him how hard he would have to work when he got well, in order to give me a rest. I spoke glowingly of a second honeymoon in New Hampshire and Vermont, but my inner fire was numb.

Now he was blind in one eye. In another few days he was paralyzed on one side. His family came to tell me what an ungodly position I was taking in not letting the minister come and help Wilbur prepare for his death. I fought every suggestion that he should know that he was dying. Even I had accepted his eventual death, as I sat near him and held Mary Lee. I helped raise his hand to touch her soft, golden hair and her pink cheeks. Her strong, healthy, seven-month-old legs were larger than her father's. The inevitable question again came up, "Am I going to die? Do you want me to make a will?"

"No, Wilbur, don't make a will. You are weak and depressed, but you have a life ahead of you." I just could not tell him. I knew if I told him to make a will, he would know that he was fatally ill. He wanted life; he didn't want death. No, I could not tell him. I forced myself to act gay and cheerful.

Christmas greeting cards began arriving and snowflakes made patterns on the window panes. I placed a little evergreen tree where Wilbur could see it and hung holly, tinsel and a bit of mistletoe. I pinned the cards on the wall, where my husband could see them. The rooms looked gay with the Christmas spirit, as Wilbur with a waxen, deathlike face looked up at me. I felt as if I were going to break and crack like the icicles that cracked outside the window. I was frightened and so desperately tired. If only I could have one night of sleep! I wired Christina in Vermont and asked her to come and give me a hand.

I didn't trust his family to stay with him so that I could sleep. They were much too interested in the welfare of his soul. I was interested in his mental well-being on earth. He had already lived two months longer than the doctor said he could, but now he had longer periods of unconsciousness. When awake, he was in acute pain, so his dose of morphine went higher and higher. One dose might have killed a normal man. At times when he moved and whimpered with pain, I was tempted to give him the extra bit of morphine that would kill him. Who would know? I couldn't. I still hoped for the discovery of a drug that would cure him.

Flowers came, plants came, plates of food came, but people stopped coming. They could not bear to watch him slipping away, and I did not blame them. The baby was fed, taken care of, but never got a smile from me. When she cried and Wilbur whimpered, I chose to go to Wilbur. How unfair this was to Mary Lee; but what could I do?

Christina, my friend from New Rochelle Hospital, answered my wire and came. Wilbur regained consciousness and asked her about her family in Vermont. What a relief it was to have another nurse in the house with me, and a friend! He was skin and bones, but I no longer had the strength to lift him and to move him in order to change the sheets. Now we were two.

Chris begged me to go upstairs and get a night of sleep, but I could not bear to leave him. I sat at his bedside, and at night I lay on the army cot next to him. I waited for his lucid moments. I wanted to be with him.

One day I fainted. My exhaustion was great, and I could not argue with Chris when she pushed me up the stairs and said, "Sleep. I'll watch Wilbur, and I'll care for the baby."

The next morning when I came downstairs Wilbur's face was covered with a sheet. Chris said, "He died in his sleep. I did not want to wake you up. There was nothing you could do."

I felt a wave of guilt come over me. The first night since his illness that I had left him, he died. A part of me died with him, on January 23, 1931.

Chris went to notify the doctor and Wilbur's mother. I sat in a daze. I was alive. I moved my fingers, yet I felt as if my body lay under the sheet with Wilbur. I wanted my body to lie there with his.

Suddenly the house was full of people. All those who had never come to help me wash a sheet or care for the baby were giving me advice. I must get black clothes. Wilbur must have a fancy coffin. I must do this and do that. All I wanted was to be left alone. I was one big gnawing ache and did not want to face life. I thought of the morphine that I had in the house. I took the syringe and placed it in water to sterilize it. If I gave myself a killing dose of morphine, there would be no hurt, no ache, no tiredness, and peace at last. Mary Lee began screaming with hunger. I came out of my daze and turned to feed her.

As I fed Mary Lee, I began coming out of my desire to die. I had to live for her. I didn't want to live, but I had to live. I wanted to weep. For months I had wanted to weep. I had not allowed myself to weep. I felt like stone, like a walking corpse. I could not cry. I envied the baby her tears.

I was taken to the funeral parlor to pick out a coffin. I had $1,000 in insurance coming to me. I paid $500 for the coffin, and the doctor got the other $500.

My sister-in-law, who had never come to help me when I needed help, insisted that I must sit by the coffin with my baby. She wanted my baby to remember her father. Mary Lee was all of eight months old.

Once I went to see his cold, made-up face, and not again. I had done all that I could to keep him alive. All was finished. This was not Wilbur lying there, but a cold, dead body, having to lie there for three days to satisfy barbaric customs. I had to wear black for the same reasons. I had to listen to a long sermon which chastised me for not letting the minister prepare my husband for his death. I rode in the car to the cemetery. I watched the coffin being lowered. I returned to the home of his mother and never went to the cemetery again. With all my guts and knowledge I had tried to keep him alive, but I couldn't. At least he had been as comfortable physically and mentally as skilled, loving nursing care could make him. This I had done. Now he was gone. If I had not had the courage to kill myself, then I had to gather all my strength and fight to live for Mary Lee.

The week after the funeral, Miss Duffy, Directress of the Visiting Nurses Association, came to call on me. I had worked with her as a volunteer, and now she was offering me a part-time paid job. Thanking her, I said that I would give my answer within a week.

I had to settle in and adjust myself to the Fuhr household. After the funeral, I just couldn't walk up those stairs where I had known such happiness and also the opposite. I told my mother-in-law to sell all my furniture. I had to have some cash.

In one large room upstairs in the Fuhr home, I put my personal effects and my baby's crib. I had a room, but it was not a home.

I had heard there was a school nursing job open in the Port Chester High School. I liked public health nursing. If I went back to hospital nursing or private duty nursing my hours would be irregular, and I would have little time for Mary Lee. Public health had regular hours and vacations with pay. It was a positive field of medicine which worked to prevent disease and needless deaths like that of my husband. I wanted to work in public health.

When I called on Mr. Knapp, the school principal, he obviously wanted to give me the job, but there was a law that the applicant had to be a high school graduate and had to have twelve college credits toward a Bachelor's Degree in public health nursing. He explained that he had to abide by the rules of the State Public Health School Nursing Division. I found this difficult to accept. Finally he said, "Go and see Miss Mary Swanson in Albany. She is in charge of the School Nursing section."

I asked Wilbur's mother if she would care for Mary Lee for a day, and I explained why I wanted to go to the state capital. All the way to Albany I hoped that I might be able to persuade Miss Swanson to make an exception in my case. I had had two weeks of public health nursing as a student nurse, and I had worked as a volunteer with the Port Chester Visiting Nurses Association.

Fortunately she was in the office when I arrived. As I explained to her why I wanted the job, she listened sympathetically. Certainly she could have eased me out of the office with a firm refusal, but she didn't. Her refusal was firm as she explained why a nurse in public health needed specific education in that field. I understood and agreed with her after awhile. How could I help the teacher to integrate health through the school program if I did not have experience and practice in teaching theory? Then she said, "You can make up the four years of high school that you lack. You can then start working for your degree in public health."

"How can I, when I have an eight-month-old baby, bills to pay, besides the seven dollars a week room-and-board to my mother-in-law for the baby and me? How can I?" I asked, and added, "I must begin earning money in order to meet my commitments."

She answered, "Begin thinking about how you can do both: Earn through work, and go to school."

Down the Hudson River Valley the wheels clicked and clacked. "Go to school, go to school," they said. I didn't know if the train wheels were crazy or I was. How could I go to school? At night I had hardly slept, thinking of Wilbur. That night I hardly slept as I thought about high school. By morning I had decided I would take the part-time job with the VNA and ask the high school principal if there was a way to make up the missing education by going to high school part-time. If I could do that, then I'd face the next step, Teacher's College, Columbia University, and twelve college credits.

When Mary Lee had been bathed and fed, she always took a nap. While she slept I walked down to Miss Duffy's office and told her of my fruitless journey to Albany. I wanted to be honest with her, so I told her I preferred the school nursing job, as it was full-time with a good salary, and I told her of my interview with Miss Swanson. Since Miss Duffy had taught public health nursing, she encouraged me to finish high school. She explained that I worked only in the mornings, which left afternoons free to go to high school.

Next I went to see Mr. Knapp, the school principal. He explained that if I passed the regents' exams with a mark ten percent higher than the full-time students, I could not only complete the high school requirements, but I could do it in less than four years. Two weeks after Wilbur's death, I was working in the mornings and attending high school in the afternoons.

I still wonder how I did it! Mornings began by feeding Mary

Lee, putting her diapers in to soak, feeding myself some breakfast. I dashed to the office to get my schedule: Give an old lady a bed bath. Teach a mother how to bathe her newborn and how to make the formula. Teach a diabetic how to give himself the important, lifesaving insulin, and so on. At traffic stops, I'd look down at the seat next to me and try to memorize chemical formulas for an afternoon class. Home at noon. Feed the baby, and grab a sandwich. Race to school to get into my physics class, or chemistry or history. I worked, I studied, and I brooded about the coldness of the home in which I existed. I worried about the poverty in the homes in which I worked. I was unhappy that my little girl rarely smiled. Was this my fault? Was she reflecting my own worry, hurry and misery? I could do nothing. I had to stay where I was. My salary was $75 a month. Where else could I get room and board for two of us for $7 a week? Mother Fuhr loved Mary Lee, and for this I was grateful. This tied me.

My life was compartmentalized. I was one person in the home in which I lived, quiet, introspective, listening and disagreeing, but keeping my mouth shut. I had to for the sake of my baby. In school, I was hungry, alert and filled the classroom with my constant questioning. In the district where I worked, I felt for the people whose bellies grumbled with hunger, and all I could give was understanding and warmth.

Noses ran, and bellies grumbled in emptiness as pathetic mothers worried about their children. Men looked for work, but there was no work. My in-laws said they were lazy Italians and did not want to work. I knew this to be untrue. I was in their homes daily and saw their faces when they came home from a fruitless quest for work. From a cold-water flat filled with wailing children, I might go to the banker's home to bathe his invalid aunt. The contrast was at times unbearable. In the banker's home there was poverty in human relations but wealth in food, and warmth created by the furnace. In the homes that I had come from there was poverty in food and coal, but not in spirit. Even in their bitter poverty, the Italians were not afraid to love, to laugh, to weep, to live. I felt closer to them than I did to my in-laws and their friends.

There was one person at this time to whom I could talk. She was my patient, and I went to her home daily. Her profession had been that of a madame in a whorehouse. After my initial prudish shock, I realized that she was one of the most understanding and tolerant women I'd ever met. I would express to her my distress with the cleavage in the town: upper middle class, white, Protestant Americans who hated the foreigners and accused them of being thieves, murderers, anarchists, socialists and communists. To Annie, the ex-madame, all were people with problems, including the upper middle class. She felt sorrier for them in their ignorance of life. I lived with the upper class, and my sympathies were with the so-called common Italians. Annie said, "When you can, you have to break with your in-laws and live alone with your child. You have to find yourself."

One morning when I entered our office, I found a lovely, white-haired woman talking to Miss Duffy. I write of her now, since she introduced me to ideas and the people who had these ideas. They were responsible for changing my whole life from the pattern it was in, a change which finally was to remove me in ideas and space from Port Chester, New York.

Mrs. Post was introduced to me as the representative of the Birth Control Clinic in Port Chester, an extension of the Margaret Sanger Clinic in New York City. I had never heard of such a clinic or of Margaret Sanger, but I listened intently as she asked us to send those women who were interested in spacing their families. Mentally, I agreed as she spoke of the right of families to have the information which made spacing possible. I almost cheered her as she spoke of the lives that could be saved by family planning as contrasted to deaths after dirty abortions. I had seen more and more deaths in the poor homes, from abortions induced by some old woman who called herself a midwife, but I didn't speak. I was still fresh out of nurses' training, where in the presence of an older nurse one only spoke when spoken to.

I awaited to hear what my supervisor would say, and I was shocked when I heard her: "We will not suggest your clinic. The unemployed should not bed together. They must control themselves. We will not advise our clients to go to the Birth Control Clinic."

I had been taught that one listened and obeyed one's superior. I had studied ethics in medicine when I studied to be a nurse, but what was ethics? To whom did I owe my loyalty — to my superior, who could say, "Don't have intercourse"? She had never been married, and she had never lived with a man. What did she know of the sex drive? Or did I owe my loyalty to the struggling mother? She had six or more children spaced a year apart. No, not spaced — they came. The ones she had she could not feed. If she had an illegal abortion done, the probability was that her children not only would be hungry but motherless. I decided I owed my loyalty to her. To work with her was ethics. I felt it was the inalienable right of every woman to have this birth control information if she wanted it. Here in this little town of Port Chester we had an information center for birth control with a specially trained woman doctor in charge.

Nevertheless, the next morning I felt guilty and hoped I would not be seen entering the Birth Control Clinic. In the cheerful waiting room I explained to Mrs. Post that I had decided to help, and I hoped she would not tell my supervisor. If I lost my job, how would I finish high school? How would I feed Mary Lee and myself? She understood. Routinely at the VNA, we called in homes where there were newborn babies. I gave this list of names to Mrs. Post and told her that I would continue giving her lists. In this way she could call on the mothers and invite them to come to the Birth Control Clinic.

Gradually, as I began to know her, I found that I had a

friend in Mrs. Post. She was gracious, loving, intelligent, with many interests, the kind of person I had wanted to know. She reminded me of my aunt in Holland. She was twice my age and had daughters my age. When I asked questions of her and expressed my doubts, she answered me with books. I had read little since my days in the mills when I sneaked off to the library. Now I devoured the books she loaned me. Most were ones that made me think, argue, agree and disagree, like Harold Laski's *Socialism*. My mind had become blocked with any word that had an "ism" in it other than Americanism. Laski's book made sense to me. Capitalism, communism, socialism, fascism, Americanism — what was the answer? Why depressions? Why unemployment? Why wars? Socialism sounded good to me. Was it workable? These were the things we discussed.

What an education I was getting without being aware of it! My friends were Mrs. Post, a social worker and a lady, and Annie, an ex-madame and also a lady. My other tutors were hungry, non-English speaking Italians, "shanty" Irish, and "nonshanty" Irish who had graduated to lace curtains. There were blacks from the South and blacks from Jamaica. The latter felt superior to the ones from Alabama. To top this layercake of peoples, I was studying courses in high school. I was changing, but my environment was not. My home with the Fuhrs, which was not a home, was unchangeable. Sometime and somehow I had to break those walls. Someday I had to be where the walls were mine, to change the paintings as my needs changed and to change the books on the shelves. Better to have a home where one had bookshelves!

I hoped that I could graduate with the class of 1932. Since I only attended formal classes from noon until 3:30 in the afternoon, I had to study many of the courses without a teacher or formal classes. By about three in the morning, my mind was a mess of prisms, transformers, what makes a bell ring, German verbs, civics, history, biology and, now, books on socialism. If the personality of a schizoid may be split two ways, mine was being split in six or seven different directions. I just hoped I wouldn't get them too mixed.

In school I had become a notetaker. The teachers didn't like questions on socialism. At work with my supervisor, I was a respectful nonopinionated public health nurse. With the Fuhrs I trod as if dozens of soft-shelled eggs were under my feet. They loved my child, and they were good to her. What did it matter if they thought of me as a queer fish as long as they cared for her? But with Mrs. Post and Annie, the possible *me* was coming out and expressing herself.

I had done it! I had crammed a four-year high school course into one year and four months by going to school in the afternoons and by studying at home. I had passed the regents' exams with honors. I, who had always wanted to have a high school education, was now a high school graduate. As I marched up the aisle to receive my diploma with the class of 1932 of Port Chester High School, I hardly believed it.

What I had done had been good for me. Through study and work, I'd had less time to brood about Wilbur's death a year and a half before. The edge was off the hurt, and I was now able to sleep at night without waking up to see if Wilbur needed me. For months after his death I had still awakened hoping he was in the room, but now I slept through the night.

I began working full-time with a salary of $150 a month. Miss Duffy was going to take a well-earned, long vacation from the VNA, and I was left in charge with part-time help. When she left, she also left me the VNA car. After work on hot nights I was able to escape from the Fuhr home, and Mary Lee and I went to Rye Beach. She loved the water, and I began teaching her how to swim. She was now two years old. I was 27.

Sometimes my new friends, whom I had met through the Birth Control Clinic, invited Mary Lee and me to spend a day on Long Island Sound. I loved these Sundays on the Sound, sitting in a rented boat. I seemed to be able to think more clearly with the sea around me. I knew that I had to make a break from the Fuhrs, but I was frightened. I was earning $150 a month. Jobs were scarce. We were in a depression. Did I have the courage to make the break and strike out for myself? Mother Fuhr loved Mary Lee and was good to her. They wanted her but not me. But I wanted us to have a chance to grow, to question, to become. What I did not know was what would or could become of us, but I wanted freedom to be free in the becoming!

I don't remember the straw that broke the camel's back, but I went off in a huff. I walked up the street to the Women's Club, a large, rambling, old house which also rented rooms. They had a vacant room under the eaves on the third floor, and I rented it. It cost no more than what I was already paying, but the price did not include food, although I had kitchen privileges. The housekeeper was a kindly person who could care for Mary Lee when I was at work, and she was glad to have the extra money. I was scared stiff as I made the decision. I was afraid to move toward freedom, growth and the future — what future?

Mother Fuhr realized that I could not live under the same roof with her "old maid" daughter, Wilbur's baby sister. She had always disliked me, had been jealous when I married Wilbur, and since his death had done all she could to make my life miserable. I thanked Mother Fuhr for all she had done for my child, and I promised to bring Mary Lee every day. I explained that I had to be on my own sometime, and this was the time. She was hurt, but she understood. The town would talk, but let them.

It didn't take long to move the crib and our few clothes. I hung the copper plate that Ome David and Tante Sara had given me for my eighteenth birthday. I filled a delft bowl with flowers, and I cooked our supper. This little room, under the eaves, was now home.

At first I seemed content to have my own one-room home. I

took Mary Lee to spend some time with her grandmother every day. I felt strongly that I had no right to influence her relationships with her paternal grandparent, aunts and cousins. In a sense Grandmother Fuhr and I were better friends than before. She did not have to take sides between her daughter and me.

Yet I was not content. School was finished. I was saving money so that I could eventually register at Columbia University and could begin work toward my degree. Life was empty again. I was brooding too much and feeling sorry for myself. I wished I could make a trip to Holland. I needed a complete change, I told myself. I tried to check this kind of thinking, as I felt it was insane. I should think only of saving money and using that for my bachelor's degree in public health. Or should I?

Of course it was impossible, yet I heard myself talking about my idea to my ex-madame friend and to my friend at the Birth Control Clinic. After all, I was 27 years old. I was a widow and had a child to raise. I had no right to think of a trip to Holland, but my friends heartily disagreed with me. Obviously this was what I wanted. I began pricing tickets on the Holland-American Line. I wrote to Tante Sara and Ome David about how much I wanted to see them. I did feel sick — not physically, but sick in that I was not whole and needed the kind medicine of Tante Sara. I knew nothing of psychiatry, but I knew I needed my family in Holland like a heart case needs his digitalis to live.

It was still 1932 when I bought my ticket for a June, 1933, sailing. Suddenly I was more aware of myself. I saw my fat hips. I had been overeating as a substitute for living. Now I began dieting in earnest and buying gay-colored pieces of material. I shed the widow's black that I had been wearing when out of my deep gray uniform. Life took on meaning again as I planned my vacation in Holland.

Of course I rationalized that I would go to the International Nursing Conference which was to be held in Brussels, Belgium, and in Paris, France, in the summer of 1933. Not that I kidded myself; I knew it was an excuse to see Paris. Grandmother Fuhr and her daughter were delighted with the idea of having Mary Lee all to themselves for five weeks. Mary Lee looked like her father, and they loved this Dresden doll-like child.

In June I sailed on the *Statendam*. Two and three times a day I changed from one bright-colored, homemade dress into another. I would not let the thought come to the surface, but obviously I hoped to meet a Man. The only man who did pay attention to me was a wonderful, warm human, Ladd Haystead. Like a big brother, this newspaper writer took me under his wing. I shared in all the drinking bouts without taking a drink. The drinking shocked me, but the drinkers fascinated me. Ladd invited me to meet him in Paris and said, "I'll take you to the opera and show you some of Paris."

It was wonderful sailing up the Maas River in a boat that towered over the landscape. One could see brightly colored sailboats skimming across the canals like ballerinas across a stage. The stately *Statendam* moved slowly up the Maas. The soft, diffused light shimmering on bits of land meant home to me. I could not wait to get to Amsterdam and see my family again. I wanted to see the leaning houses alongside the canals built on top of herring bones, the skeletons of the lowly fish which had helped make Holland rich in the 16th and 17th centuries. I wanted to see the museums again and to sit in the Concertgebouw as the music of Beethoven swirled into me and around me. The Netherlands — Spinoza, Rembrandt, William of Orange, the Sea Beggars, the House of Orange, my family, my home that really was home.

When the boat docked, I took the first train out of Rotterdam for Amsterdam. The tulips and hyacinths waved and welcomed me on the fast journey. As we slowed down to enter the railroad station in Amsterdam, I practically hung out the window looking for my family. I hoped they had received my wire. Then I spied my jolly, red-haired uncle, and hopping up and down near him was my Tante Sara.

When the train came to a stop, I ran into her arms. The first thing she said was, "Child, how thin you are!"

"But Tante, for six months I have starved myself to become thinner," I explained.

"Why?" she asked.

"It is the style in America," I answered.

"What a barbaric country that must be! Don't worry. We will feed you and fatten you up. You will look like a woman again and not a beanpole," she muttered.

Obviously my Tante Sara and Annie, the ex-madame, did not agree on women's figures. I had faithfully done the exercises that Annie had taught me, and my aunt thought I was too thin.

Ten years had passed since I had been with them, and much had happened to me. I poured it out to Tante Sara's sympathetic ears: my long illness, the story I had heard from Flora about my father, my marriage, Wilbur and his death, and my loneliness. Tears that I had never shed now poured down my face as Tante Sara held me in her arms and wiped my tears. The ten years passed by in a short while. Much of my loneliness and brooding went with the tears. I felt cleansed of my problems, and I rested in the arms of the family.

My aunt and uncle did not understand why I had not brought Mary Lee with me. They wanted me to live with them in Holland. It was hard to explain that I preferred the Netherlands but that I felt my child and I were Americans. Mary Lee was a second-generation American, and I felt we had to work it out in the United States.

What surprised me was to hear so much German spoken wherever one went in the stores, on the streets and by servants in the homes. It appeared to be an invasion of Germans. I had thought of taking a short trip up the Rhine River, which I remembered, and the Lek, to the town of Viana where my grandparents had lived and where, as a little girl, I had sat in the watchtower to see the boats go up and down the Rhine. Now I wanted to go and see what lay around the bend of the Rhine.

But Ome David said, "If you go into Germany, don't come back here." Those were strong words from my sweet uncle, and I asked him why. He tried to explain the threat of Hitler, the Big Lie, the drive to war, the persecution of free speech, the racist approach, the treatment of the Jews under Hitler, and the total menace of Nazism. He told me that the father of my young David was busy writing articles in the press about the dangers of Hitlerism and its threat to man after his long struggle for dignity and human rights. Our whole family had a refugee or two in each of their homes.

I could hardly believe what I was hearing. I had been far removed from this in the United States, but I recalled the books I had read lately and the conversations I had heard between Mrs. Post and her two daughters, who had seen Hitlerism coming into Austria. I began thinking of the world instead of separate countries, and I was afraid. I agreed with Ome David that not one cent of my hard-earned money should be spent in Germany.

Instead of spending time in Germany, I would spend a few more days in Paris. My uncle and aunt did not want me to go to the International Nursing Conference — and especially not by plane — but since I insisted, Tante Sara came to see me off. Mainly she wanted to take a good look at the airplane. I am sure that she thought if she looked at the plane it would safely carry her favorite niece to France.

I shall never forget my first moments in the air, and I have envied all flyers ever since. In the golden light, Holland lay below us, but within a few minutes the steward held up a card saying we were over Belgium. Drifting through my mind were thoughts that Ome David had stimulated: Why Hitler? Why depressions? Why wars? Why spite? What wonder was this ability of man to lift heavy metal into the air? Man now flew planes that da Vinci had dreamed of. Couldn't man individually and collectively pull himself up to match his creative abilities? Was human nature foreordained in the germ plasm? I refused to believe this.

When we landed in Paris I asked to be taken to the Ambassador Hotel. I might have to go back to Holland third-class, but I began my trip in high style. I hardly unpacked my bag, as I was anxious to walk the streets of Paris. Instead of looking for the International Nursing Conference, I found the Notre Dame, Le Sacre-Cœur, Montparnasse and much more. I fell in love with Paris, though I knew not a word of French. It didn't matter because I walked and, when tired, sat in a park and watched Paris go by.

To tell the truth, I ended up spending more time walking the streets of Paris than listening to the speeches at the Nursing Conference. When they were in English, I stayed. When they were not, I'd quietly sneak out. I had noticed women at the door of the hall carrying paper and pen and asking for signatures. Now one approached me. She was a Dutch nurse, collecting signatures against war and fascism, she said. I didn't understand fascism, but the very thought of war made me ill. I listened to talks on how to prevent death and disease, and actively worked in this field. War destroyed our work. I signed with pleasure.

Since the talks would be in French or German for the rest of the day, I decided to try to find Ladd Haystead, who had taken me under his wing on the boat. He had given me the address of a friend of his, a newspaper writer, but it was difficult to get up enough courage to call on her. I didn't want to be snubbed. I had a small opinion of myself and was extremely impressed by writers. As usual, when I realized that I was afraid, I acted by facing the problem and went to the Left Bank.

I climbed five flights of stairs to Mary Knight's apartment and found her sick, hot and uncomfortable. I saw at a glance that what she needed was an honest bit of nursing care, so I introduced myself and told her that Ladd had said to drop by and that he would meet me here any afternoon. When she told me to wait for him, I suggested that I spend the time making her more comfortable. Rolling up my sleeves, I gave her a bedbath and a good back massage. In the nursing field I felt at home and equal to all. By the time Ladd came, Mary felt better. In the process of bathing her I had thrown out my inferiority complex about writers, about this particular writer, with the dirty bath water.

As Ladd greeted me warmly, I realized he had not changed a bit. He had meant it when he told me to look for him in Paris. He took me to the opera that night. I had never seen an opera, and *Faust* will never be as wonderful again as it was that night in the Paris Opera House, thanks to Ladd Haystead.

As I look back, the highlight of my stay in Paris was not the nursing conference, but that two writers had treated me as if I were a thinking person. I had expected them to be bored, to push me aside, to snub me, but they had not. I chewed on this. Could I become an intellectual?

The nursing conference was moving on to Brussels where the delegates were to be received by the Queen of Belgium. My money was running low, and I bought a third-class ticket with a stopover at Brussels. I did want to see a queen. In the third-class compartment of the train, I tried to understand and to be understood by my travelling companions. The lunch I had bought consisted of a loaf of bread, a bottle of wine and a sausage. The passengers offered me bits of their lunch, and I offered mine. In the compartment I felt the same kind of warm humanity that one met in the wards of a hospital — friendly, cursing, laughing, weeping, and very much alive. I felt at home with them, yet I wanted to be accepted by and to be like writers, like intellectuals, like college graduates. But I didn't feel as secure with the latter. Who the devil was the real me? Where did I belong?

Where in the world is there a marketplace as beautiful as the one in Brussels? Façades of sheer lace, created in stone, fronted the old Guild Halls. The towers of the church of St. Guduel aspired to reach the sky. I tore myself away from the marketplace to go and see the queen. Hundreds of other nurses had the same idea, yet the royal grounds were not crowded. The flowers and gardens were lovely. I waited for the queen. She approached, and her nose was red and runny. A common cold had conquered her. I left the Royal Rights of Kings and Queens to the bowing nurses and went back to the earthy marketplace.

When the conference finished, I went back to Amsterdam. The train was slow compared to the rapid flight of the airplane. In my absence Jack de Vries and his wife, Etty, had arrived from Java. Etty was lovely to look at, with skin like a dusky peach. I watched my family for signs of discrimination. After all, Etty was a "half-blood," since her mother was a native of Java and her father, a Hollander. Because I had been reared mainly in the States I was aware of the color line. Although I did not believe in it, some of it was in me. When my aunt began talking, I thought, "Here it comes," and I didn't want my aunt to be chauvinistic. But she said, "Lini, you know Etty is not like a Dutch woman raised in Holland. She is helpless without servants." That was the only comment that was made, and certainly it was not racially discriminatory.

Uncle Jack bought a secondhand Ford, and the three of us went off on a trip to try to cover all the states of the Netherlands. This was easy, since it's a small country. We sat on dikes, drinking beer and eating smoked eels, and Uncle Jack tried to persuade me to get Mary Lee and go to Java. He and Etty thought it silly of me to remain a widow, with many rich planters in Java looking for wives. It was an idea, but I did not take it seriously. They wanted me in Java, and my Tante Sara wanted me in Amsterdam. I preferred Amsterdam, but the United States was my birthplace, and Mary Lee was there.

Tante Sara insisted that I begin looking for Jews in America. I did not know any Jews, and this shocked her. She impressed on me that, according to the Jewish law, I was Jewish and a Sephardite. Although she was not religious, she didn't forget for one minute that she was a Sephardite and that the family had produced men like Spinoza. I promised her that I'd look for Jews in America, which relieved her.

I could well imagine what the Fuhrs would think if I began going about with Jews. What about my mother, who denied she was a Jew? I didn't know how to begin. I told Tante about the discrimination in the States against Jews, active or subversive, and she could not believe it. Holland didn't discriminate against people; why should America? I gave up trying to explain American inferiority complexes to my secure aunt.

Ome David, Tante Sara, and my cousins Dina and Gerrit came to Rotterdam to see me off for the United States on the *Statendam*. For them it was a grand excursion, though a bit of a sad one. They were sure I would be back with Mary Lee soon, but I was not sure. I did promise them that I would make an effort to come at least every five years. I knew that I had to work toward my degree in public health and try to achieve a feeling of belonging in the States before I was free to return to Holland.

At four in the afternoon, I boarded the ship. I had told them not to wait until it sailed, but they stood and waved until I could see them no more. I don't know if they were weeping, but I certainly was. I felt strong and renovated; they had done this for me, and I wept that I would not see them the next day. Little did I know that I would never see them again.

Through a sunset of purple and golden clouds, we sailed slowly down the River Maas toward the Atlantic. I stayed on deck until I could see no more of Holland, yet I was glad to be going back to America. My little girl was there. Mentally and physically I felt much better than when I had left a short month before.

One morning as I sat in a deck chair thinking of what Ome

David had told me of socialism, and wondering if socialism was possible in the United States, a young man began talking to me. I had noticed him walking on deck, observing people and seldom talking to anyone, and I had hoped he would talk to me. I thought him handsome and interesting to look at. We talked our way across the Atlantic Ocean, and I discovered that he had a mixed-up background too. His father was German and Protestant, and his mother Jewish and Dutch, but it didn't bother him as it did me. Finally he made me admit to something that I had not been aware of: I was anti-Semitic. Obviously, I had absorbed some of this from my mother, who had become a Protestant and anti-Semitic. I hadn't been able to talk to any young man since Wilbur had died, but it was easy for me to talk to Herbert. We kissed one another goodbye and clutched one another's addresses in our hands. I wondered, but hoped it would not be "only a shipboard acquaintance."

When I returned to Port Chester, it was obvious that Mary Lee had had a good six weeks. She was glad to see me but not tearfully glad. We moved into our room in the Women's Club, which was a great change from living in the socialist housing development on the River Amstel with my aunt and uncle and cousins. But I had to lick this feeling of not belonging to America before I could choose to live elsewhere. The rest of the summer was filled with wonderful plans to enter Columbia University as a part-time student. Evenings Mary Lee and I went swimming and enjoyed one another. I saw more of my in-laws and felt less tense with them. I felt renewed in spirit and knew the trip to Europe had been good for me.

Since I had a full-time job, I was only allowed to take six credits at Teacher's College, Columbia. These I divided between one class on Tuesday night and two on Saturday morning. The Visiting Nurses Association allowed me the car on Tuesday evening. I drove back and forth to school. On Saturday I took the train. I was bursting with pride and could hardly believe that I, the ex-mill dolly, was going to college. No one whom I had known as a girl had made up an unfinished high school education and had gone on to college. Now I was going to have an education and move over to the "other side of the tracks."

I began meeting some people who were from the other side of the tracks, and I looked at them not once but thrice. They didn't smell bad or act bad or carry bombs, although they said they were "communists." I sat very quietly and listened to them fling ideas and talk thick and fast. They began loaning me books and pamphlets and made me feel as if I "belonged." It wasn't long before I agreed with them, as the dream of a new world opened up to me a way of life for the many, which seemed achievable.

My Ome David had called it "socialism." They called it "communism." It appeared to me that they were talking about the same philosophy. They acted on their beliefs in the same fashion. If in the United States they called socialism communism, it was still the same to me.

Yet it was hard to shake my ideas of communism: that it lived on hates, aggressions, and caused trouble. Revolution was a frightening word to me, one I also associated with communism. My newfound friends argued convincingly that this was not so. I watched carefully their behavior with blacks, with Jews, with different religions. They did not seem to know the meaning of discrimination. Obviously they preferred being with people who had good patterns of social behavior. I spent as much time as I could with them and discovered that out of the ten or more I knew, only two were actually Communist Party members. I couldn't understand this. If they felt this way, why didn't they all join the Party?

Still I found these people constructive and decent and the most interesting I had met in the United States. The Constitution and the Bill of Rights became living and vital through discussions with them. They were interested in all that touched life: the arts, literature, painting, music, economics. They did not laugh at ignorance, but took you by the hand and led you to the open door of books, concerts, art exhibits, and so forth. I felt as if I were beginning to find what I had been looking for.

I had promised Tante Sara to look for Jews in Port Chester, and I did find a few. One was a doctor, whose wife was a social climber; another married couple had a dry cleaning business; another sold shoes while his wife stayed home and read. I found them all dull, except for the one who read. They tried too hard to fit into the pattern of white Protestant America, although they did not appear very different from the people they were trying to ape. However, my communist friends who lived on the hill in Port Chester were never dull. Some were Jews; some were ex-Catholics or ex-Protestants; some were black and some were white. They came from all kinds of backgrounds, and they all blended into what they said was communism. I wished I could talk to my aunt and uncle and could tell them that I thought it was not a question of being Jewish, but rather a question of being alive to the inherent dignity of man and his right to achieve it to its fullest.

Certainly I could not talk to my in-laws or my nursing supervisor about the people I was beginning to know, about the books I was reading or the changes in my thinking. They would be shocked, and worse than that I would find myself jobless. It was far better to keep my mouth shut with them and start saving to get out of Port Chester. Somehow or other I wanted to live in New York City with Mary Lee, where I could go to school part-time, meet more people who were teaching me new ideas, and expose myself to concerts and other activities. I didn't know when, but I knew I would leave Port Chester soon.

By summer I had saved $500. I spoke to my mother-in-law, who was delighted to have a chance to have my little girl until I found an apartment for us. The Port Chester Visiting Nurses Association gave me a leave of absence to study. I was scared to death to make the change to New York, but I was determined to do it. Some of the communists I knew lived in New York City, and I felt I could turn to them for friendship and warmth there. I was hungry to learn and to be like others who appeared secure. Was there anyone as hungry as I was then, not always knowing what I wanted to learn and ashamed of letting people know how ignorant I was?

I found a room on the corner of 115th Street and Riverside Drive, shabby and gloomy with one window opening on an air shaft. Not a bit of daylight entered the room, but I knew I could give it warmth and color with the few things I had from Java and Holland. The electric light would keep the plant green, and that would be my garden. With the money I'd saved I had to live, eat, pay tuition, and buy books. I was fat and getting fatter, but my limited funds made me diet. I was frightened of the studies but overjoyed that I, the mill dolly, had made the break and was going to college. I moved my few belongings to Riverside Drive and was ready to register for classes.

New York City, 1933-1937

Becoming by Doing 4

Registration day at Teacher's College, Columbia University, reminded me of the days when I stood with a long line of unemployed workers in front of a factory gate, and I found myself looking for the timeclock as we were shuttled from floor to floor by unfriendly teachers. The Nursing Arts Section, where I had to register for my major, made me think of the days when we student nurses had to face frozen nursing supervisors. If these women were representative of the teachers in the T.C. Nursing Education School, I doubted that there would be any give-and-take between teacher and student.

But when I walked home that late afternoon, I was thrilled with the beauty of the Hudson River. The hoarse toots of the tugs, the plodding ferries wagging their way across the Hudson like frowsy old women trying to look dignified, the crisp air and the fall colors on the Palisades all took the edge off the frigidity of registration day. I still could not believe that I was now registered for a full-time program of studies. I intended to graduate with a degree. I did not dare think of how many years that might take. If I began worrying about how to get enough credits and the money to pay for them, I'd be afraid to begin.

Before I knew it, I was deep in study — philosophy, psychology, English, public health. As I had assumed, in nursing classes you listened and gave the teacher the responses she expected; but in sociology and philosophy it was the reverse, and you could ask questions and disagree. It was fun. I was beginning to see a glimmer of light through my muddled thinking.

One afternoon as I walked down a school corridor, my eyes spotted a large wall poster: MEETING OF THE LEAGUE AGAINST WAR AND FASCISM. I was interested. After all, I had studied how to prevent deaths, and war destroyed our work. I knew a little about the Nazis from what my uncle had told me. The words "against war" intrigued me. I recalled the lovely Dutch woman in front of the Nursing Conference hall in Paris, who had asked me to sign a petition "against war and fascism," and I had done so. I had no class at this hour, so I went to the meeting.

Timidly I entered the room and slid into a back seat. I looked around but didn't see a soul I knew. I thought other public health students might be present. The professor who chaired the meeting seemed simple, sincere and earnest. There was a guest speaker who spoke of the danger of fascism, using Hitler as a symbol. He spoke of fascism as a breeder of wars. His talk jibed with some of the things my uncle had told me in Amsterdam and the stories that the German refugees told us in Holland. He made sense to me, and I agreed that we should work against war and fascism.

When the chairman of the meeting asked for volunteers to help in the work and to join the League, I raised my hand. "I would like to work against war, but I still do not understand the meaning of fascism too well," I said. He suggested that I wait until after the meeting for further explanations. However, I signed the membership card right then and there.

After the meeting the chairman of the League and I talked and walked across the campus. I asked many questions. As he answered, at times he sounded like my socialist uncle in Holland and at other times like my friends who said they were communists; but at all times he made sense to me. He suggested that many of the questions I was asking could be answered by taking some courses in The Worker's School on East 13th Street. I explained that I had little money, and that it was for Teacher's College and to bring my little girl down from Port Chester to put her in school here. He offered to help me get a scholarship in a nursery school for Mary Lee, and this really excited me. He also told me that he could get a scholarship for me to study at The Worker's School. Since at this time the word "study" was about the most exciting word in my mind, I went back to my little dark room lit up like a bright candle.

Before long the chairman, who was also the organizer of the League Against War and Fascism on the campus, became a real friend. The other members made me feel at home very quickly. They were intelligent, alert and dedicated to the organization. Before long I was elected as an organizer of the League on the T.C. campus and as its representative on the student council. My nursing companions thought I was queer to be interested in this work, and I thought it strange and illogical that they were not.

I went down to The Worker's School and registered for two courses: Principles of Communism, and Anthropology, which I had wanted to take on the campus at Columbia, but my advisor had said that public health nurses did not need it. I remembered that I had disagreed with her, because I felt a base in anthropology was essential to public health nursing. Here at The Worker's School I discovered that I could take the same course, given by the same man (but using a different name) as at Columbia, and that it would cost me $3 instead of Columbia's price of $30.

Good Lord, I often thought that I was overburdened with required reading at Teacher's College, but at The Worker's School it was worse! I thought I understood the Communist Manifesto, but the works of Lenin and Stalin I found difficult to study. I used all the arguments that I had against communism with the teacher, especially the one that I didn't believe in society changing by bloodshed. However, he kept up a positive position on the role of the Communist Party for human rights, full employment, and so forth. Although I could not understand *Das Kapital* and soon gave up trying to study it, I did agree with what I saw of the Party's work toward full human rights. I was afraid that if I once believed in the logic of the Communist Party, I would find myself acting on it and joining them.

I often spoke to my friend, the former organizer of the League Against War and Fascism, whose place I had taken, about what I was learning at The Worker's School and about my doubts. He helped clarify my thinking, and I began to realize that I was a humanist, a liberal and an individualist. I firmly believed in man's rights and wanted to have a society where man could reach his potential regardless of race, color, creed or financial status. Was communism the answer? And if I believed that communism was the answer, then I felt that I must join the Party and play my small part in making a decent society possible.

From what I read in the Communist Party press, *The Daily Worker*, this sort of society was being achieved in Russia, and I was most impressed. Yet I had little patience with those who talked of nothing else but Russia and wanted to go there. I felt we had enough problems in the United States and that we should work toward a better America. I was definitely growing, and instead of worrying about me, I was worrying about the world. I had been assured by my teacher at The Worker's School that communism could be achieved by evolution. I needed to know this, as I had a block against bloodshed and the word "revolution."

The people I believed to be communists were the finest I had ever met. They appeared to have a purpose to their lives — not a selfish opportunism, but devotion to the many. Most of them were socially, inwardly, and financially secure; yet they risked this by working within the framework of the Communist Party. I wanted to join the Party, but no one asked me to do so.

While I was trying to make up my mind whether or not to join the Communist Party, the girl who had the room next to mine was trying to make up her mind whether or not to join the League Against War and Fascism. Her name was Elizabeth Bentley, and she had recently returned from Italy, where she had been studying. She claimed to have firsthand knowledge of Italian fascism under Mussolini. It seemed that the more I tried to escape her, the more she pursued me. This was easy, since we had to share the same kitchen and bathroom.

Whenever I got back to my room, I had work to do, papers to write or books to study. Although she, too, was a student at Teacher's College, she never appeared to study. All she wanted to do was talk, talk, talk. I heard over and over again, "I am a direct descendent of American revolutionaries. One of my ancestors signed the Declaration of Independence. I must work for the revolution."

"What revolution?" I asked. "It is evolution we need, not revolution," I continued.

She talked to me and asked my advice, but I didn't ask hers. I didn't trust her, but I didn't know why. The importance of being a graduate of Vassar, as she was, had little meaning for me. I had graduated from the mills, the stores, a nursing school, and had no conception of the secure sort of life of which she spoke. To me, she was an opportunist, since when she spoke of joining the League she said, "You know absolutely the best people are in the League: Midge is from the North Shore, Chicago; Pete is Philadelphia Main Line; and Mary is Back Bay, Boston." I didn't know what she meant, frankly. I had not heard those phrases before.

I observed her as she blithely rattled on about the importance of her family. She annoyed me, but her thinness and her lonesomeness bothered me, too. She was tall, bony and pallid; she seemed all one tone of pale yellow. I'd feel guilty when I was short with her, and then I'd invite her to share my tea and toast or a bowl of soup. I was poor in money, but I didn't discuss it. She was forever discussing her poverty, and then would go out and buy some silly hat. The hat was enough to frighten away the man she hoped to catch. If ever a woman needed a man to shelter her and love her, Bentley did. She was man-hungry, and now that she had begun attending the League meetings she would check with me, "Is Bill married? Is John Jewish? Are they rich? Who are their families?" I didn't know. I had never thought to ask. I wished she would catch a man and leave me alone.

Finally she joined the League, but she never did a thing. The grubby jobs, like running off a leaflet or making a speech at some meeting, she turned down. She was busy, she said. Yet I shared the same floor, kitchen and bath with her, and I knew she never did a thing but sit around looking for someone who would listen to her. Now she began visiting the homes of the "best people" she had met at the League, which gave me a bit of peace. When I looked at her, I often thought of our mill phrase, "Cheesit, here comes the stool pigeon!"

Funny, in a sense it was Bentley's shrinking from work, her lack of sincerity and her opportunism that made me decide that I ought to join the Communist Party. Someone had to pitch in and help make a better America. Maybe I could play a small part.

In my naive way, I went blithely around asking those who I thought were communists, "Will you please recruit me into the Communist Party?" Suddenly those who I had thought were friends and communists shied away from me. Finally I spoke to the former organizer of the League, and he explained to me why people would not tell me they were communists and of the need to be secretive. I didn't like being secretive, and I felt there was nothing to be ashamed of. He recruited me into the Party.

At the first meeting I attended, I met the same people who had told me they were not communists. Now they scolded me for being indiscreet. They tried to make me understand that it would affect any future jobs, or those who had jobs at the moment might lose them, if it were discovered that they were communists. It was hard for me to believe this, since at that time I thought communism was essentially the same as Dutch socialism or American democracy. I felt that being secretive was not a way to build a Communist Party in America. I was naive!

The U.S. Communist Party at that time was interested in black rights, adequate welfare programs, the developing of unions where there were none; and certainly they were interested in helping to further federal works programs and the Works Projects Administration. Later, from the late thirties and on, it seemed to me the Party drew the interest of Stalin and became controlled by the Soviet Union. Therefore, later, to me it no longer represented an American political party. However, at the time I joined, it met the needs of idealism, or humanism, and met my personal need to work as an idealist/humanist.

Within no time, the people I met through the Communist Party became of utmost importance to me. They became my family, my shelter, my security, through my friends who were members. Nothing was too big for me to do. I took on all the work that was given: pass out leaflets, write a new leaflet, go on a picket line, and so forth. Before long I was elected the organizer of the unit on the campus at T.C. Besides this, I was still organizer of the League Against War and Fascism on the campus and also their student council representative.

Weekends, I went to Port Chester to be with Mary Lee. I was quite sure now that I could obtain a scholarship for her at Lincoln School, the demonstration school of Teacher's College. I had received a loan from T.C. which would enable me to do another semester's work. This would mean that I would have one full year's credits toward my degree. I began house-hunting and found a small apartment in one of the condemned buildings on 124th Street. I had to walk up five flights, but there was sun and, since two rooms faced the back courtyard of Lincoln School, there was a feeling of space. The rent was $25 a month.

Since I had sold everything when Wilbur died, I didn't have a pot or a pan. Secondhand shops built my new home. My loan was for $400. I figured $125 of that for rent for five months and $275 for living. One of the comrades was a waiter in a nearby cafe, and I knew he would help me get food, leftovers that the cook might throw away. I just hoped that Bentley would not come over and eat me out of house and home.

Mary Lee came down, and after being tested she received a scholarship for Lincoln School. This was January, 1935, four years after Wilbur's death. I had a home, I had my child with me, and I had friends. I was coming along.

I had not been settled in my home very long when Bentley began bothering me. She wanted to join the Communist Party, but I told her, "Listen, Elizabeth, the Party is work. You never worked in the League. You just used it to meet, to quote yourself, 'the best people.' Why do you want to join the Party? Do you want to meet the 'best people' in the Party? Is that your reason?"

"No, I'll work. I want to be a Communist Party member. I want to work harder for an America that has no discrimination, that has jobs for all. I want a communist America. Believe me, Lini, I'll work," she answered.

I didn't believe her. I told the members of the Unit on the campus one night at a meeting that Bentley wanted to join. They all knew her, since she hung around us, and their reaction was, "Well, then, recruit her into the Party."

"But I feel that she is an opportunist and insincere. She is man-crazy, and I don't trust her," I argued.

"The trouble with you is that you are a proletarian snob," one member said. "Recruit her," they instructed.

Obeying Party discipline, I recruited Elizabeth Bentley into the Unit of the Communist Party on the T.C. campus at Columbia University.

Now that Bentley was a member of the Party, she was proving that I was right. She didn't work. She just used the Party to meet more and more people, especially men. One day she came to me and asked if I wanted to be a spy. "Spy for whom? For what? Are you crazy?" I asked her.

"I can serve the Party better by being a spy," she replied. With great drama she paced the floor, saying, "I am going to find out how I can be a spy for the Party."

"Really, I think you are mad, Bentley. We have work to do on the campus. We lack drinking fountains. The cafeteria workers are underpaid. Hitler is threatening the world with fascism, and you talk of wanting to be a spy. I think you just don't want to work. You want to dramatize yourself, make yourself important," I replied with disgust.

I told other members of the Party, and they agreed with me. Finally she stopped coming to meetings. When I met her at times, she was secretive and told me she was doing important things for the Party. She dropped names, like a dripping tap, of the important people she was meeting and working with. I listened and then said, "You have a man at last, haven't you, Bentley?"

"Yes, I am in love, and he loves me," she answered.

"That's all you really want, Elizabeth, and don't give me that line about spying. You need a man, and you have one. Don't lie to yourself or to me. Goodbye," I said. (I felt like adding, "And don't come near me. I don't like you.")

My reputation as a cook was getting around. I found it easy to get students to babysit in my home in exchange for a dinner. Although most of my classes were in the day when Mary Lee was in school, some were at night. Mary Lee seemed content, but it was hard to tell. She was a quiet, withdrawn child and always had been. Before she was born I had had guilt feelings, and I still had them, about my right and my ability as a mother. I had known that she would be fatherless, yet I had refused the offer to have an abortion. I had brought her to this strange world, New York City, away from her cousins, her grandmother, and familiar things. Yet I knew that for her to have the opportunity to reach her potential, I had to have her with me. I loved the lovely, blonde, violet-eyed child who appeared to reject me.

Even at four years of age, she seemed to weigh people and ideas. I felt she was judging me. I tried to organize my school schedule and my Communist Party meeting schedule so that I would be home when she came home from school. Then we listened to records, and I read and reread *Winnie the Pooh*. I wanted to be home with her. I wanted a father for her, but none seemed to want me. I had to keep on going the best I could, to get my degree in public health. Those without degrees lost their jobs. Those with them got old in their jobs.

The semester was coming to an end. I had done a full year's work, one semester on money that I'd saved, and the other on borrowed money. Now I had to get a job. I had no intention of going back to Port Chester to work and live, and preferred to stay in school until I finished my study, but that was impossible. From where would the money have come? I would return to my part-time study program, six credits every semester.

I applied and was accepted for a three-month summer relief job. This meant I had to make arrangements for Mary Lee. Swallowing my pride, I asked Grandmother Fuhr if Mary Lee could spend the summer with her. She was delighted to have Mary Lee, as long as I was not included. This took care of the hot summer months, but what about the fall? I recalled that Christine (who had been a student nurse when I was and who had helped me when Wilbur died) had an aunt who lived in Sunnyside, Queens, New York City, and I called on her. Chris had told me that her aunt wanted to move further into New York City.

Chris' aunt was a widow with five children, the youngest of them about twelve years old. I knew that there was an apartment available next door to me. I explained my need to have someone who was gentle and motherly, whom I could trust to care for Mary Lee after school and until I got home from work. She was delighted with the prospect of a reasonable apartment, and I was happy to have one of the Vermont Smiths care for Mary Lee in the fall. Now all I needed was to get that permanent job, with the depression still not over.

I was to be a relief nurse for the New York Child's Foster Home Service, an agency which placed children in temporary foster homes until a home and parents were found to adopt them. After a short in-service training, I was to relieve, in turn, the nurses who covered Queens, Brooklyn and Manhattan, respectively. Specifically my job was to teach the foster parents how to carry out the physician's and psychiatrist's orders.

My job began June 1, 1935, in an office on East 86th Street, the heart of the Nazi-loving community — "Heil, Hitler," photos of Hitler, the hooked cross (which formerly had meant Navajo Indian to me). They jostled me as I walked to the office. They upset me with their unscientific, inhuman and dangerous philosophy. It tried to undo by force the small gains that man had made through the ages. Their racial superiority had no scientific base. I worried about Holland so near to Germany and about my beloved Tante Sara and Ome David. I wished they would come to the United States. We had our discrimination, but we didn't burn people alive. I begged them to come somehow or other with my cousins while there was still time.

The agency where I worked appeared to be in agreement with its Nazi neighbors. They boasted that they did not have a Jew on their staff. I just kept quiet about my Jewish ancestors. I played dumb in the office and became alive and warm in the homes where I had work to do. Mary Lee's bread and butter was more important than letting them know how I felt toward them.

What amused me was the evaluation the agency gave me at the end of my three months of temporary work with them, which went on my permanent records with the Public Health Nurse Placement Service: "Mrs. Fuhr came to us as a summer relief nurse from June 1935 until September 1935, adapting herself satisfactorily to the needs of the organization. Her nursing and teaching techniques as observed seemed excellent. She appears to have initiative and great enthusiasm. She has unusual vitality and varied interests. She might be described as a PEASANT TYPE WITH LIMITED CULTURE. Her appearance is good and her personality pleasing." It was signed by the Director of the New York Child's Foster Home Service. Obviously my spark had shown through, but not the color of it.

Another report from East Harlem Health and Nursing Center had said, "Mrs. Fuhr has a mouse-like quality." I was a Communist Party member and active on the campus at Columbia. Yet if that appeared on my work record, Mary Lee and I would lose our bread and butter. I disliked not being honest and open about my ideas, but I hid them in class, on a job and in my in-laws' home in Port Chester, where I went weekends to be with my little daughter. Stepping into their home was like re-entering the Nazi stronghold on East 86th Street. The same thinking, or lack of it, prevailed.

My daughter was firm-fleshed and tanned, which was the important thing. I hoped she had soaked up enough sun to help get her through the winter months and to prevent the endless colds to which she was prone. She liked her grandmother's home and her cousins, but I could see she was glad to be coming back to Lincoln School again. She would now enter the first grade. I explained to Mary Lee that I had found an apartment across the street from where we had lived, which was a bit better. The rent was $35 instead of $25, but it was only a one-flight walk-up instead of five flights. Mrs. Temple had moved into her apartment, and I knew that Mary Lee would have the warmth and love she needed from her.

I had heard that there was an opening in the Birth Control Clinical Research Bureau, of which *the* Margaret Sanger was Director. I had read her autobiography and was anxious to have the privilege of working under her direction. I admired her tremendously and always will. Family planning to me was a logical way to help lower infant and maternal mortality. It would be wonderful to have a paying job that was, at the same time, one into which I could pour all my energies.

An appointment was made for me to meet Margaret Sanger. The day she was to interview me, my mouth felt dry, and I was afraid that I might not make a good impression and not get the job which I wanted so badly. Through her struggles to achieve the right of women to have the knowledge of family planning, she had grown into a woman with great understanding. Who was I? Nothing, compared to her. I was afraid I couldn't meet her expectations.

But when I saw her walking down the stairs to meet me, I lost my fear. This was no pompous woman filled with admiration for herself. This was an uncomplicated, good person filled with a fire for justice and decency, all directed toward the dissemination of the knowledge of birth control. As she questioned me I found myself at ease answering her about my background, my days as a mill dolly, my widowhood, and so forth. Since she had been a nurse, she understood my drive toward the preventive field in health. To me, family planning was one of the largest answers to public health. I got the job!

She explained to me that first I would have complete in-service training on the workings of the Birth Control Clinic. After that I was to help Dr. Hannah Stone gather data on the relationship of marital adjustment and the use of the diaphragm as a technique in birth control. I was also to do follow-up teaching in the homes where it was warranted. The job would take about a year to complete, and my salary would be $150 a month. A small car, a Willys, was at my service for field work.

I had been thinking in terms of birth control, but during in-service training I noted that there was just as much interest in helping women who thought they were sterile to have babies. This was Dr. Hannah Stone's favorite clinic. She and her husband also did family and marital counseling, and they had written a book, *The Marriage Manual*. I wished Wilbur and I had had it when we were first married.

What impressed me most was the careful selection of employees in the clinic. They were sensitive, tolerant, patient and gentle in response to the needs of the client. This was reflected in the teaching of small groups of five or six women before they entered the doctor's office, where they would be fitted with a diaphragm. I found myself liking this teaching section the best and was delighted when they let me teach groups of mothers. These sessions were preparing me for future public speaking on family planning. We had a Speakers' Bureau headed by Margaret Sanger, with some board members and some staff members who showed aptitude for public speaking.

Visiting home after home, it was obvious that there was an improvement in family life when the fear of an unwanted pregnancy was removed. The data piling up also proved this. I was enthusiastic about family planning, but my comrade Communist Party members took me to task. They felt I was forgetting Marxism and becoming a Malthusian. Their position was, "Why waste time on teaching birth control when the answers to society's ills lie in teaching Marxism?" I heartily disagreed with them. The problem now was to prevent an unwanted birth in any home and the unnecessary death of a mother or infant. I showed them with statistics that when there was birth control, the infant and maternal death rates went down. We continued disagreeing!

I did agree that the Communist Party should work toward a society where there would be no wars or depressions, but I absolutely did not agree with those who said, "Wait for the revolution." I felt that many spades working in different fields of social progress also helped lead to a decent world and prevented the need of revolution. I was interested in saving lives. To me, it was frivolous to compare Marxism and Malthusianism. Reality was *life versus death in 1935*.

My enthusiasm for my work had percolated up to the third floor, where Miss Sanger had her office. I was invited to spend a weekend at her home on the Hudson River. Florence Rose, her secretary and another enthusiast, drove me up. As I look back, I realize that Miss Sanger put me at ease with a homey technique. Since we both had cooking as a hobby, first she swapped recipes with me in the kitchen, and then she began grooming me to be a public speaker.

The first time I was to address an audience, I was so scared that my throat closed up. After a few more trials, I felt completely at home on a platform and learned to handle the heckler as well as the enthusiast. Now I began talking birth control two and three times a week, to young people, old people, in all sorts of places and situations. I did less Party work and more work for the Birth Control Clinic. I felt this was right and my way of working.

Margaret Sanger had gone to the Orient. She went to India, Japan and China; but she and her secretary had had to leave China because of the threat of attacking bombers sent by Japan. She brought back a birth control technique known to Oriental women; and, since it was easier and, hence, more practical for a poor, isolated area, she longed to have an opportunity to offer it to a group of women who desired it. She knew that the most efficient method was the diaphragm and a jelly. This always meant a medical examination, which meant, also, an opportunity to discover a vaginal medical problem like cancer and to have it treated in time. But there were huge isolated areas, mostly agricultural, where no doctors would touch the subject of birth control. One of these areas was Vineland, New Jersey, where I was nearly arrested.

Although Vineland was a small town, it had a large migrant population of poor farmworkers who followed the crops from Florida to the North. Their children had little opportunity to go to school. Baby after baby was born, and many died. Often the mother died too. Medical care was practically nonexistent. Miss Sanger wanted me to go there and start a study with the oriental method, which was new to the United States. I recall mentioning to her that the farmworkers were on strike against a frozen food plant and that outsiders might not be welcome, except to the strikers' wives. However, since neither she nor I were fazed by strikes, I began making arrangements to go down.

I managed to get the name of the union organizer of the agricultural workers in Vineland. I was sure he could help me. However, I was warned to approach his house unseen, as he and his family had already had one time-bomb attack on their home. Feelings were running high between strikers with their union, and the owners of the plant with the rich, secure townspeople.

With Mary Lee secure in Mrs. Temple's home, I left for Vineland equipped to teach birth control to migrant farmworkers.

When I arrived in Vineland, I registered in a hotel and waited for night to fall. When it was dark, I walked until I found the home of the union organizer. He, his wife and children sat in the dark keeping watch, afraid of another bomb attack. I had never met people like them before. Mr. and Mrs. X, as I will refer to them, were tall Northwesterners, both college graduates, and dedicated to the fight of organizing farmworkers. Mrs. X picked fruit and was on strike with the rest. I explained who I was and why I had come down. They accepted me, and Mrs. X said that she would call a meeting of the Ladies' Auxiliary of the union.

As I stood on the platform in the Union Hall the next night, the hungry, pinched faces of the women seemed to leap up at me. They wanted information on how to space their families, and I gave them an explanation of the technique as best I could. I also told them it was preferable to go to a doctor, to have a complete physical and pelvis checkup, and to use the method that had been proven the safest. They laughed ironically, and I understood why. The doctors in town were lined up with the growers and had no interest in the migrant farmworkers except to see the strike broken. No Steinbeck has written a *Grapes of Wrath* about the Eastern-seaboard migrant farmworker.

These migrants — known as "poor white trash" to the growers, "hillbillies" to the world at large — came from the crags and corners of the Southeastern United States. They were mostly illiterate whites of Scotch descent, a few blacks and Mexicans — a hungry, thin people. They worked the coast from Florida to Maine. Not only was their work difficult — almost all stoop labor — but their living conditions were bad.

One of the farmworkers promised to keep track of the materials and the records for me, to distribute them and to be responsible for them until I returned from New York City.

I had only been back in New York a few days when I received a letter from the union organizer enclosing clippings from the local newspaper. In essence, they all said the same: A foreigner, a subversive, had been in town peddling birth control information; if and when she returned, she would be arrested and run out of town.

The union organizer suggested that maybe I'd better not come back to Vineland, and my first reaction was to agree with him. Then I realized that I was afraid of cops. What factory worker who has been on strike is not afraid? When on foot the cops used their clubs, and when astride a horse they used the horses' hoofs. Yes, I was frightened; but I would go back — and do so on the offensive with the police chief.

I don't know who was more surprised, the chief of police or me, when I introduced myself to him as the foreigner who had been peddling birth control information. Since I had been born in New Jersey, I was no more foreign than he. Before he had time to open his mouth, I went on the offensive and began giving him a talk on birth control, beginning with its first known written history, the story of Onan in the Bible, and carrying it through to the present and the striking workers. I watched his face take interest and felt I had won when he began asking me questions on birth control. I advised him to take his wife to one of our doctors trained in birth control, so that she could be fitted properly. I in no way hid my sympathy for the strikers, and he didn't hide his contempt for them. However, I was free to go on spreading family planning information in Vineland without fear of arrest.

Now I was more certain than ever that the offensive is the best approach. When a problem is great, it looms greater when one does not face it. Gradually I was achieving a philosophy. In a nutshell, it amounted to: "Stew on a problem. Face it. Do something about it, even though it may be a mistake. Then forget it, and be free to face the next inevitable problem." Obviously, going on the offensive had kept me out of jail.

A typhoid germ knows no boundary line. Polio virus breeds well where the workers have to squat for lack of toilets. A fly does not know the difference between the rich man's child and the poor man's child when it alights on the bread they are eating. The killer germ knows no distinction between race, color, creed or income. My God, did we have to learn democracy from germs and flies? And the only reason the chief of police let me continue my work was because he felt that "those people" must not have too many children. Of course, this was not in agreement with our philosophy at the clinic, which stood for the right of women to make their own choices about what years to have their babies.

The strike was still on in Vineland. I saw the tragedy of the hatred on both sides. Those against the strikers called them communists, dirty, lazy, among other epithets. Couldn't the growers see that they would have better crops and more profits with better conditions for the workers? The strikers wanted a chance to earn more money so they could feed their children some of the lush foods they picked. They wanted a latrine, a privy, instead of a place to squat. They wanted water to drink and water to bathe in. They preferred working to striking. If a strike was the only means to obtaining better wages, well then, they had to strike. I understood this very well. I had learned it at the age of thirteen in Paterson.

The study was completed, and with it went my paid job. Nevertheless, I planned to continue being a volunteer worker for the Birth Control Clinic, as a public speaker and as a means of helping women secure information. I wished one of the workers would resign so I could stay on the payroll. The Birth Control Clinic worked on a very limited budget and its workers rarely resigned, as conditions were good, Margaret Sanger was a dedicated director, and the staff was dedicated to her and her work. I got another job.

The woman who had taken me under her wing in 1933, when I first began going to Teacher's College, had switched from public health to social work and was working toward her Master's degree. She was working in the social work department at the Hospital for Joint Diseases during the day and went to school evenings. Since the Hospital operated with monies contributed mainly by Jews, Jewish girls were given job preference. It was almost impossible for a Jewish girl to get a job in the non-Jewish agencies. My friend Sadie said, "Lini, your mother is Jewish. According to Jewish law, that makes you Jewish. For goodness' sake, if you want the job as pediatric social worker, put down 'religion: Jewish'!" I thought to myself how pleased Tante Sara would be as I wrote down, "Religion: Jewish." If society was so immature as to dislike people because of religion or color, it mattered not to me whether I wrote Protestant or Jewish. What mattered was that I had a job and a salary for Mary Lee and me to live on.

Since the directress of the social work department was not a qualified social worker, the entrance standards were not high.

I had had classes in social work theory and had had in-service training with the Westchester Department of Child Welfare, but certainly I was not a qualified social worker. Still, I got the job without any trouble, to begin September, 1936.

From where I lived the walk to the Hospital for Joint Diseases was a depressing one. Sometimes I walked past evidences of rioting the night before. Often I would be the only white-skinned person walking at that hour in the morning. What thoughts went on in the minds of the blacks as they walked by me, chatting warmly to one another and ignoring me as if I did not exist? Why did it bother me that they were treated as animals, and I, as a human? Through my work in the clinic, I desperately tried to establish a rapport with them, between humans and not between black and white skins. Often I wished that I didn't feel guilty for the white race in general, but I did.

Dirty streets, crowded subways, poor Italians crowding in along the East River with the shanty Irish, newly arrived Puerto Ricans crowding out both blacks and Italians, poor Jews, poor Catholics, poor people, all struggling for survival. And the poor mothers, who frantically tried to keep house and bodies clean without the money to buy a bar of soap or a meat-bone for soup. Rats, hungry rats feasted on the fingers of babies; cockroaches blithely walked over sleeping, feverish babies. This was Harlem, New York City, named after Haarlem, Holland, clean and bright with tulip-filled boats sailing up the canal toward Amsterdam. God, what contrasts!

Now the snow that fell turned a shabby gray in Harlem, and I worried about Mary Lee and her constant sore throats and colds. Between Mrs. Temple and myself, we were giving her all the vitamins and love that was possible, but still the sore throats continued. I had had rheumatic fever; her father had died as an aftermath of rheumatic fever. And now her tonsils were infected and useless as part of her defense system. There was no other remedy, so her tonsils were removed in the hospital where I worked as a social worker. Now she was better, and I breathed more freely. But good Lord, I was tired, and getting more tired every minute — school at night, work in the day, housekeeping, cooking the night before, cleaning the house, washing and ironing. The required reading lists loomed longer and longer as I tried to squeeze in time to study. To top all this, I was still a member of the Communist Party, with endless meetings to attend.

One thing I was quite sure of was that I was not meant to be a social worker. I resented the "Lady Bountiful" attitudes of the rich hospital board members. What one seemed to do was shuttle the poor client from one agency to another when the basic problem, the lack of a job, was not one we could solve. The Bible of the social worker, *The Book of Social Agencies*, did not tell how to help people get jobs. They were scarce, and the color line was strong. I refused to get rid of a client by sending him or her to another agency. What I really did was practice more and more public health nursing while on my job as a social worker. Public health was positive. It fought to keep people well. I figured if there was a job to be had, they stood more chance of getting it if they were in good health. I did refer clients to agencies like the Birth Control Clinic, Home Relief Bureau, Workers' Alliance and to Vito Marcantonio, a compassionate Representative from their district. I sent them where I was pretty sure they would get some help.

Spain, Spain! Didn't I have enough on my hands without being concerned about Spain? The year 1936 was drawing to a close, as more and more I heard talks and read material on Spain. The United States had fought their revolution; England had overthrown feudalism long ago; Germany had tried in 1848; France had succeeded; and now Spain was trying to grow out of feudalism into a democratic way of life. The legally elected government had made a mistake in sending plotting generals on reduced pay to Africa. Later I thought the republican government had been too lenient and should have killed them. The generals plotted with Hitler and Mussolini to overthrow the Spanish government. General Franco led the Civil War with the help of the Moors, Nazi Germans and fascist Italians. The people of Spain were fighting a gallant fight almost alone. The Catholic Church was waving the red flag, saying, "Communists! Murderers!" and the communists were proving in their articles in *The Daily Worker* that the organized Catholic Church was nothing but big business which owned most of Spain. The organized Church did not want freedom of thought, speech, press or schools. To the contrary, they were lined up right there with Franco. Church and reaction were as one!

I read everything I could lay my hands on about Spain. William Carney said one thing from the Franco front and Herbert Matthews said another; both were from *The New York Times*. I saw the truth in what Matthews and Lawrence Fernsworth were saying, and what to do about Spain became more and more of a problem for me personally. My first reaction was to help recruit nurses for the unit which was going to Spain as volunteers.

Volunteers were going to Spain from all over the world to fight side by side with the republicans. Those who had fled German or Italian fascism were already in Spain. I read of English, French, Dutch hospital units; and now the Medical Bureau to Aid Spanish Democracy was calling for aid in materials, in money, and in volunteers. I wanted to volunteer myself to go as a nurse, but with my responsibility to my child, and my work toward my degree in public health, I realized I had no right to such thoughts. Maybe I was only trying to escape from the maze of work. I kept on trying to convince others to go to Spain with the medical unit that was being formed.

I had always taken the position that we had enough to do to help make a better United States of America, and we didn't need to struggle for other countries or to get into arguments about other countries. Now I was doing the very thing I had denounced, worrying about Spain. I had come to feel that if the republic were victorious, world fascism and a world war might be averted. I was convinced that if I could not get nurses to go to Spain I would have to go myself.

Fascism really was only a word to me; I had not experienced it. I now could explain the word from a Marxist point of view quite glibly. I talked against the danger of World War II, and I knew nothing of war. I hardly ate or slept, filled as I was with the intense desire to volunteer to be a nurse with the medical unit that was going to Spain in January.

If Hitler and Mussolini could be stopped in Spain, then my aunt and uncle and the rest of the de Vries family would be safe in Holland. Is that why I wanted to help Spain? Ome David in in Holland had frightened me with his talk of the power and cruelty of Nazism. I had read much about fascism since, and understood better what he had tried to explain to me. Did I want to go to Spain because Ome David had briefed me on the long struggle of the Hollanders for their freedom against the same Spaniards that Franco and the Duke of Alva represented? What was it that Till Eulenspiegel's wife had said late in the 16th century, as she took the blackened heart of her husband out of the fire where he had been burned at the stake by the Spaniards? She took the ashes of her husband's heart and placed them in little bags which she tied over the hearts of her children as she told them, "I place these ashes over the hearts of all the sons and daughters of the Netherlands. As long as there is an injustice in the world, you must rise to fight it. You must defend those who are persecuted." The ashes of Till Eulenspiegel lay heavy on me.

I talked to the nurses I knew and tried to influence them to volunteer with the medical unit that was going to Spain, but none would go. Early in January I took a day off and went down to the office of the Medical Bureau to Save Spanish Democracy. I intended to ask how I could help here in America, when I heard myself volunteering to go with the unit that was sailing the next week.

I wanted to pull back into my mouth the words that I had

uttered, but I had said them to no one less than the young woman who was the chief of the nurses going to Spain. Before I had time to pull the words back, she asked me, "Do you have an American passport?"

"Yes, I have one which will expire in April, but it is good until then," I answered. I still hoped she would tell me that they did not need any more nurses, but to the contrary she told me what injections I must have against such and such diseases and to be ready to sail with them next week on January 16th, 1937! She didn't seem the least bit surprised when I said I must make arrangements for the well-being of my little daughter first. But I was surprised and shocked that I had volunteered.

What right had I to leave my child and go to Spain? I had done all I could do to get others to go, and they would not. Now I had volunteered to go to Spain and was going within one week. This drive that I had — to go to Spain and help by taking care of the wounded on the Spanish front — was the strongest drive I had had since my struggle for survival with my mother and the rat-filled cellars. I had no right to go, but I felt I *had* to go!

I was flooded with guilt feelings about myself and about my young daughter. I was leaving my classes at Teacher's College just before the exams. I was leaving my job as a social worker, and I was leaving my daughter. I rationalized that she would be happier in New Hampshire with my friends who ran a demonstration farm for Kimball Union Academy. Mary Lee knew them. Mrs. Bean was Chris Smith's sister, and they were cousins of Mrs. Temple, who cared for Mary Lee when I was at work. The Beans, the Temples, the Lovelands, the Hutchinsons were all part of a New Hampshire and Vermont family and secure in their Americanism, the kind of Americanism for which I had wholehearted respect.

In the little town of Meriden, New Hampshire, Mary Lee would be part of a small New England farming community.

She would go to Sunday School in the white-spired church and day school in the one-room, little red schoolhouse. She would help collect maple syrup and eat it over snow. I was sure that she would be better off in a healthy town than in New York City. It would be part of her education as an American. I knew I was rationalizing, but I continued packing for my voyage to Spain.

It was interesting and satisfying to find out that the majority of the sponsors of the Medical Bureau to Aid Spanish Democracy were men whom I respected in medicine. Haven E. Emerson of Columbia, who had been my teacher in public health, Walter Cannon of Yale, Henry Sigerist of Johns Hopkins, among others, were on the board. O.E.A. Winslow was also present. He was the author of my favorite definition of public health, the one most useful to me in my work. It went something like this: "A good public health approach is one that begins with the individual and his interest in his own health, working out toward the family unit, on to the community, until the community itself does that which is needed to make a healthier community, economically and physically." Going to Spain, sponsored by America's leading men in public health, helped to remove some of my guilt feelings. Be assured I had no idea what war was like. I had never seen a bomb drop. I had never heard the ping-zip of a sniper's bullet. I'd seen the photos of bombed-out Madrid, but war still had little reality for me.

Things that formerly loomed great had become of far less importance to me now. I had registered in September, 1936, for seven credits which had cost me $70. The exams were to be given in January, 1937, when I would be enroute to Spain. Rather casually, I told the three professors that I was going to Spain and would take the exams when I returned.

The week before we were to sail remains hazy in my memory. I had much to do: sublet my apartment, take Mary Lee to New Hampshire, and pack. One thing I remember vividly was the mass meeting in Madison Square Garden — our send-off and a technique to raise more money for the medical unit. We all sat on the platform surrounded by thousands. We were six doctors, six nurses, one druggist, one bacteriologist, two ambulance drivers and one interpreter. I had known one of the ambulance drivers slightly in Port Chester; all the others were strangers to me.

Photos, opposite page (clockwise, beginning with top right): Lini, five, and playmate Workum in Amsterdam. They counted boats from a third story window.

Lini's father. "A good man, an honest man," he spent his life shoveling coal into gas-producing furnaces, and could not let Lini be a strikebreaker.

Lini, Betty, and their mother. Lini endured her mother's insults: "You whore, you slut, you thing of sin!" Favored daughter Betty got the praise and the candy.

Graduating from grammar school in curtain lace at childhood's end. Lini's mother forced her to begin working as a silk mill "dolly."

Tante Sara and Ome David. His cobbling hammer banged on the low notes and squeaked on the high notes. One day the Nazis came.

Beloved David Schaap in California on his trip around the world. Lini thought his tallness seemed to shelter her. Inset: Almost eighteen, but Lini had no notion of disobeying her mother in order to marry gentle, strong David. In 1923, she was sure one didn't.

(Clockwise, beginning with top right): A frozen Jackson's Quarry where, in summer, "the water falling from the cliff caught the unseen jewels in the air." Below the falls, Lini took off her clothes and folded them carefully. If she could stay under long enough, would she go to the Dutch Reformed heaven or to the hell of the "foreigners"?

"Scottie" (Katherine Calderwood). Scottie and "Dutchy" (Lini) were the only nurses accepted by the rough-speaking patients in men's ward; their supervisor wondered what "sex madness" went on behind her back.

Lini as student nurse. Working with Margaret Sanger in her Birth Control Clinic convinced Lini to move from nursing to public health. Preventive medicine was a positive force.

Opposite page (clockwise, beginning with top left): The medical unit of the Lincoln Battalion preparing to sail for the Madrid Front during the Spanish Civil War. Lini (top left), Dr. Edward Barsky, Chief of the Medical Bureau (bottom left), Fredericka Martin, Chief Nurse (bottom center), and the others saw themselves as a bulwark against the fascism of Hitler and Mussolini. Generalissimo Franco and the FBI saw them only as Reds.

Lini, after Dr. Barsky sent her home to solicit help for Spain from the lectern. She learned to handle rotten fruit and flowers with equanimity.

Dr. Edward K. Barsky, thirty years later. Of Dr. Barsky, Earnest Hemingway had said, "I will do anything I can for Eddy Barsky who was my good friend in Spain, and who I consider to be a saint, . . ."

John T. Bernard (center), being greeted in Spain by Dr. Edward K. Barsky and Fredericka Martin. Bernard was the only member of Congress to vote against the embargo against the Spanish Republic.

Mary Lee's father, Wilbur Fuhr (above). As he lay dying, Lini spoke glowingly of a second honeymoon. Lini with Mary Lee (below). Mothering was to be complicated by childhood-long attacks of rheumatic fever.

Above: Crossing a river gorge by swinging bridge. Such crossings taught Lini to repress, th[ough] not to overcome, her fear of heights. *Inset:* Lini shown crossing one of many crude brid[ges].

Lower left: Lini and other members of the Papaloapan Commission being received by townspeople. The Commission helped rebuild the school at left. The tall smiling man, rear, [is] G. Cruikshank, engineer in charge of the Upper Papaloapan, first persuaded Lini to joi[n the] staff. *Lower right:* Lini in the field with Raul Sandoval, head of the Papaolapan Commiss[ion].

Above: The Papaloapan River at flood stage. Its repeated cresting at death-dealing levels was one reason for damming the river and relocating 20,000 of the basin's inhabitants.

Below: "Our dam," as Lini and other members of the Papaloapan Commission fondly termed it. Located near Temazcal, or "Steam Bath," intense heat and malaria-bearing mosquitoes required that an advance guard of health workers pave the way for the engineers. Lini herself suffered from malarial fevers there.

A reflective moment for daughter Mary Lee Thompso[n] 1953. Inset: Mary Lee and son Robert, eight, in 197[ ]

Top right: Daughter Toby Irene (pronounced ĭ·rĕ′nĕ) Caraza, 1978. Her children, 1978: Louis, fourteen (center left), Elena, thirteen (center right), Joaquin, nine (bottom left), and Mauricio, twenty months, with his mother (bottom right).

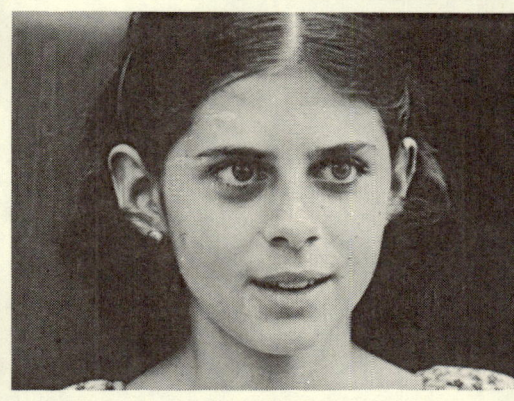
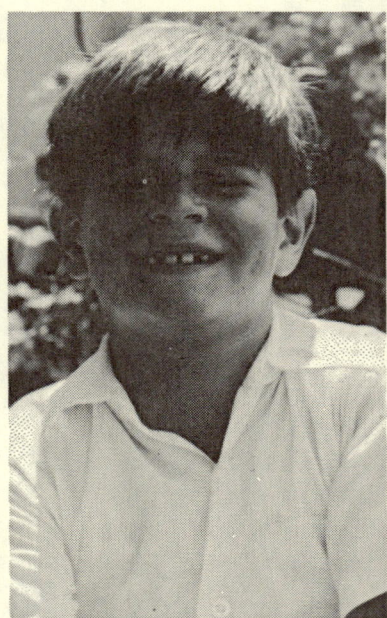

The Madrid Front, Spain, and New York City, 1937-1938

The River Ebro Flows to the Thames 5

January 16, 1937, we were on the *Ile de France*, waiting for it to sail, and being besieged by reporters and photographers. We directed them all to the Chief of the Unit, Dr. Edward Barsky. Various representatives of Spanish republican groups gave us flowers and candies and spoke to us. Although they spoke no English, and we, no Spanish, our understanding leaped over the language barriers. At the last minute, another doctor, whom I had not seen before, joined us. He was also going to the front lines in Spain. On the boat with him were eighty young Americans, all volunteers for the International Brigade. This was a surprise.

It was bitterly cold, but I stayed on deck until we had sailed past the Statue of Liberty and America was no longer in sight. I recalled the thoughts I had had before I left: "Someday you may regret having done this. If fascism is victorious, you may find yourself on the black list and/or in jail." I brushed this negative thought aside as I attuned myself to the sound of the waves and to the fact that I was going to Spain to play my little part toward shaping a decent world.

When I located the cabin to which I had been assigned, I found myself with three other girls. They were beginning to feel the effects of the ship's motion. I said, "Try to stay on deck as much as possible, and then you will have less problems with seasickness." But one of them didn't leave her cot until we landed in France.

In the ugly, strange-looking fur coat which had been contributed by the Fur Worker's Union, I warmed my body, as my spirit was warmed by the songs I sang with the young men who were going to the battle lines in Spain. I had sung with the Salvation Army on street corners; I had sung as I tied knots on silken threads in the silk mills; I had sung in the First Baptist Choir; I had sung as a student nurse. Now I was singing again, and what songs! Now I was learning songs of the people.

The eighty men were not supposed to broadcast the fact that they were going to Spain, but they said it in song. They talked a great deal, and I listened. Some were college youths, others, longshoremen, butchers, bakers, poets, writers, painters. Few seemed to agree on which method or political group worked best, in the struggle toward a better world. They were not all communists, by a long shot, even though the yellow press said they were. They represented many political lines of thought, many distinct racial heritages and religions. But they all agreed: Save Spain, Save Democracy, Fight Hitler, Stop Fascism in Spain. Of this we talked and sang. North, South, East, West, black and white — America was on the boat, onward to Spain.

We arrived in Le Havre, France, on January 23, 1937. In the United States we had held our breath, lest we be prevented from sailing, since the passports had been stamped NOT VALID for Spain. While we were crossing the Atlantic, we had been notified that the medical unit could legally go to Spain, but the men who would join the International Brigade could not. Now I wondered if we could disembark, since there were many uniformed men standing on the dock. Uniforms had always frightened me. These were policemen, customs men and soldiers, but they spoke no English. Our luggage was full of drugs and cigarettes, and every corner of every suitcase had extra drugs in it for the front lines. Fortunately, one of our doctors spoke French. He explained who we were and where we were going.

Suddenly everyone was all smiles, and cheers broke out for the American Medical Unit to Aid Spanish Democracy. We were waved through with no customs inspection. Word must have been passed along, as hundreds appeared, led by the city band, and escorted us to the hotel where we were to stay that night. We forgot the cold of the Atlantic crossing with the warmth of the greetings in Le Havre. The Popular Front arranged a dinner, where many of us drank champagne for the first time in our lives. The combination of the wine, food, and long speeches made us soon ready for bed. The next morning when we left for Paris, the tracks were lined with townspeople waving us onward to Spain.

Little had I thought, four years ago when I had signed the petition "against war and fascism" at an International Nurses' Conference, that I would be in Paris again in a group bound for Spain. The Popular Front government (made up of many political parties and headed by Léon Blum) had sent representatives to meet us at the railroad station in Paris. A reception had been arranged for us and then a meeting. I confess that I didn't want to listen to a lot of speeches in a language that I didn't understand. The young doctor who spoke French, one of the nurses with whom I had become friendly, and I sneaked out of the meeting to walk the streets of Paris. We sat in front of Notre Dame and waited for an occasional shaft of moonlight to break through the wispy fog and light up the church windows. Then we walked up to Le Sacre-Cœur, where we stood on the hill and looked at the lights of Paris. As we stood there, I wondered what a battle front was like.

We left for Spain the night of January 27, 1937, crowded into two compartments which made sleep impossible. We waited for dawn to break, and when it did we hung out of the train windows watching the sun rise on the Mediterranean. The red-tiled roofs of the little towns hugging the cliffs were reflected in the blue Mediterranean as the sun shone on them. Cerbere, our crossing point into Spain, came into sight.

In the railroad station we had some breakfast and were ready to go on into Spain. However, the fishermen and their families in Port Bou, Spain, thought differently. Representatives of the town's authorities asked us to wait until they were properly ready to receive us. When Mildred, our interpreter, asked what that meant, they answered her and she translated for us, "Chickens have to be killed and plucked. Fish have to be caught. The best wines are being brought out of the cellars. Posters are being painted, and the band is practicing a march to welcome us. In just a little while they will send the cars for us." This was to be my first experience with the Spanish *un momento*.

Meanwhile the townspeople of Cerbere surrounded us. We were queer fish to them, we women in navy blue uniforms and men in khaki. Who were we? Where did we come from? They spoke little French. They spoke Catalan. It seemed that on this border, first one was a Catalan, and then either French or Spanish. But first and foremost one was a Catalan.

Un momento stretched. We wondered if they wanted us in Spain. But when the trucks arrived to take us across the border, we could see that the welcoming posters were still damp with fresh paint.

Our hearts were in our throats as we careened around sharp, hairpin mountain curves. I wished I knew the phrase for "slow, go slowly, please." The drivers of the trucks grinned sinfully at us as they frightened us with their driving. The driver of our truck was playing with mountain curves as a bullfighter plays with a bull. When we stopped at the actual frontier, we asked Mildred to beg them to drive more slowly. They laughed. Captains and colonels they might be according to their stars or bars, but they were reckless drivers to us. We wished we could speak Spanish and flirt back with them in words instead of only eyes.

The French soldiers cleared us, and the Spanish soldiers welcomed us as we entered Spain. I wanted to close my eyes to curves we skimmed over, but I didn't want to miss the wild beauty of the Pyrenees. While we rode over the mountains, the eighty men who had been with us on the boat would climb over them. Down, down we went to sea level. We almost got thrown through the windows as the trucks braked to a stop. We were in Port Bou, Spain.

Bands played; wet posters stretched across the road; nets shimmered drying in the sun; and the loudspeaker blared as we stepped out of the trucks. We were glad to get our feet on firm ground again. The fishermen and their families gathered around us, embracing us. With smiles and gestures we thanked them for our welcome into Spain.

At last we were on Spanish soil. Here we would do what we could for the wounded from many lands who were fighting fascism in Spain. If I had thought it wouldn't look silly, and raise questions I didn't want to answer, I would have bent over to pick up some Spanish earth and hold it close to my bosom. It was a strange desire, I suppose, almost as if I had come home after a long wandering. I slipped away from the group and walked toward the sea. I wanted to be alone and let the thoughts drift to the surface. Over three hundred years ago my ancestors had fled to Holland from Spain because of religious persecution. They had fought in Holland to help liberate the country from the Spaniards in the 16th century. I was first-generation North American but had never felt at home in the United States. I had felt that I belonged in Holland, yet on this Spanish soil I felt that, finally, I had come home after hundreds of years.

I wanted to share my thoughts with someone, but there was no one with whom I could do so. What lonesomeness in which we all live! Until now the faces of the Spaniards had been a blur to me, but as I walked back toward the group I tried to penetrate their faces. Did the ancestry of the Moors, the gypsies, the Greeks, the Romans, the Gauls flow through their veins as it might through mine? Mother had been the first of her Sephardic-Spanish-Jewish ancestry to marry out of her group, who had fled Spain to England and Holland. Yet I was conceived of this stock on both sides. I looked like a Gretchen from the north of Holland, yet I identified myself with Spain. "Shades of Marxism (if there are any)," thought I. "What kind of unscientific thinking is this your mind is playing with?"

We were invited for dinner and ate in what had been a large restaurant, near the railroad tunnel. This was Port Bou, Spain, the only important supply point on the Mediterranean open for the Spanish Republic. The bomb-pocked restaurant building gave proof of German and Italian bombers. We ate a meal such as I had never had before. Course followed course of strange fishes and meats, one wine after another, each with toasts and speeches; and all the while the band played. After four hours of this, following a sleepless night, our eyelids were drooping, and we begged for some sleep.

The villagers and the soldiers escorted us to a fashionable hotel of which they were very proud. We were the first occupants since the writers, painters and tourists had left Spain, and it was in perfect condition. Mildred explained to me that Port Bou was one hundred percent anarchist, which gave me a thought to chew on. I had been told that anarchists were disruptive, disorganized, and did not believe in organized government. Yet this little anarchist town of Port Bou, an important supply point, gave evidence that all were organized against the common enemy: Hitler's might, Mussolini's soldiers, and Franco's army of Moors and Spaniards.

The soldiers ran about making up our beds until we said, *"Ya, ya, basta."* (That's enough.) "We are going to double up for warmth." An honor guard watched as we slept. At nine, we were to be awakened for supper. That gave us three precious hours to sleep in the cold, unheated, luxurious hotel.

Our honor guard awakened us promptly at nine and we supped, or rather we dined. I hoped that we would eat as well at the front. We felt refreshed after our sleep and meal, and climbed the stone stairs to the cliffs, where we could pick stars from the deep blue velvet sky and watch them drop in the deeper blue of the ocean. It was two in the morning before the villagers, the soldiers and the band would let us say, "Goodnight, and thank you." We were to leave for Barcelona the next morning at nine.

Nine, ten, and no cars had arrived to drive us to Barcelona. The villagers went with us as we walked around the fishing village. I was overwhelmed with the posters, works of art on walls, most of which gave a message in public health and preventive medicine. I wished some of my teachers could see them. We visited the new school that the villagers had built. Music blared from the loudspeaker, then announcements and speeches; but when I heard flamenco music I stood still and listened. This was music that tore me apart, music of the Moors, the Jews, the Spaniards. I wanted more and more of it.

Finally, about noon, the five autos arrived from Barcelona. Climbing, we left the sea and entered the mountains. I peeked, then closed my eyes as we seemed to fly around another narrow curve. If I looked down, I saw the ocean. If I looked up, I saw a towering cliff. When I looked at the road, I quickly closed my eyes again. Our handsome Spanish soldier-drivers scared me half to death.

Late in the afternoon we arrived in Figueras. As we waited for dinner to be served, we heard the music of the band and ran to the balcony. It was a depressing sight, our first contact with the ravages of war. Some women ran to the ranks of wounded soldiers with shrieks of joy, while others wept. Of the thousand soldiers who had left this town, only two hundred had returned. We were sobered by what we saw. War and wounds, war and death — could this happen to any of us? We ate our dinner quietly, without our usual bantering.

Gradually the scenery changed from rugged and harsh, jagged mountains to scenery softened by olive trees and orange trees that dotted the fields on the road to Barcelona. It was still light when we arrived in the city and drove down the beautiful street called the Ramblas. The streets were filled with foreigners from many lands, men coming in to fight with the International Brigade. We were told that there were many spies among them, especially ones sent by Hitler.

Barcelona and its people were Catalans first before they were Spaniards. They spoke Catalan, but they also spoke Spanish. They chose to be part of the Republic of Spain and had fought bravely on the streets against the Franco fascists. Catalans, Spaniards and foreigners walked the flower vendor-lined street of the Ramblas, where people sat on benches spelling out leaflets and posters in their eagerness to learn to read and write.

It was on the Ramblas that the Catalans had made a living barricade of their bodies as they resisted Franco's forces on July 16, 1936. On the Ramblas, the living snatched arms from the fascists to protect their legally elected government. Franco's rebellion had failed that day, and now on the same street the flower vendors pressed their wares on us and refused payment. We continued walking, bearing violets, roses, daisies, lilies in our arms. The Tibudado, a fortresslike church, loomed high over the city. Here, we were told, the rebels had used the church as a fortress when they tried to capture Barcelona. The Church had fought with the Moors, the Italians, the Germans and the Spaniards against the Republic.

What architecture we were seeing! The Roman, the Moorish mixed with Gaudí. Is there any place in the world that has a church such as that which Gaudí designed? The Catalans loved it, and it was heavily protected with sandbags. I thought it looked like a chocolate ice cream cone turned upside down, causing strange patterns in its melting. We walked past another building by Gaudí called "The Wave," where we saw curves and waves. We walked on to the place where we were going to hear that magnificent patriot, "La Pasionaria." The hall was filled, and there was utter silence as she spoke. I didn't understand Spanish, yet I felt what she was saying, and understood, "It is better to die than to crawl on your knees." A Spaniard, she generated a tremendous force. She did not ask, "Are you a Catalan?" "Are you an Andalucian?" "Are you from Asturias or from Madrid?" Or "Are you from America?" For her there was only one goal: to fight fascism at home, to free Spain of the Franco rebels, and to give Spain the right to develop and grow. Not only I, but all thought she was addressing each one of us individually.

We were impatient to be on our way to the front. When our ambulances caught up with us, we left for Valencia. Ten hours later, we were glad to stretch our legs in refugee-filled Valencia. Beds were scarce, so we slept two and three in a bed, and some slept in bathtubs. I can't say I felt refreshed when I went down to the dining room the next morning, after having tried stretching out in a bathtub! The dining room was filled with more foreigners than Spaniards, including us. From a nearby table, I heard a voice say, "Chahles, do bring me another pair of eyelashes from Paris. Mine are shedding." Can you imagine an English accent superimposed on showgirl American intonation? Later, as I got to know her, I rather liked her. She made little effort to be other than what she was, a showgirl living well off the earnings of her husband, who was one of the mercenary flyers for the Republic. I admit I stared as I heard "Lady This" and "Lord That" in the clipped voices of the British. The dining room was as unreal as a scene from *Alice in Wonderland*.

In contrast, the streets were filled with the reality of wounded and refugees from Madrid. They stopped us and asked what our uniforms meant. Opening a dictionary, we showed them the words, "Nurse, doctor, help Spain." They clasped our hands and wept as they embraced us, until we escaped back to our rooms overwhelmed by such naked emotion. When we got there, we discovered that our group leader, Dr. Barsky, the chief nurse, and the interpreter were leaving for the front to try to locate a building that we could use as a hospital.

That night, as I lay curled up like an embryo in my bathtub bed, I was awakened by sirens. I knew I was supposed to get up and go to a bomb shelter, but I was frightened and could not move. I heard loud explosions, and then boom, boom, followed by what sounded like antiaircraft guns. Then there was silence. I went out and was told that foreign aircraft were attacking Valencia, while a fascist vessel was shelling the harbor. War was coming closer to us who were from the United States. The "war hanger-ons" — ex-chorus girls, people buying looted objects, men selling guns and butter — sat around bars and in the dining room over their coffees laced with brandy. We wanted to get to the front and work, especially after meeting Dr. Norman Bethune, who talked to us about his dream, which was fast becoming a reality.

We all knew of Dr. Bethune, the famous chest surgeon and teacher, but his entrance was still dramatic to us, unaccustomed as we were to surgeons dressed as he was. He casually tossed his rifle on a bed in the room where we were sitting. He was in Spain with a small unit of Canadians with a plan to collect whole blood, bottle it, deliver it, and transfuse right on the front lines. This was revolutionary, as we had only seen blood given directly from the donor to the recipient as they lay side by side on the operating room tables.

I asked Dr. Bethune to explain his plan to us, and we all listened intently. He told us that blood-collecting centers had been set up where all types of blood were bottled, from civilians or soldiers for civilians and soldiers. (A Nazi bomb made no distinction between a civilian and a soldier.) Blood flowed into bottles and then into the arms of the wounded. It sounded visionary, and we said so. He invited us to come and see the truck that worked on the front lines with whole blood for the wounded.

The truck was compact and well-planned for delivering whole blood to the front. It had a refrigeration unit to keep the blood at a certain temperature. When he opened the door we saw bottle after bottle of whole blood, each labeled with its type, and the name and address of its donor. If the recipient wanted to write and say thanks to his new blood brother, he could. Dr. Bethune hoped to have many units like this going to the fronts. He hoped that bottled blood could be delivered by plane to the nearest first aid stations at the front, but the Spanish Republic lacked planes. The few planes it had were crates ready to fall apart. The planes that bombed us were made in Germany and Italy, and were flown by Germans and Italians.

I asked Dr. Bethune, "Why don't you have a huge red cross painted on top of these blood delivery trucks?"

With irony he answered, "Then we would surely be bombed! The fascists know very well that the International Red Cross is not doing anything in Spain, and that is why I am here and why you are here. The war is almost seven months old, and no effort has been made by the Red Cross to help, not even the civilians."

"You mean the International Red Cross believes the Big Lie?" I asked.

Dr. Bethune answered, "Unfortunately, yes. The Red Cross, which should not take sides, has taken sides with the forces of brutality and fascism against progress and democracy."

The Big Lie, a tool of Hitler's, was to call everyone a communist loud enough, often enough, to say it over and over again so people would believe it. The newspapers said Spain was communist, and the republicans were communists. The Church shouted that priests and nuns were being murdered. The Church had owned and controlled one-third of the lands and riches of Spain. Is that why they called the Republic communist? The monarchists hoped that Franco would bring them back to power, where they had ruled as cruel, absolute kings.

Were they paying the press for the written Big Lie also? Foreign business also owned one-third of Spain. Were they putting pressure on the newspapers, some of which they owned, not to report the truth? What was the truth? The majority of the people of Spain were behind their legally elected republic, for which they themselves had voted. The truth was coming through — although with difficulties put in the way by their own press — from men like Herb Matthues, Leland Stowe, Lawrence Fernsworth, Ernest Hemingway and others. Now I saw the truth all around me — the people of Spain behind their government and we, the foreigners, bringing medical aid. And I was one of those foreigners who, for once in my life, had the opportunity to work for democracy and for humanity by taking care of the wounded. I was filled with pride to be here among the Spanish people. I was proud that we were the bulwark between the fascists and other free nations. How often we heard, we said, "The River Ebro flows to the Thames!"

Finally Dr. Barsky sent word that we were to begin leaving Valencia for Albacete. A building had been located that could be converted into a hospital. Within a few hours, four ambulances and six trucks carrying our goods and personnel slowly climbed up from sea level to the Plain of Castille. We were on our way to the Madrid front, but we did not know the exact location. Trucks passed us going the other direction, toward Valencia, with wounded, with women, but mostly filled with children and one or two adults watching over them. They shouted at us, *"¡No pasarán!"* (They shall not pass!) We answered, *"¡No pasarán!"*

Through fortified towns, around roadblocks, past cave dwellers and cliff dwellers, swerving for the many burros, we sped through the purple-pink sunset toward Albacete. Next we drove around huge bomb craters, as Albacete loomed ahead of us. As we entered the town, we saw walls half-standing, with bits of furniture hanging out defying gravity. Here there were more bomb craters that were fantastic and frightening. Soldiers everywhere spoke many languages. This was the supply depot of the International Brigade. No wonder the town was bombed often! I hoped we would not stay too long.

As we waited at headquarters to be assigned sleeping space, Dr. Bethune walked in, looking dusty, pallid and sad. As I embraced him, welcoming him, I asked, "What is the matter? You look awful. You look sick."

"I feel sick, morally sick, that man can be so brutal as to fly low and deliberately machine-gun helpless women and children fleeing from a burning town. We were at Malaga delivering blood. The town was thoroughly bombed and captured by the fascists. We fled, and the people fled. We squeezed as many children as we could in our blood bank truck. The German and Italian flyers flew low, almost low enough for us to see the horrible grins on their faces, as they deliberately machine-gunned fleeing mothers and their children. I am lucky to be here," he answered me.

Believe me, I felt guilty to have been preoccupied about where I would sleep that night. When we were assigned space in the hospital X ray room, I humbly looked for a spot on the floor to stretch my cramped bones. After the light was out, we opened the blackout curtains. The positions of the sleepers and the X ray machines were weird as the soft moonlight filtered in on us. It was cold, as the windows were all shattered from the frequent bombings. But we were still alive!

We awoke stiff and cold. Our faces were dirty, our teeth unbrushed. We hoped we would get a little water. We did, and began what we later called a "whore's bath" — a bit of water for our teeth, then some to wash our faces and hands and under our arms. Finally we placed the basin on a chair and sat over the water to wash our genitalia. I don't know who named it a whore's bath, but I felt sorry for any poor prostitute who had to use cold water in such a bitterly cold room.

The bright sunlight of the day began warming our cold bones as we walked to headquarters to look for some bread and coffee. The streets were filled with men, old men and young men, in nondescript clothing that was supposed to pass for uniforms. The foreigners were more uniformed than the Spaniards. This was February, 1937, when young and old had left fields, crops and looms to go to the front. It was a people's army, as yet unorganized. The International Brigade had some organization. Many of them approached us and in their language asked what language we spoke. We smiled and answered, "American." Then came some who asked in halting English where we came from. I recognized their Dutch accent and replied in Dutch, "My parents are from Holland, but the rest are 100 percent Americans."

From then on, while in Albacete, the Dutch Brigadiers became my escort. I was not too surprised when they told me that in relation to size and population of their country, the Dutch had more men in the International Brigade than did other countries. What Hollander had not studied of the long, hard fight for freedom against the persecution of the Spanish Church, the Spanish royalty and the Inquisition against the Hollanders? The same forces were the enemy today. I, too, had been influenced by Dutch history to go to Spain. It was the same church, the same aristocracy, the same family of the Duke of Alba, who were trying to prevent the Spaniards' transition from feudalism to democracy. We Hollanders marched down the streets singing the 16th century songs of the fight against Spain. It was good to be with them here in Spain.

We are not born nationalistic, but we certainly acquire it. When I was with the Hollanders, I was all Dutch. When I was with the Americans, I was an American. Now I took sides with the Dutch soldiers. They disagreed with the judgment of the American Medical Unit, of which I was a member, about a German who had attached himself to the Unit. We had met many Germans in Barcelona, some who had managed to escape Germany years ago when Hitler came to power, and some who were still escaping to "fight Hitler on Spanish soil," as they said. But this particular man, whose name was Rudolph, claimed to be an ardent anti-Nazi. We Dutch, who had little love for Hitler's Germany, smelled a rat. He was all "spit and apple polish" with the so-called important people, and arrogant and Prussian with people who didn't count, especially women. It was true that he was extremely handsome and uniformed almost to perfection. Had Hitler equipped him? When he walked with us Dutch, he asked questions. When he was with the Americans, he asked questions. He gave up walking with us because we showed our suspicion of him. Stool pigeons always ask questions, I remembered from my mill days. Queer things, like slashed tires and motor troubles, had been happening to our ambulances ever since we had been in France. I voiced my suspicions, but no one would believe me — perhaps because they thought I was a woman reacting to his misogyny— when I said, "There is something fishy about Rudolph. I don't trust him. Maybe he is a spy or one of Hitler's men in Spain." He was nothing like the refugee Germans I had met in Holland in 1933, or like the many soldiers of the Thaelman Battalion. He acted like a Nazi, filled with the superiority of a Master Race. My Dutch nationalism was stronger than my Americanism.

One night we were awakened and told to dress quickly, as we were going to the front lines. Walking through the cold, blacked-out town, avoiding bomb holes by the light of the moon, we wondered where we were headed. At the car pool we stood and listened to our instructions: "Drive without lights; soon it will be dawn. We hope the convoy is not known to the fascists. We hope there has not been a leak in information about the convoy. If you hear a plane or planes, jump, run, bury your face in the earth. Don't let the white blur of your face be a target for a machine gunner in a plane." I had a fleeting wish to be sleeping in New York City, with my child in the next bed.

Our instructor continued, "Throw yourself into the nearest ditch when bombs drop. Keep the trucks a good distance apart in case one catches fire. Keep moving. Keep moving."

I hoped we would not be caught. We had a complete fifty-bed hospital ready to set up. Spain had no medical supplies. They came from other countries, and we were bringing ours. The Neutrality Act of the United States, England and France prevented Spain from buying arms to defend herself, but at least medical supplies could get across the border. When I discovered I was riding in the ambulance that contained our highly flammable ether supply, I was more scared than ever, for myself and for our hospital unit.

As the drivers watched the road, we passengers watched the sky. I began suspecting stars as plane lights, until I caught myself — an enemy plane would not be using lights! At one alert, we jumped into the ditches, but we had not been spotted.

We were tired, hungry and thirsty when we entered the small town of Lillo. We had been told that there was a big, new building in Lillo that we could use for a hospital. The only big building was a large, old church with beautiful gothic lines, but dank and dirty inside. The villagers told us the building we wanted was in the very next town, Romeral; but they insisted on giving us breakfast. First they brought us water to wash ourselves. While we waited for the goat to cook, they fed us peanuts and muscatel wine. Our medical chief had gone on to check about the building. We couldn't talk to one another, but there was really no need. The whole village, women and children and old men, surrounded us, beaming at us and embracing us. We no longer asked where the young men were.

Dr. Barsky sent word that we were to proceed to Romeral. The day was warm and sunny, and windmills turned against the incredibly blue sky flaked with white fleecy clouds, as we drove on. It was early February, and the olive trees were already garbed in their slate gray-green leaves. Only Don Quixote and his Sancho were missing from the scene as we entered the outskirts of the whitewashed village. To our right loomed a large building. It was not Don Quixote who stood there motioning us to stop, but Dr. Barsky.

It was obviously a new school building, and we watched children and teachers moving out desks, maps and books. We walked into the building, weaving in between outgoing school furniture, and saw the huge rooms lighted by large glass windows. However, there was no heat, no plumbing facilities, no water, no electricity, no kitchen, no stove. It was just a new, two-story building, the first school Romeral had had, which they had recently finished building themselves. They offered it to us with great pride, to use as a hospital. It was late, and we took only the mattresses off the trucks.

We walked through the deep blue, star-studded night, past the silent windmills to a home where we were to be given our supper, which included the last eggs we were to see in many a month. We listened to speeches from the village authorities welcoming us to the Madrid front. Each speech was translated either by Mildred, our interpreter, or by Rudolph the German, who somehow was in Romeral ahead of us. Outside the door we heard women's voices arguing louder and louder. When we questioned our interpreter, she told us that the villagers were fighting as to who should be chosen, who had the right to work with us in the hospital. One voice, which later I was to know well, kept saying, "I have more right than Elvira. My father was killed, and my two brothers were killed defending Madrid. I am the only one left who can serve."

What people! The closer one got to the front, the stronger they appeared.

In the morning the villagers brought us water for washing, and coffee and bread to eat. Women and children kept arriving from far and near, milling around, all wanting to help us. We begged the village authorities to settle the argument, since we could not possibly use all of them. We needed a fixed number to be trained as nurse's aides, for the kitchen, for our ambulances, and for other jobs. Off they went to the mayor's office, and I felt sorry for the poor mayor, a dignified old man, being confronted by women who all insisted on their "right to serve Spain" by working with us.

We had exactly 48 hours, Dr. Barsky told us, to have the hospital set up and ready for patients. Thanks to the wonderful organization of the fifty-bed hospital materials from the States, our task was made easier. Boxes and crates of every size were painted with a broad stripe, one of five colors, each signifying whether it was to go to the kitchen, the operating room, supply room, and so forth. We nurses were accustomed to pitching in and not letting one another down. Our training had lasted three years, beginning with menial and often heavy work. We had learned through sheer necessity how to lift and move heavy patients and heavy objects without straining ourselves too much. We had waited on interns and doctors hand and foot, opening more doors for them than we wanted to remember. We had stood on our aching feet while they sat. So now we enjoyed the doctors' discomfort and grumbling as they pushed and hauled like anyone else. Some of them balked and complained that they had come to be doctors and not stevedors. Dr. Barsky, our chief, who was not well because of his gastric ulcer, was working harder than any of us.

The posters said, *"¡Ahora todos somos iguales!"* (Today we are all equal!) We gloried in this, but we recognized the physical differences between men and women. The doctors and ambulance drivers had to carry in the heavy crates and had to be carpenters to uncrate them. We helped the ones who cheerfully worked side by side with us by showing them tricks in leverage. Within 48 hours we were ready, but those hours will always remain a blur to me, since we hardly took time off to eat or sleep. Our group of 17 was more than doubled by helpers from the village. Wires were strung for lights. Holes were dug for waste materials. Water was carried on women's heads and burros' backs. Food came in from nearby villages, and the stove was assembled. The dirt and rocks that flew out of the latrines were carried to the road and used to fill the chuckholes. When André Marty appeared, he gave us a pat on the back in praise.

Lillo, the nearby town where we had almost put up our hospital, had been bombed. We did not put a red cross on our roof because it would have meant annihilation, as had happened in Madrid, where hospitals had been bombed by German planes. I looked again with suspicion at Rudolph the German. He had known that we might set up in Lillo. And he could have conjectured that if we were bombed, though we could run to the fields, would we? Of course not; we would stay with our helpless wounded. I began worrying about bombings seriously.

Now it was February, 1937, and we were to serve the Jarama, on the Madrid front. The men of the Abraham Lincoln Battalion there sang a song to the tune of "The Red River Valley": "There's a valley in Spain called Jarama./It's a place that we all know too well./It was there that we gave of our manhood./It was there that our first comrades fell./We are proud of the Lincoln Battalion/and the fight for Madrid that it made./For we fought like true sons of the soil,/as a part of the International Brigade." We who left part of our hearts in Spain, who left a job unfinished, will never forget this song. "A place where our best comrades fell" — the wounded were pouring in from the battle raging on the Jarama front. The Lincolns were bearing the brunt. Within four hours after the battle had begun, we had 93 wounded. Our hospital was equipped for fifty. A little later, the same day, we had 200. I was on the first floor, where they came in. Those who had died enroute to us were left in the bitter cold courtyard. Occasionally from among the dead we heard a moan and found life.

The wounded lay on the floor, and two or three lay on each bed. First we fought to keep them alive. Later we got their names, in order to list them as wounded. When we had time, we went through clothing matted with blood on cold, stiff, dead men to see if they had letters on them or any identifying information. I cut through clothing of boys I had danced with on our way to Spain. My eyes were heavy with lack of sleep and unshed tears. This was no time to cry! The crying would have to come later.

Men coming out of anesthesia cowered, remembering the Moors on foot and horse at the Jarama front. Others shuddered when they heard planes overhead. Spain, a recognized, legally elected government with representation in the League of Nations, was being brutally attacked by Germans, Italians, Moors. We were outnumbered in everything, but the front still held. I, too, trembled with fear of the Moors. Thousands were dying, of which a small part were foreign volunteers, like the boys from the United States, here to hold the front, to hold Madrid.

Precious blood flowing from wounds was being exchanged for that from ampules brought to us by Dr. Bethune. I hated what I saw and the forces responsible for this suffering, anguish and death. I hated the hand grenades, the shrapnel, the dumdum bullets, the machine guns, the mortar shells. I hated seeing the bleeding wounds, the living wounded, and the dead. A part of me died with every one who fell. The wounded became a part of me. I burned my living red cells trying to keep theirs alive. We had not slept in four days, other than in catnaps taken leaning against the wall. It was impossible to walk in shoes, so we put on the peasant *alpargatas (espadrilles)*. We worked as one body, as a unit, to keep men alive. Day and night Dr. Barsky operated, by good light and by candlelight. He was our best surgeon for major surgery, and to this day I don't know how he did it. Despite his burning gastric ulcer, Dr. Barsky never lost his patience with or his kindness toward the many men from many lands with their many languages.

The wounded were given first aid at the front under fire. Those who could not survive the ambulance ride to our hospital at Romeral stayed at the hospital at Colmenar. As fast as we could, we put the treated men who could travel on the ambulance train to lines further back. Our fifty-bed hospital was jammed with hundreds of wounded, but it was easing up. The front had been held fast at the cost of thousands of lives.

Now we took turns to go off-duty to get a few hours of sleep. When it was my turn, I walked past the operating room and heard Dr. Barsky ask for me, so I stepped in. A pallid, fair young lad lay on the operating table. Dr. Barsky said, "He is Dutch. He does not understand English. Please tell him that we are going to operate. Tell him we are going to give him a spinal anesthesia; then help him get into position for the anesthesia."

The boy's eyes lit up as he heard my voice explain to him in his language what had to be done. His name was Peter. "Stay with me. Don't leave me. I am dying, I know. Don't leave me," he begged.

The doctor who was giving the spinal anesthesia said, "Okay, Lini, you can leave now and get some sleep. You need it badly."

Peter clasped my hand firmly as if he understood. "Don't leave me. Don't let me die alone," he whimpered.

I answered the doctor, "Later. I must stay with this wounded man now." Softly I spoke in Dutch to Peter about the streets of Amsterdam, about the beach at Scheveningen, as I watched his abdomen being opened, exposing a shattered spleen. I also knew it was hopeless now.

"Promise me before I die that you will keep on fighting for Spain and for what is right," he said. I promised him. "Sing me the cradle songs. Sing me the folk songs. Sing to me," he begged.

With a pinched throat and unshed tears, I sang to Peter as softly as I could. I thought again of Till Eulenspiegel's wife as she placed the ashes on the hearts of her sons and daughters: "As long as there is injustice in this world, you must fight against it." Peter had heard these words; he had read them in school. I was hearing them through the din of the bombers overhead trying to locate our hospital. Dr. Barsky finished operating by candlelight as our lights went out. Silent sobs caught in my throat as I felt Peter's pulse fading to nothingness, to death.

The long days without sleep resulted in an infectious sore throat. For two days I lay delirious with fever and exhaustion. Nightmares of Moors capturing me, of bombs falling on our precious hospital, of death, held me. But the body is a tough fighter when not completely snuffed out by a bullet or a bomb. Within a few days I was back on the wards again, as one after another of our staff had to go to bed, sick with fever and exhaustion.

The Battle of Jarama was over. Not a dead body lay in the courtyard. Most of the wounded had been evacuated by the ambulance train. Every bed was full, but with only one patient to a bed and not two and three as before. The floors were clean and being used as floors and not as beds for wounded. Maybe now we could also practice our nursing arts, give a bedbath, rub a hot, tired back, be nurses again, and make the wounded men's stay a bit more pleasant.

Death was brushed aside as men felt better after the grime of the front had been washed off them. They began joking and singing, and we sang with them. Miraculously, they were alive, and so were we. One morning, as I gave bedside care, I heard a very British voice say, "I will say that in our British hospitals the corners on the beds are fitted more neatly, but we don't have the song and the warmth of the American hospital." It was Lady Hastings, who had walked in while I was singing along with the wounded. When she had been in Barcelona, sick and feverish, I had given her bedside care. She was on her way to the British hospital at Colmenar and had stopped by to see our hospital. Forgotten was the Revolution of 1776 as British and Americans worked side by side to help Spain in her fight against the rebels.

Now we were on regular schedule, with time off to sleep and time off to eat. We began griping about the food we ate — chick-peas and more chick-peas with bits of an old, tough burro thrown in, flavored with rancid olive oil. We wanted a shower put up for the staff. We wanted to leave the hospital and walk. We wanted to see the village again. We had not been out of the building for a month. One by one we were allowed to go out and poke around the village. I got a ride to Lillo, where our driver was going to search for food other than chick-peas. Except for the huge, old church — where the fascists thought we would have our hospital — which had been bombed, the village looked quite the same. We did not find fresh vegetables, but returned with many bags of peanuts and bottles of muscatel wine. I didn't like the wine, but the peanuts were a welcome food.

In the afternoon dusk we drove back to our hospital. The windmills of Romeral beckoned us on. Although nights were bitter cold, the days were getting warmer and my bones ached less. Even the hospital looked homey as we entered the courtyard. In the few hours that I had been away, things had changed. Crates were being packed, and the staff was bustling here and there. I asked, "What's up?" The reply was, "The Jarama front is secure, so we are moving nearer the lines to Tarancón."

Someone who had been there told me that the town had a history of daily bombardment, since it was the last place where one could get gasoline on the road to Madrid. The fact that Rudolph the German was also in Tarancón made the news less pleasant. We hated to break up our efficient working unit where many had lived who otherwise might have died. We had had an unusually low mortality rate, considering the condition the wounded were in when they came to us. Now we were going to Tarancón, where there were three hospitals and many other doctors and nurses from other lands. I hoped we would continue to work as a unit.

I was ordered to stay behind with one doctor to get the last men ready and onto the evacuation train. After that I was to pack what was left and join the group in Tarancón. I hoped they would forget me for awhile, since Carl, one of our ambulance drivers, had just finished rigging up a shower. I had visions of a daily shower and walks through the village with Modesta, my assistant nurse whom I had trained.

Modesta and I vied with one another as to who could give the best backrub. The wounded Americans, Italians, Poles, Greeks, Spaniards, English, Austrians and Germans had not had such attention since they had left their homes and families. My only problem was that I could speak only Dutch, English and German; but somehow we managed. Human warmth superseded the language barrier.

I had one pack of cigarettes left. I searched and searched until I found the boxes with emergency food, where I knew I would find chocolate bars. Then I made sixteen packages of one chocolate bar and one cigarette each to slip to the wounded men when they were ready to depart on the train. (I should say when the train was ready to pass by for them.)

One afternoon the train came in. We took the wounded, four at a time, to the train. As I got each one settled in his berth, I gave him the little package of chocolate bar and cigarette and kissed him *hasta luego* on his forehead. Yes, a kiss! In Spain I had lost awareness of sex with a capital S. These were my brothers, my comrades, my patients and my friends.

As I stood alongside the train in the cold March wind, waving good-bye, I was happy that they were on it and going back behind the lines. I had never seen a train like it before. It had an operating room, almost perfectly equipped. Male nurses were on duty and a capable surgeon, in charge. I had heard of him. He had managed to cross fascist lines to get back to the Republic in order to serve. He was a military medical doctor, and his train showed the discipline in the service it gave to the wounded.

With the help of Modesta and some village women, we soon packed what was left for the move by truck. All I had to do now was wait for someone to come and get me and the equipment. I hoped they would take their time. I wanted to call on Modesta's mother and urge her to let Modesta come to Tarancón with us. Modesta was an amazing person. She was about 19 years old, compact, sturdy, with flashing black eyes. Her voice had been one of the most strident months ago, when we had looked for helpers. She insisted on working with us. She had lost her father and two brothers at the front. The other girls had not liked her much at first, because she was insistent and opinionated. I liked her for those very qualities and was delighted when she was assigned to me. I had studied three years to become a graduate nurse. In no time at all she had picked up the nursing skills and was invaluable. Despite our language barrier, we were close.

With a dictionary in my hand, I went with Modesta to call on her mother. I tried to explain our need for Modesta. All she would say with her hands was that she would consider it, *"Pero, al momento, no"* (But not right now). Modesta kept on saying, *"Pero me voy contigo, quien sabe cuando, pero iré."* She repeated it often until a smile broke on my face and I replied, "You will come — you don't know when, but you will come!" We shook our heads in unison and understanding.

When we returned to what had been a hospital, we saw trucks unloading desks, books, blackboards and maps. I was glad to see the bright-faced children getting their school back instead of its being filled with wounded. I was impressed again with the most vital force I had encountered in Spain: not the war, but the drive to learn and progress!

Our chief nurse, Frederika, whom we affectionately called Freddie, arrived in one of the trucks to collect the rest of our equipment and me. I had become attached to Romeral, its people and its windmills, even though I had walked through the town only twice in a month. I hoped I could leave behind the memories of the battle of Jarama and the wounded and dead who had been poured into the hospital, but I have never been able to do this. A part of Romeral is always with me.

It got colder and colder as we drove on to Tarancón. Freddie was not the least bit impressed with the situation at Tarancón, but all she would say was, "See for yourself. See what your reaction is. I think it a mess and impossible to work in, but Rudolph says that we can."

Even the nurses were becoming suspicious of Rudolph. We

could not understand why our doctors could not see through him. Yet we had no grounds other than his arrogance and the open contempt with which he treated the Spaniards — or, rather, all others except Aryans. Then, too, his emphasis on the place of women in society made us wonder about him.

When we got to Tarancón, it was after midnight. I searched among my sleeping friends to find one into whose bed I could crawl. My flashlight spotted one of our thin nurses. I crawled in and hoped she wouldn't object to my cold body. She was so exhausted that she didn't even awaken.

The next morning I saw what Freddie meant. A tower of Babel was around us and in our ears. It appeared that at least every language represented by the International Brigade was being spoken. The Americans only added to the confusion. In an area of about one square block stood three hospitals, all near the station where ambulances, trucks and other vehicles got their last gasoline before they arrived at the fronts at Madrid or Jarama. Sometimes thirty to forty trucks would be lined up for gasoline. No wonder the town was being bombed. I wondered whose crackpot idea this was to have the representatives of foreign medical aid all working together in a town that was rarely without bombers overhead.

Freddie told me that I was to be in charge of Hospital No. 3. Great, I thought, it is diagonally across the street from the gasoline station! It was also directly across the street from the only house Dr. Barsky could locate, where at least our unit could eat and sleep together. He wanted to keep us as a team as much as possible. I only hoped that we would have few moonlit nights and that the Germans were poor marksmen with their bombs. Gasoline dump, waiting trucks, Hospital No. 3 filled with patients, and the living quarters of our unit of seventeen — I longed for Romeral!

Hospital No. 3 — what a mess it was! There was not a window intact. They had been blown out in the last bombing. Rubble, rubble everywhere, yet I found myself dreaming of how this hospital could be left intact as a general hospital for Tarancón. Although its location was excellent for bombers, it was also excellent for a city hospital. I had visions of outpatient departments, of a visiting nurse service connected with the hospital, of well-baby clinics — all of this with the emphasis on preventive medicine. I hated war more than ever, especially this war, which had been forced on the Republic of Spain and kept them from doing that which was more important to them — growth in democracy, in schools and in medical services. I even dreamed of bringing Mary Lee over when the war was won, and of helping them set up public health units.

Dreams, dreams — yet the reality was that I had two patients in every bed. They were mostly men from the Lister Battalion — Italians, Poles, French and Spaniards. A male nurse from England was on night duty; a Polish male nurse helped in the daytime. I longed for Modesta to help me make sense in this international disorganization.

As far as I could understand, the idea was to have all the Internationals under one direction — Spanish, of course. But it seemed as if everyone wanted to be boss, even we Americans. This was easy to understand, as there was disorganization all around us, although the front was quiet. Poles bickered. The French hated the Italians. The Irish teased the British. The Spaniards bickered among themselves. I had not been conscious of political differences for a long time. How could I be, on an active front? But now I was hearing it — socialism vs. communism, the UGT (Unión General de Trabajo) and the FAI (Federación Anarquista de Trabajo), the anarchists and the Trotskyites. It annoyed me; there was only one fight — that against fascism.

There were rumors that we had spies and saboteurs among us, which increased suspicions. When I saw blood oozing through a cast, I reported it. The sutures had been loosely tied.

Adding up case after case from the three hospitals, one particular doctor seemed to be doing deliberate sabotage on humans. It appeared unbelievable, but it was true; he disappeared. All lights were to be out. Blackout curtains must be on the windows, and fires must be put out in hospital courtyards. One night coming home late from the operating room, I spotted burning coals in the shape of a cross in the hospital courtyard. No worker had set this fire for warming a cup of coffee. I kicked it aside with my feet, but the bombers were already overhead.

Half my time seemed spent chasing down soldiers who wanted to return to the front. We had orders to keep them until discharged as ready for the front. I found them on a truck waiting for gas and then would begin my long argument as to why they should stay in the hospital until completely healed. I had never heard of soldiers going AWOL *toward* the front, but these boys from many lands and from the many provinces of Spain wanted to fight, not lay on a hospital bed. Not that I blamed them much; at least at the front they had trenches to cower in when bombs fell.

Romeral had been cold, but Tarancón was colder. My hands and fingers became swollen with rheumatism. Beds were emptying. All I had to do was supervise. With my hands as they were, all I wanted was to sit in the sun when it appeared. Freddie gave us time off, and finally I got to a beauty parlor and had the sweat and grime washed out of my hair. Such a luxury!

There was still a lull on the front. Dr. Barsky set out to look for two buildings for us, one to be used as a base hospital and one as a convalescence hospital. We had news that another unit was arriving from the States. We did not want those supplies to disappear as they were doing in Tarancón. We were determined to work as a team in Spain in our hospitals. During this quiet period, some had been to Madrid. I, too, longed to see Madrid, but I settled for a ride in an ambulance to Colmenar, the first front-line emergency hospital. Typhoid vaccine was to be delivered to be given to the front-line soldiers and to the staff at Colmenar. One of their nurses had typhoid, and some of the soldiers had it. I readily settled for a ride to Colmenar since I hoped to see the front-line Lincoln Battalion doctor who was quite special for me.

Fleecy white clouds drifted across a breathtakingly blue sky over a flattish landscape bordered by the purple mountains of Guadarrama as we traveled toward the front. It was hard to believe that a war was going on. When truckloads of children being evacuated from Madrid passed us, I was again aware of Moors on the front and Germans and Italians overhead. But those bomb craters at the entrance to the bridge reminded me again that it was best to enjoy the scenery while I lived. I relaxed with the clouds. Within no time we were at the hospital, in time for tea. The operating room table served as the tea table. I was graciously asked, "Do you prefer lemon or milk in your tea?" This was a part of England running the hospital at Colmenar. They had had it worse than us during the Jarama battle, since they were within range of the battlefield. Of this the British did not talk as they served tea! They were more nonchalant and casual than we were. These British are amazing people, I thought.

After tea, Percy, the British ambulance driver, collected the materials that he was to take to the front, a short distance away. I begged him to take me with him. "It's against the rules, and you know it," he replied. "Snipers, machine guns, hand grenades, mortars, and she wants to go to the front," he muttered.

"The front is quiet; nothing will happen. If anything does, I'll take all the blame," I coaxed. I wanted to see my favorite doctor at the front.

"All hell can break loose in a moment on a battlefront. If I let an American nurse get killed, the Revolutionary War between the British and the Americans will begin all over again," he continued.

"Please, Percy, let me go. I won't tell anyone," I begged as I hopped on the running board of the ambulance.

He gave in. We started down the dirt road, past a happily gurgling brook lined with purple violets under branches of yellow mimosa. The slate graygreen leaves of the olive trees whispered in unison with the sounds of the brook, "Percy, drive slowly." The road was one shell hole after another. I looked at the violets and the mimosa to avoid seeing the reminders of war. But now I began hearing the sounds of war that I had never heard before. Percy said, "Hear that? It's a mortar — that was a machine gun — now that was a bursting hand grenade. Be careful now. We will go through an area that snipers have covered. Duck low."

I associated the sounds with the wounds I had seen in Romeral. It was too late to turn back now. We had arrived.

Near the top of the hill, sheltered by trees, we could see the headquarters of the Lincoln Battalion and the cookhouse. As we walked up the incline carrying the materials being delivered to the front, it still seemed peaceful, except for the occasional loud noises. I don't know who was more surprised, the men at headquarters or me, when I walked in. They had not been away from the front at Jarama since their arrival in early February, and they had not seen a woman in months. My favorite doctor scolded me for coming up to the front, but his eyes told me that he was glad to see me. One by one, men slipped out, and others took their places in the first aid station. They asked about their companions who had been in our hospitals, and they wanted other news. The few of the Lincolns who were left slipped out of the trenches to chat a bit with me.

Over a cup of muddy coffee, the doctor described a road that he had conceived and was helping to build. By using this road the stretcher bearers would not have to walk so far and would not be in the sights of the snipers' guns. He was as enthusiastic as a newly diplomaed road engineer, to be building a road right under the noses of the fascist rebels. In his enthusiasm, before he realized it he was showing me the new road. We walked among the olive trees, and at irregular intervals I heard a ping and a zip with a bit of a whine close to us. "What is that sound?"

He replied, "That is the whine of a sniper's bullet. Here, take my helmet. Put it on."

I did as I was told, but soon took it off. It was uncomfortable. I gave it back to him, and turned up my cape collar.

As the ping-zip-whines became more frequent, the doctor shouted, "Drop!" We dropped and lay on the sun-warmed earth. I saw beauty over our heads where the sunlight filtered through the olive leaves and the yellow mimosa. The ping-zips played a minor note to the music of our whispered words and acts. We must have fallen asleep, both of us, the doctor and the nurse. Then the sun was less bright, and gone was the sound of the whining bullets. Maybe they thought us dead. We were very much alive, alive with the joy of two people who cared for one another.

When I returned to Tarancón the next day, I was greeted with the news that Dr. Barsky had found two huge buildings isolated near the front. His plan was to set one up as a base hospital and the other for convalescent care. We were thrilled with the prospects of getting away from Tarancón. The bickering bothered us more than the bombs. We had been frustrated by wanting to do our best and being handicapped in doing it. The second unit would soon arrive from the United States, more doctors and nurses with supplies. We had enough staff for the two hospitals, we hoped.

By the end of March, 1937, we moved to Villa Paz, or House of Peace. Villa Paz had been one of the country houses of Spain's royalty; they had certainly done well for themselves. It was as if they had walked out yesterday, instead of years ago. The servants, who lived in the nearby caves, had kept the summer palace immaculate and intact. They warned us to keep it in good condition, as they hoped it could be an agricultural college after the war. People of Spain — cliff dwelling, cave dwelling, slum dwelling — you deserve to be free!

We had a crack operating-room nurse in our group, Ann Taft. I have never seen one better. She had worked with Dr. Barsky in the New York hospital where she had trained. It always surprised me how this little bit of a young girl could make an operating room out of nothing. Her lovely face bubbled over as she discovered beautiful glass jars etched with the Royal Crown, filled with preserved fruit. We helped eat the fruit, in order that the jars could be sterilized. Instead of preserved peaches, the jars would hold preserved catgut sutures.

Again we were bustling. Not that Dr. Barsky told us in so many words, but he hurried us to get the hospital ready for service. He was pushing us as if he knew there would be another big battle. The operating room seemed to be one big maw with its demand for more and more sterile packs. At least here, as one folded gauze or rolled bandages, one could look through the big windows and see the green of the trees as we were accustomed to doing in the United States. This was not the parched, sun-scorched, dry earth of Romeral or Tarancón. Best of all, the bombers left us completely alone.

I was notified that Dr. Barsky wished to see me in his office. I wondered what on earth the problem was. I had never been called to his office before. I soon found out. He told me to take Modesta — who had now joined us — and take over at Castillejo. The hospital there had fifty patients and a Dutch doctor in charge.

"I want you to get Castillejo organized so that it can handle three hundred convalescent patients. Two hundred and fifty cots will be delivered soon. You will also get the needed hospital supplies. I am counting on you to handle all the rest — feeding, laundry, care, and so forth — for a potential three hundred patients," Dr. Barsky said very calmly.

I said to myself, "My God, how?" as I replied just as calmly, "Yes, Dr. Barsky, and when do you want me to begin?"

"Now," he answered.

Down the hill, past the tumbling trout stream alongside the ruins of an old Moorish castle, Modesta and I rode on a small truck, carrying our clothing and supplies for Castillejo. When we entered the patio, I saw that it was even larger than Villa Paz. Two beautiful great Danes guarded the entrance and barked furiously at us. I wondered if they had been left behind by the royalty. Modesta and I braved the dogs as we entered the patio in search of the doctor.

We found him in the kitchen, sterilizing instruments. I told him that I had been assigned to help. Dr. Theo van Reemst seemed to know all about it. Jokingly he said, "Let's hang up the Dutch flag, seeing that a de Vries will be working with a van Reemst." He continued in a more serious vein, "I have one right-hand man, Peter. Let him show you about, find you a room, and then see what you can do about converting this into a three hundred-bed hospital."

I found Peter a serious, rather fussy, Prussian-type German. We conversed in a mixture of Dutch and German as we crossed the patio to the wolf calls of the Italians aimed at Modesta and me. I picked the room that had been the "Infanta's," and Modesta chose one nearby. The bed was not as soft as it looked, and the Royal Crown hung a bit precariously at its head. Peter wanted to take it off, but I said, "Leave it! This will be quite a new experience for me to sleep in a bed with a crown at my head."

Peter said, "But it may fall off and hurt you."

"It is not that heavy, and my skull is thick," I answered. One night, alas, it did fall on my forehead as the Infanta rattled in her grave!

Peter next insisted that I take a delousing bath, like all incoming wounded or staff. I insisted that I had no lice, but he insisted on law and order and obeying the rules. I stopped objecting. I could think of nothing better than sitting in the Queen's huge bathtub and letting myself soak. Of course there was no running water, but Peter had buckets of hot water poured into the tub. I traced over the symbol of the Royal Seal with my wet fingers as I deliciously soaked in the Royal Tub. Now I was on the deloused list. If this was the way to get a hot bath on occasion, well then, I'd look for a louse now and then to report to Peter.

Glowing with cleanliness, I made the rounds of the building. It was fantastic. The dining room had been and still was an art gallery. The library was filled with the soft colors of leather-bound books, most with their pages uncut. In the kitchen were crested glasses. The dishes gleamed mellow with their gold finishing. I saw nothing of the vandalism I had heard about. Except for the plumbing system, everything was cherished and cared for. Nightingales sang in the dusk, and the brook murmured. I fell in love with Castillejo.

At first I didn't say a word about my being sent down from Villa Paz to administer the hospital at Castillejo. I felt I had to earn this right. I explained to Modesta that we must pitch in and work side by side with the six young girls who were already there. By seeing us working as hard or harder than them, they might gain confidence in us.

As their confidence in us increased, the complaints increased also. "It is hard enough with fifty patients. How can we do the laundry, the cooking, the cleaning, and the nursing when the patient load increases? There are men who could help us carry the water, help us in the work, but they just walk around. They forget that today we are all equal according to our constitution," they grumbled.

"Of course you are correct, girls, but you can't expect the men to change their Moorish, European attitudes overnight. However, I have an idea. Leave it to me," I answered.

"What is your idea?" they asked.

"My idea is to call a meeting of the ambulatory patients, the whole staff, and just about everyone who can be walked or carried, to discuss how to run the hospital. I'll get the wounded Lincolns to help me by volunteering for chores," I replied. This was a new lesson in cooperation for them. I hoped it would work!

The girls said, "We want to learn to read and write. We are too tired at night and have no time in the day. The soldiers are learning in the trenches and in the hospitals. Why not us?"

"I think we will be able to do all of this. We will ask the men to help us," I answered, hoping the Lincolns wouldn't let me down.

I knew that no Spaniard or other European of his own free will would scrub a floor, wash a dish, wring a sheet, peel a potato or do what they thought was "women's work" in any way. I had to find a way. The Germans of the Thaelman Battalion might volunteer, but who wanted to listen to long speeches on women's rights with quotes from Engels, Marx, Lenin and Stalin? Neither I nor the others. We wanted helping hands and fewer words. I looked for the few Lincolns. One had a leg in a light cast; two had their arms in casts, and so forth; but they all were able to walk. I spoke to them and explained the need for them to volunteer at a general meeting that would be called. "Please set an example. The Spaniards admire the Americans more than any other nationality group. Please volunteer for squads or committees of potato-peeling, washing in the brook, carrying water to the hospital, washing dishes, making your own beds. Please, won't you help?" I begged.

They griped, which I expected, but they said we could count on them to volunteer and to help get others to volunteer. I knew that with this, 90 percent of the problem was over before we were loaded with 300 or more patients. Dr. van Reemst walked by and stopped to chat with us. I told him of our idea, and he said, "I'll volunteer for the latrine-digging squad."

"That's real public health: Build latrines, and cut down the dysenteries," I replied. "'A toilet or latrine in every home' used to be a slogan in the United States Public Health Service, sparked by Dr. Mountain."

Dr. van Reemst was wonderful to work with. He was a great man, like Dr. Barsky. He did not need his ego flattered every minute as did many men I had known. It was a pleasure to call him Chief; he was.

We called the meeting for that night. The bed patients sent from each ward a delegate who could walk. I had interpreters ready: Greek, French, Italian, German, Spanish and English. Dr. van Reemst opened the meeting, and then I presented the problem confronting the women nurses, of doing all the work for a hospital which now had fifty patients but might soon have 300 or more. I said that I knew there was great desire on the part of all of us to learn Spanish, and the Spaniards wanted to learn to read and write Spanish. If all able people helped, we might be able to have an efficient hospital and also an educational program. I called for discussion.

It came, but hot and heavy. Through many languages the gist was: They came to fight, not to do women's work. The men of the International Brigade here were of all political shades: anarchists, communists, socialists, democrats, monarchists who hated Franco, and so forth. One of the Americans asked, "Don't you believe what you preach — the right of women to develop?" With that, bless their hearts, the Americans began volunteering for dishwashing, scrubbing, washing, digging latrines, and so on! The first Spaniard to follow was a replacement who was very proud to be in the Lincoln Battalion, now known as the Lincoln Brigade. Slowly other Spaniards volunteered, and a few from the other European groups followed suit. I was happy with the results, and the assistant nurses were beaming. For them, this was revolutionary. I preferred thinking it was evolutionary, but either way we were on the road toward progress in human relations right here at Castillejo. I had always felt that progress should begin in the situation in which one found oneself, and the less talking about it, the better. I had seen in New York and now in Spain that the more political or other discussion, the fewer the deeds!

President, secretary, treasurer, and other officers of the Hospital Volunteer Association of Castillejo were elected. We closed the meeting, setting the date for the next one within the same week.

The next morning, with some dirty sheets in a pillowcase, I

walked down to the brook. I heard voices arguing and stood sheltered from their sight by the willows. I peeked through and saw the girls pounding the sheets on the flat rocks. Two of the Lincoln Brigade, with their fractured arms sticking out like angels' wings, were wringing sheets. They were Irish-Americans from Boston. One had his right arm in a cast, and the other, his left. "The angels," I thought fondly. Two Spaniards, who had been with them at the front, were pounding sheets along with the girls. A few Germans were stretching out the damp laundry on the grass to dry. A Spaniard leaned on his crutch and sneeringly said to the other Spaniards, *"Tú no eres macho. No eres hombre. Estás trabajando como mujer."* The youngest Spaniard answered with anger, "You sound just like one of those Hitler Germans or Franco Moors," as he leaped up to attack him. The Lincoln men quickly handed him the end of a sheet to wring as the Germans began their political lecture to the protesting Spaniard leaning on his crutch.

Stepping out, I handed the girls the laundry and said in English, "Thanks a lot, men." I didn't translate it or ask for translation. It was the Lincoln men I was thanking, not only for the present but for the past. If they had not held at Jarama, neither I nor any of them would be here today. We would have been raped or slaughtered by the Moors — little Ann, bright Helen, our lovely Freddie, all of us, and it probably would have been worse for the Spanish girls who worked with us.

The Italians of the Garibaldi had not volunteered for any of the "women's work," but they volunteered to help supply food. Chick-peas became boring meal after meal. They began bringing in fish from the stream. When they hobbled back on their crutches clasping live chickens, I didn't ask them where and how they got them. I hoped some day they might manage to bring back a whole pig. After all, had not I, too, become adept at stealing? It was a strange rationalization in war: I did not steal for myself, but for the many. The Italians were doing the same. Before I spoke to them, I recalled the nights I slipped up to Villa Paz ostensibly to visit the other girls there, but really to steal some supplies for my hospital. To them Villa Paz, being the base for major surgery, was the most important. To me the hospital at Castillejo was the most important. They hung onto their supplies, so I stole what I thought we needed, which was more than that given to us. I stole alcohol, bandages, sheets, anything I could lay my hands on for Castillejo.

The people who lived in nearby caves asked permission to use the chapel for a meeting. "Of course," I replied. "This is your building. We are only borrowing it for awhile to use as a hospital." They graciously invited us to sit in on the meeting. I wondered what it was all about. I hoped we had not offended them or stolen too many chickens. But no, the meeting was about the fertile land not in use around the two summer palaces, Villa Paz and Castillejo. It was almost painful to watch the careful articulation and slight fear with which they voiced their ideas. Then one voice timidly said, "I have a plow." Another offered seeds. The ambulatory wounded soldiers who had not offered help to the hospital suddenly were offering to help plow the earth and plant the seeds. A cooperative was being formed right here. I saw democracy aborning among the cave dwellers, former servants of the royalty.

Italians and more Italians — the hospital was full of them, and more were pouring in. They certainly couldn't all be of the Garibaldi Battalion. Many had bullet wounds in their backs. What was this? Through interpreters and through the ambulance drivers who were bringing the wounded in from the front, we pieced the story together.

Thousands of Mussolini's Italians under Black Shirt command were fighting the Spaniards on the Guadarrama Front. They had been successful at Malaga, and they were going to show how to break through to Madrid. Every Garibaldi Italian who could move was at the front fighting side by side with the Spanish republicans and the Internationals. And a new type of warfare was going on. Our Italians had loudspeakers going, saying, "Why do you fight us, your brother Italians? Why do you fight brother workers? Join us. Desert! Fight with us! There will be no reprisals. We will pay your way back to Italy if you so want." They were deserting to our side, all right, and getting bullets in their backs from their officers.

The poor souls had thought they were going to Africa and instead found themselves in bitter warfare fighting brother Italians. The famous, invincible Black Shirts of Mussolini had been routed by the Italians of the Garibaldi. A carbon copy of a cartoon from a British newspaper circulated through Castillejo, showing Mussolini boasting, "Well, only the Italians of the Garibaldi could beat my men. It took an Italian to beat an Italian."

I was making rounds early one morning on the second floor of the palace to check on the number of bed patients and the number of patients who could come downstairs to the first aid room for their dressings. I noticed a group of Italians clustered around one bed. I examined the soldier who was surrounded by his countrymen and found he had a clean bullet wound on his back, a scratch really. He also had a cold, but his temperature was normal. Obviously he could come downstairs to have his wound dressed, and there the doctor might give him an aspirin for his cold. The wounded around the bed objected to this. "Our countryman is a sick man. He escaped the Black Shirts to join us. He must have extra-special care," they said.

"Nonsense! I am not aware who of you is Garibaldi or who is Black Shirt. You are wounded soldiers. If you can walk, help us by coming downstairs," I replied. The soldier with the cold and the slight back wound did not appear, and I found that the Garibaldis were not speaking to me. They had reported to the doctor that I had discriminated against one of their fascist refugees and that this matter should be raised at a meeting. What really bothered me was not the proposed meeting where the problem would be raised, since this meeting could be utilized for other matters as well. What bothered me was the big fat hen they had acquired. I saw it being plucked, and then odors of chicken soup wafted from the steaming caldron in the patio. Later, when I went upstairs to check on the Black Shirt's temperature just to be sure, I found him surrounded by doting Garibaldis and being fed hot chicken broth. I got nary a wing. Formerly they had always saved me a wing.

At the regular meeting of Castillejo, of its staff and patients who were now also part of the staff, I raised the problem of men staying in bed who could walk down for dressings. I surprised the Garibaldis by going on the offensive. Dr. van Reemst, whom everyone respected, explained the problems of numbers — over 300 patients, most of whom could walk, and an official staff of only one doctor, one registered nurse (me), and eight nurse's aides. The Garibaldis were a bit sheepish, grinned at me, and offered to help more in the hospital. After that they again whistled at me when I walked by, calling me the Blonde Dynamo; but I had lost one chicken wing.

The Battle of Guadalajara had been won. Hardly any new wounded were arriving directly to us, only the ones sent down from the base hospital. These days, in a sense, were more difficult. The idle soldiers, those who had not volunteered to help, argued. My God, how they argued — anything from art to politics! Right now I had a vehement Greek who was a dogmatic communist and a fanatic anarchist from Barcelona who argued through the use of interpreters. The argument grew from two persons to twenty to forty. Words got sharper, and before it became fists I thought I'd better do something. I asked the Greek to write a speech in honor of the Republic of Spain for April 16th, the date of its founding. I asked each nationality of the Internationals to write a few words of greeting. This kept them out of mischief.

I had hoarded sufficient oranges so that at the fiesta I could give an orange to every cave dweller and their children. April 16, 1937, came, and with it came some trouble.

Several of the French soldiers had found some potent brew. The only intoxicating liquor we had in Castillejo was a horrid, sour wine, which was served in lieu of water at meals, due to the shortage of water. The French were quarreling drunk. Words flew, and crutches waved to accent them. Raised, white-plastered arms were the exclamation points. Fists shook. The fight was in many languages. I understood nary a word, but I felt the anger. We could have quieted the fighters. By now we had experience in how to handle soldiers in moments of boredom, but we were not prepared for the fool who had run up to Villa Paz and had reported a riot in Castillejo. In walked Rudolph the German with a gun which he pointed at the group. To a man, they turned on him, "What right do you have to appear in a hospital with a loaded gun? Guns are for the front! It is absolutely illegal to have a firearm in a hospital. Get out!" they said. I was delighted to see the arrogant bravado crumbling in Rudolph as his gun was taken away by the now sober French, and they escorted him off the grounds. Then it was as if nothing had happened. The Greek made his speech. The Catalan talked. Songs were sung, and oranges passed out. We closed the fiesta with the Hymn of the Spanish Republic.

Not a week later we heard that Rudolph had been arrested. The military police had been watching him. He was a German officer who had infiltrated the republicans' ranks, part of a spy ring. His fountain pen, which he would never let a soul borrow, had contained the proof. The talk was that he had sabotaged our unit all along and had been responsible for the many bombings our unit had suffered. At Castillejo he had tried to convert a simple fight into bloodshed. I hoped that the republicans would not be too easy with him.

Perhaps never again in my life will I be with such idealistic, intelligent, gentle people from so many lands. This was a crusade for the freedom of man. Maybe you bickered once in awhile, gripe you certainly did, but you were all united toward one goal: man's right to be free! In 1937 I was seeing almost pure idealism. Yet I had a guilt complex for being here in

Spain: I had left my young daughter in the States, even though I'd left her well cared for. The photos which came to me from New Hampshire showed her busy and happy. I was torn between my feeling of guilt and the love I had for service. Anything that I had ever learned, any skill I had, any belief I had in humanity was working here in Castillejo. I was seeing all the principles I believed in coming true in one spot. I was seeing men of all races and creeds working together. I was seeing democracy aborning in Castillejo. You, my fellow idealists, were teaching me. The illiterate peasant was teaching me.

If I learned nothing else, I learned something most important, proven over and over again by these "teachers" — something which I had vaguely learned at Columbia University that I was witnessing here in real life: There is no direct correlation between intelligence and education. Here were illiterate farmers and soldiers whose social philosophy was superior, it seemed to me, to any I had seen before. War was being fought near them, around them, over them; but their most vital consideration was life with a future. Clinics sprang up where none had been. Trenches were dug with a special section for classroom work. Small theater groups performed to people who had never seen theater. Paintings, as in our hospital, were carefully cherished. The desire to increase knowledge was the most exciting force in Spain.

In Castillejo, our wounded Catalan schoolteacher-soldier conducted classes in the library ward on how to read and write. It was he who told me of the work being done in the trenches which began with every soldier who could read and write teaching his *compañeros*. Then the Spanish Federation of Teachers, the FETE, began placing materials in the trenches. A form card was worked out, and when the student could write the data on it, he had learned to read and write. It was mailed to the FETE. The last report from FETE gave information on about 900 classrooms in trenches on the fronts. In the 18th Brigade alone, illiteracy had been reduced by 60%. The schoolteacher told me that once, when they lacked reading material, a group of volunteers raided a deserted village in no man's land and brought back textbooks from the village school. Indeed, I had seen evidence of such attempts at learning.

For the first time in my life, I kept a diary and into it went such data. Here are some notes I made: "In 1935, during the monarchy, 943 schools had been established. Since July 1936, the Republic of Spain had established 10,000 new schools. These were school buildings, not classes in trenches. Salaries for teachers had trebled. Fourteen million pesetas had been set aside to build and equip more schools." I know that the building at Romeral, which we had used for awhile, had been the village's first school. I had seen many sitting on curbs in Barcelona, and groups in the parks at Valencia, studying reading and writing. I had never in my life seen such a flow of well-thought-out posters on health and sanitation. I was constantly being overwhelmed by the Spanish republicans and their desire to win the war in order to build for peace. The people of the Spanish Republic were combating the invaders with their blood, their agony, their tears; but they studied while they fought.

My American passport would be invalid after the middle of April, so I went to Valencia to get a renewal. I did not doubt that I would get it, since a new ruling had ostensibly been passed by the U.S. State Department that nurses, doctors and medical units could legally be in Spain. We were not combatants like the men in the International Brigade. I disliked leaving smooth-operating Castillejo. The front was quiet, and I had time to study and to read among the wealth of books in the library. Still, I did not want to have to stay illegally. As usual, there was not a bed to be had in Valencia. I met Lady Hastings in the hotel, and she offered to share hers. She and her British friends doubted that I would get a renewal of my passport, and they chuckled at my naivete. "Just wait till you meet and speak with the American Consul, and you will understand," they said.

I went to the American Embassy in Valencia and asked to

speak with the consul. I was introduced to an exquisitely groomed man, Mr. So-and-so. I explained what it was that I needed. In his high, falsetto voice, he began by asking, "What is a nice girl like you doing in Spain, helping those murderers? Why, do you know 30,000 were murdered right here in Valencia just because they wore neckties?"

"Did 30,000 own neckties in Valencia?" I innocently asked as I gazed at his bright, flowered necktie and wondered how he felt walking the streets wearing it.

He appeared to quiver with fright as he told me that they were all communists, they raped nuns, they had no respect for the monarchy. My God, I thought, is he the representative of the United States of America?

I tried to tell him something about the people and what I had been learning from them and about them at the front. I explained the problem, as I saw it, of trying to change from feudalism to a democracy in the 20th century and at the same time fighting off Hitler's Condors, Mussolini's Black Shirts and Franco's Moors. I spoke of the similarity of the Constitution of the United States to the new constitution of Spain, but I was wasting my breath. His thin face pointed like a bitchy cat at the people and said, "They are all communists." How he hated them! It was obvious. I felt like spitting in his face, but he was not worth my spittle. Of course, I didn't get an extension of my passport. He told me to go back to the United States. I told him I'd stay till the job was done. He swished back to his desk, and I walked out.

I told myself: But he does not represent the best of America. America is Catholic, Protestant, Jew, Democrat, Republican, socialist, communist, Irish, Pole, Italian, German, tenth and first generation Americans — buried at Jarama — waiting for relief in the rain at the front — impatient with their wounds in the hospital. This is America — of thee I sing!

When I returned to Castillejo I was told that Dr. Barsky wanted to speak to me. Now what? When he told me what was wanted from me I could hardly believe my ears. I was to return to the United States and go on a speaking tour for the Medical Unit to Aid Spanish Democracy.

"But why me? I don't want to leave the work here!"

"You are the only one of us who has had experience in public speaking. I heard you once hold forth on birth control," he said. "We can depend on you to do a good job, and to get more and more medical supplies moving to us."

I had identified with Castillejo, and it was hard to leave. I was leaving a part of me behind. I left a job unfinished. Perhaps someday I might be able to return to Spain and finish my job, but in public health. Was it possible that I had been in Spain only a relatively short time? I had sailed from New York on January 16, 1937. I had been in Spain only approximately three months, yet it seemed I had been there forever. Now it was the first week in May, 1937, and I was returning to the United States. I had played a small part in the uneven struggle of the Spanish people defending themselves against Hitler's forces, Mussolini's Black Shirts, and the phony Neutrality Act which forbade a legally elected government to buy arms with which to defend itself.

I had received far more than I had given to Spain. I had received daily experience in valor, courage, bravery. I saw idealism expressed by men from many lands. I saw democracy in the making. Spain had given me the chance to work, think and act at the highest level of humanity that I was able to attain. In this action I had had a chance to grow.

In 1935 I had joined the Communist Party. I had been dogmatic. I had little patience with all other shades of liberals who did not join the Communist Party. Spain had changed me. Although I still thought of myself as a communist, I just as strongly felt that the important matter was not the label at all. I didn't even like labels any more. What counted was what I had seen in Spain at the battlefront, men and women of all races and creeds and of all political viewpoints working together in order that man could grow and obtain his ultimate stature.

By car, by train, by boat I was going home to the United States and my child. The voyage home was a blur until the wonderful, magnificent skyline of New York loomed before my eyes. Tugboats scooted toward us. The pilot came. Many men came off the little boats, and I wondered who they were. Suddenly I seemed to be surrounded by them. They were newspaper reporters. I was being interviewed, and it scared me. One man sidled up to me and said, "Be careful of the man in the yellow shirt. He is from the Hearst press." I smiled in thanks, as I thought, "The truth can't be smirched. I'll answer the questions as honestly as I can." I figured that the objective papers would print what I said and that the Hearst press would distort what I said anyway.

The immigration authorities wanted my passport. It was invalid, but I refused to part with it. It was mine. I had paid for it, and I would not let them have it! Finally I was off the boat and being greeted by the Medical Bureau of Spanish Democracy. On the way to the office I told them that before I would depart on any speaking tours I must spend some time with my little girl. They agreed. In the office of the Bureau, parents and relatives were waiting for me. Naturally they wanted to hear about their loved ones. I wept with the mothers of boys who had died on the Jarama Front as they pleaded for any information I could give them about the time before their sons' deaths, their burial places, and so forth. It was less heartbreaking to talk with the relatives of the nurses and doctors of the Medical Unit, since we had had no fatalities.

When I got to New Hampshire, I found my daughter happy in her environment: the Little Red Schoolhouse, living with Uncle Clarence and Aunt Clara. It was difficult to believe, in peaceful Meriden, New Hampshire, that only a short while ago I had been under bombs in Spain. Frankly, they were not interested in the fact that I had been in Spain. They were interested in crops, cattle and fowl, and in keeping Mary Lee with them through the summer, which could be unbearably hot in New York City. Since I was going on a speaking tour, we decided that Mary Lee should stay with them until the fall. Playing with her, I knew that I would not return to Spain during the war. I knew that I must stay in America, raise my child, and help Spain by speaking about her. The fourth medical unit was enroute to Spain. It was not so much the personnel they needed now as the continuous medical supplies. This meant money, which I hoped to raise.

I was to make my first speech in Trenton, New Jersey. I shall never forget that night. When I stepped on the platform, my whole body was pulsating with fear. I felt my heartbeat in every muscle of my body. I told the audience that I was badly frightened and that this was my first talk on Spain, and I felt the audience responding to my frankness. I tossed the written speech aside, forgot myself, and let the work of the nurses, the doctors, and the people of Spain speak through me. Never was I frightened again: From the Mississippi to the Shenandoah, in the Hippodrome in New York City, or from a pastor's pulpit or in a union hall, I let the heart of Spain pour through me. In some towns, like Wheeling, West Virginia, I had bodyguards; in others, I had none. I was entertained, and I was heckled. Tomatoes or roses were thrown at me. Nothing mattered except the chance to *talk Spain* through the eyes of a nurse who had been there. I have never again been able to hold an audience in my hands as I did then. It was not me; it was the right of Spain to be a republic.

June, July, August — airplane propellers whirled, trains clacked as I pushed myself through rain and heat, town after town, city after city, sometimes three and four talks a day. In September, 1937, I was scheduled to speak at the Congress of American Psychologists in Madison, Wisconsin. I had a pain in my back which got worse and worse. That was the finish of my speaking tour for Spain.

One doctor said that I had tuberculosis of the kidney! This I refused to believe unless it was checked and rechecked. I noted that he took a smear of germs from my vaginal area. He placed the slide under the microscope and said, "That is the tubercular organism." He began talking about removing my kidney. I got out of his office as fast as possible. I was quite sure that he had confused the harmless smegma bacillus, which is always present in the vagina, with the tuberculosis bacillus. I knew that the only way to be really positive that it was tuberculosis was to stain the germ in carbol fuschia dye by boiling it. He had not done that. Ethics or no ethics, hurt feelings of the doctor or not, by God, these were my kidneys, and no one would take one out until I myself was sure that it was tuberculosis! I went to a renal specialist.

Guinea pigs were injected with my microbes, and I impatiently awaited the results. In the meantime, I felt better and had to have some work in order to eat. Mary Lee and I were together again in our apartment. Fortunately, there was a three-month organizing job open with the Congress of Industrial Organizations, better known as the CIO. It was specifically to organize hospital workers, mainly nurses.

In public health we had decent hours of work and wages; on the contrary, hospital workers had miserable hours and wages. Only recently, in New York City, the small Hospital Workers Union, by publicity and pressure on the mayor and on hospital leadership, had won an eight-hour day for 20,000 city hospital employees. Naturally, I joined that union. However, it was extremely difficult to organize nurses. They had the wrong impression of Florence Nightingale, who did believe in labor organization. We did make a dent, sufficient enough to permit the official nursing organizations to begin establishing committees to study wages and hours.

In the meanwhile, when I was in Spain, nurses had organized a union in New York City. When I returned, at their meeting to elect officers they elected me president — president of the first nurses' union in the United States.

I kept track of the pigs who had my germs in their bodies. One day I was notified that they had died of tuberculosis and that I should prepare for surgery — prepare for losing a kidney. One hour later — and bless the honest doctor! — I was informed that the pigs had been mixed up and that they didn't know which were mine and which were of another suspect. Back to the hospital I went for an uncomfortable cystoscopic to extract more urine to inject more pigs. Six weeks later, plus ten negative Mantoux tests and fat healthy guinea pigs, proved that I had never had tuberculosis. What a relief!

Now I had to get a permanent job and finish my work at Teacher's College, Columbia, which I had left when I went to Spain. I took a job in a nurse placement service, which was establishing hourly visiting nursing service for people who could pay. Most of my work seemed to be washing out intestines (colonic irrigations) of those who had been drunk the night before. I didn't like the job one bit. What a contrast to my working with all I could give in Spain! But I was in the United States facing the reality of making a home, raising my child, and finishing my degree.

The year 1937 was drawing to a close when my little girl became very ill with rheumatic fever. Her father had died as an aftermath of it; I had had it, and I knew the statistics. Out of every ten who have it, five die ten years after the first attack. Her father had been one of those five. Three manage to survive with damaged hearts; I was one of those three. Only two out of ten with good care come through with undamaged hearts. I was determined that she would be one of those two. At this time there was no medicine known to combat the cause of rheumatic fever. Mary Lee was hospitalized at Mount Sinai Hospital under the service of Dr. Bela Schick. Four long months the poor child had to stay in bed, completely inactive. Then she had two months in a convalescent home.

In the meantime a book on rheumatic fever had come out, written by Dr. May Wilson. The groups that had been sent to warm climates had not had recurrences of rheumatic fever. I began trying to get a job in a warm climate. I was accepted for the State of New Mexico. Since it was in the Southwest, I assumed it would be warm. My appointment was as of September 1, 1938.

Frankly, I was glad to get out of New York City. Something had happened to me in Spain. I no longer saw politics as all black or all white. I saw the shades of gray between. I got annoyed at my former companions in Spain, who wanted only to talk Spain and to live in the past. We had a future to make in America. I was tired of talking "-isms." The farmer at the front knew nothing of isms; yet he was a dedicated fighter for his country against the rebels, the Germans, the Moors and the Italians. Many of the communists in the United States seemed more like dictators to me. I began wondering if I were a communist. What was I? I still didn't know.

I got a job in a summer camp as a senior counselor in order to be near Mary Lee during her convalescence. I had enrolled her in the eight-year-old group. This camp was run by liberals, but they seemed more down on liberals of other shades and labels than against reactionaries. I was not against any ism, as long as that ism furthered man's progress. To me it seemed, especially since I had returned from Spain, that it did not matter what a political cause was named, as long as the group or the individual worked and lived for the betterment of society. This could be in an organized way, but also might be in an unorganized way, as an individual, within one's family environment, or within one's community. More and more I thought honest liberalism began first at home within one's family unit. In 1935 I had joined the Communist Party. I had had my dogmatic period; now it was over. I didn't resign from the Party; I just tapered off in activities. I hardly ever went to meetings now. My concern was my daughter and getting the money to go to New Mexico.

When I went up to Port Chester to try to borrow money from my mother-in-law, I ended up getting $500. However, to get it I had to sign away any rights I had to Wilbur's estate. My mother-in-law promised to give any share that I would have obtained to Mary Lee. (This never materialized.) I had to accept this, as I needed the $500 then. I still had a half-year's work toward my degree at Teacher's College, but that, too, would have to wait. First came my daughter's well-being.

I did not know a soul who had been west. The interpreter, who had gone with us to Spain, came from Las Vegas, New Mexico, where I was to go. Mary Lee and I looked on the map of the United States. New Mexico was right above Texas. Boats sailed from New York to Galveston, Texas. We thought it a fine idea to go by boat to Texas and then to take a short ride by train to New Mexico. Later, on the boat, I realized that I was taking a long way around. I didn't mind, since the sea journey was doing marvels for Mary Lee.

The endless stretch between Galveston, Texas, and Las Vegas, New Mexico, took almost as long as the boat trip, it seemed. We were experiencing the vastness of the United States. Entering the northeast corner of New Mexico, I thought I was back on the plains of Castille. It was like the Madrid plateau.

*New Mexico, Puerto Rico, the Southeast
United States, Chicago and California, 1938-1948*

McCarthy's Hordes 6

I fell in love with New Mexico — blue skies, massive white cloud formations which were forever changing colors, tall green pines over the little piñon trees, encircled by the mountains. Again I had the feeling of being Home. The people helped me find an apartment, register Mary Lee in school, and locate things I needed. They were friendly, warm, sincere, individualistic. I liked the West and its people. However, I was not in the tropics. Stupidly I had assumed that New Mexico, being south, would be warm. Parts of it were, but I had come to work in the San Miguel County Public Health Demonstration Unit. The town of Las Vegas, where I was to live, was about 6,000 feet above sea level and far from warm, although it was a dry climate. I hoped that Mary Lee would not have a recurrence of the dread rheumatic fever.

I had arrived in time to attend the monthly staff conference of the three counties which comprised the health officer's district. Typical problems were raised: how to secure safe drinking water, how to encourage the building of latrines, the importance of registering births and deaths. Rain poured all day. An

Indian, a Navajo, stood outside selling silver jewelry and bows and arrows to the passengers of the Super Chief train. We were holding our meeting in the Harvey Hotel on the railroad line of the Atchison, Topeka and Santa Fe. And I had taken the boat to Texas, not knowing of the El Capitan or the Super Chief trains that traveled the old Santa Fe Trail. I stopped musing as I heard, "Don't urinate behind a bush or near flat rocks. A rattlesnake might bite you." The doctor continued, "Take antivenin along in your bag, but best of all don't go behind the bushes — urinate out in the open. Only the prairie dogs will see you." He chuckled, but I did not!

The public health nurse whose district I was taking went over directions with me. I tried not to show my bewilderment about the area which covered 1,000 square miles and contained 32 known villages, some of 1,000 inhabitants and some as small as 25 inhabitants. Some areas had dry farming, some had irrigation, and some had no crops, just sheep. In some villages there were feuds between families, and at other times there were feuds between villages. Few spoke English in any village! After leaving the paved highway, one had only dirt trails and excuses for roads. She continued, "Watch out for flash floods in dry arroyos. Try not to get your car hung up on high centers. Don't drive across the Pecos River to get to Garmabullo if there has been a rainstorm. If snow obliterates the trail, set your eyes on Starvation Peak and drive toward it. You will eventually come to the highway." I thought, "Good Lord, help me!"

She gave me notes with written instructions on how to get to the villages. I took them home to read. For the village of Sena she had written: "Go up the road to Villanueva about eight miles. On the right you will see wagon tracks which cross the mesa. Usually a white mare is standing near the piñon trees. Turn right. Drive through two prairie dog towns and stop. Look down at the narrow wagon trail going down the side of the cliff. Be sure that no wagon is on its way up. Check that there have been no rock slides. Proceed in low gear and pray."

I'd never seen a prairie dog town. White mares, excuses for roads, cliff-hung drives, rattlesnakes, deep ravines and slippery adobe mud — I decided I'd say nothing until I had conquered the situation. I didn't want to show my ignorance or fear, but I was just plain scared of what lay ahead of me.

As I studied the record system, the bag techniques, and so forth, I was so scared to go out on my own that I hoped the in-service training period would last a good long time. I wanted to get out to the rural areas and see what stuff I was made of, but the mountains looked formidable. Could I manipulate roads like those? When it rained they became like an ice-skating rink, but with deep ravines into which one could slide. Could I break down the antipathy that the Mexican-Americans had for the "gringos"? Since I liked people, I had never had difficulty working with any foreign group. But the faces of these Mexican-Americans, who were warm and alive with one another, froze in my presence. This was understandable, as they were supposed to have retrieved their lands and rights after the Treaty of Guadalupe in 1848; instead these lands were lost to Anglos.

I began. Pink slips meant newborn babies in my district. The rural, untrained midwife had been taught to make a cross on a slip of paper and to report the birth of a child. A newborn baby was my entry into the home. With the sheer force of my personality, my love for the babies, and my meager knowledge of the Spanish language, I began breaking down their barriers against what I represented to them — a *gringa*. Gradually, I was able to organize maternal clinics, groups of midwives for teaching, well-baby clinics, and teachers' conferences on how to integrate health through the school program. The teachers, who were Mexican-Americans, had had limited opportunities, and they, too, were suspicious of me at first. Gradually I won them over to accepting me as me, and not as a *gringa*.

I never got over being frightened of the slippery adobe roads after a rainstorm. Trying to change a flat tire on such a road was hell. Being stuck after nightfall in the mud, alone on a wagon trail, wasn't fun — especially when the coyotes howled. Yet the sunny days and the long mountain drives made up for the horror of slippery mud. When I ate my lunch in a quiet spot on the side of a mountain, there was such peace in the blue-purple quietness of the Sangre de Cristo Mountains.

Gradually, as I discovered the 32 known villages in my 1,000-square-mile district, I became aware that others were working in the same district. Farm Security Administration was active in El Pueblo. Soil Conservation seemed to be working in other areas. The Works Projects Administration appeared in still other parts. Probably there were others of which I wasn't aware. The chap in charge of WPA was a trained social worker. I talked with him, and we came up with the idea of organizing a Council of Social Agencies. He sent out a call to all agencies that dealt with people's welfare to send representatives to a dinner meeting at the Harvey Hotel in Las Vegas. Through the consecutive meetings I learned many things. Each agency reported on its objectives, and where we overlapped we tried to work together. For example, I found out that Farm Security was using El Pueblo as an experimental village, to teach improvement in livestock, housing, latrines, canning — all things related to healthful living. I was working toward the same goal through the well-baby clinics, the maternal clinics, immunization round-ups, and so forth. From then on we worked together, pooling cars, materials and efforts.

I loved the northeastern corner of New Mexico where my district lay. In many ways I had never lived so well or been as happy as I was in Las Vegas, New Mexico. After working there for three years, I felt like an oldtimer and could stay on a horse with the best of the cowboys. I was socially useful, which obviously was necessary to my well-being. I had earned the respect of the New Mexican Spanish-speaking Americans. The occasional scorpion that interfered was the visits of the FBI.

I always heard about it when the doctor would jokingly ask, "What on earth has the fact that you were in Spain got to do with reducing infant mortality?"

"Oh, the FBI were checking on me," I answered. "What did you tell them?"

Our wonderful health officer, Dr. Eilers, had been born and raised in the West. He had lived on Indian reservations as a child. He had helped his doctor father practice medicine among the Indians. To me, he represented the honest, straight-thinking Westerner. I admired and respected him. He had done his postgraduate work in public health in a large Eastern university. He was always cagey with newcomers from the East; but once we earned his respect as workers in the health program, he backed us. He had told the FBI that I was dedicated to my work in public health, the infant death rate was going down in my district, my relations with other agencies were good, and that he could not see what that had to do with the fact that I had gone to Spain or that I had been a communist, as the FBI had said.

Next the FBI approached our maternal and child health physician. She gleefully told me, "And you know my dog never bites, but he bit the two FBI men."

Later I heard that they had gone to the State Directress of Public Health Nursing, another Westerner and an amazing, competent leader in the field of public health nursing. At Teacher's College, Columbia, I had studied public health; but here in New Mexico, and under the direction of the health officer and supervisors, I was really learning and putting into practice good public health nursing. The proof was the lower infant and maternal mortality rate. In the state office, the FBI men were also rebuffed. I knew of few agencies or organizations that would have done this. Most organizations fired workers if they were suspected by the FBI.

I suppose they were trying to add material to my dossier. As I said before, they were like scorpions, and I never knew which of the scorpion bites might prove fatal. Naturally I was always upset after discovering the FBI had made the rounds questioning about me. Maybe my acute, almost hysterical fear and complex about police and the FBI went back to my factory days. But the health authorities helped me feel safe, since they always protected me on the basis of my work as a public health nurse. I might never have left New Mexico, and I certainly had no intentions of leaving, but Mary Lee became ill again. This was her fourth attack of rheumatic fever. The first had gone unrecognized in New York City. The second attack had kept her in bed almost six months. The third attack in New Mexico had been very mild, but this fourth one was serious.

The night the diagnosis was verified, I burst into uncontrollable chills and weeping. It was almost too much to bear. I had to do something drastic. Dr. May Wilson's book on rheumatic fever had demonstrated that the number of cases sent to hot, humid climates had had no recurrences. They had gone to New Orleans and to Puerto Rico. Where we were in New Mexico, the temperature sometimes dropped to 13° below zero. At noon it might be warm enough to shed coats and sweaters. When a cloud passed over the sun, the temperature would drop with a bang. Mary Lee just could not take these extreme changes without getting a cold, a sore throat, and rheumatic fever.

I tried to bring my weeping into control. I did not want her to hear me and become frightened. Her father had died from it. I had a slight lesion. And I knew that if Mary Lee had another attack like this one, statistically she could be dead before she was 25 years old. I had to fight against another recurrence. She had escaped heart damage up to now. Would she, could she escape it with this severe attack?

I had to get her to a tropical climate. How? I earned $150 a month. I lived from paycheck to paycheck. Tires had to be bought, car repairs made. Our cars took an awful beating on the rocky wagon trails. I had no money saved. Payments on the car came every month. But I had to get her out of this climate — for her very life. When I came to New Mexico, I had thought I was coming to a warm climate, but had found it far from warm. With real regret, I planned to leave New Mexico. The state had a vastness, a dignity, a oneness with which I felt at ease. My heart wept to leave this part of the United States, which at last I had felt was home.

The red chilies drying on the walls of pastel-shaded adobe houses, the aspens turning golden on the mountain sides, the fluid, soft song of the Spanish language, the trips by horse up Old Baldy at the top of Gallinas Canyon, and even the discomforts of dangerous roads when muddy or the fording of the Pecos River by car I would miss. Yes, I loved this corner of New Mexico and did not want to leave; but if Mary Lee was to have a future at all, I had to get her to the tropics.

I applied for a position as a public health nurse in New Orleans, Florida, Hawaii, and Puerto Rico. I received good offers from the Hawaiian Islands and from Puerto Rico. I tossed a coin, and it fell for Puerto Rico.

By selling everything I absolutely could do without, like car chains for ice and snow, I managed to get enough money together for the trip to Puerto Rico. But first I had to get Mary Lee settled where she could continue her convalescence. She went on ahead by air to her grandmother's in Port Chester, New York. The passing years had made things easier between us. This was especially true since she and her daughter had come out to visit us in New Mexico, and I had had a chance to give them the hospitality of my home.

When I got to Port Chester, Mary Lee's sedimentation rate showed that there was still some rheumatic fever activity. The doctor felt it was better that she stay there until I was settled in Puerto Rico. It was summer, and there was no danger of bitter cold weather, which she could not take. Of course, I had no idea that it might be difficult to find a home on the island. Hitler was blasting his way across Europe. It was 1940, and our armed forces were moving into Puerto Rico. I just told Mary Lee that in about six weeks she would follow me to Puerto Rico.

Lounging on the boat I tried to push out of my mind the fears of a new job, a new environment, the problem of housing and furniture, the language difficulties, and a good school for Mary Lee. The important matter was that Mary Lee had again escaped heart damage. My car, containing the few things I never parted with, was in the hold of the ship. Public health nursing positions demanded that one own a car. I had driven my Ford across country, and now it was ready to be driven off the boat.

The island of Puerto Rico loomed in sight in the incredible blue Caribbean Sea. Big, powerful, white clouds played overhead in a blue sky reminiscent of New Mexico. Green mountain tops stuck out of the ocean. It was a beautiful island. The Directress of Nursing met me at the pier. As soon as I got a chance, I asked her about housing. It was difficult, but she would help me. I didn't tell her that to have my own home was a psychological must. By baking a cake or cutting and sewing a dress I often dissolved my insecurities and depressions based on fear — fear for Mary Lee's health and the fear of losing a job. In the evening I felt sheltered if I could peek in and see my daughter happily asleep and could go back to an armchair and listen to a record. This island of peace was essential to me. I had not had what one could call a loving home when I was a child.

Puerto Rico had been the fourth most densely populated is- Air Force, the WPA, the NYA, the FSA, and all the rest of the letter agencies of Roosevelt's period were on the island. All I wanted was a kitchen and two rooms. Although I had never accepted the word "impossible" since childhood days, I had to accede to it temporarily. The chief of public health nursing took me to a home where I might get room and board. She said, "Of course, they are more Spanish than Puerto Rican."

This she said in a manner as if to say the Spanish belonged to the human race, but she doubted if the *puertoriqueños* did. I had already suspected that she was on the other side of the fence from me and that, to her, public health meant only statistics and not men, women and children.

Out of necessity I rented a large room and bath in a house where the bloody red and gold flag of Franco's Spain was draped around the dictator's picture. I earned $175 a month. My room and board for the two of us was $100 a month. I had to take the room and keep my mouth shut until I could find an apartment for just the two of us. They were a boring family, but when I heard that their married daughter was leaving New York City for Puerto Rico with her children, her maid, her nursemaid, and so forth, I could not resist asking if Mary Lee could come down with them. They agreed, and I made necessary arrangements to have Mary Lee brought to the boat.

In the meantime, I threw myself into studying what was to be my job and how it was to be carried out. My job was that of maternal and child health consultant in the Public Health Department of the island of Puerto Rico. I wanted to know the morbidity and death rates on the island, since with that information it is possible to figure out the economic conditions of the people and the health services offered to them. I went from one corner of the island to the other. I saw the health units and the hospitals. I had never seen such filth, poverty, hunger and disease as I saw in the fall of 1941. Physically, it was the most beautiful bit of land I had ever seen in my life; yet the canker sore of poverty blighted it. In New Mexico I had almost forgotten all the isms — socialism, communism, fascism, among others, in the daily struggle against the elements and in the need for only one goal: Help people help themselves to health. They had disliked us at first, true; but gradually we had won the people with our sincerity and actions. How could one climb over or break the intense wall of hostility the *puertoriqueños* had for us Americans from the United States, the mainland?

On this little island feelings ran high. Many were Nazi

sympathizers; others argued the virtues of Hitler versus Franco; and it seemed the so-called "best people" were mostly Franco admirers. The sugarcane workers, the unemployed *puertoriqueños*, didn't like any of them, including Americans. How could I tell them that I was for them and with them? Could I say, "I hate discrimination too, which my countrymen are bringing into the island against darker skins"? I also looked like a *gringa*. I knew that in time, by actions rather than words, they would accept me and not discriminate against me for looking like a *gringa*. This was somewhat like New Mexico, but more difficult. At times there were overt acts to show we were not wanted. The *puertoriqueños* wanted independence from the United States. I wished I had one liberal I could talk to. It was lonesome keeping my mouth shut when I wanted to shout, "Look out for those Nazis! Look out for Franco's Falange! We, too, may be in this war. They are our enemies."

Then one afternoon I was asked to go to a cocktail party at the home of a public health physician, a black from Harlem who was doing a study in one of the health units. As I listened to some of the university professors talk openly in positive terms of ideas that I believed in, I felt at home. They tried to find out where I, the newcomer to the island, stood. I took a drink and played dumb. I felt like shouting to the professor who asked the most leading questions of me, "Don't you remember me? You organized a meeting for Spain on the campus of the University of Chicago. I was the speaker." I kept quiet. Their boss was Rexford Tugwell; mine was a reactionary Catholic. Tugwell had a long record of intellectual honesty. I wanted to join in the discussion, but I had to keep my job and not be stranded.

I did ask leading questions to find out more about the island. They were answered by the professors, a mixed group of teachers from the United States and Puerto Rico, all of whom taught in the University of Puerto Rico. I heard that the majority of the working population earned less than $200 a year. The illiteracy rate was 41%. The death rate from tuberculosis was 258 per 100,000 population, a ratio which accurately indicated the economy of the given population.

On this poor island all foodstuffs had to be imported. The ocean abounded with fish, but dried fish was imported. Rice could grow here, but came from Louisiana. Every bit of available land was cultivated for sugarcane, and I suspected many of these plantation owners had never seen Puerto Rico.

Absentee landlords and feudalism, Puerto Rico and Spain — how similar it was! In New Mexico, no matter how poor the farmer was, the land was still his *tierra*, his land. We were the foreigners in New Mexico, but the state was big, and we didn't crowd them out. Here in Puerto Rico, with nearly two million people living on 3,500 square miles, the incoming Army, Navy, Air Force and federal workers were crowding the natives. Most of the incoming Americans acted superior to the natives and discriminated against them where it hurt the most, in wages. The mainland American got five or ten times as much money as the native Puerto Rican did for the same work. For example, I had a job which should have gone to a well-trained native public health nurse. There were not too many, but they did exist. In New Mexico, I used to feel guilty once in awhile for the behavior of Anglo-Americans, as we were called there, but here I felt guilty most of the time.

The stateside Americans called the Puerto Ricans "lazy" as they themselves sat at the bars every chance they got to drink their rum Collinses or Cuba libres. The Puerto Ricans who were lucky enough to have a job worked even when they felt sick, and most of the time they were sick. Eighty percent of the population had energy-sapping hookworms. When the majority of the population does not have enough money to buy sandals or shoes, hookworm is the result, especially in the tropics. Not only did they have the hookworm burrowing in their muscles, but the malaria organism was also rampant. I wondered how many of the "let's have a drink" Americans could cut sugarcane with either hookworm disease or malaria in their bodies and sometimes both! The infant and maternal death rates had been about four times as high as those for the United States in 1939 and 1940. Needless infant and maternal deaths especially infuriate me!

Where a bulldozer was needed to do effective public health, a little beach shovel was being used. Then the bulldozer arrived. I say that affectionately, since Dr. O.C. Wenger of the United States Public Health Service was a man who moved mountains to get work done in public health. He cursed like an old army man, especially if he liked you. I adored and admired him. I knew him from New Mexico when he had come out to see what we were doing in the Venereal Disease Program. Many a time he shocked doctors and staid nurses with his gusto and his use of any and all publicity methods to achieve results. Who in the Venereal Disease Program will forget the parade and the publicity in Chicago that he and his pal, Dr. Herman Bundensen, sponsored? Of course, he had a one-track mind — venereal disease. That never bothered me, since when searching for VD, other conditions could be uncovered and prevented.

Most public health workers have their special interests. Dr. Mountain used to say, "Every home that does not have an indoor toilet must have a latrine. A latrine in every home, and death rates will come down." My special interest was maternal and infant welfare. Dr. Wenger was happiest when he had hundreds and thousands being tested for syphilis. I think one of the funniest things I have ever seen was Dr. Wenger walking ahead of a group of nuns, leading them to have their blood tested for syphilis. I wonder what he told them.

Federal Works Administration announced it was going to set up a work project in health. There was some fantastic sum of money available to employ unemployed doctors, nurses and social workers, and also to train thousands of lay health workers to place in existing health units and in those to be established. Many were sure that America would not be neutral much longer and that Puerto Rico was a major defense for the

Canal. Dr. Wenger applied to the Health Department for me, and I became the Administrator of the WPA Health Service for Puerto Rico and the Virgin Islands. Of course, although Dr. Wenger's main idea was to use the funds for VD, mine was that the blood test for syphilis be a part of a complete medical exam to fight existing disease and to work at preventing more diseases. However, most important both to him and to me was that every cent of these government funds be spent honestly and effectively.

As usual with a new job, I was frightened, especially with this one. I was the first employee on the staff, and I had to build up a 1,600-worker project. I already knew the existing health services on Puerto Rico, so I crossed over to the Virgin Islands to study their needs. Doctors, nurses, nurses' aides, social workers, hospital workers, laboratory technicians, janitors, charwomen, and so on were being placed in existing units under the supervision of the Health Department. I had to develop and give in-service training to all incoming workers, introducing them to our objects and aims. Nurses' aides had to be trained in the arts of practical nursing. By now I had assistants, capable women who in time could be trained to take my place. (I was the only mainland person in the program.)

We divided the island into districts for supervisory purposes. We all learned about work flow and organizational charts. Through work and the possibility of achieving results, the miserable poverty and disease conditions on the island bothered me less. I was active in doing something about it. As the work developed and grew, I learned and grew with it in our efforts to make Puerto Rico a healthier island for its residents and the incoming armed forces and construction workers.

My salary had increased fifty percent on this job. I began looking for an apartment. Housing that had been built for those who came from the States with mainland wages was now available. Mary Lee and I disliked the home where we were boarding, and its inhabitants. We didn't like the food, especially when we competed with the flies as we ate it. We didn't enjoy the mosquito larvae floating before our eyes in the flower bowls as we ate. I did not enjoy having Franco stare at me from the wall.

We moved to a lovely, modern, new apartment. It had two bedrooms, living room, kitchen and bath. I bought the basic furniture needed. This was easy, as many families were leaving the island because of the threat of war. Mary Lee was doing well in school, and the climate of Puerto Rico was doing wonders for her. I liked my work very much. What I could not understand was why I should feel lonesome. I admitted to myself that I wanted to have dates, to go to dances, to be looked at as a woman, to marry again. Maybe I would not be lonesome if I made a point of associating with liberals on the island, but I was afraid of losing my job. If I lost my job, it might also mean upsetting a program which gave needed employment for necessary medical services to 1,600 workers. I could not afford the friendship of the liberals, with the FBI still chasing anti-fascists instead of chasing Nazis and fascists.

After a day's work, Mary Lee and I went to the beach. On Sundays we went to the beach. I met many men, naturally. Wives and children were leaving Puerto Rico for the United States, but the men stayed behind. They wanted a woman, but I didn't want them. I wanted a man who saw in me more than someone with whom to go to bed, a man who saw *me*! Yet when I met men who read, knew music, whom I thought of as intellectuals, I got tongue-tied. Or if not tongue-tied, I became bossy. I had a deep inferiority complex. Even the fact that I, too, had now gone to college didn't do much to obliterate it.

I was secure in my ability to do a job. I was most insecure in any relations with men. I was 35 years old, and yet I felt as if my insecurities were getting worse. My only creative outlet seemed to be cooking. The armed forces and the construction workers used rum and whiskey to ease their lonesomeness, and I used the cookbook.

Pearl Harbor! I was angry. I was shocked. I wanted to do something for my country. Yes, I say "my country." I had always loved America, even though I felt that America had never accepted me. I admired its past. I felt that Roosevelt was helping us through a difficult transitional period. I longed for the potential greatness of America. I thought of myself as an idealist, a socialist, a humanist, a democrat, and an American. At this time I belonged to no political organization. I was paying dues to the American Red Cross and the National Organization for Public Health. I was definitely an antifascist. I had been one of the preliminary ones in Spain. I wondered if we who had been in Spain would now be recognized as preliminary antifascists. Perhaps the FBI would stop harrassing us, stop causing us to lose jobs. We had fought fascism in 1937. Americans had died in Spain. Hardly anyone had listened to us then. Now we had to fight Hitler and Japan.

The training of lay workers for hospitals and public health units was now more important. We were the gateway to the Canal. Submarines sank ship after ship at our doorsteps. Horribly burned sailors were rescued. I threw myself into the work of preparing lay workers for more nursing care. It was the best way I knew to help my country.

It was fascinating to watch the turnabout of many people who had loved Hitler, Mussolini, Franco — the racists. They had believed in fascism, in anti-Semitism, in keeping the black in his place. Suddenly they were not 100 percent American, but 150 percent antifascist. They became active in civil emergency organizations. I hoped that some of them were not spies, informing on ship movements. I was quite sure some of them must be, as ships kept on being sunk. The Nazis seemed to know all about our maritime movements. The FBI stopped harrassing us and began collecting data from the anti-Nazis. For example, one doctor had kept a photo file of all Nazi and fascist meetings on the island. The FBI now cultivated him for information. What a relief! I no longer had to keep quiet about having been in Spain, for fear of losing a job. Now we were all in the same fight together. America had been attacked by the Axis.

The harder I worked, the more lonesome I became. I did not have the courage to admit to myself that I needed a man in my life. I created messes in my personal life. I thought I loved a *puertoriqueño*. Yet the man I liked around me, who often came to eat with us, was a photographer twelve years younger than I named Lee Pitman. When he began dropping by my home and sitting with us at the beach, I was thrilled. He had written poetry. He was making a movie for the National Youth Administration when I first met him, and he did not make any passes at me. I was flattered. Maybe he was seeing me, the inside me. Now he had finished the film and talked of joining the Army.

As I was being transferred to the mainland to work on a national, federal-level project, I hoped Lee and I would meet again. My job was being taken over by a young woman I had trained, a *puertoriqueña*. This pleased me, as I felt strongly that we outsiders should be used for training persons, leaving the nativeborn in the jobs.

Very few boats were getting through to their destination. The submarine pack of the enemy was in full operation. Insurance was high on anything being shipped. Again I sold my furniture and, this time, my car. I packed one trunk with things important to me, and I hoped that the boat would not be sunk. It was out of the question to go home by boat. We had to go by airplane. I had few regrets about leaving the island, though I had learned much through my work there. I had been lonely, but my daughter was in better health than she had ever been and was brown from the rays of the sun.

Puerto Rico was fantastically beautiful, geographically speaking; but it was an unhappy, impoverished island. Americans from the States were coming in by droves. The islanders called us "carpetbaggers." They did not like us, and I felt it. I felt uncomfortable because of the behavior of drunken Americans. I resented the brash, discriminatory practices they brought with them. The Puerto Ricans, also our countrymen, were being treated worse than the New Mexicans of Mexican and Indian extraction. I liked the Puerto Ricans, but to them I was just another American. Did that account for my frustration and loneliness on the island?

Mary Lee was glad to be leaving the island. She had never made friends with the sons and daughters of the officers of the armed forces in the private school she attended. As she often said, "They fight the battles of the Army, the Navy and the Air Force instead of studying." The Puerto Rican children didn't make friends with the American children, since most American children had been forbidden to play with them. It was not a good situation for a sensitive, intelligent, basically democratic, growing child. She remembered her grandmother with love and was anxious to go back to a place where there were four distinct seasons of the year. She wanted to see snow again.

I had priority to get out on a plane, but my daughter didn't. With the help of the Traveler's Aid Society, I managed to get her off the island and to Port Chester before I could leave. After two weeks of waiting at the airport, I managed to get to the United States. I had been concerned about Mary Lee, since I had had no word from her. But when I arrived at Grandmother Fuhr's home, I heard Mary Lee asking, "Where have you been, Mother? You took so long to get here I was worried about you."

It was summer when I left for Washington, D.C., and my child was well and happy with her grandmother. In the crowded city I managed to rent a room to use as a base. Most of the time I would be traveling, since my area of work would be from Washington south to the tip of Florida and west to the Mississippi River. Although many of the Federal Works Administration's projects were closing down due to rising employment, this was not true in the Southeast, where projects were being established specifically to help the war effort. I was to work with projects to bring men to treatment for their venereal diseases and to help them become noninfectious so they could be drafted into the Army or Navy.

As usual, I liked my job but was disillusioned with the top staff. I had thought that in the Service Division of FWA I would find people with real idealism. I was surprised to find myself the only one in the Health Section to have had specific training in public health. No wonder Dr. Wenger wanted me there. My own immediate boss pompously sat at his desk checking race sheets. Whenever I returned to Washington from a trip in the field, I first wrote my report, after which he had me check race sheets. He thought more of winning horses than of winning the war.

I traveled through Nebraska, Louisiana, Mississippi, Georgia, Florida, Tennessee, Kentucky and Alabama. The more I covered the territory, the more I wondered how a liberal white could live there. I would certainly not want my child to grow up in the South. Liberals had to accept discrimination in the South or get out. People who did not believe in racial discrimination had to live a lie.

I think what bothered me most was the senseless waste of money in hospitals. There were duplicate hospitals — one for blacks and the other for whites — duplicate sterilizers, duplicate pots and pans and dishes, duplicate staffs. I wondered why no one had thought of a means for separating the very air we breathed into two parts. The oxygen we breathed fed the same type of red cells, expanded the same kinds of lungs; but all externals had to be separate. The look of the second-class citizens, the hurt in their eyes, disturbed me. I did my job, but I didn't like the South one bit. I pitied any white liberal who had to live there. I thanked my ancestors for their white genes; but for an accident, they might have been black. I could think of nothing worse than to be a black person in the South of the United States.

Quite properly, one after another of the work projects we set up were taken over by state agencies. Unemployment no longer existed. There was work for all in the United States.

Naturally, the FWA, which had been set up in the Depression days to provide useful work, was closing down. We were to be the last. I knew that my job would not last many more months. Fortunately, I was able to save money on this job. While I was East, I intended once and for all to finish my work at Columbia toward my degree in public health. I planned to get some sort of housing close to the campus, to bring Mary Lee to New York City, and then to head west again.

My scheduled layoff was convenient, as it coincided with the beginning of the spring term at Columbia. I located a small room with kitchen privileges near Teacher's College. A widow friend of mine had the room across from me, with her daughter who was slightly younger than mine. Since my friend hated cooking and I loved it, we made a fine arrangement. I would do the cooking for the four of us, and my friend would do the cleaning. This meant we were sort of a family unit, two widows and their daughters. This gave at least a semblance of home life for our children. It was good to get away from the madhouse in Washington, and I hoped I would never set my feet in the South again.

Mary Lee got a half-scholarship to a private school, but I had to make $400 stretch for four months. I knew that as soon as I had my degree in public health I could almost pick my job. It was early 1942, and the heat was off the veterans who served in Spain. Russia was our ally. Franco was our enemy, and the veterans of the Lincoln Brigade had been among the first to enlist in the armed forces. I felt a bit guilty working as a student instead of working in the war effort, but I rationalized that when I had my degree I would get a more important job toward winning the war.

I loved being a student again. I always had to earn the tuition and food money first before I could go to school. Perhaps this made school more vital to me. Sundays were an extension of learning. Mary Lee and I lived in the museums of art and history.

I got long letters of endearment from Lee, the young man I

had met in Puerto Rico. He was now in the Army and editing the Army newspaper. By letter our friendship was developing faster than when we knew one another in Puerto Rico.

Bacteriology, sociology, mental hygiene, among other courses, kept me busy doing research and writing papers. The months flew. I had to begin thinking of work and where we would go. I was offered a position in Texas by the Farm Security Administration, which at this time was in charge of the health care of the Mexican farm laborers and the American migratory workers. I wanted nothing to do with Texas. The bigotry of the South had bothered me, and I was afraid that it might be the same in Texas. Chicago had an opening in the Venereal Disease Program for a Director of Epidemiology, Case Holding and Case Finding. My old friend, Dr. Wenger, hoped I would go there, since the first Rapid Treatment Center to use fever therapy and penicillin would be established in Chicago. With this method it was hoped that syphilis could be made noninfectious in a shorter time.

I was interested enough to take a train to Chicago in order to be interviewed by Dr. Herman Bundensen. En route, I wondered about my interest in Chicago. Was one reason the possibility that I wanted to be closer to New York in case Lee might come up from Puerto Rico? Through our correspondence I was beginning to fall in love with him. Another reason was that I had always admired Dr. Bundensen and his reputation in public health. He was unconservative at times, and so was I. The techniques used in Chicago got the job done, and it had the reputation of being one of the best public health setups in the country.

Following my interview with Dr. Bundensen, I knew I was hooked. The job sounded fascinating: Find the case, treat the person, search for the contacts, observe them, treat if needed, try to prevent the spread of more venereal disease, get the men ready for induction into the armed forces for World War II. This was called epidemiology, and I would be the Director. I worried about whether or not the climate would play havoc with my daughter, predisposed as she was to rheumatic fever. The doctors assured me that since she was now of menstrual age the danger was over. Her heart was undamaged after four attacks. I wanted it to remain undamaged.

In New York I finished my work and made arrangements to have the sheepskin mailed to me. Finally I had a degree in public health, eleven years after Wilbur's death. I had completed the four-year high school course in a year, but my degree in public health had taken me years. I wished I had the money to go on to study medicine, but I realized that this was improbable.

Puerto Rico, Washington, New York City — they all had housing shortages, but Chicago was the worst. Finally I found a one-room kitchenette apartment. In this apartment the bedbugs discovered me. I went to the office in the morning with either one eyelid swollen or my lips enlarged to twice their normal size. It was impossible to work all day and to do without sleep at night. The bedbugs conquered my Dutch thrift. I took a cab, found another place, and left the bedbugs and their landlady with the balance of the month's rent.

The second apartment was larger, with a living room which became a bedroom at night, a room for my daughter, and a decent size kitchen. Not a ray of sun filtered into the place, but it had no bedbugs. It was on 43rd and Drexel, one block away from the black district. This bothered others, but not me. I worked six days a week, eight to ten hours a day, and spent Sunday cooking, washing, ironing and cleaning. The term "venereal disease" was not allowed in our home on Sundays. I had enough of it during the week.

My office was in the largest Venereal Disease Clinic in the world. We had a caseload of 50,000 on file. The building had been the Red Schoolhouse. Now it was a clinic, which rattled and shook as the elevated trains went by. Dust and heat blew in the windows in summer, and in winter I froze. My job required trying to find all cases of veneral disease, their contacts and their sources, then holding them for treatment until noninfectious. This sounds easy, but since the organism which causes venereal disease usually enters through sexual contact, we had to deal with the problems of mores, guilt, social stigma, shame, and so forth, as well.

The left hand of the FBI never seemed to know what the right hand was doing. In the office I was helping them in their work, but two others went to call on the Director of VD Control for the city of Chicago and asked him, "Isn't she subversive? Don't you think she is a communist? Isn't she a socialist?" To this day I think his answer was priceless, "No, I don't think Mrs. Fuhr is a socialist. She has thrown out the social work approach on the job and put in one based on the germ, a public health approach." He further told the FBI that our department was breaking the record for the nation in getting cases under treatment, keeping them, and sending them into the armed forces. I heard all this from a co-worker, who happened to be in the main office when the FBI called on Dr. Bauer, the Director. I felt secure that Dr. Bauer would not fire me, since he was more interested in the control of venereal disease than the fact that I had been in Spain. Someday I might be fired for this, but now I hoped that fascism would be defeated in this war and that a brave new world would arise.

This was the first and last time that I cooperated with the FBI. They had molested me and had threatened our bread and butter, yet now I was working with them. They had to find missing draft evaders. We had to find the missing draft evaders who had a venereal disease. Often they were one and the same. I took an impish delight when our staff found them first.

The FBI boys generally followed the same pattern: young lawyers, crewcut, with little sensitivity or imagination. Now we were working together. I wanted fascism defeated and prayed that my beloved aunt and uncle and my cousins would survive the Nazis in Holland. The FBI had to help get the men into the

Army, and I did too. But when they questioned me about one of my staff, I felt like telling them to go back to school and study what socialism and communism and idealism are all about. The woman about whom they questioned me had never been a communist. She was a liberal of the New England school of democracy — philosophical, nonorganizational liberals. I tried to explain to them that she was not a communist and felt like saying, "Good Lord, boys, I was a member of the Communist Party. I know who is and who isn't."

I thought it strange that they did not realize at the time that they were talking to an ex-member. Not that I was down on Russia at that time, not at all. I admired Russia's fighting, but somehow or other, after my return from Spain, I had less and less patience with the individual, dogmatic Party members. I had not rejoined in New York or in Chicago. The Communist Party seemed to be making all efforts through their membership to help win the war. I was doing the same, but through the channels of my job.

During this period, two things occupied my mind besides my job. One was a great joy, and the other, a worry. The correspondence with Lee that had begun when I left Puerto Rico had become more meaningful. Letters came to me almost daily, and I wrote daily. We began talking of marriage when he came home on a furlough. He was scheduled to become a photographer-reporter for the Army magazine *Yank*. All the love and warmth of which I was capable I poured forth to him in my letters. Overlooking the fact that there was an age difference of twelve years between us, I hoped we would be married when he came back to the States before he went overseas.

On the other hand, I was frightfully concerned about Mary Lee. In the uneven, damp, cold winter climate of Chicago, she had cold after cold. Her red blood count was going down. Tests showed activity against a disease. We were giving her sulfa drugs in small doses. Penicillin was not available. The Rapid Treatment Center had some, but it was scarce. I was afraid I would have to leave Chicago and get to a warmer, more even climate again to prevent another rheumatic fever attack.

In January, 1943, Lee came to Chicago. We talked about marriage. I raised my objections about the age difference, yet I wanted to marry him. I loved him, and I wanted to be a wife and mother again. Mary Lee liked him. We married. Within a few days after our marriage, he left for the China-Burma-India theater of war as *Yank* correspondent. I was sad to see him go, but happy to be his wife.

I worried more about Mary Lee as she grew more and more pale. Her red blood count went down to a dangerous low of 55%. The doctor began doing cultures on samples of her blood, looking for the *hemolytic streptococcus*, strain A, which had killed her father. Mary Lee was almost thirteen years old. She was in danger, and we had to get to a warmer climate. I explained my problem to Dr. Bundensen and asked for my release. He understood and gave me a letter of introduction to the Director of Venereal Disease Control for the City of Los Angeles. I hated to give up my job, which had been exciting, but it could go on very well without me. The staff was united and well-trained. One of the supervisors of the Women's Section of the clinic took my place. By now it was late spring, 1943. We left for California.

I hoped that the FBI would be far behind me in this change and would not catch up with me until I had had a chance to prove myself on a new job. It appeared as if they had been catching up with me at closer intervals. I wished they would spend more time chasing Nazis instead of anti-Nazis. I often wondered why they seemed to concentrate more on me than other nurses who had been in Spain. I was to discover the reason later. Outside of occasional meetings where I spoke on the right of Spain to be free after the war was won, I was only fighting disease. What on earth was subversive about fighting venereal diseases? I felt as if I were a hard-working American patriot while on my job, and certainly when I gave pint after pint of blood to the Red Cross. I had never done anything destructive against the United States. All my working years had been constructive in the field of public health. Obviously, the FBI did not agree.

Within a week after my arrival in Los Angeles, I began working in the Venereal Disease Control Section of the Los Angeles City Health Department. The idea was to put into action the system of IBM cards we had used with such success in Chicago. This saved much manual labor, and the time saved could be utilized in finding the case and the contact and getting them under treatment. Unfortunately, Los Angeles had no Dr. Bundensen to sweep away objections, deadwood, and antique methods of work in public health.

I was shocked with the lack of quality of the people who worked in the VD Section. Most had been swept in with civil service when they should have been swept out very fast. They were untrained, but what was worse and what made them impossible as workers were their biases. I have never met so many haters under one roof in one service. They hated Jews; they hated blacks; they hated Protestants. They were filled with hate against people instead of hate against that which destroys people — in this instance, the germs that cause venereal disease. No wonder patients hated to come here for treatment. The top leadership in the Health Department were good people, but their hands were tied by civil service plus the wartime shortage of trained personnel. My hands were tied also, and I could accomplish nothing. Organizational and supervisory lines recrossed and got fouled up, with the result that the venereal disease rate was rising in Los Angeles. My abilities were not being used. I was disgusted.

Only three months after I had come to work, the FBI called on my boss, the doctor in charge of the program. It followed the same pattern, "Do you think she is a communist? She was a nurse in Spain, you know. Does she act subversive?" The doctor told them to call on me and ask me. He thought it amusing and told me about it. I was annoyed and phoned the FBI and told them to come to see me personally if they wanted to find out what I was doing, and I'd give them a good explanation of my work on how to control venereal disease. They paid no attention to me, of course.

Mary Lee was fine. The change to a sunny climate had done wonders for her. Her color was good, and the danger of another attack of rheumatic fever seemed to have passed. Lee was excited about his work as a *Yank* correspondent. His letters constantly flowed to me and mine to him. All the allotment checks that I received I put into the bank, since I thought he could use the money after the war to buy equipment for his work as a photographer. We had a nice apartment, which Mary Lee and I had painted. We had scraped and polished early American furniture until the pieces gleamed like amber. The only thing I didn't like was my inability to work, through no fault of mine. The doctors, who liked their soft jobs, preferred us to do nothing — to not "stir things up." When I was offered the position of Supervisor of the Medical Services for the Health Care of the Mexican-imported Nationals and the American Migratory Workers, I took it. The Director of the VD Section understood and accepted my resignation.

Frankly, I was fed up with the word "venereal disease." It seemed that during the last few years all I had done was work in this field, as if no other preventable death existed. I had always preferred the generalized public health program, where one saw the individual as a whole and as part of his environment. In the job I was going to, I would have the opportunity to put democracy into action in supervision. I could acquire staff workers who were not filled with hate for their fellow men, but rather those who would join me in trying to lower the illness and accident rates among the Mexican workers.

I had known of the work of the Farm Security Administration since the time I worked in New Mexico, and we had kept in contact with one another ever since. When they offered me the job in Texas, I had refused it. During the depression years they had set up a health care program for the migratory workers' camps. Now they were no longer called the FSA, since Agricultural Workers' Health Associations had been set up. However, the funds came under the budget of the Department of Labor, which placed the workers and moved them to the areas where they were needed, and the Health Association was responsible for their health care. California was one of the most important states and had the most imported farmworkers, mainly from Mexico. There was a contract between the U.S. government and the Mexican government relating to conditions of work and health care. My responsibility was to see that adequate health care was given to the Mexican *braceros* and the American migratory workers in southern California.

The medical chief of our program was a public health man, which meant that he saw the program as one of preventing accidents and illness. We hoped to achieve the lowest accident and illness rate, in terms of loss of work days, through an educational approach, by setting up medical services where the workers picked the fruit and worked the fields. This meant teaching the growers, mainly the Orange Growers Association. It meant teaching the workers to report any illness or accident, no matter how minor, in order to prevent major problems.

It was not always easy to sell the growers on the need of cooperating in the establishment of clinics in the camps. This was especially true with the small growers' associations, who used stoop labor to pick vegetables. The larger growers' associations, like the citrus fruit growers, were interested in getting the most fruits picked. It was easier to show them that giving the Mexican the food he liked to eat, which was adequate for nutrition, giving him a place to bathe, a good cot to sleep on, and safe drinking water helped lower the absentee rate. They also understood and helped in the program of evening entertainment such as English classes and movies. Near every camp where the Mexican workers lived, prostitutes had established themselves and were particularly active on payday. Entertainment might keep down the incidence of syphilis and gonorrhea. I knew the workers would not be problems. They wanted to work, keep well, and send money home to Mexico.

When I joined the program, it was a mess. Mexican consuls were disgusted with us. The growers didn't understand and were angry. Work camps were striking. With well-chosen help, nurses selected for their warmth of heart and lack of bias, things improved rapidly. We secured physicians to be on the medical panels where the workers were, so that medical care could be secured rapidly. Naturally, the men were screened first by the nurse. For example, often the new men came in and complained of colds, grippe, headache. We had discovered that what they needed was some attention. A soft, gentle word from the nurse, a word as to their importance in helping get the crops in, a question about their family and children at home, followed by an aspirin, usually cured them.

I had tried to acquire public health nurses for our rapidly growing staff, but they were not to be found. Then I located some of the nurses I had known in Spain. They knew some Spanish and would not act superior to the Mexican worker. When a work camp felt a superiority complex on the part of the *gringo*, they became uncooperative and started what they called *tortugismo*, or turtle action, which was nothing more than a slowdown strike. As standards went up in our organization, nurses who did not or could not comply with the standards resigned and were quickly replaced by nurses who could help us meet the government's contract with the workers as it related to their medical care. These women had not had public health training, so I began monthly in-service training courses. I encouraged those living near the university to take courses in public health. In areas where I had four or five nurses at work, I chose as local supervisor the one who already was the best liked and to whom the rest always turned for help. This worked fine and made my supervisory job easier. I could not be in every nook and cranny of southern California, south to the border and north to the San Joaquin Valley.

Within a year we had the lowest accident and illness rate in the nation — a fact attested to by the Public Health Manual of the USPHS for that year — and were running it at $2 per man per month. Certainly, I had not done this. I was only the catalyst, the administrator. It was the result of democratic action in supervision and the work of the staff all over southern California.

I had never had a job that I liked as much as this one. I had begun it with less fear of the FBI bothering my boss about me. As usual, I had been worried that I could not do it well. Now, due to an efficient and warmhearted staff, it was running smoothly. Naturally, there were problems — especially after a Mexican national holiday when the men had had a few too many drinks while celebrating Mexican independence, and a brawl, with injuries, followed. Yet in the years I was administrator of the program, no Mexican national was accused of robbery, rape, or any other offense. They had fights between themselves on occasion, but my district supervisors were well-equipped to handle the problems as they arose. Major problems were cleared with me, emergencies by phone and non-emergencies by discussion at the site where the worker was located. My technique was to ask the supervisor, "How would you solve it?" Nine times out of ten the answer was correct, and she had needed just a bit of reassurance.

My daughter was in high school and doing well scholastically. Her girlfriend from Taos, New Mexico, was spending the summer with us. The Russians were beating the Germans at Stalingrad. We were retrieving lost ground in the Eastern Theater of war. My husband was safe in Calcutta, India, and I hoped that he might come home soon. Perhaps, finally, I could achieve my cherished dream of being a wife, a mother (I hoped to have more children), and a homemaker. I had not had that chance since Wilbur died in 1931. Life was good. The

FBI seemed to have forgotten my existence. Mary Lee and I had many friends by now in Los Angeles. It appeared as if a happy future stretched ahead of me.

It was interesting how our circle of friends had begun. I had been busy almost every waking hour of the day. No matter where I was, I had to be near a phone or had to check in. I was on call every hour of the day. This meant I had little time for social life. But one day I was in the elevator going to my office when I noticed the symbol of the International Brigade on the other passenger's lapel. I couldn't resist asking about it. With surprise in his voice he answered, "How do you know this symbol?"

I answered with pride, "I know it. I was a nurse in Spain on the Madrid front. I cared for many a man from the International Brigade."

He had been with the Lincolns of the International Brigade and introduced me to other veterans and their wives, many of whom I had known in Spain. We began having picnics together on Sundays and reactivated the chapter of the Veterans of the Lincoln Brigade. We wanted to organize meetings, speak and keep the concept of the Spanish Republic alive in the eyes and ears of Americans. Of course, we thought that when Hitler, Mussolini and Japan fell, Franco would fall with them. On many occasions, at small house parties, I now spoke on Spain from the viewpoint of a nurse who had been there.

These veterans had been wonderful soldiers in Spain. Now I saw them as family men, good fathers and husbands, working in responsible jobs. I hoped that Lee would find friends among them. Since I wrote as much as I could in my daily letters to him, he knew something about them. He knew who played chess, who were interested in photography, and so forth. Men need men, as women need women. I remembered Lee from Puerto Rico as a rather shy man who liked to be near me but who did not make acquaintances readily. I was outgoing, and he, the reverse, which seemed to be good for both of us.

Now I discovered that Lee would be transferred to San Francisco. Suddenly I got panicky and felt insecure. I recalled that he did not like fat women, and I was fat. I wore a size 16, so I began dieting like mad. Judy, a friend of mine, took me to Bullocks's and helped me pick out clothes. I remember them well: a huge hat, a smart dress and high-heeled shoes, the sort of clothes I normally never wore. Actually I liked clothes, but paid little attention to them other than keeping them neat. I never bought makeup of any kind, although once in a while I used a bit of lipstick. Now Judy showed me how to use makeup.

I was in such a nervous state that Lee and I missed one another at the train station and met at home. I felt him withdrawing from me. I was happy to see him. I was proud of the home I'd gotten together, and I showed him the bankbooks with all the allotment money saved — for him. He resented my caressing him. At night I woke up with nightmarish sweats, trying not to face the truth that my husband didn't like me or my clothes or the home. In the daytime I would not allow these thoughts to rise to the surface. I loved him with an adult love. I dreamed of sharing a future together with children to raise. What did he want? I could not ask him. I was in my late thirties, and he, in his late twenties. Yet it was not the barrier of age between us.

When we wrote to one another while he was in San Francisco, it seemed all right again. When we were physically together, a wall appeared. Now he was discharged from the Army and would be home for good. I hoped I could do all in my power to make him happy, and us, too — Mary Lee and me.

Mary Lee had liked Lee in Puerto Rico, and she had been pleased when we married, but now she was changing in her attitude toward him. Mainly, Mary Lee liked her canvas and paints. Lee liked photography. He taught her how to make solutions for developing and darkroom work. He teasingly called her "the darkroom slut," and that finished Mary Lee as his helper. I had enough to do and had no intention of doing darkroom work. I found myself getting a complex against photography and the money it cost. All that I had saved was spent, and to what purpose, since Lee was turning down jobs as a photographer? When I asked him, "Why do you turn down photographic jobs?" he answered, "I am lucky to have escaped death, flying over the Hump to China. I'll never do what does not interest me. I will only work at that which is creative for me. Now I want to write."

Since he would not make any effort to work for money, I had to do so, but I had patience with him because I loved him and thought perhaps this was an adjustment period. I gave up my cherished dream of staying home and instead kept working, but little things bothered me as time went on. Now it was washing and ironing for three — men's shirts, dishes, cleaning on Sunday, shopping on my way home from the office, cooking for three and never having anyone say, "Gosh, this tastes good." Mary Lee had withdrawn into a shell. I was afraid of losing Lee, so I shut up.

He wanted a child. Maybe that would help. I was happy to tell him that I was pregnant, but it didn't help, because now I had the discomforts of pregnancy also. I wanted to quit my job and force him to take over the role of husband, but how could I? I could not ask him to assume responsibility for Mary Lee.

Fundamentally, I was such a healthy peasant that I managed my work, my home, and everything. Emotionally, I was under a strain, getting fatter, heavier all around and protruding in the front. My husband was uncomfortable seeing me, especially if others were present. Fat women repulsed him. Not only was I fat, but I was pregnant, too. It was a relief, after serving breakfast and washing the dishes, to go to the office where I forgot him and my personal problems.

One morning in the office the phone rang, and my assistant handed it to me saying, "It is for you."

I answered, and a man's voice said, "This is the Federal Bureau of Investigation."

"And what do you want?" I asked.

"It has been called to our attention that you are vulnerable under the Hatch Act. We want to talk to you. You can refuse to see us. Will you call us?" he asked.

This took my breath away. I was frightened. My baby flipped and tossed in me. My secretary asked, "What is the matter? You look upset."

I replied, "Oh, nothing. The baby is doing cartwheels."

I pondered. From what I recalled, the Hatch Act made it a criminal offense to mix in politics if one was a federal employee. I had not done so. I had been too busy helping workers keep healthy. I did know that if I refused to see them, they had grounds to report their suspicions to my boss. Consequently, I could lose my job. Good Lord, I was working for three, and a fourth on the way! I could not be without work. Then I got angry with myself for my fright. I phoned San Francisco and told my immediate superior about it. I told him that I was going to see them and not let them browbeat me. He told me that the Colorado supervisor had refused to see the FBI. (Her husband had been a communist, they said.) Consequently, the report of the FBI was sent to our main office, and she was fired. The director asked me, "Have you been active in politics? Are you vulnerable under the Hatch Act?"

I replied, "I am quite sure that all they want is information as to whom I knew in Spain or before that."

This was the first time that the FBI had contacted me personally. Usually they had gone to my place of employment and asked questions about me. It was spring, 1946. Since June, 1937, they had checked about me on every job I had held. Usually the worker got fired after such a visit, but I had been lucky so far, probably due to my interest in the job I was doing. I spoke to my husband, and he was panicky.

I decided I would let them interview me, but I'd be damned if they would get any names or places out of me. I'd talk public health, and maybe they would learn something about patriotism through fighting disease. I phoned them. They set the time for the very next day in their office.

I think I was in my sixth month of pregnancy. I remember wearing a gold-colored dress, but nothing hid my pregnancy. I entered the FBI office and was taken to a rather bare room with one desk, three bright standing lights, and four straight chairs. Three FBI men sat facing me.

They took turns asking me questions, and one with a steno pad took down the questions and answers. I no longer felt that I was on the offensive. I felt on the defensive. The whole setup frightened me. Was I in the United States of America or in Hitler's Germany?

The questions came fast, and I had no time to think. Whatever they wanted from me, they did not get. They asked, "Of those you knew in Spain, who are in Los Angeles? What are their activities? Are there people here whom you knew at Teacher's College in 1935? Why did you go to Spain? You were seen at a recent political meeting of the communists."

To that statement I replied, "It was not a meeting of communists. The meeting I attended was one in which a doctor delivered a speech on the proposed Wagner-Murray-Dingle Health Bill, which was a bill to further public health and preventive medicine; public health is my field of work. To all other questions and statements, about whom I knew, I questioned back, "What has this got to do with the Hatch Act?" I told them to give me proof of political activities, since they knew very well I spent my time fighting disease. Who I knew in Teacher's College or in Spain had nothing to do with the Hatch Act.

They mentioned names, and I contested with, "What has that got to do with public health?" I insisted on explaining what a good program of public health entailed. "If my long years in public health was politics, was unpatriotic, please explain that to me." My baby kicked inside of me as I got angrier and angrier at them for wasting my time trying to get information from me.

Three times I had to see them. Three times the questions were the same, about Spain and about my Teacher's College days. They wanted me to mention names, to agree I knew so and so. I contested with program planning in public health.

I was given my testimony to read. I corrected the spelling in spots and initialed my corrections. I told them this testimony was a good foundation for a paper on public health to present as a thesis. It was false bravado. The whole experience had frightened me. Policemen knocked down strikers with horses' hoofs. I remembered the brutality of police toward us when I was a factory worker. These men gave me the same fear, but they did it in a refined way with words and questions.

Of course I knew most of the people they were talking about. The majority of them were hard-working husbands and fathers, patriotic Americans who had done all they could to help win the war. It was none of the FBI's damn' business how they thought. Not even by a flicker of an eyelash would I admit to knowing them. I'd completely lost track of the people they asked me about, whom I had known at Teacher's College in 1937. Once in a while I might read about this educator or that one, but I knew nothing — except public health.

Obviously there was no evidence that I had been vulnerable under the Hatch Act, since no report to that effect was ever sent to our main office. I kept my job, my honor, and my self-respect. Communist Party people felt that I had been incorrect to take the position that I did. They said I should have refused to see them, but I didn't agree.

I wondered why they were bothering me personally at this time. Although we had won the war, obviously we had not destroyed fascism or those who believed in it. True, I was a member of the Los Angeles Chapter of the Veterans of the Lincoln Brigade and made occasional talks on Spain when requested. I would talk to anyone who would listen to me about the need of a national health bill, like the Wagner-Murray-Dingle. Fundamentally, the very program that I was in charge of was socialized, and I had been employed to establish it. It was working in all states where there were imported foreign workers, such as Mexicans out West and Jamaicans in the East. We were getting pats on the back for running this program at $2 per man per month, with the lowest number of workdays lost in the nation. Florida was costing $7 per man per month, but California was spending less federal funds with a better program. Basically the federal government ran this socialized medical program which employed me. It was the only obvious way to meet the terms of the Mexican and U.S. governments' contract relating to the health of the Mexican nationals.

I was interested in the Communist Political Association, as it was now called, but I was not active in it. I had a full-time job, which forced me to cover all of southern California and, once a month, to work in San Francisco. I had a growing daughter and a husband. I had a kicking bit of humanity within me. I was cook, laundress, seamstress and housekeeper, as well as Director of Medical Services for the Health Care of the Mexican National and the American Migratory Worker for Southern California. I had no extra time.

I told myself to stop worrying and fussing about my visit to the FBI. My husband had not liked it. I liked it less. I had the present to think of. I was almost due to give birth. Yet I did have a bit of extra time, which I gladly gave to Spain. Spain had done much for me, and I was honored to be part of the Veterans of the Lincoln Brigade. I am still honored to be able to be part of the Veterans of the Lincoln Brigade. I am still honored, and I shall always be honored because of how they fought to defeat fascism in Spain. They were idealistic, humanistic, and still are. I was not a veteran in the sense of being a soldier on the Madrid front, but I had been a nurse there. I was honored to have any veteran, from any country, who had fought in Spain against Franco, invite me to be with him. Was this anti-Americanism?

It was early evening, September 8, 1946, and the veterans were giving a small house party combined with a piano recital. The baby was quiet, which was rare, since it seemed to spend most of its time kicking me. I wondered if I would give birth soon. I still had about a week to go, I thought. I looked big. I felt huge, but this did not prevent me from singing, along with the vets and their wives, the songs we used to sing in Spain. It disturbed Lee that I had no shame in being out in a social gathering when I was emphatically pregnant, but it did not seem to bother him that I went to work daily. I had always thought and still think that pregnancy is a beautiful phenomenon, so I paid no attention and went on with my life. I refused to be ashamed of my figure at this point.

When we got home, I lay tensely beside my husband. I was miserable. I could feel his tug to break away. He was not happy. How could I be? I could not sleep and slipped quietly out of bed so as not to disturb him. I walked to the front yard and sat on a stone bench. Under the stars the smell of the night-blooming jasmine comforted me, and I had a feeling that the baby would be born soon, but I hoped not for a few days. The next day the state and national level people were to meet with me to plan how gradually to liquidate the program. The Mexicans were beginning to go back home, now that the war was over, and the program would be closed. After that, what? Jobs would not fall into my hands as before. The labor shortage was over.

The night fog came in, and I felt cold. Quietly I slipped back into bed. A sharp contraction awakened me about 1:30 in the morning, and I knew that this was it. I asked my husband to drive me to the Queen of Angels Hospital. The contractions came at frequent, regular intervals, and at 2 a.m. I was admitted. As the intern ordered the routine delivery procedures, I begged him to get me to the delivery room. But he was sure of his book knowledge of obstetrics, which assumed that, since I had just had my fortieth birthday and had not had a baby for sixteen years, my delivery would take hours. He ordered me to wait it out in the labor room and made me walk there, when I knew the baby would be born soon.

At 2:45 I rang the bell and hit the iron bed with a tin pan. I wanted a doctor! My child was demanding to be born. I felt the head coming. The nurse arrived and got me onto the stretcher, saying, "Pant! Hold your legs together! Don't let the baby be born!" I was too busy having contractions to answer, "You fool, and kill the baby?" Let me be torn due to bad obstetrical practice, but let me have a live baby, I thought as I worked along with the contractions.

I recall only vaguely getting on the delivery table. A tremendous upheaval was taking place within me, pushing at me, tearing me, as the baby fought to be born. I could feel the baby pushing downward, rotating. When they slipped the gas mask over my face, I felt the head come out. I was too busy helping with the work to push the mask away. I did not want anesthesia. I wanted to finish my work without it.

I heard the baby cry. What a glorious feeling! I looked at the delivery room clock. It was 3:15 a.m., September 9, 1946. Our baby was a girl, only seven-and-a-half pounds, and such a wriggly, noisy baby. I hoped that Lee might be happier now that he had a baby girl and was a father. Since he was almost always moody, I hoped he would express pleasure. I needed some warmth from him also. He did seem pleased and went home to sleep. I had worked hard in the deepest and most satisfactory sense as a woman. Come what may with Lee and our marriage, I would take care of Mary Lee and her new sister. I turned over and went to sleep.

Lee wanted the name Toby for our little girl. I wanted Roberta. She was named Toby. I wanted de Vries to be her middle name, in memory of my aunt and uncle who had died in German camps. One of our nurses who had been in Spain was named Toby — Toby it would be. Toby she is.

I am sure Queen of Angels Hospital and the nuns had never seen such goings-on before. My secretary came daily, and I dictated. From the phone near my bed, I supervised the job.

We had the meeting relating to the liquidation of the program on the 10th instead of the 9th. On the fifth day I went home and worked from there. When the baby was two weeks old, I returned to the office daily. I had hoped Lee would suggest that I stay home, but no such luck. Lee wrote and wrote and continued turning down any photography job which was not creatively stimulating to him. What could I do?

Although I had found a woman to care for Toby during my hours away from home, it was really getting tough: Push through the crowds at Grand Central Market before I went home. Pack myself with my bundles into the trolley car. Cook for three. Feed the baby. Sometimes stay up all night with a cross child. Mary Lee had a full-time high school schedule, and I couldn't ask her to help me. I preferred waiting until she asked to help with Toby. If I tried to make a slave out of Mary Lee, she might resent Toby and me.

Another problem was of great concern to me. A hard bone growth on my left wrist was growing rapidly, and I could hardly use my left hand. My hand was turned inward due to the growth, and the doctor suspected bone cancer. There was no way of knowing for sure until I could be operated on and a bone biopsy could be done.

Toby was now two months old, but I had to wait for the operation until the Christmas vacation in order to have Mary Lee take care of her. Mary Lee had become fond of her little, squirmy, opinionated sister. She was responsible, and I could depend on her. In that regard, Mary Lee was unusual at 16. She had been a quiet baby, but not Toby. I had never met such a determined baby. She napped when she wanted to. She ate at her convenience. Even at three months of age, when I entered the hospital for the bone operation, she had a forceful personality. I was constantly amazed. It was as if she wanted to walk, talk, express herself before the appointed age.

I could not rest until I had the report of the biopsy. It was negative for cancer. My arm was in a cast. Lord, it pained where they had sawed the extra bone away, but I didn't have cancer!

Now a real bombshell dropped on us. The landlady asked for the apartment we had fixed up so nicely, plus we would lose the expense of setting up the darkroom. The landlady's son was home from the Army and needed it. Los Angeles had an almost impossible housing shortage, but my husband rose to the occasion and thought of using his G.I. Bill rights to buy a house. He found a gorgeous view which had a horrible house on the land. It leaned in queer ways. The bathroom was unfinished. Termites ate the beams. It sat on the side of a steep hill. On the grounds were perhaps two places which had level spots of about two square yards. The rest was hill and more hill. Toby was not a mountain goat, and I feared for when she would begin to walk. The gardens were exquisite, but I wondered who would water and care for them. It had been one room, and the present owner, a retired carpenter, had added a small room after small room. On the ground floor were the kitchen, the bathroom (which lacked a toilet), a living room and a bedroom. Upstairs were two rooms. Lee took the largest room for his study, and another room became the darkroom, but there was still room for all of us.

I borrowed $2,000 from personal friends of mine to help buy the house. I did not like the house or its location, but I was glad to see him take over on something at least, so I said nothing. After we moved, I made it as attractive as I could. The five-minute climb up the steep hill, laden with bags of food after a hard day's work, didn't help my disposition. Lee had a car, which he said he needed, but I did without one.

It was 1947, and I was busy liquidating our program. Naturally I was liquidating myself out of a job also. I had to think in terms of continuing to earn a living for four of us. I took the civil service examination for a public health school nurse. I had thought it out carefully. With such a job I would have eight-hour days, all holidays, and the summer vacation, giving me more time for my home. The examination was easy for me. I never considered the fact that I might not be wanted: I had had a good education and experience in public health. After the exam, the applicants were interviewed by a group of women, all nurses. I assumed I stood a good chance of getting the job, since I met all the qualifications and then some.

Imagine my surprise, fear, and frustration when I received a notice that I had not been approved by the committee! I went to the school superintendent's office and showed him the card of introduction to him I had not used, as I had relied on my preparation and on civil service qualifications. He admitted that which I had suspected: I was considered undesirable, since I had been in Spain. The FBI had supplied lists of those who were considered undesirable, and I was on the list. The blacklist had reached me.

I was not desperate yet, since I was still employed closing down the program. Most of our equipment was being bought by a newly organized medical group which planned to give health care at low cost to the middle class and to union groups. Thank God, they offered me a job. The job would cover many aspects of administration, writing out and selling health insurance plans to unions, publicity, public relations, filling in as a nurse, and so on. I would have to continue to work more than eight hours a day, but since I was on the blacklist, I considered myself lucky to have a job — and especially with such a wonderful group of socially conscious doctors. Soon I loved my new work. I heard myself singing on my way to work, and I kept up the humming at work, where I felt wanted and useful.

At home I felt unwanted. When it came time to go home, black depression came over me. This splitting of my personality played hell with me, but I didn't get thinner, which might have helped Lee to like me more. Never before and never again did I have such nightmares. They are still vivid. Large, threatening, dark waves rolled toward me, and I could not escape. A man with a black sheet covering him approached me with a long, sharp knife. Trucks loomed on the road, trying to run over me, and I could not flee.

I worked bleary-eyed from lack of sleep. My headache and my heartache combined into one big ache. My menstrual periods became irregular, and I became suspicious that I might be pregnant. The day the doctor told me I was, I began having intermittent bleeding, and I hoped I would have a spontaneous abortion. Toby was only one year old, and I could not take lightly another pregnancy. I was breaking. If Lee looked crossly at me, I wept. I was desperate and, at times, wanted to die.

Early one evening the blood gushed out of me like a freshet. I asked Lee to phone the doctor and have him send an ambulance, but the doctor could not be located, and the hospital said they could not send an ambulance without a doctor's order. My pulse was fading. Air hunger set in. I knew the symptoms; I was bleeding to death. I whispered to Lee, "Tell them my pulse is imperceptible, and I'll be dead in less than an hour if they don't come with plasma ready to give me. Tell them I am a nurse and know!"

The ambulance came, and before they lifted me onto the stretcher, life-giving plasma was flowing into my veins. This was my third entrance into the hospital in one year. I knew that the doctor must scrape away the placenta that had not passed, from which the hemorrhage flowed. I heard him say, "She is in no condition to be operated on. We will pack her vagina and keep on giving her transfusions. Maybe, if she's alive, we can operate in the morning." They thought I was unconscious, but I wasn't.

Blood dripped into my veins on both arms. Plasma leaked into my thigh tissues. Suddenly I felt myself choking. Big, itchy welts swelled my lips, skin, throat. I felt myself hemorrhaging again, but I could not reach the bell to signal the nurse. With all the strength I had left, I hit the iron bed with a basin. Interns came; nurses came; a doctor came. I had been given the wrong type of blood. "Her blood pressure is 55 over 40," I heard the intern say. According to the textbooks, this meant death; but I would not die. I had to live for Toby and Mary Lee!

The doctor said, "Prepare for an emergency D and C. Her

only chance to live is if we do it immediately. She is near death."

I whispered, "I can't die. I must live. I have a baby."

He looked surprised to find me conscious and said, "Save your breath."

I was getting adrenalin intramuscularly. My body, too, was shooting out adrenalin, I was sure. I fought to live. I knew my chances of coming out of anesthesia were slight, but I kept fighting. I was alone. Lee was home sleeping. I hoped he would care for Toby if she awakened. I could count on Mary Lee if he did not hear her. The mask slipped over my face, and I slipped away into nothingness.

Light filtered through to my eyes, and I opened them. I was in a hospital bed. I was alive. I had won. My arms were pinned down with needles giving me life through whole blood. My legs were immobile with the dripping of plasma. God, it was good to be alive! Again I was living on borrowed time. I vowed to try to straighten up my messed life, but the nightmares returned as soon as I went home. Now I had a pain over my heart. I knew it was psychosomatic; nevertheless, it was a pain, the pain of an unsolved problem. How could I solve it?

Two weeks later I was back on the job, weak and exhausted but working.

Mary Lee finished high school with the highest honors and worked as a telephone operator in the summer vacation of 1947. She planned to go to the University of California at Berkeley, but not because she really wanted to go. She had been painting furiously and was influenced by a teacher who thought a painter did not need to go to college. I insisted, in my discussions with her, that she should go to college at least one year and then decide whether she wanted more education or not. With the example of her stepfather in the home, I pointed out that we were living in the 20th century and not in the days of patronage by kings in the 17th century. (Lee obviously was living in the wrong century. I had told him this when he said, "You are not an artist. I am. You must work in order that I can create.") I clinched my arguments with Mary Lee when I asked, "How will you earn the money to buy the tubes of paint and the canvas? Do you want to remain a telephone operator, or would you rather earn the money to buy materials by working in a field related to the arts, especially painting?"

She went to Berkeley and lived in one of the cooperative dormitories, working part-time as a telephone operator to help pay her way. I could not give her a cent. The money I had saved for her education had been used by Lee. The only future I had was to admit the fact that our marriage was a nightmare. He wanted to leave, but who would feed him? I didn't have the guts to say, "Get out!"

A small lump in my left groin was getting larger. I went to the Ross-Loos Medical Center, of which we were members, and asked about the lump. The doctor assured me that it was a slight infection of a lymph gland. I doubted this but took his word for it. One night a knifelike pain shot through my abdomen. Lee was asleep. I sat in the rocker stewing on my problems, our problems. It came again, frightfully sharp. The lump got bigger and harder. I awakened a doctor and explained the type and site of pain. Perhaps I was passing a kidney stone, I suggested. Maybe the doctor, our medical chief at the center where I worked, recalled the well-known story and thought, "Wolf, wolf, wolf." I had been neurotic the past six months with one pain after another, plus cardiac arythmia. He suggested that I send my husband over to his home for a quarter-grain of morphine to quiet the pain. I woke Lee and asked him to drive over and get it, which he did. He returned to bed, and I gave myself the whole quarter-grain of morphine by hypodermic.

I went to bed quickly, since I knew that the morphine would knock me out cold. It was three in the morning. At six a.m. I was awakened by vomiting fecal matter that shot straight out of my mouth and almost hit the far wall. This was projectile vomiting, and I knew it was serious. I could not move. The pain had me in a cast of iron. "Lee, please call the surgeon of the medical center, and tell him to come. This is an emergency."

The surgeon came and was furious at my self-diagnosis and treatment. By taking morphine, a hernia had the needed hours to become strangulated, and it might be gangrenous. Again I left by ambulance for the Queen of Angels Hospital. This was the fourth time in a year. Due to my poor condition, a spinal anesthesia was given. All I could think of was Peter, who had died in Spain from a shattered spleen: "Live for me. Remember the words of Till Eulenspiegel's wife," he had said when dying. Was this my final moment? How many more close shaves could I have with death?

They cut once. I felt them pulling my guts up to the surface. I felt the doctors untangling them. They sewed me up. Then they opened me up again, just to be sure that the blood was returning to the gut, which had blackened from loss of circulation. I heard them say, "The color is returning. We won't have to cut a piece of her intestines away." I breathed a sigh of relief. I knew my chances were better now.

Peritonitis set it, and I was sick. Again, I fought to live. Ten days later I went home, weak, and with orders to take it easy for a month.

Mary Lee had been writing to me. Her dormitory was having open house for parents on the weekend that coincided with the end of my month's convalescence. I went up mainly to talk to Mary Lee. Maybe she could help me face my problem marriage and help give me the courage to break it. I was extremely mixed up and could not think clearly. I didn't want to lose Lee, but I had lost him. He had a girlfriend, whom he saw a great deal. She was better for him than me, obviously, since he spent so much time with her. He certainly was not good for me.

Probably just knowing that I would see Mary Lee and have a chance to talk to her helped me have a night's sleep without nightmares. I drifted off to sleep with the clack of the train wheels taking me to Berkeley. It was unfair to put the burden of myself and my problems on her, but I had no one else to whom I could turn. Who would believe me that this charming man could be such a sadist to live with? He had the ability to find one's weak spots and twist the screw. Mary Lee had seen it and had lived with it. I sat on her bed that night and let it pour out while she listened.

Then she said, "Now listen to me, Mummie. You have no right not to give Toby the same warmth you gave me. You act frozen, dull, dead, unhappy. You have changed. You never sing anymore. You don't sparkle. This marriage is killing you and will destroy Toby's growth. You managed to raise me without a father, and I have good memories," she said emphatically.

"But what did I give you? You had no father. We were poor when I was going to school. The first years of your life I was numb with your father's death. I did my best, but what have I done? You didn't have a father. I want one of my girls to know a father," I answered tearfully.

"Living in the dorm with many other girls has taught me something. Our favorite topics of discussion are our parents and boys. I only had you. But you know, Mummie, of all the girls here I've had the most secure home life and the most feeling of being wanted by my parent. Sure we were never rich and were often poor. But our home was always rich in color, warmth and friends. There was never a dull moment living with you, and now you are dull. You act broken. Sever it. Don't be afraid. Begin again," she told me.

Returning to Los Angeles, I thought I must do something. But I did nothing. I lacked the courage to say anything that would precipitate the breaking up of our home and our marriage. I still wanted Toby to have a father.

I returned to work. My salary had not stopped. The medical center had been most decent to me, and I was happy on the job. Among other things I was teaching a group of pregnant women, helping them prepare themselves to have their babies without anesthesia, using a natural childbirth method. I helped in a group psychiatry clinic and worked on health care plans for the unions. It was the kind of a job that I loved, where I learned more than I gave. My nights were filled with nightmares, but my days were useful and busy. I often forgot, for minutes at a time, my problem marriage and a husband who appeared to dislike me, was bored with me, yet whom I served.

It was early spring, 1948. Sundays I worked in the garden while Toby scrambled like a mountain goat among the flowers up and down the steep slopes. She was a year-and-a-half old, sucking her thumb day and night. She was not a secure baby or a happy baby. Mary Lee was planning a year's work at the Art Students' League in New York City. I was existing from day to day when the worst blow of all fell on me. I was about to find out why the FBI had focused on me.

A friend of mine came to my home carrying a Hearst newspaper. Big headlines announced that Elizabeth Bentley had been the Spy Queen. She was beginning a fantastic story in the Hearst press, to be carried in every Hearst paper all over the nation, about her work as a spy. I doubted that she had been a spy. I knew her as an opportunist who wanted to be a spy while at Teacher's College and who was looking for importance. We had laughed at her. She began her story by saying that I had recruited her into the Communist Party. The article said that I would be called to Washington, D.C., to testify! I was panicky.

Headlines continued, and suddenly I was notorious. Many whom I had thought of as friends did not speak to me since finding out I had recruited Lizzie into the Party. Others would not speak to me, since I had been a communist. It said so in the newspaper. Where I worked, suddenly great coolness reigned when I appeared. I wanted sympathy and understanding. Instead it looked as if they hoped I would resign.

My husband worried how this would affect his future. I had visions of going to jail, since I knew damn' well that I would not be a squealer and name names as an informer. What about me? What about Toby? What about Mary Lee? I didn't know what to do.

The threat of being called to Washington, D.C., and my insecurity brought my marital problem to a head. I'll always remember the specific occasion when Lee told me for the last time that I was fat and ugly. I was bathing Toby. She wriggled in delight and was trying to swim. I called Lee to come and see how she actually was trying to swim. I turned to him and asked, "Please, Lee, take Toby and me to the beach someday. I could have a swim. Toby would love to splash in the little waves as they break on the beach."

"You in a bathing suit? My God, I'd be ashamed to be seen with anyone as fat and ugly as you are," he said as he walked out of the bathroom. He had said this often, but somehow this was the first time it really hit me, and something snapped in me.

"Listen! I work for the food you eat. I wash the clothes you wear. I iron them. I cook for you. I loved you. Now get out! If you are not out in two weeks, I'll call a moving van and have you moved out with your photo equipment," I said quietly. A surge of some of my old self-respect swept back into me.

He stayed on, day after day. Fourteen days later I had the moving van come. He left with the equipment that my savings had bought and the two typewriters, one mine and one his. The car went with him. He also left me with a $2,000 debt. I loved him, and I hated him. I had to learn to feel nothing when I thought of him.

The house had to be sold and debts paid. I had to make more money than my salary provided. I took in seven boarders. I cooked for them. I washed and ironed for them. My greatest concern was the $2,000 that Lee had borrowed from very dear friends of mine, who now needed the money back, which Lee had told me had been paid but had not. He did manage to sell the house, which helped liquidate other debts that he had incurred which I hadn't even known existed. Lee was managing to live on his G.I. Bill student money by eating at his girlfriend's house. These months were difficult, and I have trouble remembering them, since I'd rather forget them. The medical center where I worked implied that it would be better for them if I resigned. The publicity which was continuing in the press didn't help me or them. I had to move somewhere, and I decided to move back to New Mexico, where I had felt wanted and where I'd loved the people and my work. I wanted to be far away from Lee, and I wanted Toby to have some security.

I packed into a truck the furniture that Lee had not taken, my pots and pans and linens, and sent it all off to New Mexico. I bought a secondhand car which was not much, but I hoped it would take Toby and me to Santa Fe, New Mexico, where we had a friend with whom we could live until I found a home. I was quite sure I could get a staff job as a public health nurse. Toby quietly sucked her thumb from Los Angeles to Santa Fe, while I was throbbing with an aching void. In time I would divorce him, but I missed him. Yet I knew I must put distance between us, mainly for the sake of Toby, who was unhappy and insecure. She was a baby, but she reflected my insecurities and unhappiness.

I was a mess. I was at one of the lowest points in my life both physically and mentally. I could not seem to unravel my feelings of being unwanted, stupid, unattractive and a failure. I had gone to a psychologist and to a psychiatrist. The latter wanted to analyze me, but I didn't have the money for that. The psychologist thought I had worked out quite well my plan for a transition from marriage to a working life without Lee, toward a future in another state where I had been wanted. I recall the psychologist said, "You sure have to learn the hard way, by your guts."

Guess so!

I was putting miles between myself and the *Los Angeles Times*, which was running the Bentley story. The first third of her book, which was running serially, was about me. I lived in fear of being called to Washington. If I had to go there, I planned to give her a piece of my mind. I had told a lawyer this, and he tried to show me that I would not stand a chance before a Congressional Committee with my attitude of "telling Lizzie off." He told me, "If you answer one question, they have you. From then on, you will be caught in a net. The best thing is not to say anything." Coming or going, they had me. McCarthy prevailed in the Congress. What chance had I?

New Mexico and California, 1948-1949

Farewell, United States of America 7

The black, volcanic, rocky pools between Grants, New Mexico, and Albuquerque didn't help my mood, but then I began going up the road to Santa Fe. The unbelievably blue sky of New Mexico hung over me. Clouds reflecting the colors of the earth scudded overhead: here a rosy one, there a golden one or a white one, in the distance a black one discharging its burden of rain. A double rainbow arched over us as Santa Fe came into sight. I found my friend's home perched on a high hill over the town. She could put me up there until one of her little houses nearer the center of town could be renovated. Bless those who have helped me when I needed it most!

I took the exams and was able to get a position as a public health nurse for the City of Santa Fe. This was great, as I'd loved Santa Fe when I worked in New Mexico before, and it had been my dream to live there one day. I would stay here for the rest of my life if the FBI would leave me alone. I hadn't been working very long when I wondered if that would be possible. One of the girls whose name I had used for reference had sent them all the clippings about Bentley and me from the *Los Angeles Times*. I don't know how she got them.

This was a girl I had helped — helped in such a way that it endangered me, back in 1940. She was unmarried, in an important position with the Department of Welfare in San Miguel County, and she was pregnant. She had had an abortion, but it was not well done. The doctor had not removed the placental tissue, and she was hemorrhaging, wide open to infection and death. She told me about it, and I spoke to our staff doctor. Behind closed doors and stuffed keyholes, we finished the abortion to prevent her death. I had never told anyone, and neither had the doctor. Now she accused me of being subversive by the materials she had sent in the mail. I could not say anything to her, since I was not supposed to have access to the private files in the State Health Department. I didn't, but a friend of mine did and told me. Thank God, I was kept on despite her.

The town of Santa Fe was thick with FBI agents because of Los Alamos and the work being done there. The residents of Santa Fe called Los Alamos "the shadow on the hill." The red glare of smoke and fire hung over it at night. I had never thought of atomic energy, atomic bombs and New Mexico. I had jumped into a fine kettle of fish, and I wondered how long the Health Department would keep me if the FBI complained.

I worked, loving my work, but I never knew at what moment the subpoena would come from Washington. I knew I would stand on my rights under the Constitution, but as far as I could see I had no rights. It seemed you became an informer or you went to jail or you were blacklisted. I did not have a cell in my body which would allow me to be an informer. I would not name names, and I had nothing to confess. I was and had been an American who had served her country and served it well in one of the most important areas, helping people keep alive and well. I believed that the health of a people was the vital concern of the nation, and I was not ashamed of being me. If only the FBI would stop bothering me, not threaten the loss of a job, so that I could continue in my beloved field of public health work. I didn't want much. I wanted to help lower infant and maternal mortality rates and to live quietly and raise my child in peace and security.

The golden leaves of the aspen trees streaked the Sangre de Cristo Mountains that loomed purple around Santa Fe. Adobe walls turned red with strings of chilies drying in the sun. The smoke of piñon wood fires scented the air. That fall of 1948, flakes of snow began to cover the tops of the mountains earlier than usual. Toby was now two years old. I went back to Los Angeles on a quick trip for a hearing on my divorce, which would be final within a year, I hoped.

Toby stayed in a good home in the day as I worked, and I picked her up at five. Our little adobe house on Canyon Road was lovely and warm, with the big fireplace in the flagstoned living room. Before I put her to bed, she sat on my lap as I read *Winnie the Pooh* and *The House on Pooh Corner*. These were books which Mary Lee had loved, and now Toby liked me to read from them. Mary Lee was working part-time at the Museum of Modern Art and going full-time to Barnard, Columbia University, where she had a partial scholarship. I was beginning to respect myself again. My confidence was coming back through the process of work in public health nursing. I was content to drum up business for the well-baby clinic, to organize the tuberculosis clinic. I was proud that from the 13 cases of typhoid in my district, no new cases had occurred. I was sleeping like a log with nary a remembered dream or nightmare. I began to be Lini Moerkerk de Vries again, alive, energetic, singing, trying to learn the guitar, loving my children. It looked as if the FBI had forgotten me and that I could work and live in Santa Fe the rest of my life. I loved New Mexico, my adobe home, my children, and my work!

It was December, and the Christmas tree stood green and tinselly in the living room. The fragrant fire threw light on it when I opened the door to my friend who worked in the State Office of the Health Department. She looked glum. I invited her to have some hot coffee as she shook the snow off her coat and left her boots by the door. "What is the matter?" I asked.

"I don't know how to tell you, but I want you to be aware," she said.

"Aware of what? What's wrong?" I questioned.

"Well, two agents of the FBI called on the boss today," she answered.

My heart sank as I asked, "About what? What did they say? How do you know?"

"I heard it all through the thin partition. I don't think they realized that I was typing there in the outer office. They told him that you had been associated with Bentley, the ex-spy, that you were a communist, that you had been a nurse in Spain, that it was dangerous to have you near the atomic bomb plant. They said that you would soon be called to testify in Washington. I know that the only thing that may be true is that you were in Spain."

"I knew Bentley, too. I lived with her, that is true, but what in hell has the atomic bomb plant got to do with public health nursing?" I asked.

She said, "That is exactly what the chief asked them, but they are going to give you the opportunity to resign."

I resigned as of January 1, 1949, and thought, "I will look for a job in another place. If they keep hounding me, I'll leave the country." I didn't know where I'd go, but someplace where I could work in public health and raise Toby.

Not long before that, I had been phoned by a doctor who was now working with the health care plan of the United Mine Workers' Union. He had offered me a job, but I had said, "No, thank you. I want to remain in New Mexico." Many of the men I had known working with the Mexican imported workers were now with the expanding UMW plan. I headed east with Toby to see if I could still get a job with the UMW. Since that union formerly had been attacked as communist, which it never had been, I felt that they might be sympathetic to my problem and pay no attention to the FBI. The physician who had called me was in charge of a district which contained West Virginia. I left Toby with dear friends of mine in Washington and took the train to see him.

He was glad to see me and told me the job of nursing supervisor covering a few states was mine if I wanted it. It would mean leaving my child in the hands of others for days at a time, but it was a job and paid $6,000 a year. I was ready to agree when he began telling me of the problems he had had with the FBI. He told me that he had had to resign from the United States Public Health Service because of FBI pressures early in 1949. I felt that I owed it to him to tell him of the problems I had had, of which he had known nothing.

He almost froze before my eyes as I told him the story of Bentley and her book, and the FBI follow-up on me. He said, "Lini, I have an invalid wife and four children. I need this job. If you come on, I might be called a Red for hiring you. (This, coming from an ex-Red, was something.) If there is any Red-baiting or witch-hunting in the Mine Workers' Union, I'll not protect you. I'd rather see you fired than me. After all, I was not in Spain, and I didn't know Bentley. If there has to be a sacrificial lamb, it will be you."

I was shocked as I listened to him, yet I was not angry. He was more scared than I.

"Nevertheless, you can have the job if you want it," he said hesitatingly, as he watched the expressions flit across my face. "Think about it."

The clack of the wheels did not lull me to sleep that night as I returned to Washington. I was weighing the constant threat of being fired and living in the East versus $6,000 a year. I hated the East with its uneven cold-hot-damp climate. I didn't want to be stuck on a blacklist in the East. If worst came to worst, I'd rather be a cook, a servant, a dishwasher back west in sunny California than blacklisted in the East. I lacked the old notion of security that doing a job to the best of my ability protected me.

Besides, both Toby and I were vulnerable to the infections caused by an allergy to the *hemolytic streptococcus*, strain A. She was already beginning to have strep, sore throats, and asthma attacks. I preferred to face job insecurity in Los Angeles, where the rheumatic fever incidence rate was lower, so I wrote and said, "No, thank you. I don't want the job."

I felt strongly that I'd never see the East again. I took Toby to her grandparents' home in Pennsylvania. This might be their only chance of meeting her. Lee's parents understood the divorce problem and helped me with money to head west, but first I stopped in New York City a few days to see my older daughter. She was busy doing what she wanted to do: study, work and paint. It was difficult to take her pity for me. This I was not accustomed to.

We began traveling west by train, the El Capitan from Chicago to Los Angeles. I made a bed of pillows on the floor for Toby. Three nights and three days I sat sleepless and tight with worry. I knew Lee would not help. He found it difficult to give me the $50 a month that he had said he would give in the divorce agreement.

In Los Angeles, a nurse I had known in Spain, Rebecca Durem, took us in. She hated cooking for her family of four. I was grateful for a room, and in payment I did all the cooking. I jobhunted. Two agencies wanted me. Then I was told that I was on the "undesirable list." I was surprised that even the nongovernmental agencies were being told by the FBI whom to employ. I managed to get social security payments, and I wrote and answered advertisements offering myself as cook and governess, but my child was not wanted on these jobs. I wanted a job. I wanted a home. I wanted security.

Finally I heard that a Jewish home for the aged in Receda, California, was looking for a resident director. They required that she be a registered nurse. I really pleaded for that job and got it. I was hired on three months' probation at a salary of $150 a month, plus room and meals for Toby and me. Over one of the workshops, I had a little apartment consisting of a kitchen, a bedroom and a living room-bedroom. It was good to have a bit of a home again.

I shopped for thirty, and drove those who needed to see medical specialists in the little secondhand car I had bought. I was on call 24 hours a day, and I went mad with the constant bickering of the old people. I had lost my guts and spunk. I didn't like the job, but thought — I can grow old here. Toby will have lots of grandparents. At least no one can say there is anything political about managing a Jewish home for the aged. I can even be buried from here, thought I.

Twenty-four hours a day I slaved. Weren't old people ever happy? I guessed not, not in a home for the aged filled with dissention and bitterness. Board members fussed at one another. Tattling ran rife. But I was ready to stay.

My three months of probation were hardly up when I was fired. I had not been fired from any job since I had tried to learn quill winding in the factories when I was 13. Now I was 42 years old. This was a blow! I asked the president of the board of the home the reason, and he said, "Your work is unsatisfactory. The old people don't like a little girl roaming around."

"But she has been in a nursery school in the day. How can you say that? I bet the FBI has been to see you," I retorted.

His surprise and the flash in his eyes made me realize I had hit upon the truth. After seeing him I went to see one of the board members whose daughter had been a classmate of mine at Columbia. We had renewed our friendship in California, and I was sure she would tell me the truth. I had to know. If it were the FBI hounding again, I had to start planning anew.

I drove over to her home and begged her to tell me. With all my problems, I could not stand any inference that my work had not been good. She told me, "No, Lini, your work has been good, but the FBI said you had been in Spain. You might be called to Washington. They said that you are working actively as a communist in the home." She smiled ironically, and so did I. Cleaning up cases of scabies, preventing bedbugs from entering the home, bathing sick old men and women, listening to their constant complaints, especially after Sunday afternoons and no visitors had come to see them. "This is communism to them?" I asked.

"Seriously, we are Jews, and the home is Jewish. There is enough dislike for Jews. Anti-Semitism did not die with Hitler. The home can't afford the publicity you would bring if you were subpoenaed," she said. I understood.

I went back to the friend's home I had left three months before. I could always depend on the veterans of the Lincoln Brigade or the nurses who had been in Spain to help. The nurse's two daughters and Toby ate the cake that I baked for Toby's third birthday, September 9, 1949.

When I graduated from nurse's training school in 1928, I had said that I would never do private duty nursing. Now I began doing it. I took night duty in order to be at home with Toby in the day. My feet hurt, my belly hurt, my heart hurt. I kept on looking for jobs in public health in the day, when I should have slept. No matter where I turned, I was not hired. The publicity in the *Los Angeles Times* about Bentley and me, plus the visits of the FBI had thoroughly blacklisted me. I had lived in nine homes with nine different families following my separation from Lee. Toby was a whiny, thumbsucking, unpleasant, unhappy little girl. I knew she could not change until I was secure again. I wasn't even welcome in many homes. People didn't want it known that they knew me — with a few exceptions: the veterans of the Lincoln Brigade and one Hollywood writer and his wife.

What peace pervaded me when they invited me to their home for dinner or to go on a picnic with them! I couldn't tell them how very miserable I was. I was stewing as to what to do about it. Finally I told them that I was thinking of leaving the United States, going to Mexico to make a new life for myself and again to work in public health.

It was still just a thought. I had not quite given up hope of getting a job as a public health nurse. I had worked hard and long to become one, and I was determined to work again in my field. My mother and the rats in the coal cellar had not destroyed me. Was I going to let the FBI and its hounding destroy me? Like a punch-drunk boxer, I was stumbling to my feet. The last round had not been fought yet. I heard myself saying, "Why did you have to go to Spain? Why did you join the Communist Party in 1935? Why should you worry about discrimination, anti-Semitism, social rights? Why do you have to be different from other public health nurses? Who are you anyway?"

I was ashamed of being me. I felt homeless and unwanted by my friends and my country. I was losing my self-respect for allowing such thoughts to enter my head. I still had ten weeks of social security unemployment insurance to go — and then what? I had begun my conscious life with rats after me. Now I felt they were after me again. I looked at Toby's unhappy, unsmiling face. She must have a chance to grow up proud of her mother, proud of her country. This could be only if I could be proud of myself, which I could achieve only by useful work, which was denied me in the United States. Slowly the punch-drunk fighter was rising to her feet.

Again I tried to get work, this time with the Heart and Cancer League, which was looking for someone who had knowledge and experience in the fight against rheumatic fever. Certainly I had both, but I was not hired.

On Thanksgiving Day I was having dinner with my friends who lived in Hollywood. I began telling them of the years since 1946, when Toby was born, of my fruitless search for work. Just the telling of it helped me make my final decision, and I said, "I will leave the United States and go to Mexico. I will make a new life there. I should have a chance. Mexico has never recognized Franco. They still recognize the Republic of Spain. Maybe one of the Spanish republican refugees there will give me a hand to get started."

"Do you have the money to go? Do you know anyone in Mexico?" they asked me.

"I neither have money, nor do I know anyone, but I know *of* a woman, Constancia de la Mora, who might help me. I don't know how I am going to go or when, but I'll go," I replied.

Once more I looked for work in the United States and had no luck. It was the same complaint: I had been a member of the Communist Party, I had been a nurse in Republican Spain, and worst of all I had shared a kitchen with Elizabeth Bentley, the "Spy Queen."

Again I couldn't help thinking that if I had never joined the Communist Party in 1935, I would not have hit the blacklist in 1947. I pushed the thought angrily out of my mind. I had nothing to be ashamed of. When I joined the Communist Party, it had been like joining a faith, a faith in mankind. I had thought through communism man could reach his potentials. Under communism I had hoped discrimination and inequality would cease.

I had been a humanist, an idealist, a fighter for what was just, long before I had joined the Communist Party. I still was a humanist, with a great sensitivity for man. I had never been a political scientist. I never could wade through political tracts. To me in 1935 communism was humanism. I knew that the meaning of the word "communism" in the dictionary and the action of the Communist Party were very different, but I didn't even want to think in terms of politics. The only politics I wanted was in the sense of the Greek definition of the word, "the art of living." Yet the joining of the Party in 1935 and my gradual disillusionment with the direction and leadership of the Communist Party had all been a very important part of my growth. I was almost a religious liberal, in the sense that liberalism of mankind was my faith. If this was un-American, then it was time for me to leave.

By letter I tried to explain all of this to Mary Lee. I asked her to phone me what she thought. Then I wrote to Constancia de la Mora and explained why I wanted to come to Mexico. I asked her if I could manage to live there on $50 a month, until I found work. She did not know me, and I did not know her, but we knew of one another from the days of the Spanish Republic. The book that she wrote, *In Place of Splendor*, tells better than I can of the gallant role she played in Spain and after Spain.

My first answer came from Mary Lee, who phoned me at the number I had given. She asked, "Mummie, since when have you been afraid of change? You did it for me. You owe Toby the same good life you gave me. Go to Mexico. Don't be afraid." I needed those words!

About a week later a letter came from Constancia de la Mora. She doubted that I could live there on $50 a month, but she told me to come anyway. It appeared that she had a small guest house and wanted to leave it in good hands while she took a trip. I had offered myself in my previous letter as a cook and housekeeper. She wanted to leave right after Christmas and asked if I could come shortly, in order to come to know the house before she left.

Newspaper publicity had begun again. Bentley was yelling, "Spies!", and my name was being mentioned. I had a hunch that I'd better sell all, raise some money, and buy a plane ticket before I was subpoenaed to Washington. It seemed that the congressional committee was running out of names with which to foster publicity for themselves. McCarthy fed on it like a cannibal.

I began feeling a hysterical fright with every strange male face that approached the house where I boarded. I sold everything from which I could possibly make some money. I wished I had an American passport just in case it was requested by Mexico, but I knew I could not get a current one. I didn't know of any nurse who had been in Spain who had been granted a passport. Certainly I would not get it when I was threatened to be called to face McCarthy. I'd better get out.

My tickets were for December 12, 1949, leaving from Tijuana, Mexico. I lay awake the last night and reflected on my past. My struggle to become me had not been an easy one. The threat of being called before the House Un-American Activities Committee hung over me. I was unwanted as a public health nurse unless I named names and became an informer. That I could not do and live with myself. I had no home. I had two daughters: The elder was managing to see herself through college, and the little one, age three, was a whiny, unhappy child. The United States was doing this to her by persecuting me. In the eyes of the average American, I was no good. Yet, where I had worked, infant death and maternal mortality rates had gone down. Whole areas had been freed of typhoid through my teachings. Venereal disease had come under control in Chicago. Our program of health care for the Mexican workers had been a factor in winning the war. I had helped build future Americans through my public health work in the schools.

No, these agents of the United States of America would not destroy me. I had been a good American citizen, but I did not want to be one any more. I wanted a country that would allow me to build a constructive life for my child and me through public health work. The United States did not want me or my work. I would leave the next day, and I had a hunch I would never return.

The old fright I had had for my mother had returned the past few months. The fright I had had when she used to say, "Get to the cellar, you damned child!" I now had for the United States. I had been having nightmares, but instead of the beady, black eyes of the rats in the coal cellar with which I'd lived in childhood, they were humans with bodies of men and the faces and hearts of rats. These human rats were betraying the decency, the greatness, the dignity of the America I had loved. Had these rats never read the words by Emma Lazarus on the Statue of Liberty? Didn't Thomas Jefferson mean anything to America any more? Had they forgotten the greatness of Lincoln? Was Walt Whitman forgotten, too? Was the Bill of Rights subversive? Had Thomas Paine been a communist, and

Jesus Christ, also? All of that was America to me! It hurt to be rejected by America. I ached at leaving America. What America?

I was plain scared of the America I was leaving and of what it was becoming. For me, it had already become a country that denied its glorious history, its Bill of Rights and its Constitution. Could I get out of it in time? Would they catch me before I got on the plane? Minutes and hours dragged until the time I envisioned I could be safe on the plane over Mexico.

December 12, 1949, a friend drove me to Tijuana, Mexico. All the way down I kept looking over my shoulders for FBI agents. I was hysterically frightened. Nothing must stop me now.

With $100, my duffle bags packed with our clothing, and thumbsucking Toby holding my hand, we entered the airport in Tijuana. We were in Mexico, but still too near the United States for me to feel safe. At nine sharp we were on the plane flying to Mexico City. I watched the lights of the United States fading from sight and wept for what had been my love. I wept for the good that is in the United States of America. I wept for myself. I wept for all of us.

As the night passed, we flew deeper into Mexico, and I dried my tears. I began planning our future in Mexico. Toby and I would somehow work, study, grow and serve in Mexico. Mexico would be my home!

Mexico, 1949-1962
The Victory 8

December 12, 1949, and the plane sped through the midnight skies. The whimperings of my sleeping child, Toby, just three years old, heightened my apprehension. Every turn of the propellers brought us deeper into Mexico, the land I had chosen for us.

Forty-four years I had spent in the United States. Except for brief periods in the Netherlands, 32 of those years had been spent as a silk-mill worker, a telephone operator, a nurse, a social worker, an educator, a teacher, and a public health administrator. The United States had made it possible for me to complete, against many odds, a full high school course in one year; it had enabled me to study at Teachers' College, Columbia. Yet the same United States, at that time, was making it difficult for anyone who as much as disagreed with Senator McCarthy's witch hunt to find a job. Unable to work, blacklisted, refusing to have my daughter grow up as a second-class citizen, I was leaving the United States, by choice.

Dawn was breaking over the wings of the plane. It was now December 12th, the Day of Guadalupe, most beloved of

Mexican virgins, symbol of nationalism and religion. Was this an omen? Was it to be a new day, a new world for Me? Could I work in Mexico? Could I make a home for myself and my daughter? Could I learn to speak Spanish? What had I to offer Mexico? Mexico had not asked for me.

Begging the gods of Mexico, her old and her new, to help me, I bent down to kiss my child. In the womb of the plane I felt safer than I had for many years. I had never been convinced that the North American culture had accepted me, not even the first-generation Americans with whom I had worked side by side in the silk mills of Paterson, New Jersey. In Amsterdam, in the sheltering warmth of our family, I had felt wanted. But that family had been wiped out in Nazi concentration camps.

What did I know of Mexico? Through previous work, I had come to know the Mexicans who lived in San Miguel County, New Mexico. Few spoke English; most resented the fact that New Mexico was no longer part of Mexico. After the Treaty of Guadalupe Hidalgo put an end to the U.S.-Mexican War in 1848, the Mexicans living in New Mexico became, perforce, U.S. citizens; but their culture remained Mexican. Many of their young men lay buried in Bataan or the Philippines; to many I had given typhoid injections before they had gone off to die for democracy. Like me, they had never been accepted into "the American way of life." To them, New Mexico was still Mexico, and with them I had felt at home.

In California, during the war years, I had met many *braceros*, immigrant Mexican farmworkers. And as health service administrator, I had gotten to know Indians from Oaxaca, from Michoacán, and other states. Through the years of knowing them, I had admired their individualism, their warmth and humanism. From them I learned even more of Mexico. Had some of Mexico and her culture penetrated me?

As the plane circled the Valley of Mexico, I was grateful that we had a new home to which we could go. We were expected at Constancia de la Mora's home in Acapantzingo, on what was then the outskirts of Cuernavaca. I had not met her, but to all of us who had been in Spain, she was a legend. A refugee from Franco's Spain, she had become a Mexican citizen. Her grandfather had been Prime Minister to the King of Spain, but she had worked hard for the Republic. Her book, *In Place of Splendor*, still stood out in my mind.

Dazed from lack of sleep, I tumbled out of the plane. It had been an eight-hour flight in a four-engine plane. No longer remembering even the bit of Spanish I had learned in Spain and New Mexico, I was tongue-tied; I understood nothing. Somehow or other, we managed to get to the limousine service that ran hourly to Cuernavaca. The tremendous beauty of the snow-capped volcanoes, the sweeping fields, the tall pines, and the glowing earth colors helped lift my depression. I wondered about the home to which we were going. Constancia had written me she would soon be leaving for Guatemala as the guest of an American friend, but that there would be time before her trip to show me how to manage her small guest house, manage the servants, and learn something of Mexican cooking.

Through lush tropical green and brilliant flowering shrubs, we drove the short distance to Acapantzingo. We approached the gates of what seemed to me to be a huge estate. Inside, a handsome, brown-skinned man left his rake to take our luggage. In the attire of the proud Indian women of the Isthmus of Tehuantepec, Constancia de la Mora came to the door to welcome us.

Our quarters were at the side of the house. Vines and plants sent tendrils into the sun-filled room. Its ceiling was fortified by black, time-worn beams, and the furnishings were simple, with bright accents of color in the Mexican rugs and pottery.

When the gardener brought our bags into the room, Constancia introduced him, saying, "This is Fidel, my *compadre*." Following him came a three-year-old girl, bronze-skinned, her black eyes sparkling, her braids swinging. "And this is my godchild, Constancia Moreno." Spanish aristocrat and Indian blended here into newly adopted kinfolk.

Over coffee, Constancia told me of her *compadres*, Fidel and Delfina Moreno, who were from the nearby village of Tepoztlán. They had asked her to be godmother at the christening of little Constancia. In New Mexico, I had already learned of the deep responsibilities of the *compadre* system, so I understood when she explained that her *compadres* were *de confianza*, completely trustworthy. Fidel would be my right hand, and Delfina would help me run the house. As they spoke no English, I would be entirely responsible for the North American guests and their meals. Aside from Delfina and Fidel, there were two maids, Tarascan Indian girls from Michoacán.

Within a few weeks, Constancia would be leaving for Guatemala. I had to brush up on my Spanish, but it seemed even more important to me to earn the respect of her *compadres* and the two maids. It was already obvious that they worshiped Constancia and silently, unsmilingly treated me as an intruder.

By the time Connie left on her trip, I had learned the workings of the house and how to run it, but I had not yet won over her *compadres*. Their faces masked, they were chilling in their politeness. To them I was merely a *gringa*. They were putting up with me until Connie returned. A constant turnover of guests kept me busy, and they realized I was needed, inasmuch as they spoke no English. But when Connie returned, I was certain they would not make my life pleasant. The Tarascan girls had already warned me that Delfina, of whom they were not too fond, would even practice witchcraft to get me out.

The witchcraft threat did not bother me, but I did wonder if Connie would need a foreigner and her small child in the house when she returned; I was occupying a room that could accommodate two paying guests. Not that she had even hinted at this; she had been wonderful, but I began planning to leave. I was grateful to Connie, but I did not want to impose upon her.

My daughter whined, fretted, threw temper tantrums, kicked people. Rarely did she smile. The more the servants and guests were shocked by her behavior, the worse she behaved. To give her the security she lacked, I needed desperately to make a home for us. Upon Connie's return, I planned to move to a small apartment I had found.

The terrible blow fell a few weeks after Connie's departure, when we learned that she had been killed instantly, the only fatality in a car accident in Guatemala. Olga Costa, the painter, came to tell us that Connie's neck had been broken. The *compadres* wailed, servants wept, friends called. I tried to help prepare for the funeral, ignoring the heightened resentment against me in the household — Connie had been accompanied by a *gringa* at the time of the accident.

Constancia de la Mora y Maura came home beautifully embalmed. One expected her to sit up and smile at the hundreds of friends who came to pay their last respects to that fine, dynamic woman. She lay in the house she so loved, built with the money earned from her book. Now it was filled with tears for a life snuffed out. In place of splendor, she had chosen to be a part of the Republic of Spain. She had lived with the splendor of her warm heart. Now she would lie under a great, spreading Indian laurel tree in the quiet cemetery of Acapantzingo, Morelos.

Months later, on All Saints' Day, I returned to her grave. On her tomb I lay marigolds, the flower of the dead, and sat with the many families picnicking and keeping their dead ones company. Bands played, children flitted from grave to grave, admiring the gold and purple floral displays, and the settings of food for the visiting dead. Constancia lay peacefully in the Mexican soil that had given her refuge in 1940. For ten years she had known the vitality and wonder of Mexico; now its warm earth sheltered and embraced her.

We moved into what I called "my penthouse." It had four tiny rooms that could have fitted into one large room of Connie's home. The kitchen permitted a two-burner stove, a small icebox, and me. Next to it was a small dining alcove. From its window, Toby and I could see a riot of bougainvillea and lilies of all shades, even a small swimming pool. At night, the living room became my bedroom. It hung over a ravine, the one depicted by muralist Diego Rivera in the Palace of Cortez, only two blocks away. From the living room, a door led to a tiny nook that held a cot for my little girl, and from there — best of all — one stepped onto an open roof overhanging the ravine. We would sit there as I read aloud from *Winnie the Pooh* until the light faded. Then I rocked her to the twinkling of lights on the other side of the ravine, and the lightning bugs. We watched the vultures settle in their roosts at the same height as our penthouse roof.

Toby was then in nursery school, and relaxed. Envying her ability to speak Spanish, I struggled with verb endings. The more I studied the worse it became, until one fine day I closed all books and merely listened and copied, as Toby was doing. Stumblingly, I tried to converse with my landladies, the Blanco sisters, who helped me generously. They fascinated me. From them I began to soak up Mexican history. I could not read their books in Spanish, but I could listen to them tell of their family history.

Margarita and Argentina Blanco had been refugees in the United States during the Revolution of 1910. Their brother, General Lucio Blanco, had been killed. He was one of the first to distribute or, rather, redistribute land under Article 27 of the 1917 Constitution. Their family had been active on the side of Mexican progress for 300 years, as demonstrated by photos and books they showed me. I was stimulated to study all I could on Mexico's long travail toward becoming a nation. With every book I read, I acquired more and more respect for this new country of my choice.

My rent was $15 a month. When I got it, child support amounted to $50 a month. I earned what I could by private English lessons and occasional night nursing jobs, mainly with alcoholics — which I disliked, but we had to eat. As long as the people in the compound where I lived did not borrow from me,

I managed. Altogether, about ten other apartments and bungalows were occupied by compatriots, many of them escaping through alcohol. Increasingly, I found myself feeding people "the day after the night before," or giving them Vitamin B shots. In the evening, when some of them squabbled, we watched and listened as if it were theater — though I did not think it was particularly good children's theater.

This compound was not the Mexico I was looking for. It might take me six months or a year, but I would have to move, even though I loved the Blanco sisters. They helped me get a small teaching job at the University as an English teacher. It paid five pesos an hour for six hours a week, or 30 pesos a week. To me, that was two days' food. Best of all, the president of the University was going to write to the Immigration Department, asking for my services as a teacher. Should I be able to obtain legal status, my road to becoming a Mexican citizen would, I hoped, be less difficult.

Nevertheless, my house hunting continued, and the Blanco sisters understood. I had heard of a place near an ancient Indian temple on the outskirts of Cuernavaca. When I saw it, my common sense told me the rent was impossible, yet I had to have it. Countless lime, avocado, and orange trees shaded the lovely old house. Flowers covered the stone walls, and the nearest neighbor was about a block away. A large swimming pool filled the back part of the garden. Actually, there were two houses on the property — a large one, and a smaller one at the gate for the gardener or caretaker. I could visualize living in the gatehouse. By renting the large house and by acting as gardener and caretaker, perhaps I could live rent-free. The rent was more than my income. I rented the house.

With the few pieces of secondhand furniture I had gradually accumulated, I moved. The two-story house was quickly rented to a wonderful family who came to Cuernavaca for weekends and vacations. Their daughter was just a few years older than mine, which helped. I pinched myself. What mill dolly, factoryworker, telephone operator had ever had it so good? The nursery school that Toby attended was down the street. I taught English there. Friends of mine had moved in across the road, and to their children I gave fifth and sixth grade classes, using the Calvert system. I was learning, and they were learning. What had been the gardener's porch became the classroom.

In the early sun in the garden, Toby and I took breakfast. We swam, we glowed with suntan, both of us. I knew the house was for sale, but I planned to enjoy it as much as possible, even though I was not yet achieving my objective. I heard only English, and spoke only English. The few houses on the street were inhabited by North American families. Toby's school companions were from the States. Would we ever absorb this new culture, learn, and work and become part of Mexico? Was this at all possible for a foreigner? I felt like an outsider peeking through the window at a large, warm, affectionate family. I wanted to be inside, but how?

Not that I had cause for complaint. The sun shone over me; fruit was to be had for the picking. My best friends lived across the street. It was sheer joy to have a pool and to be able to dive in at any time of the day. Yet there was another Mexico I wanted.

Feeling thwarted, I recalled the psychiatrist-teacher at Teachers' College, who had told me, "Write, and write your problems out of your system." He said that after reading the term paper I submitted to comply with his assignment "to write that part of your life that is unbearable to remember." And he added, "When you feel the need for psychiatric help and can't get it, try writing it out."

Late evenings, Toby asleep, the house quiet, I would let memories float to the surface, and as they became clearer I noted them down. Early in the morning after I had walked Toby to school, I would begin writing from my notes of the night before. Writing, writing, month after month, I covered the period from my earliest recollections down to the time I came to Mexico. Then I would read it over, and it helped me. I understood myself better in relation to the time in which I lived.

One truth was most important to me, and there was no point in trying to escape it: I was a doer, a do-gooder. Obviously, the urge to work in my field, public health, was strong. In a tentative way, I began to play with the idea of moving to southern Mexico, where there were fewer foreigners. Perhaps it would be easier there to find the work for which I was prepared. But I was not in any real rush, for as long as the house was not sold, I could continue to live in that Shangri-la world and, even if for only a year, the memory of it would always be wonderful.

Should there be the chance of a ride to Oaxaca, however, I planned to explore the possibilities of work there. Perhaps in Oaxaca Toby would be able to attend the government primary school, like any other Mexican. Meanwhile, I was enjoying sunny Cuernavaca, the gatehouse, and the estate. I was tutoring children, learning with them, and most of all, pleased with my relaxed, happy daughter, swimming like a fish in complete security.

Late in 1951, an old friend drove down from the States, wanting to go to Oaxaca. So did I. On December 30, 1951, we drove from Mexico City to Puebla, the snow-capped volcanoes always in sight, then from Puebla to Oaxaca through semi-deserts, narrow canyons, and weird-shaped organ cactus. We climbed up and up into the pines on narrow ridges of mountain tops, and descended through gashes of red-purple adobe earth changing color in the fading light, blending with the green, jadelike, rocky upthrusts. There were few villages in which to buy gas. It was dusk when we dropped down to the level floor of the Valley of Oaxaca.

Night fell abruptly, and suddenly in the blackness we saw brightly colored globes filled with flickering lights. It was a long procession of lights dancing up and down in time with a band. We drove on toward the electric lights of the city of Oaxaca, and by nine o'clock we were registered in the Hotel

Marqués del Valle. Dining in the outdoor cafe, we watched the dignified Indians on the square. The band had just finished playing. Under the huge Indian laurel trees, the kiosks glittered. The calm of Oaxaca entered me. This was it.

After our 14 hours together on the long, slow trip, it was not difficult for my friend to read my mind. When I said, "This is it!", she asked nothing other than, "When do you think you will move?" I replied that when I had finished the school term late in May, I would then calculate how to make the move and meet expenses. I did not want to leave the children I was teaching in midterm. I hoped the house would not sell until May or June, though more and more people were coming to see it with the idea of buying. Since I would have to move eventually, I was planning on the long change, Oaxaca.

Now it was imperative that I find my friends who had spoken to the president of the University about me. We went to their home, but discovered they had left for Cuernavaca. The president, also, was away on vacation. That meant I would have to come back. I had to find some sort of job in Oaxaca, preferably teaching public health. But since we were already there, we decided that, for the moment, we would simply be tourists in Oaxaca.

Sunset found us overlooking the city, which lay in a cup at the foot of the classic archaeological site of Monte Albán. How had it appeared centuries ago, when games were played on the ceremonial ball court? We went from one tomb to another, then sat on pyramid steps watching the sun go down as lights began to shine in the city. The next day we visited Mitla, the city of the dead. It was more compact and equally exciting as Monte Albán with its hidden mysteries.

Early in the morning, Indians, in a hopping motion (similar to that of the cheese carriers in Alkmaar, Holland, I recalled), ran down to the market carrying hot, fresh tortillas. Later, from the hills came Yalaltecas and Triquis, among other groups. North Americans having their early coffee, enroute to the market, tried to distinguish the Indian origins of the passing women by the *huipiles*, the loose overblouses they wore. At night the band played, and if the band didn't, the marimbas did.

I fell in love with Oaxaca and was hungry to know more of the region and its people. But I had to go back to Cuernavaca, to my child, to the "for sale" sign on the house, and to teaching. I would return, that I knew. I could picture my little girl going to school, blending with the *oaxaqueñas*, even though she was fair. There, at least she could become part of Mexico faster than was possible for me. The deadline I gave myself was June.

In early March I had the chance to go to Oaxaca again, as a part-time driver and interpreter. I met with the president of the University, a wonderful young doctor, Jorge Pérez Guerrero. I did not realize then how he was sticking his neck out to give work to a foreigner in a state where all aliens were suspect — even Mexicans who were not born in Oaxaca. Our agreement was that I would teach English in the junior college, where I was needed. Also, I had permission to teach public health to the nursing students, though that was not required. The latter I would do gratis, but for teaching English I would earn five pesos an hour.

In a renovated colonial house, still bearing the shields of the religious order to which it had belonged in the late 16th century, I begged the owner to rent me the upper left-hand corner. Housing was scarce in Oaxaca; old buildings were shared by many families. This landlord was one of Oaxaca's coffee millionaires, and it really took some coaxing to get him to promise me a part of the house for June 1st. The corner I wanted had two baths, five ample rooms, a kitchen, and a large terrace. It was across the street from the University where I would be teaching. Just to be sure, I left him a month's rent.

First thing I saw when I got back to Cuernavaca was that the "for sale" sign was down. A general had bought the house, and the faster we could vacate the better the owner would like it. I explained that I had an obligation to teach four students until the end of May; then I would leave. We had had one glorious year in the gatehouse, an almost perfect climate, a garden and pool; my daughter was tanned and secure. My older daughter had come down from Barnard College in New York, and we three had shared this lovely home. I wondered if I would ever live as well again. But it was the working Mexico I wanted to be in, and that was not possible in the tourist town of Cuernavaca, the playground of nonresidents since the time of Moctezuma I in the 15th century. Before me lay Oaxaca, a gleaming green emerald hundreds of miles south, with Monte Albán guarding it.

Rings that were meant for my daughter on her 18th birthday were sold for enough to pay our way down to Oaxaca. (Later I replaced the rings with jewelry Toby liked.) I borrowed a bit here and a bit there. Toby had just recovered from measles, so we had to fly down; the truck with Fidel Moreno, a few sticks of furniture, and my potted plants would follow. Fidel was now my *compadre*.

Little had I thought, when I met Fidel and Delfina Moreno and their two children in Connie's home, that one day they would be my *compadres*. But then Fidel and Delfina had come to make a formal call, and asked me to be the *madrina*, or godmother, of little Constancia's first communion. I told them how honored I was, but explained that I could not be her *madrina* for I was not a Catholic but christened in the Dutch Reformed Church.

To this, Fidel replied, "My people were worshipers of the one God long before Cortez arrived. Our village has always followed Quetzalcoatl, who believed in one Great Spirit beyond all man-made gods. It was the Spaniards who made me a Catholic." After a pause, he added, "So will you be her *madrina*?"

I answered that, with the greatest pleasure, I would try to take the place of Constancia de la Mora as little Connie's godmother. Within a few days they came for me, and we took a cab to the Cathedral, where I became the *madrina* of

Constancia, for life. Just how he managed that, I never asked.

Now my *compadre*, Fidel, was en route by truck to Oaxaca, while I arranged a flight for Toby and me.

When we arrived, it seemed as if the landlord did not want us. It was fortunate that I had left the month's rent in advance. He must have been sorry that he had promised me part of his mansion. Nothing had been done since I had seen it two months before. I jumped over bags of cement, piles of loose wire and tiles. Not that I blamed this newly rich coffee grower, who didn't need my paltry 200 pesos a month, but I surely needed that apartment.

We moved in and, little by little, a certain friendship developed. I listened to him, but did not agree with most of his opinions. One day he told me that the best president Mexico had ever had was Porfirio Díaz. A life-sized oil painting of Díaz hung in the room where we talked. In a tiny niche stood the patron saint of Oaxaca, the Virgin of Soledad. He also muttered something about the people of Oaxaca not liking their governor.

I was shocked to hear him denounce the rights so hard-earned in the struggle Mexico had waged for 400 years, culminating in the Revolution of 1910. The peons on his coffee plantation were treated as if the Revolution had never happened. By that time I was in a position to quote various facts to him: 9,500,000 Mexicans were landless in 1910, starving as agricultural slaves, while 50,000 other Mexicans owned everything. But I needed the apartment, so I kept my mouth shut. To get to my place, I had to pass his living room, and often he captured me as an audience. He was a lonesome widower, but I was not lonesome. Once I quietly asked him about that great liberal president who had come from Oaxaca, Benito Juárez. It was all to the good that I only asked, and did not state my opinion, or I would have been homeless, his hatred for all that Juárez represented having burst forth so insanely.

Gradually I learned to recognize the social currents in Oaxaca, the strong black and white with little gray between. The more my landlord clarified his position, the more provoked I felt to study Mexican history. One took sides there, and as I learned I was beginning to choose. Being a foreigner, I had no legal right to take an open position, but I had to know where I stood. To me, only the dead were detached. My landlord's heroes were Iturbide, Santa Anna, Porfirio Díaz. Those were men who had championed the selected few. I hoped my own Mexican heroes would not mind my choosing them. They were the priest, Miguel Hidalgo, who began the long road to independence from Spain in 1810; José María Morelos, the humble priest who kept the independence movement alive with his *guerrillas*, and drafted the marvelous Plan of Apatzingan in 1814; the Lerdo de Tejada brothers and their Laws of Reform; magnificent Benito Juárez, an Indian from the Zapoteca village of San Pablo Guelatao, who rose from sheepherder to become one of the greatest Mexican presidents; and Lázaro Cárdenas, the pet peeve of *gente decente*, the decent people, who enforced the Constitution of 1917 and, by the expropriation of oil properties in 1938, finally freed Mexico from foreign domination.

Then I noted in my own home an effect of the drawn lines. Toby was attending the Sacred Heart grammar school (the public school had been much too crowded and too great a walk) when she asked me, "Whom do I believe — the nun or you — on Benito Juárez?" I replied, "If you are my daughter, don't believe the nuns *or* me. Look it up, and think for yourself." Later she told me she thought her teacher, a Spanish nun, was wrong.

When I arrived in Oaxaca, the people had just won their strike against the governor and his "gangsters," as they put it. The lines were sharply drawn. The barely literate newly rich tried to run their lives and those of others, as Don Porfirio would have done. The majority of the people — farmers, workers, teachers and the mountain folk — took their courage from their own man, Benito Juárez.

According to what the students told me, the governor had been planning to take away all popular gains, bribery and corruption were on the increase, and his threatening gunmen were covering the market stands, demanding more and more money. Businesses were not exempt. The students organizing resistance were most hated by the governor's *pistoleros*, who grew bolder every day. Fearing the consequences of any group assemblies, the governor forbade the traditional ceremonies, *calendas*, and fiestas for the Virgin of Soledad, Oaxaca's patron saint, for the Virgin of Guadalupe and all others. This was the biggest mistake the governor made. The Virgin of Soledad was the protectress of the people of Oaxaca, and the Virgin of Guadalupe had fought side by side with them against the Spaniards, the Americans, and the French, and was the symbol of nationalism for them. Forbidding homage to Soledad and Guadalupe was like forbidding them to live.

Early in 1952, a delegation of businessmen and students called on the governor to protest his actions. Hired gunmen shot down many students that day. The University closed its front door and flew the flag at half-mast; but the students of the University of Benito Juárez entered through the back door, and classes continued. All commerce in the town, including vendors in the huge market, went on strike. Anyone involved with the governor's group could not buy food; servants of that group would not, or could not, buy from any stall in the market. Scrip tickets were issued to all those opposed to the governor; only with those could one buy food. Would it be possible to starve the governor and his men out of office?

First it was just the city of Oaxaca, then the small villages in the Valley, then on through the mountains and, before long, the whole state was on strike. The governor asked the president of Mexico for troops; armed tanks with soldiers arrived. The tanks surrounded the *zócalo*, the plaza in front of the Hotel Marqués del Valle. Church bells stopped ringing. Neither the band nor the marimba played. Only two people at a time could cross the *zócalo*, enroute to the market. Red and black flags denoting "strike" hung over the closed doors of shops. Only the birds sang. All was quiet in passive resistance. The people were determined not to give the soldiers a chance to shoot at them.

Food stalls were permitted in the *zócalo*, and from them came the aroma of *carnitas*, or crisp, deep-fried pork, the black *mole* of Oaxaca, tortillas, tacos, and *chalupas* — among other tasty offerings. Anyone with scrip tickets could buy; the young soldiers could only smell. Those soldiers were sons of Mexico, humble bronze boys hungering for the taco behind the smell. Often, some little grandmother, feeling sorry for them, would sneak a taco to one or another. Later it became the custom to take care of the "poor young man so far from home," and his usefulness to the authorities was soon weakened. He, too, came to agree with the people of Oaxaca. Munching the rich tamales of the region, filled with black *mole* and chicken or pork, and shouting "good luck" to the strikers, the soldiers were recalled to Mexico City.

Stories about how the Virgin of Soledad was protecting the strikers sped from mouth to mouth. People said she stopped the tanks on the way to Oaxaca, warning the soldiers not to harm her children. It was said that a woman had appeared on the highway, stopped the lead tank, and exhorted its occupants, "My children, I forbid you to hurt your brothers, who are also my children." Then she disappeared.

Another story that made the rounds was that the governor had told the soldiers guarding him not to allow anyone to pass to see him. One late afternoon he dashed out of his private office demanding to know why they had permitted a woman to enter. The soldiers insisted that no one had crossed the threshold all day, that no woman had asked for an audience, that no mortal could get by their fixed bayonets. The governor insisted to his aide-de-camp, "She was dressed in blue. She told me to leave and let her people be, and said, 'I am the Virgin of Soledad.'"

Not much later, the governor, his staff, and his gunmen

crept away in the dead of night. A note of resignation was found, stating that he was leaving Oaxaca for reasons of health. Firecrackers and fireworks crackled and sparkled; the church bells rang and rang; the bands and marimba played. The Mexican flag and the University banner again flew on high. People danced in the streets. The strike was over. The governor had retreated.

Not only was I reading about Oaxaca and her history, but I was asking my students to explain the significance of certain customs. I was hungry to know more about Oaxaca. Teaching became sharing. When I taught English, the students helped me with my Spanish; when I taught public health and anthropology, they helped me accumulate more knowledge of their cultures, the Zapoteca, Mixe, Mazateca, Mixteca, and so forth. People knew me before I knew them. In the market, as he weighed the meat, the butcher would ask, "How is my son doing in class?" The vegetable vendor would give me an extra tomato, and when I seemed surprised by the gift I was told, "It is because you help my daughter to learn." Parent-teacher relationships became solid in the market, and I found myself patronizing the stalls where the vendors' sons and daughters were my students. Not that the learning of English was so important to the men and women of the market, but learning for learning's sake was. They were proud to have their children attend high school and college.

Many of the students were from the Sierra de Juárez, their native language, Zapoteca. They had learned Spanish, and now, English. Some of them were also my public health nursing students. Others were from Zapoteca villages in the Valley of Oaxaca. They spoke Spanish somewhat better, and we improved our knowledge of that language together. Because the educational system was so different from that to which I had been accustomed, I set out to learn something about Mexican education. Rarely did one of my students have a parent who could read and write, especially if he came from the mountain region. Few had the chance to go to school. How hungry they were to go to school and become professionals if possible!

For 400 years the Church had dominated education. It fought bitterly against schools being controlled and developed by the State for the many, instead of only for a few. In 1823, and again at the time of Juárez, there had been a spurt forward, in accordance with the Constitution of 1857, toward the separation of Church and State in relation to schools. During the Díaz dictatorship there was little improvement in State-controlled free education, but after adoption of the Constitution of 1917 — Article 3 — schools developed rapidly.

The Church, however, fought the application of Article 3 tooth and nail. Finally, President Calles became so angry that the *ley Calles*, the Calles law, was introduced in late 1926. It meant the closing down of practically all Catholic schools in the country. The Church was driven to play its highest trump card: Either the law was repealed, or the Church would abandon Mexico. Calles refused, and the Church went on strike.

It is to Ambassador Dwight Morrow's credit that he helped to heal the breach between Calles and the Church, but not before much damage had been done by the *cristeros*, who were at their strongest in 1927. This was a group dedicated to defending the Church and to destroying sinful education by the government and its humble representative, the rural schoolteacher. The *cristeros* were mainly ignorant farmers who had been propagandized to protect the Church. It had been 400 years since the first priests, the great early Franciscan friars who believed in educating the masses, came to Mexico, only to have the Church turn its back on the people later. There were still forces that would not give up, but the separation of Church and State was inevitable.

With the expropriation of oil properties, Mexico's true Independence Day — a feat achieved on March 18, 1938, by President Lázaro Cárdenas — Article 3 of the Constitution took on a galloping movement. Schools for Indians took on new life, and cultural missions moved into the mountains. Primary schools, high schools, colleges, and technical schools sprang up all over the country. Meanwhile, there was a huge oil debt to pay, and not a trained man available to run the expropriated wells and processing plants. Old and young were studying.

It was now only 14 years later, and I was sharing the textbooks on Mexican history with my students, helping them with their homework. I was learning; we were all learning. I was teaching three groups of English students at the University of Benito Juárez, and two small groups at home. By using more direct methods, such as audiovisual aids, I was having some success. It was in the public health class that my teaching became decidedly lively. Most of the students were from the Sierra de Juárez. Their deep brown eyes sparkled with intelligence. Their long hair hung in braids. My pale skin looked drab compared to their lovely, bronze-toned faces. They were taking the combined high school and nursing courses, and my youngest student was 16 years old. (She became supervisor of the Outpatient Department of Mexico's big medical showplace, El Centro Médico.) I was teaching the third year.

In the group were three sisters who more or less reflected the whole of my student body. One was in my college English class; she hoped to study medicine. Her two younger sisters were in my public health class. Their home was in a small village in the foothills of the Valley of Oaxaca. In the city they had rented a room for four dollars a month, where they did their cooking over charcoal and rolled out straw mats on the floor to sleep.

The eldest sister was in charge. She checked their homework as they studied by candlelight, munching tortillas curled around a few beans. Once a week their father brought them a week's supply of corn for grinding, some beans, *chiles*, and any other extras that could be spared; there were three more children at home to feed. This man and his wife were the rural schoolteachers of their village. As we became friendlier, he invited me to the village, making a special point of the fiesta honoring their patron saint.

How the sisters ever found anyone with a jeep, I'll never know. As we drove toward the foothills of the mountain range, the jeep twisted and turned and bounced over dirt trails, and mounds and more mounds covering Zapoteca tombs not yet excavated. Less and less did we see people dressed as they dressed in the Valley. Women on their way to the fiesta wore dark red, woven woolen material wrapped like skirts around their waists, tied with a wide, handwoven belt, and topped by a snow-white *huipil* reflecting the white, fleecy clouds above. Around the last turn we came to the church whose spire had appeared from a distance. It was a lovely old 16th century church, built under the supervision of the Dominicans — the same Dominicans who were in charge of the Inquisition in the New World.

Facing the church, a temporary bullring had been built, where a rodeo was in progress. Dust flew from horses' hoofs, cattle lowed, pigs grunted. The band, or bands, played louder and louder as the visiting feather dancers from Teotitlán del Valle enacted the coming of Cortez, the role of La Malinche, his Indian interpreter-mistress, and the death of Moctezuma II. Indians sat at the entrance to the church, playing the piercing sweet music of the pre-Hispanic flute, accompanied by old drums that had been carefully cherished for 300 years or more. The audience sat as close as possible to the musicians while heating their tortillas and beans over a charcoal flame. In and out of the crowd wove vendors from the city of Oaxaca with their ugly plastic wares — ugly in contrast to articles produced in the village.

It must have been nearly two o'clock in the afternoon when one of the little brothers came to call us away from the fiesta. Dinner was ready. It was a short walk to where the parents lived. Eight of them, in addition to Toby and me, sat around the long table eating the festive dish of black *mole* with turkey, as well as beans and tortillas — the tortillas used as fork and pusher. Mr. García, the girls' father and director of the village school, begged us to eat more and more. To divert him from that insistence, I asked him to tell me about their school.

It went to the sixth grade, equivalent to eighth grade in the States. He and his wife both worked as teachers, and also studied in the three-year Teachers' Institute, including vacation periods. Three teachers served the six grades. The students walked from nearby villages and, when the distance was too great, they stayed with kinfolk until the end of the school week. Most of the first graders had to learn Spanish, since their mother tongue was Zapoteca.

After dinner they insisted that I see the school of which they were so proud. It was a small, two-room building, the walls covered with the gaily colored artwork of the students. The *parcela escolar*, the piece of fertile land worked by the children and their fathers, produced enough to pay for school repairs. Surrounding the school and the village were *ejidal*, or communal lands. Before Cortez, as now, land was held sacred by the Indians. One gave to the land and, in turn, was sustained by the land. Private ownership was unheard of, until after the Conquest. Following the Revolution of 1910, agrarian reform brought about wholesale redistribution of privately owned lands to communal farmers.

Our visit over, Toby and I thanked Mr. and Mrs. García for inviting us to their home, to their *tierra*. On the way back to Oaxaca, I thought how admirable they were to manage, with their combined incomes of $80 a month, to keep three daughters in the city and three more children at home. This family was typical of the Zapoteca people from whose children I was learning so much. It was a system of mutual education.

From my students I had begun to learn about the Comisión de la Cuenca del Papaloapan. What on earth was a *cuenca*, and why were you so lucky if you lived in it? *Cuenca* means river basin or watershed. If you lived in it, there was more hope of getting a school in your village, or a connecting road to the highway that was being built. I found that fascinating, and began to investigate the Papaloapan Commission. A branch office in Oaxaca was helpful in obtaining material. It was somewhat like the Tennessee Valley Authority in the United States. Not only was it concerned with building dams, electric power plants, roads and bridges, but it also seemed to be greatly concerned for the people who lived in the watershed of the Papaloapan River. That was of special interest to me.

It was the fourth largest project of its type in the world. The Papaloapan River Basin contained 17,582 square miles, half of that area lying in the high mountain range of the state of Oaxaca. There was born the river network that swept the soil of Oaxaca down to the sea. Inhabiting that area were ten distinct Indian groups, with a population of about 200,000, most of whom spoke no Spanish. Once the Río Tonto was dammed, 20,000 Mazatecas would lose their homes; therefore they had to be moved before the closing of the gates.

In the hot, humid, low part of the basin, malaria was the third most important cause of death. In the area where the dam was under construction, a disfiguring disease called *mal del pinto* was commonly found. It left ugly, white blotches on the skin as the spirochete ate the pigmentation cells. This disease kept the people from being welcome in areas to which they would need to move. In another part of the Sierra de Juárez, among the numerous blind, the least affected — the youngster — led the blind parent to his work: digging a hole in the ground with a stick wherein the child then placed a kernel of corn. The disease these people suffered was onchocercosis, caused by the bite of the black fly. Engineers hated to go into the region to prepare for road building; they were afraid of the black fly which was found in rapidly flowing water.

But what a challenge to work there, studying each culture, trying to learn how to apply public health teaching to each!

With a chuckle, I recalled how my advisor in public health at Teachers' College had disagreed with me, scolding me for my insistence on taking anthropology courses offered by Columbia University. That was in 1936 when she thought it was not essential, not at all necessary, in fact, a waste of time. I had felt that as long as I was taking the required courses, there was no reason why I could not take others, since I was paying for what I felt I needed.

I had tried to point out to her the upward curve in morbidity and mortality rates. They were particularly high among the non-English speaking Sicilian people of Port Chester, New York; the Spanish speaking New Mexicans; and the Deep South blacks who had migrated to Harlem. Her reaction had been, "We don't feel that anthropology is needed for public health work." Of course, that was way back in 1936. After reading the report of Dr. Alfonso Villa Rojas on the Indian cultures in the watershed of the Papaloapan, I was glad that I had been so ornery in 1936, and later continued my anthropological studies whenever I could, by reading.

Because I had so many unanswered questions, it was especially thrilling to be invited to the inauguration of various projects in Guelatao on Juárez' birthday. I was to go with Mr. Cruikshank, an engineer from the Isthmus of Tehuantepec, who was in charge of the Upper Papaloapan. He towered over most of the Mexicans around him, a blend of Scotch and Tehuana ancestry.

So often I had been captivated by the hills surrounding the Valley of Oaxaca. On that day, March 21st, the birthday of Benito Juárez and, in a sense, my birthday (for that date was to mark the beginning of my life as a Mexican — though I was still to earn my citizenship) I was finally to have a glimpse of the works in the Papaloapan Basin.

Turning off the Pan American highway, we bumped along on the new dirt road, and part of the trip was over another road built in the days of Porfirio Díaz. Inasmuch as the latter was paved with cobblestones, we bounced and jiggled. The new road would eventually tie in with one under construction from Ciudad Alemán. When they met, there would be a road all the way from Oaxaca to Veracruz. Now it was merely a bleeding gash in the red adobe earth, weeping for the tall pines that were being sacrificed. Not only was the scenery breathtakingly beautiful, but I was grateful to the climatic belt that the rainy season had not yet begun. I had slithered and slipped enough on wet adobe roads in New Mexico to be properly fearful of that kind of mud.

As we climbed, villages could be seen perched on the slopes of sharp mountains. It seemed much too densely populated for all the erosion in the valley. We crossed the divide, at the top of which Mr. Cruikshank stopped the jeep and said, "As far as you can see, and even farther, is the watershed of the Papaloapan River." He pointed out the highest peaks, cloud-covered, where the Mixes lived, five walking days from where we stood. The nearer Zapoteca villages that we could see were one and two walking days away.

From villages like those my nursing students came. I began to understand their shyness, coupled with an intense desire to learn. Questions tumbled from my lips. How did the villagers survive? Why had they moved from the valley to those peaks? Were there health services? Were there schools? All I saw around us was eroded red earth. What was being done for these people?

Now that we were on the Gulf Coast side of the divide, purple mountains covered with white wisps loomed far to our right. We were in a thick, green pine forest. Orchids hung on trees; bush oak hugged the pines. As we began the descent into a narrow valley, we could see before us two villages perched on crags. The first was Guelatao, and the next, on the upper level, was Ixtlán de Juárez. The engineer was telling me about the intensive program to build schools. Many had been started three years before, and classes formed up to the third grade. Those with the complete six-year grammar school program were still rare, but Ixtlán had one.

The Commission had a director who was responsible for the staffing of schools, in cooperation with the State and Federal

Directors of Education. When I asked Mr. Cruikshank what he knew about disease and other health problems, he could tell me little. Finally, in desperation, he said, "Look, we are engineers, roadbuilders, dambuilders, and so forth. We need someone who understands human engineering. We have agronomists, road experts, soil experts, civil engineers, electrical engineers, sanitary engineers — but how can we get people to come to a clinic when we know nothing of their language or their culture?"

So I began to wonder about the rural schoolteachers — whom they taught, what and how they taught, and if teaching health could be integrated with the official school program by instructing the rural teachers. How could it be done? Saying nothing about my thoughts to Mr. Cruikshank, I pleaded with him for more history of the project. When was it begun? Why? What was the plan?

In the 16th century, Mexico's first foreign anthropologist and ethnologist was a priest, Bernardino de Sahagun. Though he himself did not realize he was behaving like an anthropologist, he investigated and collected data from the Indians on their life and cultures. As it had been recounted to him, he wrote of the dangerous flooding of the Papaloapan River. In 1944, the flooding was again so serious that Tuxtepec, caught between the Río Tonto and the Río Santo Domingo (which join to form the Papaloapan), was buried under seven feet of water, and three-fourths of its population drowned. Papaloapan means "river of the butterflies," but this river was no fluttering butterfly when it went on a rampage.

Overall planning for control of watersheds began during Lázaro Cárdenas' presidency. Plans were conceived for the control of the Papaloapan, the Grijalva, the Lerma, and others. When his term of office came to an end, Cárdenas began work in the small Balsas basin in his native Michoacán. Many of the men who were now in the Papaloapan Commission, established in 1947, had worked with him. In the Papaloapan Basin, studies were undertaken. Anthropologists, civil engineers, road engineers, electrical engineers, agronomists, physicians, educators, and mining engineers set out to determine what was on the land and under the land, and what kind of people lived there. Anthropologists made studies of the various Indian groups in the watershed, soon to become a lake. In general, the problem was how to help the Indians meet the encroaching culture of the 20th century with minimum shock, the soundest approach being that their fortification lay in retaining the best of their own cultures.

Medical studies needed to be made of those diseases that could impede the building of dams and the big hydroelectric plant. For example, malaria was endemic. A crippling and killing disease in the hot areas, it was worse where the main dam was planned. Hookworm, other worms, intestinal parasites, typhus, tuberculosis, blindness, *mal del pinto* would not help Indians to confront the modern world. Also, the workers going into that area were in danger. Germs are democratic. As it was practiced there, medicine was of the pre-Conquest variety, with a gloss of the worst methods introduced by the Spaniards. Strange rites were practiced by witch doctors, herb specialists, bonesetters. Magic and religious rites were a mixture of pre-Hispanic and the colonial period. Science was unknown.

In single-engine planes, photographers and engineers studied the basin from aloft. Others walked into the almost impassable rain-belt jungles, studying and planning for roads, step dams on feeder streams, river control, and forestry. Seven cuts were to be made to straighten the river at the delta so that, during the flood season, the waters could rush out to the Gulf.

Toward the mouth of the mighty Papaloapan, the villages of Cosamaloapan and Tlacotalpan nestled on its banks. Previously, the only communication with these towns had been by boat; now they would be connected with Ciudad Alemán by a dike road. The dike was being built with the help of a Dutch specialist.

The more Mr. Cruikshank talked about the future of the watershed and its inhabitants, and the almost impossible task of teaching for the changes, the more excited I became. Then I heard myself offering three days a week as a volunteer on "How to Teach for Health Through the School Program and the Rural Teachers." As at other times in my life, if I had known what I was getting into, I probably would not have done it. Little did I suspect that I was volunteering for the chills and fever of malaria, along with chicken pox while riding a mule five days from Oaxaca — not to mention the constant plodding up and down the mountains through pouring rain.

To this day, I wonder if Mr. Cruikshank did not invite me to go with him to Guelatao anticipating that I just might volunteer. Ever since December 12, 1949, when I first arrived in Mexico, I had been saying I wanted to dig my feet into the earth of the country and to play a part in its development. Now it looked as if I might be going to do so. But I had not visualized myself knee-deep in mud. That was still to come.

Zapotecas from far and near were climbing the hill alongside our jeep, going to San Pablo Guelatao. First we heard the brass of the bands; coming nearer, we heard the marimbas. Where we parked the jeep we could see bronze young lads shouting, cheering for their basketball team. The basketball court was to be inaugurated, together with other installations, such as the retaining wall brightly painted with the yellow letters "C.P." (Comisión del Papaloapan). Behind the wall was a swimming pool that also served as a dam to check the overflow of the enchanted pond where, legend has it, Benito Juárez used to dream while the sheep he was supposed to be herding sometimes drifted away. Glistening, snowy white ducks sped across the pond that reflected the blue sky, where fleecy clouds skimmed in rhythm with the ducks, the bands and marimbas. It appeared as if every band within walking distance of Guelatao was playing in honor of Juárez.

Before the ceremonies began, the engineer took me to the Indian School, attended by Mixes, Mazatecas, Chinantecas, Mixtecas, and boys of other groups. From the far-off Mixe area, it had been an eight-day walk to enter school. Not only did they have the equivalent of grammar school there, but they also learned the essentials to help them develop a better life for themselves and the villages from which they came. They cobbled the shoes they wore, baked the bread they ate, made the furniture they used, and learned the rudiments of agriculture from the Papaloapan agronomist in residence at Guelatao. They also learned to care for small and large animals. The engineer was most proud of the electric lathe and power tools that were to be used in the carpentry shop. These, too, would be inaugurated during the day's ceremonies.

Successive booms of fireworks initiated the activities. A brass band headed the procession of students from the Indian rural schools, followed by the villagers, the visitors, village bands and more bands. All of us marched to see the various installations, such as the swimming pool, the basketball court, and the new electrical equipment for the carpentry shop. Then came basketball games on the new court, exhibitions of folk dancing and, of course, long speeches. Airplanes from Mexico City zoomed overhead dropping flowers on the statue of Juárez that stood on the small plaza.

It was almost four o'clock when dinner was served at the rural school. Teachers and students flitted around with platters of duck in the deep brown Oaxaca *mole*, rich with nuts, fruit, *chiles*, chocolate, and thirty-five or more spices. Huge piles of tortillas disappeared as they helped the *mole* and duck into hungry mouths. About 100 persons were being fed by the village authorities. Soft drinks of all colors blended with the prize gladioli that were raised for cash crops. Although my fair Dutch skin and blonde-red hair seemed to me incongruous with the lovely, bronze faces around me, in no way did I feel like an outsider with the Zapotecas of the Sierra de Juárez. I was made to feel that I belonged with them.

Near me sat the federal inspector for that zone. From him I discovered that the teachers met for in-service training three times during the school year, and that the next Teachers' Training Institute would be in session the first week of April. Mr. Cruikshank told the inspector that I had volunteered to teach "How to Teach for Health Through the School Program." As the inspector questioned me, I explained how I thought it might be done by integrating health through the school subjects. He invited me to the Institute, to be held in about a week's time.

The die was cast. My plan was moving faster than I had expected. Now I was frightened. I knew too little of the Zapoteca mountain culture. My Spanish was not fluent. What nerve I had!

Through the rose-gold sunset, driving back to the city of Oaxaca, I pondered over my ideas and worried Mr. Cruikshank with them. He kept telling me, "Whatever you know, it is much more than we know. We can measure for a road, build a dam, make technical plans; but we can't teach about diseases." Within a few months the direct road would stretch as far as Tiltepec, where most of the people were blind. Mr. Cruikshank continued, "Many of the engineers don't want to go into that area. Someone must begin to make it safe for the road engineers to work, and also to prevent further blindness."

If I had been fresh out of Teachers' College, I might not have been able to do it. But having taught in the hills of New Mexico, on the plains of Puerto Rico, and on the Madrid front, I hoped I could do it. I knew I needed, immediately, the textbooks that the teachers used; I would have to study them in order to determine how to use them properly in teaching for health.

I was aware that teaching was done directly in Spanish throughout the whole Papaloapan area, except at the National Indian Institute Unit in Temazcal, where the Papaloapan dam was being built. I agreed with those anthropologists who felt that, first, the student should learn his indigenous language, get it down in black and white, and then go on to the second language, Spanish. It was felt that in this way there was not only less trauma, but the results led to better acculturation, because one became prouder of one's own history and culture before transition to the mestizo culture. The engineers, however, felt that the sooner the people learned Spanish, the sooner they would be integrated into Mexico. They regarded the Spanish language as the one possible common denominator. But at that time I really could not say which approach was the wisest. All I knew was that teachers were not supposed to speak Zapoteca to the children. I myself would find it sufficiently difficult to lecture in Spanish, without having to learn Zapoteca.

The immediate problem was to present, within the next 48 hours, a plan, albeit tentative, for a Teachers' Institute. One copy was to be delivered to the director of education in the Papaloapan Basin and another to the director of health and medical services. My proposed teaching plan was related to both.

How does one teach for health and prevention of disease in the face of such handicaps as these? Distances were great. Roads were nonexistent, except for the one under construction to connect Veracruz and Oaxaca, now only a gash in the red adobe earth. Telephone and telegraph service did not exist. Spanish was spoken in villages near the road; but the farther away one got from the road, the less Spanish was spoken. Altogether, ten different Indian tongues were spoken in the watershed. There were barriers between Indian groups. Mixtecas and Zapotecas did not like one another. Mixes had never been conquered by any group, including the Spaniards; nevertheless, the Zapotecas felt superior to the Mixes. Deep ravines and lack of transportation perpetuated cultural barriers and ancient dislikes. Medical practice was in the hands of the herb lady, the witch doctor, the bonesetter, and the empiric midwife. Faulty nutrition encouraged parasite and germ growth. Poverty in the semieroded area was obvious. Only the rural teacher was likely to have some scientific knowledge, along with the obligation to teach science. Usually the teacher was respected in the community.

In New Mexico I had discovered that the rural schoolteacher could be my right hand in program-planning for health. In the mountains of Oaxaca, the teachers might not have completed Teachers' Training courses, but their motivation was high. As teachers from Indian cultures themselves, they had already gone beyond the need to say, "I am a Mixe" or "I am a Zapoteca." They could now say, "I am a Mexican." Besides the rural teachers, who would be my key, I had another positive factor working for me — the natural curiosity of the student. He, in turn, would carry the knowledge home to his parents, translate it into their native language while, at the same time, he was preparing for his future adult role, to come all too soon.

I planned my class presentation of the various systems of the body and their functions. Anatomy and physiology would come to life in a brief course. Germs that aid and germs that destroy were to be shown in a simple way so that, even without a microscope, the student could visualize them. The constant battle between the host and the invader, the condition of the host and the virulence of the invader — all this would be discussed, as well as the control of invaders. Diseases prevalent in the area in which they lived would be defined, and emphasis placed on prevention and control.

The plan included methods of training lay health workers, *promotores de la salud*, in areas where there was no scientific medicine. How could we impart scientific knowledge to the existing *yerbera*, *huesero*, *brujo* and *partera* (herb lady, bonesetter, witch doctor and midwife)? How could this new knowledge be integrated with the official structure of the school program, extending only through the third grade? Could health instruction be threaded through the regular classes in reading, writing, arithmetic, civics, geography, history and science? I hoped that the teachers, the students, and I, together, could solve this problem, using the unit method, or the global method as it is called in Mexico. John Dewey's concept of the interaction of the individual with the environment, and vice versa, had always worked in public health teaching. I was sure it could be applied here.

The tentative plan to instruct teachers how to teach for positive health through the school program, with the purpose of training lay health workers, was accepted. In the few days remaining before leaving again for San Pablo Guelatao, I studied the textbooks of the first three grades. In the first grade the pupils were to learn the construction and function of the skeletal system, followed by the circulatory and the gastrointestinal systems. I was beginning to think of games and tricks for integrating my ideas into the curriculum.

It was good that I had my own program to think about, for there were changes in the University. A new president had taken over, and teachers were being dropped, especially those believed to be loyal to the outgoing president. And since the latter and his wife were close friends of mine, I assumed I might also be dropped. And I was.

For the first time I had to leave my little girl for as long as four days; but I was not worried, because with us was a wonderful young woman, Celia Vázquez Paz, who was both maid and housekeeper.

She turned up the very day after I had mentioned to my classes in public health nursing that I needed such a person. One of my students, together with her grandmother and her Aunt Celia, appeared at my house, and the interview was conducted by them, not by me. The grandmother decided that Celia would be permitted to work in my home, though she was not to sleep there until they were sure of my way of life, my moral conduct.

Señora Vázquez, the grandmother, came from a small Zapoteca mountain village called Ixtepeje. She was the matriarch of the family, her position as such even more solid, since she was a widow. The granddaughter became a nursing supervisor, and all members of the family are still my friends. Years later, my only complaint about Celia was that every two months I had to permit her to go home for five days; the call of the Oaxacan earth and family ties being as strong as they are, there would have been no staying for her should I not allow these regular visits, even if I were to be forever on my best behavior.

Toby and Celia were by then inseparable. Toby, nine years old, was as Oaxacan as the black *mole* she ate. Whatever she did and whatever she thought tended toward the dramatic. Since Celia was a devout Catholic, Toby felt she was one too, and soon became more Catholic than the Catholics. It was not always easy to explain to her that ever since man's appearance on earth, he has had gods, and what he called his god depended on the age in which he lived. The only common denominator there seemed to be was that man needed a god. To keep her from becoming too fanatical a Catholic, I stressed the many religions down through the ages, beginning with Amon. Inasmuch as I was not a Catholic, she did worry me. But, being such a strong believer in individual rights, I felt I could grant her the right to become a Catholic while I insisted on my own right not to be one. However, I acquired some wonderful *compadres* through my daughter's baptism as a Catholic. Again I realized that living with Toby was never dull. Toby, in Zapoteca, meant "one" or "god," I had told her — at the same time cautioning her not to think of herself as a goddess.

On April 1st, the jeep took me to Guelatao. This time I was less concerned with the beauty surrounding me and more concerned with doing a good piece of work. The directors of education and health services for the Papaloapan Commission would be there to listen to me. I was scared. Who was I? What did I really know of Mexico? What did I understand of the problems of the rural schoolteacher? I knew so little of the Zapotecan culture. Spanish was not my language. English had become mine, though when excited I still lapsed into Dutch, my first language. From experience, however, I had learned that I always worked better when I was unsure of myself.

I wondered how little Guelatao, with a population of about 1,000, would sleep and feed the 100 teachers of the Ixtlán Sierra de Juárez school district. I was to report to the home of Josefina Luna, director of the rural school and also a member of the board of municipal authorities. In Guelatao, despite the superimposed PRI (Institutional Party of the Revolution), Mexico's predominant political party, the old system of government continued in effect. It worked like this:

From the age of ten years, one began serving his community. He became a *topil*, and his work, his *tequio*. He served according to his ability and according to the needs of the community until he reached age 35, when he became an elder, or *anciano*. The governing authorities consisted of both men and women, about 35 in number. To become one of them was to achieve the highest honor. Everyone served without pay. Obviously, to accomplish anything, one had to work through these village authorities.

Josefina Luna's tiny house was on the hillside road entering the village. It was built of native stone and cement, covered with flowering vines. On the porch, basins and pitchers of water were ready for hand-washing. One room, her own, had been prepared for the director of education. Mine was the small living room. The privy behind the house was nestled in a niche over a small ravine that drained into a river hundreds of yards below. It was beautifully papered with "Eradication of Malaria" posters. Water for washing and cooking was carried to the house from a nearby community tap.

Teachers came walking up the hill, tired and disheveled. Some carried small babies; others had children at their sides. Men and women, mostly young, were arriving. Some had been walking the entire day, and others, as many as three. From behind the flowering plants on the porch, I watched the bone-weary teachers as they stopped to catch their breath and to greet Miss Luna.

In the long dormitories of the Indian school, the men would sleep on cots in one room, and the women, in another. The boys had been moved out temporarily, to sleep on straw mats in classrooms. Although it seemed quite rustic and primitive to me, I did not then realize how fortunate Guelatao was to have adequate electricity and water. I was to learn that later, at teaching centers where one cup of water a day was my supply for all purposes.

When the school bell rang for supper, teachers walked down the hill to the rural school, passing the enchanted *laguna*. Sheets were used as tablecloths, and gladioli graced the tables. Chattering, singing voices filled the air as we ate our beans and tortillas and drank hot chocolate.

The opening ceremony was held early the next morning in the rural school. Following the plan of the Papaloapan Commission, all major works like dams, electric plants, and state roads were paid for; but all other works were on a 50-50 basis, the village contributing its share in labor, local materials, and so forth. Even though the Commission contributed fifty percent, the work belonged finally to the village.

The Mexican flag was raised. Everyone, his hand on his chest, solemnly sang the national anthem. I had not forgotten the anthems of the Netherlands, of the United States, and of the Spanish Republic. Now, with deep feeling, I was singing another, the national anthem of Mexico. After breakfast, the program began on the huge terrace, or porch, which had been set up as a classroom.

Professor Antonio Barbosa Heldt, director of the Commission's educational program, stated that the three-day Teachers' Institute would cover "The Role of the Teacher in Helping to Lower Morbidity and Mortality Rates Through the School Program." First there would be an explanation of the new five-year program for the eradication of malaria. It was given by one of the newly trained specialist doctors involved with this dynamic, radical program. It was the first time in world history for such a campaign to be launched. With the help of

UNESCO funds, it would begin to take on the unprecedented scope it envisioned. Eagerly I strained my ears in order to not miss a word. It was said that every home, every shack in malaria-prone areas would be specifically numbered, to be included in a master list. At the same time, a training program would be set up for those responsible for spraying. Teachers would be taught how to make slides and how to report suspected malaria. Talks about malaria would be given in all schools: what it is, what causes it, and the importance to Mexico of its eradication.

To find these dwellings was not an easy job. In the Oaxacan mountains, teams would have to walk as much as ten days to reach certain areas. After all had been well charted, the spraying would begin. Throughout this period teachers would be giving classes, hoping that information on the urgency of wiping out malaria would make its way to those at home.

The difference between the proposed technique and those used before, both in Mexico and elsewhere, was that an attempt would be made to keep the disease from spreading by killing the mosquitoes before they could transmit it from infected persons to healthy ones. Walls were to be sprayed with a substance that causes the mosquito to drop dead. All of this had been done in one area, the basin of the Papaloapan River; otherwise the dam could not have been initiated, or the hydroelectric plant. Malaria was the third highest cause of death in the nation. In the Papaloapan watershed it was nearly extinct, and the malaria program of the Papaloapan Commission would pass over to the National Eradication Program.

What an exciting fight this could be! To liberate an entire country from malaria! Cold wars, hot wars were far away from us here in the open classroom in Guelatao. This would be our war, a fight to the finish, a constructive war where enemy germs were slain. This was the kind of combat to which I could give myself wholeheartedly.

The next talk was given by engineer Morales of the Papaloapan Commission, on onchocercosis. It was important to him to know from the teachers how the brigades would function, those that would be going to the villages where the disease was prevalent. A sanitary engineer, the speaker was world famous for his knowledge of the subject. Its cause had been discovered by Dr. Larumbe, a former health officer in the state of Oaxaca: The vector was carried by the bite of a black fly found in rapids and swift rivers. Once bitten, blindness of the victim was inevitable, unless the nodule that contained the vector was surgically removed — and the operation was painful. Upon the arrival of medical brigades, people were known to flee and hide. The approach had been all wrong, of course. No explanation had ever been given to the people themselves. There had been no teaching on the disease in the villages. I was becoming more and more certain that teaching the teacher how to teach for health was essential, especially where medical services were nonexistent.

Then it was my turn. After apologizing for the errors I would be sure to make in speaking Spanish, I asked if it had not occurred to them to wonder, "What right does the foreigner have to teach us?" I said that, while in general I might agree with that view, I was hoping I would be granted the privilege of earning that right.

I had asked Miss Luna if the first three grades could have a sample lesson. Expectant faces were before me. In the rear were the teachers; on the porch wall the village authorities were seated. In the open court outside the classroom, the boys from the Indian school were listening attentively.

A chart of a skeleton hung on the wall. It was a fixture; everyone ignored it. In that culture, its only significance was for the Day of the Dead, when charming candy skulls and skeletons were placed on altars. How could I make the skeleton, the actual bones of the body, come to life? How could the knowledge of bones be taught through the school program? Could we say "drink milk" in an area where there were no cows? Addressing the first three grades, I asked, "Do you want your bones to stay the same size they are now? Do you want them to grow bigger? What makes a bone? What makes it strong? When is it brittle? Is it up to you to make your bones? Whose body is it? What is heredity? What is environment? What is the best way to get good bones?"

I answered my own questions as simply as possible. Then I walked to the white wall of the schoolroom terrace and, directing my questions to the first-graders, I asked, "What is this wall made of?" One boy answered, *"Cal"* (limestone). "Would it stick together and hold if only *cal* were used?" I asked. They looked at me as if I were a total ignoramus. Then they shouted, "Our fathers used *cal* and *mezcla* (mixture, in this case mortar). We helped them build it." One interrupting the other, they explained how a wall should be built.

Now I pulled out of my pocket a series of bones — turkey, chicken, fish — and asked, holding up each in turn, "Guess what this is made of? What color is it? Is it *cal*? Does it need a mixture to make the *cal* stick together? Let us all feel our bones in the forearm and upper arm. Juan, how many bones do you have in the lower part of your arm?"

He answered, "Two." I continued, "And in the upper arm?" He answered, "One." I glanced quickly around at my audience and couldn't help smiling as I watched the young and old feeling and counting bones. "Now, Roberto, can you add two and one? Can you write it on the blackboard?" Roberto went proudly to the blackboard and wrote, "2 and 1 are 3." We had just used three subjects: reading, writing and arithmetic.

"Now guess, children: What is hot? It is all around us. It is free. It shines."

"The sun, the sun!" they shouted in unison.

I went on to explain that the sun has a certain substance called Vitamin D that enables the *cal* to stick together. "It is the adhesive tape. But if the vitamin helps the *cal* and other minerals to stick together, where do we get the *cal*? The textbooks say that milk has calcium, but there is no milk in these mountains. Now, students, think. Where will you, or where do you, get the calcium that makes your bones longer and stronger?"

Teachers were raising their hands, but I had to motion no to them, again smiling at their eagerness. "Try to think, children. What does your mother put in the corn at night to make it swell, so that by morning it is puffy, and she can grind it for tortillas?"

Now they guessed, and their answer was *cal*, lumps of *cal*. How satisfied they were as they drew bones, added bones, and talked bones. We drew tortillas and little rays of Vitamin D coming from the sun. Not a word was written on the drawings they would take home to their parents, explaining what the tortillas and the sun did for bones. I hoped some mother would be grateful that she no longer had to say, "Juan, eat your tortilla."

We had added drawing to our school subjects, showing bones. Now that we had demonstrated the importance of *cal*, we had to show, through geography and history, how erosion had taken place and how it could be contained, prevented and changed so that the limestone would not take over as it had done in the Alta Mixteca, where for miles one saw only limestone and where nothing could grow. Civics and science were easy; we had just been proving as much. The bell rang for dinner, and I promised the audience that, later, I would help them discover how the black beans they were about to eat, accompanied by *chile*, worked in their bodies.

Duck soup, duck in *mole*, black beans and tortillas made up our dinner. Ducks were the only protein in the village, aside from beans. After three days of duck, I preferred it in its natural habitat. Teachers all around me continued asking questions. I was glad that the dinner hour was from two to four o'clock in the afternoon, so that I could later escape to my room to be alone a few moments and to restore my energy for the four-to-eight session.

Knowing that before a pupil finished the third grade, the teacher was supposed to have imparted the necessary knowledge of the circulatory, respiratory, and gastrointestinal systems, I thought I would begin with the circulatory and show it as a life-giver, a huge transportation system carrying foods, life-giving oxygen, protectors to fight invaders, and a means of carrying away waste materials. Here, also, the teacher had large drawings that she had bought in the city of Oaxaca. The students copied them with little or no idea of what they signified, and perhaps even the teachers had no idea of their significance.

Apparently, word had spread that a foreign woman was speaking at the school. The villagers stood six deep at the wall, ostensibly studying the school's demonstration vegetable and flower garden.

Since water had recently been piped up to community taps in their village, the children knew what a pipe was, as well as a pump. These objects I could use as analogies for the circulatory system. Trying to capture their interest at once, I asked, "Do you have pipes in your bodies like the water pipes the village now has?" They looked at me as if I were mad. As they shook their heads, I continued, "But you do have a piping system, and a pump that pumps a river carrying many things to all parts of your body." Drawing a pipe on the blackboard, I gave it three layers, explaining that the middle one was of elastic tissue. "Now let's prove it. Each of you place your three middle fingers — not too hard — on your wrist just below your thumb. Press gently. What do you feel?"

Swiftly I slipped through the room and placed the children's hands on their pulses. Teachers waved their hands for help. I had to keep them waiting a bit, for I did not want to lose the attention of the students, their interest centering now on themselves, making them more attentive, creating a better learning situation. "Now, Juan, count your pulse. Now you, Julia, and you, María. Feel it pulse, feel the elastic in your piping system." Great excitement reigned as they felt their pulses, while I, who could hardly draw, was sketching a pump, the heart, on the blackboard. It did not look much like the professional chart hanging on the wall, but I was holding the interest of the students in their own circulatory system.

"Where does the liquid in your pipes go?" I asked. "Does the mouthful of tortilla you bit off and ate — does it go as such to your big toe? Is there oxygen in the liquid? Hold your hands as tightly as you can around your leg. Does it feel cold? Does it turn blue? What is happening? What is the liquid? What is blood?"

Drawing a big, yellow river, I made it change color by adding red cells, red with oxygen and iron. I added farmers carrying machetes, who fought off invaders, germs that were harmful. Now, with another colored chalk, I added bits of food broken down by the digestive system, separating the fats, proteins, carbohydrates, minerals, vitamins, and so forth. On the blackboard we listed all that one of the boys, then one of the girls, had eaten that day. We checked the river to see if what was needed for growth had been fed to their bodies. Had they supplied the river in each of them with the needed materials for their proper destinations? The pupils were learning a lesson in nutrition and the circulatory system without being overwhelmed by frightening pictures and words.

We began to draw rivers, pumps, foods going into rivers, farmers fighting disease germs with machetes. Children were to take these drawings home to explain what they had learned to their parents. The sun was sinking as we finished the afternoon class. Teachers came up with questions popping with the criticisms I had requested when I dismissed the class. Here and there in the patio, men and women, parents, were teaching one another how to count pulse. They had been fascinated by that. Now I could see the beginning of what I wanted to do: to place the responsibility for eliminating or controlling a disease on the afflicted person, who would combat it actively because of, first, his personal interest, then community interest, through an awareness of technical aids.

The teachers crowded around me, asking questions. We decided to have an informal round-table discussion after supper, group the questions in proper order and try for answers.

Hearing no English, speaking no English, seeing no English in print, it should not have been so amazing to me that I was hearing, thinking and speaking in Spanish. I had discovered a trick: If I took a word like *idea* and pronounced it as in Dutch, it became good Spanish. The vowels were pronounced the same in Spanish as in my native Dutch. I was glad that no linguist was present at the Teachers' Institute to hear my mixed Dutch-American accent.

Boys from the Indian school came trotting down the hill with the fresh sweet rolls they had baked for our supper, to be taken with hot chocolate, then the black beans. It was strange to me that one ate the sweet roll and hot chocolate first, followed by beans and tortillas. I would have preferred the reverse — the sweet for dessert — but this was acculturating.

We ate in the indoor classroom, which had a blackboard the full length of one wall. For teacher participation, I had them group the questions as they came up on the floor. This was doubly useful, as I could not spell in Spanish. It was fascinating to watch them group. Problems of pregnancy, how to distinguish the normal symptoms from the abnormal. These came mainly from teachers who lived at great distances from a town. Male teachers requested the rudiments of how to deliver a baby. Some of them were motivated by the death of local midwives. Could I explain the delivery process to couples so they might help one another, the husband actually performing the delivery? Of what should a school first aid cabinet consist? What to do for this emergency or that? My answer to them was that, at this point, I would have much thinking to do and that I would devote extra time to another conference, perhaps even two.

When the three days were over, I felt close to the rural teachers of the Ixtlán de Juárez school zone. After the closing exercises, everyone was inviting me to visit him at his school. They were promising to develop practice-teaching plans to demonstrate what they had learned. For my part, I promised that at the next Teachers' Institute I would work on the problems they had presented to me. At least I was less frightened than I had been before I started. I was learning. They were learning. It was an exciting mutual help society. I'm afraid I was becoming biased in favor of the Zapoteca Indian culture.

Since the rains had not yet begun, there was no adobe mud to get stuck in this time, and within two hours we were back in Oaxaca.

How I longed for a hot tub bath, but water was a scarcity in the dry season. If the house one lived in did not have a water deposit and an electric pump to make the big stationary tank on the roof function, pressure from the street line could not be counted on to send up the water that was pumped into the street lines only a few hours each day. Sure enough, my longings for a hot bath were thwarted; there was not a drop of water in the building. The only supply we had was the five-gallon jar of purified water. Well, it was neither the first nor the last time I went unwashed while working with the Papaloapan Commission. Next best — a plan Toby highly approved of — was to go to a swimming pool, La Serenita, the next day.

As soon as I could get to it, I made out a written report on the Guelatao Institute and, with it in hand, went to the offices of the Commission and gave it to Mr. Cruikshank. He thanked me profusely and said, "I'll let you know when we have the next Teachers' Institute." I reminded him that I had volunteered to help several days a week. I wondered why he was so indefinite about giving me a date. Little did I realize how difficult it was for him to sell federal school inspectors on the use of a foreigner. By the time three weeks had passed, I was feeling disappointed not to have heard from him. What had I done wrong? Where had I offended Mexican cultural patterns?

On April 30th a man came to call on me. He was the paymaster of the Oaxaca office of the Papaloapan Commission. In a most bureaucratic manner he asked, "Why have you not prepared for work? You have been *nombrado*."

I asked, "What on earth is *nombrado*? What does that mean?"

He then explained that I had been named, appointed in charge of health education for the entire upper section of the Papaloapan Basin, where 200,000 Indians lived in isolation. A month's salary was awaiting me, retroactive to include the center in Guelatao. One of the persons present there, whom I had not met directly, was the engineer, Raúl Sandoval, in charge of the whole Papaloapan Basin; but they had neglected to tell me so. So he had observed my teaching and had seen to it I was *nombrado* for the appointment. My salary was $72 a month.

May 1st, Mexico's Labor Day. Tomorrow I would be working as a federal employee. With that in mind, it was thrilling to watch the May Day parade pass by the Hotel Marqués del Valle where Toby and I stood watching. First came the governor and his staff; then, of course, the state band, followed by the unions — electrical, railroad, teachers, among many others. The large banners they carried captivated me. "Remember the Haymarket Martyrs! The Haymarket Dead Gave Us an 8-Hour Day!" U.S. labor history was certainly honored there in the streets of Oaxaca!

On May 2nd, I reported to Mr. Cruikshank. With typical Mexican courtesy, he guided me around the offices and introduced me to the staff. I met architects, agronomists, engineers of all specialties, masons, carpenters, clerks and secretaries. I would share office space with the radio operator and the young man in charge of physical education, David Rodríguez. Last but not least, I met the pilot of the Commission's single-motor plane. Everyone was polite, but chillingly so, with a "let's see what she's like" attitude. I felt it all around me. I was older than most of them, old enough to be the mother of most. I was a foreigner. Above all, I was an American. What had a foreign woman ever done for Mexico? Would I prove I could take it? I could sense their attitude and hear their questions in their whispers, see them in their eyes. They were distrustful of me.

And quite rightly, I thought — at least, from their point of view. I had to prove myself first, and I could earn their respect only through work, given time.

Day by day in the office I read reports on the area to which I would go and studied information on the works that had been accomplished there. Soon my very naivete began to make the first cracks in the wall of ice around me, but not with Memo, the engineer in charge of road building. I asked David, my coworker, who had never been distant with me, the reason. He explained that Memo nourished a special resentment ever since U.S. warships bombarded Veracruz on April 21, 1914. Many in his family had been killed in the defense of the unarmed town. Understandable in Memo, I thought, and determined to read more on that period of Mexican history.

Staff workers would gather by the huge wall map, especially when we saw new pins being stuck in it. Like Joseph's coat, it was a map of many colors. Each color meant a new bridge, a new school, a new step dam, or a new section of road. But most important to the field workers was when the pilot, Captain Silva, placed a pin indicating a new airstrip. In time I would learn that ten minutes in the Cessna equalled ten hours on a mule.

"Profie," as David Rodríguez was called, told me that the next institute would be held in San Isidro Huajapan, in the Mixe region. The only study in English I could find on the Mixes was a brief one done by Ralph Beals. He had stayed in Ayutla, the first village he encountered upon entering the Mixe area. David gave me more data, and explained that the Mixes had never been conquered, neither by other Indian groups nor by the Spaniards; that they numbered about 50,000, and lived in the most inaccessible part of the state of Oaxaca. In President Lázaro Cárdenas' time, they had tried to break the rigid hold of the *cacique*, local bossman. But Luis Rodríguez was an all-powerful chieftain in the Mixe area, controlling everything. Many were afraid of him. David told me how once the federal troops had arrived at Zacatepec, where Rodríguez lived, asking for him. No one understood Spanish except one person, who told them that Rodríguez had left for another village four days distant. They never knew they had been talking to Rodríguez himself. Another tale was that he had 100 wives. That one I considered improbable, but the story of his private cemetery and the feuding, quite believable.

When David began to describe the difficult trails, the dangerous downgrades, and how one had to lean toward the cliff and hang loose in the stirrups should the mule slip and fall into the ravine, I did feel slightly panicky — but I couldn't tell him so.

I sneaked a look at the map to see if there were any airstrips in the vicinity, but there weren't. On the relief map, it looked like abrupt terrain. The federal inspector, when he came to the office to plan the Institute with David, made it a point to tell me that it was about the most difficult terrain in the Mixe area. "However," he reassured me, "it is only two hard 14-hour days on muleback. The first day you do part by jeep, part on foot." Good Lord, I had never ridden a mule!

David advised me that the jeep could take us some of the way, over a new road that was being built by the Papaloapan Commission from Mitla and which would eventually reach Ayutla. But we could walk from where the road ended to Santa María Alvarado, and there we could sleep the first night, renting mules for the rest of our journey. Santa María was mainly Zapoteca in culture, but had become more mestizo as a result of its proximity to the Valley of Oaxaca. The people earned their living by renting mules for transporting coffee from the Mixe area, where it grew under banana trees on the Veracruz rainbelt slope.

Foolishly, I had suede boots made, thinking they would be softer. Levis, a straw hat to keep the sun out of my eyes, blankets, a flashlight — all the things I considered necessary I gathered together. My teaching plan I wrapped up in plastic to keep it dry. I was certainly not anticipating what might happen to suede boots, straw hat, and rolled blankets in pouring rain.

The Victory

Early in the morning, one of the engineers was to take us to the end of the road. But it was two o'clock when he finally picked up David and me. That meant we would be caught in the rain. The rainy season had begun, so the road engineer decided to stop and visit a bit in Mitla. The ruins were exquisite, but walking about among the old tombs when we had to reach Santa María Alvarado was more than I was prepared to do willingly. We slithered and slid to the end of the dirt road, which was a mass of adobe mud. David and I scrambled out with our packs.

Fortunately David knew the trail. To me it looked like an impenetrable maze. Soon my straw hat — meant to protect me from the sun — hung, a sodden mess around my face, directing streams of water down my back. My new suede boots squished water with every step I took, climbing and climbing. My braids were drenched.

I had wrapped my poncho around the birth atlas, for I hoped to begin instruction on midwifery. Stumbling up the hill in the dark, I slipped, fell, twisted my ankle, but had to go on. Lights blinked ahead. We heard voices in the impenetrable night — other teachers, stumbling, making their way up the trail. We had arrived at Santa María Alvarado.

The villagers directed us to the schoolhouse. Under the protecting eaves, we built a fire to dry ourselves. Nacho, a Mixe teacher, as well as Flora and Guadalupe Fuentes, two sisters whose native tongue was Zapoteca, had joined us. So now we were five. We found a tiny store where we bought huge, blue-corn tortillas, and a hardboiled egg for each of us. That was our supper. David had begun trying to get mules for our use in the morning. The not too friendly mestizo villagers preferred to have their mules carry coffee beans. Would we pay? Could we be trusted to treat the animals well? Finally David managed to arrange for two mules, with the proviso that the owner's eldest son, Santos Cruz, accompany us to be sure they were not mistreated. I was far more concerned about how the mules would treat us.

Nacho had borrowed a guitar, and while I sat by the glowing fire, shaking my long hair dry, I listened to the sweet voices of Flora and Lupe as they sang "La Llorona" in Zapoteca. Then Nacho sang in Mixe, followed by David in Spanish. When my turn came, I sang Dutch songs and American folk songs. Almost dry, we pulled the long school tables together. It was cold, a wet, penetrating cold. Rolling ourselves in our damp blankets, we lay down close to each other for body warmth. I was at the end, then came Lupita, Flora, David and Nacho. Wrapped up on a hard table, body to body with Mixe, Zapoteca and mestizo, I certainly did not feel like a foreigner. But the fleas must have recognized me as one, for they bit and continued to bite me.

Scratching away, unable to sleep, I began to think of my four bed-table companions, snoring peacefully and with great gusto. Ignacio, or Nacho, director of the rural school at Totontepec, had walked for many days some years ago to enter the Indian school at Guelatao. Upon graduation, he returned to his village to become a teacher. For the past three years he had gone to Oaxaca every vacation to attend the Rural Teachers' School. From Totontepec, it was a four-day walk to Alvarado where we lay on the table. Within another few years he would have his teacher's certificate. So far, he had been shot at only once, but could expect more, since the *cacique* in the Mixe area did not like young moderns.

Guadalupe and Flora were two of the five children of a deaf-mute woman who understood them by reading their lips. They, too, went to the Rural Teachers' School during vacations. In fact, they and Nacho had just returned and were now on their way with us to the Teachers' Institute. The girls were particularly proud of their elder brother, a product of the same Indian school at Guelatao. He had gone on to the National School of Agriculture at Chapingo and was then on scholarship in Grenoble, France. He spoke French, English, Spanish and, of course, his native Zapoteca. Another sister was a teacher in a different zone. The youngest brother was studying at the

University in Oaxaca and lived at home with their mother, who did dressmaking to help sustain her family, as she had done since the death of her husband.

These people, to me, were Mexico and her future.

As dawn broke, the sleeping forms awakened, bright and cheerful. Following the leader, I washed my face in icy cold water, more to wake up than to clean up. The dry, blue tortillas and hot beans tasted good. Four mules and a horse awaited us. The saddles were wooden and looked most uncomfortable. I was given a mule, a big beast. She stared at me, and I, at her. I hoped she did not guess how scared I was. David glanced at me and said, "Don't worry. It's *mansa* (tame) and easy to handle. This mule has been carrying coffee out of San Isidro for many years. She knows the trail."

I decided then and there to let the mule and the rest of the company lead the way. I was quite sure that I could not. David showed me how to hold the reins, how to guide the mule for left and right, but he forgot to tell me that stirrups could be adjusted. Mixe guides had come down in the night and were waiting for us to take the long trail. Of course, I had Santos Cruz, watcher of his father's mules, to keep an eye on me. I had wanted to work as a Mexican, with Mexicans. Well, now I could. Did I really want to so badly, I wondered, as I was being instructed how to mount the mule? But how did one get off? I decided simply to wait until the time came.

In the heat, in the clouds of dust, over rocks and shale we climbed and climbed. Five hours the horse lay down and refused to move. The trail was too rough for a horse. Santos said, "Let him alone. He will rest and then find his way home." How I wished I could do that too! But I had to see this thing through. When it was hot, I shed clothing, but now it was getting colder, and I added new layers. Another five hours later we were approaching the last of the three Alvarado villages, a few huts. It was the very last before reaching Ayutla, the gateway to the Mixe area. The fact that it was a Zapoteca village meant warm and friendly people. The others jumped off their mules. I waited until David helped me off. My knees were without feeling. I could hardly walk.

First the mules had to be fed their *zacate*, or dry corn stalks. Then we had good tortillas, black beans, hot black coffee — plus the luxury of a fried egg each. I was told that the worst of the day's trip would now begin. That was easy to imagine as I studied the cliffs ahead. Climbing again, we were among huge boulders that rolled at the touch of a hoof. Now, on the downgrade, I felt like a Westerner as I stood up in my stirrups, leaning backward as the others did, so that I would not go headfirst over the mule. Very soon we all had to dismount, as the narrow trail down the cliff was too dangerous for riding muleback. The mules went first, tested the trail, and the riders followed. Rushing rivers had to be crossed, and the mules swam while we crossed over narrow swinging bridges made of jungle vines. Through it all I admired the incredible beauty of waters spurting out of cliffs and falling in spray. By then other teachers walking to San Isidro had joined us.

We were still climbing when night fell. What had been mist now became a hard rainfall. In the distance were the flickering lights of Ayutla. I wondered if this agony would ever end. My knees were sore. My body ached, the pain acute, but especially in my knees. I wanted to weep, and I did, but in the dark and quietly, while the others were singing. I hoped the mule really knew her way, for I had given up and was just trying to hold on. I had been at the tail end of the party for the last few hours. I could not hasten the mule. She did as she pleased while she plodded toward Ayutla. Suddenly, around a bend, we were there.

As Santos Cruz led the mules to water and food, we were taken to a long, low building, partly roofed, the water dripping where the roof had given way. Sleeping figures stirred as we moved toward the kitchen and the open hearth. Now the tortillas and beans tasted like ambrosia.

As the oldest member of the group, I was honored by being offered the teacher's room. David told me it had a bed. How I looked forward to that bed! Of course, I assumed that a bed meant a mattress too. Not that I expected sheets or blankets, and I was not surprised that the springs sagged, but a mattress was nowhere evident. By that time I no longer cared. Mattress or not, fleas or not, I fell onto the springs and was awakened at four the next morning.

About fifteen more teachers milled around us. They had been the sleeping forms we had stumbled over the night before. Together we drank our hot coffee, ate our tortillas and beans, and got ready for the worst part of the trail. As dawn broke, and I looked back at the trail we had covered the night before, I was grateful it had been pitch dark and that the mule had known the way.

My mule had a distinctly stubborn personality. She was always the last in line. She paid no attention to me when I told her to hurry, to catch up with the others. When she came to grass that was appealing to her, she looked back at me with bright eyes and stopped to eat. I could only sit and wait until she was ready to go on again. Yet I had learned to trust her. When we went around curves on a narrow path not more than two feet wide, with sheer crags overhead, a drop of thousands of feet below, she would make her way with amazing caution, while I leaned toward the cliff wall just in case she might slip. Over and over again, I heard myself saying under my breath, "Please, God, take care of the mule."

When there were steep, muddy slopes to climb, I leaned back, and the mule sank almost to her knees in mud. Plodding along, hours later we came to a lovely little valley, a tumbling brook, a few shacks, and a delicious drink right out of the stalk of the maguey plant. It was called honeywater, and it certainly was, served in a gourd that looked like a Dutch wooden clog. I admired it so much that the farmer gave it to me.

Again we climbed, now to Cacalotepec — only a few hours more to go, David assured me. He would come racing back on his mule every so often to see if I were okay. He would get the mule to go faster, but the minute David rode ahead, the mule slowed down again. By that time I was so tired and hungry — but with stirrups adjusted to my height — that I simply let the mule take over. Eight hours later we at last saw a village perched precariously on a crag.

That was Cacalotepec. It was the highest we would climb. Now we saw it, now we didn't. We were riding in mist and clouds, climbing the trail on the side of the cliff. We moved along, passing Mixe straw-thatched huts. When the clouds broke over the schoolhouse, we were on a narrow level which held a few other buildings too.

Bless the Mixe runners who had gone on ahead. Waiting for us were hot cabbage soup, rice, beans and tortillas. Should the mules make good time, we had only three more hours to go, and all of it downhill.

With the mules sliding in the mud, we rode along the trail to San Isidro. Not too often the sun would show through, and we could see the lush, tropical green ahead. We had long ago crossed the divide and were now on the Gulf Coast side. It was becoming hot and muggy, with an occasional shower of rain.

Was it a mirage now? What was that flat, shiny object in the distance? It seemed suspended in air. "David," I finally asked, "am I seeing things? What is that shiny surface on the other side of the ravine, there in the distance?"

He told me it was only the tin roof of the new school at San Isidro.

"How did it get there?" I insisted.

He replied, "The *topiles* brought it from Oaxaca. That was their *tequio*." He didn't seem at all impressed.

Numbly, I hoped I wouldn't slip off as the mule kept sliding down. I had been in that wooden saddle for nearly twelve hours. At times I swayed, in rhythm to the songs being sung by the large numbers of teachers who had joined us, emerging from almost invisible trails. Now came the sound of a band, many bands, fireworks — the bands played, the firecrackers boomed. We had arrived.

Again David had to help me off the mule. I had blisters

where no respectable lady should have blisters. I heard him say, "That wasn't too bad, was it? It's only three days from Oaxaca!"

The bands were lined up along the trail as we entered, and the mist had lifted to reveal a level terrain. David whispered to me, "They shaved the mountain top to make a place for the basketball court and the school." A basketball game was being played. Tables filled the court, the teachers were seated, drinking — of all things — Coca-Cola. Facing the court was a beautiful three-room school with glass windows and, of course, the tin roof. Nearby I saw another house with a sign reading "La Casa de los Maestros" (Teachers' Residence).

I could hardly believe I had made it. The federal school inspector walked toward me. He greeted me, saying, "You are late. It is 6 p.m. Can you give your first class at 7?"

Boldly I answered, "Of course." But in the mist that was changing to rain, I looked longingly at the teachers' home.

I had one hour to freshen up. On the way to the home, the mingled sounds of band and basketball filled the air. I was glad to see five army cots set up in the house, as well as pitchers of water and basins for washing purposes. The latrines were a long, muddy slope away. It was good to change to a dress and to pile my hair up high. Mixes had already been touching my braids with curiosity as I walked to the Teachers' Residence.

One hundred teachers of the Mixe zone sat on low benches in the schoolroom, waiting for me. Since I had only one hour before supper, I outlined what I hoped to teach in the next three to four days, such as basic anatomy, physiology, how to teach for health through the school program, diseases current in the area and how to fight them, some first aid and home nursing, as well as special evening classes on pregnancy, delivery, and care of the newborn. Though I had gotten soaking wet on the trip, my precious teaching aids were dry.

Candlelight flickered in the scattered huts. The serving committee of the day began setting up the school tables in the classroom where I had outlined the program. A line formed like a bucket brigade, bringing plates heaped with food. Where had it all come from, enough to feed 100 teachers? Who was paying for all this? I knew that the village consisted of 300 *ranchería* families scattered over the slopes. Judging by the rags they wore, they were poor. But I knew I could not draw conclusions like that in an Indian culture, for the people thought us crazy for having so many clothes, and for changing once or twice a day. They had certain clothing for work, which they wore until the patches gave out, and their fiesta or holiday garb, always fresh and white, ready for use.

After the tables were cleared, the meeting resumed. Through the windows the people of the village watched us, listening and translating into Mixe what the inspector was saying. Their heavy wool *gabanes* kept the mist from penetrating. The inspector's main emphasis was on the importance of going to school during all vacation periods and working toward a teacher's certificate. That sounded easy, until I recalled the trails I had covered in the past three days.

The group broke up to go to bed, the male teachers on straw mats in one classroom and the women in the other. The only ones who had cots were the inspector, his wife, David and I. We were to sleep in the Teachers' Residence. I wished they had plannned latrines when they built the school.

Who could be so cruel as to serenade us with "Las Mañanitas" at four in the morning? Rockets shot off. Bands competed to see which could play the brass the loudest. I had heard that the Mixes had the best musicians and bands in the mountains — but at such an hour? Half asleep, I muttered to the inspector, "Tell them, please, to stop and wait until 6 or 7 o'clock." He replied, "But it is the custom to serenade visitors at 4 a.m." Trying to clear my head, I thought, "Part of acculturation . . ."

It was damp and cold as we walked to the classroom for breakfast. The bands played on and on. Through the wet mist, the mysterious Mixes continued to come from nearby ranches. For what? To listen to us? To hear the music? Or to simply visit? I could not distinguish one group from another, but David could, by the way the women were dressed. Those with white *huipiles* were from Cotzocon. Gradually, with David teaching me, I began to recognize women from specific areas of the Mixe region by their dress.

That day I hoped to make the germ groups come to life dramatically. As a teaching aid I would take the position that there were four races of men — though another theory held there were three — and four races in the germ world. Man wanted to live, to adapt to his environment. Man ate, slept, had different food preferences. Well, so did the germs. Man had parents — Spallanzani proved that germs had parents. Man had cousins, aunts, uncles, brothers, sisters — so did the germs. Germs also struggled to adjust to and live in their environment, the human. And they were most democratic: They couldn't care less about color, race or creed.

Although I would be discussing such groups as the *cocci*, virus and bacillus, my emphasis would be on the spirochete. I hoped to make the spirochete that caused *mal del pinto* such a vivid threat that teachers would carry the instructions back to their villages even before the campaign to eradicate the disease began. Why, at this point, should we expect a Mixe to allow anyone to plunge a large needle into his body without knowing the reason and without being allowed to make his own decision as to treatment?

Teaching how to recognize the disease was easy. Anyone who lived in the Sierra Mixe knew that the *mancha morada* (purple blotch), followed by the *mancha blanca* (white blotch), meant *mal del pinto*. If it took so many years for a human family to develop, how many weeks did it take for a family of spirochetes to develop? (I was following the book, *Control of Communicable Disease in Man*, published by the American Public Health Association, but I stayed away from words like "incubation" until I had used sufficient analogies.)

What did the Mixe like to eat? What was his favorite bean, the black or the brown? What was the spirochete's favorite food? If this was the enemy, how could we destroy him? As I drew on the blackboard pictures of the skinny, snakelike spirochete — breathing, eating, living — I heard whispers of the bilingual Mixes at the windows translating what I was teaching. Integrating this project through the school program could be done by teaching the systems of the body. The more dramatically the student could describe it to his family, and the stronger his aversion to having ugly marks on his face and body, the more effective would be the medical program.

This spirochete was not a killer like the syphilis spirochete. This one liked to eat only the pigmentation of the skin, but it sure was ugly to look at. It was endemic in the Mixe zone. And when the gates of the dam were closed, making it necessary to move 20,000 Mazatecas, groups in other areas would not want them to come and live nearby, looking as they did after the disease had claimed them.

Heads were nodding a bit, so I changed tactics. I called on Jesús Siguenza, a tall, thin Mixe teacher, and said, "Look at the blackboard. See that snake trying to bite the girl? Go to Guadalupe Fuentes, and bite her cheek." The entire room awakened, tittered and giggled as Jesús, with pleasure, bit Lupita's cheek. And such rapid translation going on outside the windows!

Next we worked out a simple play that could be put on in each school for the parents' benefit, stressing the cause and prevention of *mal del pinto*. Much later we did the play in puppet theater. Skinny boys imitating snakes, lovely girls as victims, the doctor and his nurse approaching on muleback to set up a clinic for giving hypos. Some really delightful plays were worked out that day.

Later, as I taught the teachers how to give hypos intramuscularly, I showed them how to teach others to do the same, how to better prepare future health workers from among their students. I had brought a supply of hypos and needles with me, also alcohol and cotton. The alcohol didn't matter; one could always use *aguardiente*, or burning water — pure, unadulterated alcohol made of sugar cane. When the doctor came, with one nurse, to treat every Mixe epidemiologically, he would need extra help to give hypos. He would be able to do that job only to the degree that teachers taught the student and that the student relayed the information to his family.

Months later, at another Teachers' Institute in the Sierra Mixe, I met the doctor. He reported that attendance at the clinic had been almost 100 percent effective. That, I told him, was due to the teachers and their efforts. The teacher, having come from an Indian community, knew that in order to work effectively, explanation on the project first had to be made to the village authorities, as well as to the elders.

Pregnancy, delivery, and the newborn — how on earth to teach that in an area days away from the nearest medical services? Fortunately, I once had had a scholarship to attend Maternity Center, New York. The scholarship had been granted me because there were plans afoot then to establish a Home Delivery Service in Las Vegas, New Mexico, and one of the major aims was to hold classes with the existing midwives, to raise their level of knowledge in an attempt to lower maternal and infant mortality rates. Since then I had also read a marvelous short book on the subject, written by Dr. Leo Eloesser and published by the Inter-American Indian Institute. Before leaving for the Sierra Mixe, I bought ten copies of the manual and teaching guide. That material, plus the huge birth manual published by the Maternity Center, had survived the rain and dampness on the three-day trek.

Beginning with conception, I carefully reviewed symptoms to be considered suspect, possibly abnormal, so that the pregnant woman could give herself enough time to get to the city of

Oaxaca. After we had discussed the abnormal as thoroughly as possible, we went on to the normal: the relationship of the passenger to the passage, the smallest door the passenger would come through, and how to help at that time. I had brought a small doll, a nylon bag to be inflated, and a few other aids with which to stage a delivery. I would add information on how to cut the cord, why drops in the eyes, immediate care of the infant, and so on.

Never in my life did I have such a fascinated audience. How I hoped that, later, we could do some work with the practicing midwives. Teacher after teacher begged me to get them books to guide them on pregnancy, delivery and the newborn. Within a year I had distributed over 400 books in the Upper Papaloapan.

Classes went on for four days, in rain, mist and cold, on systems of the body, how to integrate teaching for health, first aid, home nursing, midwifery. The first class began at 8 a.m., and the last one ended at 10 p.m.

Meanwhile I tried to soak up all the Mixe culture I could. The village government had requested help from the Papaloapan Commission in building the school in which we worked, and the Commission matched the 50 percent they had readied in labor and materials. Over the ghastly terrain I still had to cover to go home, these people had transported the essential materials like cement, glass, roofing, and so on. Not only had they secured food for us for four days, but they had also brought cots, soft drinks and cigarettes. They had scraped off a mountain top to make way for a basketball court and the school. They were dressed in rags, because every cent had gone into the new installations. They followed the communal pattern of government, each individual earning the right to become a village official by serving the community from the age of ten years.

The Teachers' Institute was now drawing to a close. At supper that evening we discussed how much we owed the village. One hundred teachers had been served three times a day for four days, or 1200 meals. These meals had been cooked on open hearths and carried to us through mist and rain. We all chipped in and presented the village authorities with a sum of money which they refused to accept. The food, the Coca-Colas, the cots were their offerings to us. Much of it had to be carried for days up the brutal mountain trail.

When the village authorities left us, after refusing our contribution, the discussion of how to pay them really became excited. Someone suggested we buy an electric clock for the school, to mark the new times; but someone else argued that it might be years before electricity reached this particular mountain top. Another proposed books for the library; but others questioned the wisdom of that idea, as most of the people couldn't yet read. Like the housewife I am, I suggested a sewing machine. There was unanimous approval. But someone asked whether the Papaloapan Commission would match the fund 50-50 so that a good sewing machine could be purchased. I reassured them on this point, meanwhile wondering how I would sell the idea to the new engineer in charge, Mr. Jiménez. (Mr. Cruikshank had left for a tour of Latin American countries, to help organize regional development.)

And then the fiesta began, with village bands playing for us until almost dawn as we danced the mountain dances.

At dawn we held the official closing ceremony of the Institute on the basketball court in front of the new school, the only level spot in the village. Clouds hung low. Through the mist our mules appeared. They were well-fed and better rested than were we who had danced the night through. The school children, their parents, and the bands lined up along the hill slope. We began climbing to the strains of the "Canción Mixteca."

It was hours of climbing before we reached Cacalotepec, where we stopped for hot coffee before the long downgrade. My blisters had healed. I knew that stirrups could be adjusted, so I sang along with the others as we moved ahead on the trail. We were riding in the deep, black night, trying to reach Ayutla, when David said, "I have lost the wallet with the 1,500 pesos in it!" But what could be done? We had to move on. Hours later, two Mixe *topiles* presented the wallet! They had retraced the trail and, with a borrowed flashlight, found the wallet. What a relief! San Isidro had not lost the sewing machine.

Days passed quickly, and we reached the end of the trail, where the jeep was waiting to take us to Oaxaca. I have never loved a jeep as much as I did that day. When I saw the Willys with a winch, I knew it had rained a lot. The new cut was a quagmire, but with a winch one got through. My skin itched, my long hair was a snarl, scabs still clung to my blisters, my knees were black and blue, but I felt good. We had worked well together. I longed for a hot bath and the sight of my daughter. I wanted to tell her about the wonderful teachers of the Sierra Mixe. I hoped they had learned from me as I had learned from them. Interest, cooperation, sharing, brotherhood had taken on added meaning.

As I entered the office the next day, I was reminded of the lines from the song "Jericho": "and the walls came tumbling down." Limping in later than usual, I realized there was a new warmth in the greetings and smiles of the staff. David, having come in early, must have said something to the effect that "that foreigner" was now "their foreigner," for I was definitely one of the staff at last. And I was treated as an equal even by the paymaster, the point where bureaucracy can show itself at its most vexing:

The mule had cost 50 pesos a day, and I had had it for ten days, or $50 U.S. The *zacate* and corn to feed it had cost about $15, a total of $65 U.S. I was shown how to make out the original-and-four-copies request for my per diem, plus expenses for the mule. I was asked for my receipts, but no one had previously informed me of this.

"Neither the Zapotecas nor the Mixes can write," I told the paymaster. "At least, not those I dealt with."

His reply was, "Well, you should have gotten thumb prints."

No receipts, no money. There went almost all of a month's salary. I was paid $72 a month, and I had spent $65. An expensive learning experience, to say the least.

But it was only money, and my ignorance of bureaucracy was to blame. Could I convince our director, Mr. Jiménez, to match the 1,500 pesos we had collected to buy a sewing machine for San Isidro? I had already noticed that he shared the special philosophy of the Papaloapan Commission, that the fate of the human beings who lived in the watershed was as important as the dam itself. I told him of my promise to the teachers of the Mixe zone to secure matching funds. And, since this coincided with the basic view of the Commission on procurement of funding, he approved. But I had to put it all down in writing, original and four copies. Also, he reminded me, I was expected to write a report of the work I had done in the Sierra Mixe — original and four copies. Horrors! My written Spanish was disgraceful, but I was pleased to be treated as one of the staff. I wrote the report in what I hoped was understandable Spanish; then the secretary put it into proper, flowery Spanish — an original and four copies.

With that bit of bureaucracy behind me, I could go to the State Health Department and report what I had observed in the Sierra, and what I had taught. I always tried to get whatever I could for nothing from the Health Department — such as hypo needles — but since they were trying to conduct a state program, both preventive and curative, on the basis of one peso per man per month, they were always broke. They told us our Commission had sufficient funds to work with, and I suppose, in comparison, we did.

Down the street from the Health Department was a small shop that sold Singer sewing machines. There I found a heavy-duty model costing no more than the amount I had available. It was the tourist season in Oaxaca, and some of my friends from the States were there, so I found myself telling them the story of the sewing machine for San Isidro. It did seem as if all the Americans wanted to help the "poor Mexicans," so I suggested they buy four-meter cuts of material with matching thread, each donor to place his name and address on the package, and I would see to it that all these contributions were delivered together with the machine.

The Mixes did not feel poor, and I did not feel "poor Mexico," but if the foreigners felt better buying material and thread for the people who could use them, fine. By that time a nice bundle of packages had piled up on my desk, waiting for the four Mixe *topiles* to come as far as the new road to pick up the machine. One of our jeeps would deliver it to that point.

I wished I could be in San Isidro to hear the band and fireworks welcome the new sewing machine. Later I was told what happened. The Mixes raffled off the pieces of material to make money with which to buy other material better suited for work clothes. But the best thing I heard was that they had written to the State Department of Education requesting a sewing teacher for the school and village. When I taught, in the study of civics, that it was important to know your state and federal organizations and how to have them work for your community, little did I think it would end up in a request for a sewing teacher.

In the time remaining until the next session of the Teachers' Institute, I began writing plays that could be presented by the students. Never having written a play in my life, it was exciting to have characters like the louse that carries typhus, the spirochete that brings *mal del pinto*, the vector of onchocercosis — of blindness, the blood stream with rivers and all sorts of shipping on the rivers. Some of the plays I cast with pretty girls and iodine, showing that a lack of iodine was the main cause of the goiter condition prevalent in some areas of the watershed. In another I used bats that bit animals; if one ate the flesh of the dead animal, encephalitis was probable. I thought if we could include this in puppet theater, as it worked in the Lower Papaloapan where the dam was being built, all the better.

I made written requests for paper, envelopes and other items, original and four copies. I was delighted to be going back into the field to attend a Teachers' Institute in Cuicatlán, in the canyon near the railroad that went to Mexico City. This time I could go by train — but no one warned me about bedbugs on the train.

La Cañada, or The Canyon, stretched up from Oaxaca to Tehuacán, Puebla. David decided we should take the day train to Cuicatlán, in order to see the canyon and to follow the rivers that added up to the big Río Santo Domingo. By now I had become Mexican enough to realize that I benefited if I let the man (David) handle all details and feel that he was taking care of me, the helpless female. Just lovely!

At Huitzo, still in the Valley of Oaxaca, we passed mound after mound (usually indicative of ancient pyramids or temple bases), corn growing high around them. This must have been a huge Zapoteca center. We entered the canyon, and it became increasingly narrow. A rushing stream, crashing over great boulders, jumping over rocks, falling in misty waterfalls with rainbows brightly ribboned, was to one side. The bedbugs were biting so badly in the first-class coach that I had to find myself another seat, on the steps of the car. Holding on to the rail for security, the red-purple cliffs on both sides, I was well aware that the canyon was becoming even narrower. No wonder there were washouts in the rainy season. The railroad bed felt much more than 100 years old; and, in fact, it had been built about a century earlier, during the presidency of Benito Juárez. Soot blew back from the coal-burning engine that was helping us over the divide. Soon we began dropping to where the canyon widened, and then we changed to a diesel engine.

In Tomellin, engines had to be switched. Dinner, which David told me never varied, could be eaten there. Chicken soup, chicken and rice, tortillas and beans, followed by *flan*, or custard. It was hot, and the flies tried to eat the food faster than we could. I gobbled up each serving so that David could show me where the four rivers met and became one: the Upper

Papaloapan. A long, high railroad bridge crossed it. I shuddered when David told me that today we would cross it by train, but that on the way from San Pedro Chicozapote to Valerio Trujano, we would have to cross it on foot — with the hope that no train threatened to pass. When we went over the bridge by train, I observed the space between the track and the rushing rivers below and was glad that today, at least, I was not making it on foot.

Now we were in a wider section of the canyon, with sugar cane and rice growing. When the train stopped at San Pedro Chicozapote, the town could hardly be seen because of the density of trees laden with chicozapotes and mangoes. Atop the canyon walls in the distance lived the Chinantecas, who had fled the Spaniards. In the canyon lived the descendants of black slaves who had been imported to work in the cane fields. These black slaves were brought in when the laws of Las Casas declared that the Indians were men with souls and therefore could not be enslaved, and that they did not have to work in sugar fields or mines. It was no wonder that so many of the passengers who boarded the train at San Pedro had negroid characteristics.

After traveling since eight in the morning, it was nearly three in the afternoon when we arrived in Cuicatlán. Later we changed the name, among ourselves, to Chinchicatlán, or bedbug town. A long, hot walk brought us to a home where cots had been set up; sleeping space could be rented. From there we walked a bit farther to the school building. Cuicatlán was the main town in the area, with more than one primary school, but no high school. As teachers began to arrive for the afternoon session, David introduced me to the federal inspector for that zone. A young man of 70, he had been a participant in the Revolution. He was a very dark-skinned Zapoteca Indian from the same village where Benito Juárez was born and, at age 70, he covered his district by mule and horseback.

In this Institute David took the main role, teaching games and folk dances to help the teachers prepare for the Independence Day festivities on September 16th. For every basketball team that David helped to organize — they would receive balls, uniforms, and other equipment on a 50-50 basis — he would say, "One feud less" — the feuds of hundreds of years were worked out on the courts. Except for the Indians on the cliffs, it was a mestizo area of blacks, Indians and Europeans, the black strain predominant.

I was to play a minor part in teaching, for it was that kind of area. The teachers were mestizos; the people were mestizos. They were known to be envious, suspicious and lacking in cooperation. How very different it felt from an Indian zone. Here the government consisted of the leading political party. There was none of the communal type of service to one another and for one another. Here the walls of Jericho were rising against the foreigner. I would have only six one-hour sessions of teaching in three days, but I hoped to break down some of the suspicion.

The first night, in what approximated a village inn, I tossed and turned on the cot. My flashlight showed hundreds of bedbugs, not big ones but really hard-biting ones. Having squirmed the night through, I begged the school inspector, as tactfully as I could, to move me to a private home. That night I relished the clean, white, lace-trimmed, embroidered sheets; but I awakened scratching, covered with welts, and turned on my flashlight. Huge bedbugs were plying the white sheets. I dressed and took a walk in the moonlight and, for the three nights in Cuicatlán, or Chinchicatlán, I did not sleep.

Bedbugs climbed up legs of chairs, fell from the beams. I learned that the whole canyon was infested with bedbugs. The spraying against malaria had not touched a whisker on their bodies. I don't think I did a particularly good job of teaching in that town. I had to learn to take my own air mattress, to spray on it and around it, to cover it with Nexo powder, to sleep under a net, and to hope.

But I did meet the staff of Cultural Mission No. 25 that worked in San Pedro Chicozapote and Valerio Trujano. The director was a teacher, a normal school graduate. There was a social worker who taught how to improve home conditions, a nurse-midwife who was a Mixe, a former student of mine from Oaxaca; a carpenter, a mason, an agronomist, and a specialist in music and dance. The cultural missions were established, soon after the Revolution of 1910 came to an end, to work in areas where schools and villages needed help.

I promised to visit them and to see how, in the very next week, I might help.

Now that I had learned to take Nexo powder and to spray the train, I managed to get to San Pedro Chicozapote the next week without too many bedbug bites. It was a small, compact town with perhaps 1,000 inhabitants, the population increasing somewhat in mango and chicozapote picking time. The town seemed to be a solid mass of large trees filled with fruit. Since the canyon was not very wide there, other crops were scant. Unfortunately, crops were presold on the trees before the fruit was ripe, and earnings were quickly spent, so there was always a shortage of money. In the main square stood the beautiful new school, built by the people and the Papaloapan Commission, with the ever-present basketball court. What a delight to roll out my sleeping mat to sleep in the clean school, which had both toilets and showers!

This was not a water-shortage area. On the contrary, in the rainy season the waters rushed down from the cliffs, down eroded canyons, washing away arable lands. In the triangle formed by Tomellin, San Pedro and Valerio Trujano, four rivers converged to become one.

The staff of the Cultural Mission lived in private homes or in rented rooms. They had one large building which they used for teaching. The rural teacher, his wife who was also a teacher, and their three small children lived next door. The social worker, Emilia Canales, and my former Mixe student, Sabina Alcántara, the nurse-midwife, walked me around the village before dusk. I noticed how careful they were as they greeted people passing, and asked, "Why do you greet everyone the same way, with so little emotion and so formally?" They explained that in this village there was so much jealousy between families that they had to be careful not to show favoritism. As Sabina said, "They are so different from our people, the Mixes, where cooperation is a way of life, and where we believe in communal government." I agreed, for I found it much easier to work in the Indian culture than the mestizo.

Sabina had been trying to raise the standards of the empiric midwife in the village, without much luck. I suggested that we give the pregnant woman more knowledge of her pregnancy, the normal and abnormal warning symptoms, and not only prenatal but also well-baby classes. The woman's awareness of good obstetrics might motivate her to demand more of the midwife; and if she encouraged the midwife to attend classes with her, it would help. Sabina was shy and felt sure she wouldn't be able to talk before a group. I was certain she could, if she observed me a few times, then stepped in to take over. She also practiced first aid, and taught home nursing in the home where needed. We mulled over the idea of establishing a first aid and medical center, in time, in San Pedro Chicozapote, as an outgrowth of home nursing classes. Perhaps we could even find a doctor who would come for one morning a week.

Walking with Emilia, I wondered about her. She was tall, fair, blue-eyed, about 35 years of age and looked like a model. Her accent was that of Catalonia, Spain. She took me to homes where families were able to maintain their cultural patterns of closeness by living around an open hearth, the hearths there having been moved up two feet from floor level, circled by adobe. Other homes, where obviously the young bride had visited the big city, or perhaps had even worked there, revealed major innovations in the form of kitchen tables and chairs. In the classroom Emilia showed me her dress patterns and equipment for sewing, the cooking ovens, and other homemaking facilities. Crocheting, knitting — so many skills she encompassed in her teaching!

Finally I could stand it no longer; my curiosity got the better of me. I asked, "What are you doing buried in Chicozapote and Valerio Trujano? With your charm and ability, how is it you did not choose instead to go to cosmopolitan Mexico City?"

She proudly replied, "Mexico gave me refuge in 1940. I am a Spanish republican. This is my way of paying my debt to Mexico." She looked at me to see how the foreigner would react to that.

I said, "I, too, am repaying Mexico for the home it is giving me and my daughter. I was a nurse on the Madrid front."

Such excitement! Such *abrazos*, such embraces! We had to hurry back to the center so that Emilia could bake a cake to celebrate the happy occasion. She had already educated Sabina on the Spanish Republic.

Emilia sent word to all members of the Cultural Mission, as well as to the rural teachers, inviting them for cake and coffee in the evening. When they arrived, surprised that there was cake on a no-cake day, and curious to know what had happened, Emilia introduced me as her *compañera de España*. Professor Lomelí, the music and dance teacher, led off with songs of the Spanish Republic. Emilia added some Catalán songs, and we all ended up singing the songs of Mexico — the *corridos*, the *huapangos*, the songs of the south — until our voices gave out.

Mr. Lomelí, balancing a cup of coffee in one hand and appearing to wave a baton with the other, explained to us how he sought out old dances and music and, in order to preserve them, taught them to the school children. And then the other members of the Cultural Mission explained their tasks and that of the Mission as a whole. The normal school graduate helped the local rural teachers. The student agronomist helped with seed and planting techniques. Last, but not least, was the carpenter-mason, who not only worked at his skills, but also taught them.

They spent three days a week in Valerio Trujano and four days in San Pedro Chicozapote. They would stay put for the entire year, and perhaps another, if the village so requested. Later they would move on, the whole group, to another area in the state of Oaxaca, or to another state.

I was later brought up-to-date on achievements in San Pedro. Sabina organized the classes which the young mothers started to attend. Eventually, out of curiosity, even the two local midwives arrived. Sabina was especially gratified about that for, having watched me in my prenatal, postnatal and child care classes, she paid particular attention to the midwife, as I did, asking her always for her advice and special knowledge. A home nursing and first aid class was initiated. I taught only four times; then Sabina took over, and I became part of the audience.

With the help of the first-aid workers, trained by Sabina, a room was whitewashed and set up as a clinic. There the well-baby clinic was operated, and midwife classes began. Best of all, the young man who had finished his six-year medical course and was then doing his year of social service was persuaded to ride over once a week on a horse the village sent to him.

Where formerly women were delivered on the hard-packed dirt floor, with the constant danger of cord tetanus, one of the chief causes of death in the newborn, women were now being delivered by Sabina or the local midwife on a wooden cot covered with a straw mat, and babies were getting drops in their eyes.

Emilia, in sewing class, taught the first-aid workers how to make their uniforms and masks, which they loved to wear, as well as other clothing. She also taught them how to preserve the mangoes and chicozapotes that did not sell. It was all happening so fast! Tables and chairs being built; old songs becoming new songs; old dances, new dances! New vegetables were being introduced by the agronomist.

I thought of this village as being an especially progressive one, but Emilia said, "Wait until you see Valerio Trujano."

Emilia kept saying, "Hurry, hurry! A freight train is due to cross the bridge!" There I was, making every effort not to look down to where the four rivers met below us while we stepped along the ties, repressing my fear of heights and listening to the singing rails. Glad for a mule on the narrow, Himalayalike trail in the Sierra Mixe, I did my best to hurry. I was terrified.

Two things had always frightened me — no, four: small enclosed spaces; rodents; slippery adobe mud roads; and heights and the compulsion to jump from them. The worst seemed to be that almost mile-long, high railroad trestle crossing the rapidly converging rivers. Finally, when Emilia gave me a helping hand on the last ties, she said, "Were you so afraid when bombs dropped on the Spanish front?" Truthfully I answered, "No."

We had reached Tomellín where, sure enough, a freight train was pulling in. We crossed one of the small rivers to a bluff where two horses and a young lad were waiting for us to ride to Valerio Trujano. On the big map of the state, the village was called Guendalain; but since 1812 the village inhabitants had called it Valerio Trujano. I learned all this while slowly riding, in the early hours of the day, over a level plain covered with cactus, aware of the rice and sugar cane cultivation around me.

The lands we were traversing, and as far as the eye could see in that part of the canyon, once had belonged to a Spaniard named Guendalain. The Indians had fled to the high bluffs, where their descendents still lived. Black slaves were brought in to work in the sugar cane and rice fields. (By 1810, 250,000 blacks had been brought into Mexico.) In accordance with the law, the son or daughter of a black slave was born free, and blacks mated with the Indian girls of the area. Exercising his feudal rights as Lord of the Manor, Guendalain added a Spanish strain. The soldiers who guarded the manor added even more. But the present population was largely negroid in appearance, according to what Emilia told me, and from what I could observe.

The Victory

With Hidalgo in 1810, the long, hard road to independence began. Hidalgo declared an end to slavery. He was killed, but one of his followers, Father José María Morelos, continued the struggle with the guerrilla army he raised in the states of Guerrero, Morelos, and Veracruz. One member of his staff was Colonel Valerio Trujano. Guendalain had armed the blacks to enable them to help his Spanish soldiers repulse Trujano. In Tomellín, as the Colonel was approaching the bluffs, the blacks decided to kill Guendalain and his soldiers and to welcome the forces of Valerio Trujano. They did exactly that.

Trujano became the father of the black town. From then on, the blacks were always on the side of the liberals. They were with Juárez in the War of Reform, and they were crushed as rebels during the time of Porfirio Díaz. Again they won their freedom with the Revolution of 1910; but it was not until 1934, under Cárdenas, that they obtained title to their lands, formerly Guendalain's. Now Emilia was telling me that they were pressing a court case in Oaxaca for possession of the old hacienda headquarters, which were in ruins. When I asked her what they wanted it for, she said their feeling was that they would be really free only when they had that to use as a community center. "But they still live in the most horrible, rat-filled, bedbug-infested huts they lived in as slaves," she added.

They followed the communal system in the operation of their lands. They had a school government that Emilia told me I would witness with my own eyes that day. By then we were approaching the village square, and Emilia pointed out the school, the *ejidal* offices, the city hall, as well as the two jails left over from slave days. One was used by the school children for the detention of burros that broke into the school rice fields or sugar cane patches.

We walked silently into the rear of the schoolroom and observed what was happening. The weekly change of school government was about to take place. Seated at the teacher's desk, the president for the week called for reports from his various officials. The treasurer, all of ten years old, gave his report of funds collected: María had come to school with her hair uncombed — fine, 10 *centavos*. Juan had been caught urinating against the school wall — fine, 10 *centavos*. Juan's father had committed the same offense — one *peso* fine; and a committee would call on each offender to discuss civic responsibility. Julia had three lice in her hair, 10 *centavos* for each louse found (and the committee would call on her mother). Five burros caught in the school corn patch were in jail — 25 *pesos* in fines.

The health committee read its progress report on the latrines they were building with the aid of the Cultural Mission's carpenter. This would be the first old school in the canyon to have latrines. A few more points, such as hairdos, lesson plans and substitute teachers for the week were discussed. Then elections were held, and new officials took office. The outgoing group handed over its caps, together with the badge of office, a soldier's khaki cap.

All this was guided by a wonderful teacher, a man with mild, shaking palsy. No longer a young man in age, he was young in enthusiasm and ideas, and his name was Professor Severiano Osorio. He had served in the Army of the Revolution as a youth. I felt honored to meet him.

Next I was introduced to Mrs. Aguirre, wife of the president of the *ejido*. She had only one arm, and on that hand three fingers were missing. Emilia told me that Mrs. Aguirre had been a rural teacher in the days of the *cristeros*, when many rural teachers were murdered. Attacked by peasants armed with machetes, she was miraculously rescued by other teachers. Now she was married to the chief of the *ejido*, whose black arm embraced her white shoulders as we chatted.

We were shown around the village, deeply shaded by mango trees, and I was shocked by the huts the people lived in, the old slave quarters. The village authorities were delighted that Emilia had brought me, because to them I represented the Papaloapan Commission. When their bridge had been washed away, a new one was built in four days of nonstop labor, with the 50-50 aid of the Commission. What they wanted to discuss with me now was the possibility of building new homes on the slopes of the hills, which had never been allowed. There was no water there. How could water be gotten up? What type of house? Would the Commission help? I thought of the rammed-earth technique of building houses, and said I would ask our engineer about it. I was sure we could help them with pipes to take up the water.

Together we ate lunch, prepared by Mrs. Aguirre. I had already noticed how different the food was in the canyon. It was Creole-Spanish-Indian, with sauces of crushed almonds, and cactus fruit for dessert. Mrs. Aguirre was a natural leader, so we began planning how to add well-baby clinics, prenatal and postnatal classes, home nursing and first aid, plus more sewing and cooking classes. Since the students comprised the most progressive force in this progressive village, we asked the committee of the week to meet with us.

I was going slightly mad with bedbugs all over the place. They resented me. Was it my imagination, or did some of the blacks resent me too? Emilia had told me that they could not understand the racial discrimination in the United States, and I was not to be surprised if at first they kept their distance from me. I had not felt any such attitude in the school or with the village authorities, but I did feel it with the teenage boys who were out of school, the ones who had come to ask if the Commission would go 50-50 on a basketball court. I told them I would speak to David Rodríguez, the physical education teacher, and was quite sure the Commission would help. They seemed to be expecting me to say no.

The Cultural Mission certainly did not need me, and neither did the village of Valerio Trujano. They were getting along fine with the active school government groups and their wonderful director, Professor Osorio. They wanted me to come up at least twice a month to help in the teaching program, and I was delighted, for it was such a positive mutual learning experience. Out of the school would come health workers, carpenters, masons, gardeners, musicians — all stimulated by the

Mission. Adult committees were being formed in the community.

The band played loud and long when the other jail was converted into a spic-and-span nursing station and teaching unit. The doctor, on leaving San Pedro Chicozapote, would go on to Valerio Trujano one day a week. What I most enjoyed was seeing the well-baby clinic held in the old jail room, watching Sabina Alcántara weigh babies on a fish scale, and the lay health workers as they gave the first hypos with the triple vaccine against tetanus, whooping cough and diphtheria.

On July 27th Emilia and I rode over to Valerio Trujano to attend a meeting of the public health committee. Halfway there, children lined the road to offer me garlands of flowers to hang on my saddle. Entering the village, people old and young came running toward me with more flowers, while the band played, "Happy Birthday to You." I then learned that Emilia had sent a messenger over the night before to tell them it was my birthday.

Valerio Trujano, a village very proud of its black heritage, had accepted me as an equal.

The Mixtecas, draftsmen of pre-Hispanic Mexico, lived in the Valley of Oaxaca. One has only to see the treasure found in Tomb 7 at Monte Albán to appreciate their artistry in gold, ivory and feather work. In the entire long valley, a single village remains where Mixteca is the language spoken, the village of San Jacinto. Here they make cooking and ornamental pottery in shades of green. In my opinion, it is better than Corning Ware. Milk can be boiled in a pitcher, which may be placed directly in the icebox and, ice-cold, placed again on the flame without breaking. The cooking ware tends to be simple, but invariably reflects the artistic capabilities of the craftsmen. Playful musicians, flower jugs with hovering birds and bees — their work is captivating.

Toward the Pacific Coast, in the watershed of the Río Balsas, lived a large Mixteca group. In our watershed, another group lived in a badly eroded area above Nochistlán. I was told that the Mixtecas had once taken this area from the Zapotecas, then abandoned it. When the Mixtecas returned, they could not re-enter the fertile valley, again in the possession of Zapotecas. Now the major portion of the Mixtecas lived in the heavily eroded, nonfertile areas stretching up to the semidesert area where Puebla and Oaxaca meet.

Until then I had not gone into the Mixteca area, but finally I decided to accompany some of the Commission's agricultural specialists to the big fair held in honor of the "Virgen de la Concepción" on December 8th. They would present an agricultural demonstration, and I would help in the mass immunization program planned by our young medical intern, to be carried out at the four entrances to the huge outdoor chapel of the church.

Leaving the valley, kept so green by irrigation, we climbed through pine forests, crossed the divide, and were in Nochistlán, the beginning of the area that in Spanish is called La Mixteca. Not a tree was in sight, and winter wheat struggled to survive. Soon we came to Yanhuitlán, where a huge old Dominican church and convent loomed high over the landscape. Memo told me that prior to the Spaniards' arrival, 200,000 Mixtecas had lived there, and the area had been covered with trees. He said the Spaniards ordered the trees cut down to make a level terrain resembling the plains of Madrid. Whatever the reason for the devastation, it was depressing to see deep, red-purple gashes in the hills, and white limestone showing through the top level of earth.

At Tamazulapan, site of the rural normal school, we turned off the highway. Now it got rough. Jolting between and over the rocks and boulders, we passed sulfur springs and white limestone glaring in the sun. Where there should have been a field of earth and greenery, there was *puro caliche*, limestone. I sat in the middle between Memo and the agronomist, and my knees were black-and-blue from hitting the truck's gearshift. In the back we carried thornless cactus that animals could eat, as well as flowering plants, fruit trees from hot and temperate regions, olive trees, grapevines, and other flora. In a second truck we had a special breed of goats, prized both for their long hair and for their milk and cheese production.

The fruit trees had been grown from pits our agronomist collected in Guelatao. For every 40 pits that a school child brought in, a mature tree was contributed to the area in which he lived. In Guelatao we had an agricultural station with a full-time agronomist. On the road we passed many people walking to the fiesta of the Virgin of the Conception. Memo told me that folks came from as far away as Mexico City and Puebla for this particular fiesta in this village, Buenavista.

Bouncing over the rocky road, we came to white houses huddled together, the high walls of an enormous church, Gothic in style, seeming to protect them. Most of the churches in this area had been built by the Indians under the direction of the Dominicans. White limestone glittered in the setting sun; white limestone dust filled the air. The little town was crowded with pilgrims. I was given a place to sleep in the back room of a *cantina*, a bar.

At first, as I tried to sleep, I rationalized, "How nice to listen to the mariachis playing." But as the night wore on, voices became more hearty, the mezcal and tequila, more effective. By dawn I was exhausted from trying to sleep. I begged for another place to lay my head the next night. I felt filthy, but our water allowance was one cup per day for all purposes. I spent the rest of my nights there on the kitchen table in a rather large home, the servants sleeping on the floor. Fortunately, I had learned to carry an air mattress with me no matter where I went. With the open cooking hearths, at least I would not freeze as I had during my sleepless first night.

After breakfast I walked to the church and peered inside. The Indian flutes played, and the village bands made noises with drums that beat hard and loud as Indians carried lighted candles into the church, richly decorated with festoons and garlands of flowers and ribbons. Later the Virgin would be taken out of her niche and paraded in the village by her followers. People bowed and scraped as I walked by. Their servility to me was so apparent, and I wondered what it was that made them so different from the Zapotecas or the Mixes.

I went to work at the rear of the church, where the open chapel patio was to be utilized by the health department and our doctor. These open chapels had been used for mass christenings in the 16th century and now, in the 20th century, we would catch the people as they entered with their small children and immunize them. I could not agree with this technique of "catching them." I much preferred the slow way of working by teaching in the schools.

The nurse in charge lived in the village and was a health department employee. Her husband helped her with the vaccinations. I was not needed and went looking for the rural schoolteachers, with whom I could always work. But no one was interested in working. This was a fiesta. Stands and booths were set up in every available inch of open space. So many things were displayed for sale, including lovely straw articles, woven from the local *palma*, pottery for cooking, and *petates*, straw mats for sleeping. The agricultural fair exhibited new kinds of vegetables raised in some of the areas where there was now more water, since we had built a step dam at Tepelmeme. In one large room were the plants and trees that the Papaloapan Commission had sent. They were to be given as prizes. In a pen in front of the building, the prize goats were trying to grab the shirts of passers-by.

As the day drew to an end, and the wails of vaccinated children filled the air, I noticed that more and more men were becoming tipsy. Not that matters got rough or tough. No, in drunken voices they fervently cheered the Virgin. Our own representative in that area, Cayetano, was weaving back and forth as he transferred the goats from the outdoor pen and locked them up for the night.

I wished that I liked tequila or mezcal as I walked with our

Papaloapan men to the banquet in honor of the Queen of the Fair and her princesses. The Virgin was toasted before and after we ate the hot Mixteca *mole* with turkey. Then the Queen was toasted, then her girl attendants. Even the Papaloapan Commission was toasted. Tequila flowed and voices were raised in shouts and songs, and more toasts to the Virgin. She was the Virgin of Conception — and the way our men were gathering around the Queen and her court, I thought there might very well be more conception that night. Of course, I was cold and sober, a disgusting condition to be in at a banquet for such a Virgin. I gave up and retired to my hard kitchen table covered by a fine air mattress. Dozing in fits and starts, I heard the noise of fireworks and bands all night long.

Swiping some extra water out of the jug — the water to be used for cooking — I tried to rub the sleep out of my eyes. I was stiff; the hard table had come through to my back. I was eager to leave this village, but I could not go until the men decided it was time. After drinking what was meant to be coffee, and filling the corners of my grumbling stomach with hot beans and an egg, I walked to our fair building.

The drums were still beating, the flutes, still playing, but wearily now. Cayetano, practically in tears, stood in front of the building and, when I asked him what had happened, he silently led me inside. All I could see were tin cans and two well-fed, happy goats. He had locked the goats in with the prize plants and had not tied them up. But worst of all, his mother-in-law had lent him her beautiful red pepper plant, and all that remained were cans, bits of stem, and scattered earth. The goats had eaten even the labels. How sad! How funny!

Only the well-fed goats could be used as prizes. Old and young stood around, weaving hats, laughing about what had happened. The only thing that grew around this town was *palma*, anyway. As soon as a child was old enough to coordinate his fingers, he was put to work weaving straw hats, which were sold unblocked to a Spanish blocking firm that paid 15 *centavos* a hat. The people looked half-starved. When I asked, "Why don't they move away?" the question was repeated to a group of them, who answered, "How can we leave our dead? Who would keep them company on All Saints' Day? Who would put food out for them to smell? Who would play their favorite songs?"

I knew we were relocating people who had to be moved out before the gates of the big dam were closed, but they didn't want to leave their dead.

I had not been home a week when a letter came from Professor Berzunza, the federal director of education, requesting my services at a Teachers' Institute to be held in Huajuápan de Léon. It said that the Institute would not be held in the Papaloapan area, although three of the six school zones involved were within the Basin. Each of the zones had an average of 100 teachers, for a total of 600.

Professor Berzunza had been fascinated once at a meeting by teaching tricks I had used to achieve integration through the school program. But what had really established our lasting friendship was a long, two-hour stretch of waiting together for the train to leave Oaxaca for Cuicatlán, and then the slow ride up the canyon. On the train I told him, "Take off your jacket. I can pick the bedbugs off a white shirt easier." Then I spread Nexo on the seat and covered it with newspapers. The bedbugs continued to climb, but in controllable numbers. We had been friends ever since.

There would be leading authorities from the Department of Education, plus representatives from the National Indian Institute. I was to have two hours daily on integration for health through the school program. Huajuápan de Léon was noted for being extremely conservative, both religiously and politically. The town was filled with signs, such as, "This is a Catholic home. No Protestants wanted." I could not understand why it had been chosen, except for the fact that it was the geographic center of the six school zones, three of which lay in our watershed. The other three, where the Triqui Indians and more of the Mixtecas lived, lay in the Río Balsas watershed.

Huajuápan had one hotel and a movie house where the classes were to be held. It was halfway between Oaxaca and the city of Puebla. Since it was on the international highway, it was a mestizo town, Mixteca Indians forming the basis of the population, adulterated by passers-by.

The hotel would lodge the so-called important people, the speakers from Mexico City, Oaxaca, and elsewhere, while the teachers were spread around the town. I had heard, however, that we would sleep two to a narrow bed, and I was hoping for a companion on the thin side.

When I arrived at the hotel, I was assigned to my room and told that my roommate was in it, inasmuch as the key was not in the assigned slot. Climbing the stairs and turning toward my room, I heard a loud voice saying, "I will not share my room with a *gringa* and, above all, will not sleep in the same bed with her!"

I waited for a reply, then heard a man say, "But she is different! She works as hard as any of us, even harder. They tell me that often they send her out first, before the engineers, because she works well with the people." That was nice to hear.

Again the woman spoke. "I don't care. I hate all *gringos* and *gringas*. I won't have her in the same room with me."

This I had to face. I had known enough of the U.S. type of McCarthyism. I had lost all my family in Holland because of Hitler racism. This type of thinking was a blight and, in these people, meant a lack of security and cultural development. I knocked at the door, opened it, and said, "I am Lini de Vries, the *gringa*. Since we have to sleep together, I will sleep in this room, and I will sleep with you because you are thin and because you are all wrong, so why not have it out this minute?"

The young teacher scampered out as fast as he could. He probably thought the hair was going to fly. It didn't, but the words did.

A teacher slightly under five feet tall faced me, her hands on her hips, sparks flashing from her eyes. "Sleep some other place," she cried, "and if you don't, I will!"

"Go ahead," I answered. "But are you not curious about the play you are to present tomorrow, the puppet play on *mal del pinto*?" I had noticed her puppets sprawling over a chair and realized she must be the teacher from the State Department of Education, the one who taught puppetry.

"What has that play got to do with you?" she asked.

"Well, since it was I who wrote it," I replied, "I thought maybe you would like to know more about the disease so that your puppets can make it even more dramatic."

And then I really took the offensive. "Do I judge Mexico by your ignorant statements? Do I judge Mexico by its *malinchistas*? (Malinche was the Indian woman who became the mistress of Cortez; therefore, those who betray Mexico are often called *malinchistas*, which is really quite unfair to Malinche.) Do I judge Mexico by some of its generals who got rich in the Revolution? No, I judge Mexico by the people who are building Mexico: her engineers, her teachers, her architects. What right do you have to judge Americans by government acts in 1847 or 1914? What do you really know about the United States? What do you know about the great American dream of 1776 and the Bill of Rights? Do you even know any North Americans?" And so it went, far into the night.

Her position was that all the United States had ever done was to hurt, rob, and thrust her culture on Mexico. She belonged to a political party that was ultranationalistic. I think I even helped convince her that extreme nationalism meant an inner insecurity and that such an attitude stunted her own growth. I suggested that she read Octavio Paz' book *Labyrinth of Solitude*, that she think of the process of becoming truly Mexican and of the importance of pride in being Mexican.

Finally we went to bed, thin Eva and big Lini in a single bed. By four in the morning she had accepted me, and I, her. The delightful thing that happened the next day was that my play,

Mal del Pinto, directed by her, won first prize in the puppet shows.

I had heard of her before meeting her. She had been teaching with puppets in cardboard boxes, puppets in small theaters and, one after another, her student-teachers were demonstrating how to teach through puppet theater. At first she did not like going to the far-off areas to which I went, but soon she was traveling with me to institutes, teaching how to make and animate puppets. And through it all I recall having to temper her now-enthusiastic rapport with, "Please, Eva, now don't judge all North Americans by your impression of me. You say I am a sport, a bit different — but it is as you are different from many Mexicans."

There was a man who had a daily spot on the program, showing huge graphic photos of the work that was being done at the National Indian Institute (INI) Center in Jamiltepec and Tlaxialco. Both of these were in the Mixteca area — one in the lush tropics, the other in eroded lands. I had met Julio de la Fuente years before. Apparently he did not remember me, for he ignored me. I went to his lectures and noted that he came to mine.

That night at supper he asked if he could sit with me. After having read his study, *Yalalag*, about a Zapoteca village within my work area, I had been eager to know him better. Respecting him as an anthropologist and as a person, I was curious to know why he had pretended not to recognize me. "Were you testing the *gringa*?" I asked him, with a smile.

He answered, "*Sí*. I wanted to hear your approach to teaching first."

I teased back, "But good teaching crosses nationalistic lines, don't you agree?"

I left it at that as we went on to discuss the marvelous display of the INI on the theme, "How to Teach from One Language to Another — from the Indian Language to the Spanish." The approach of the INI had always been to teach the individual the technique of writing and reading in his own language, then to teach him Spanish. Thus they could incorporate into their materials the legends and history of the Indian groups, stress their greatness, and help them make the transition into the 20th century with less trauma.

It was 1940 when those interested in Indian affairs in all countries on the American continent met at Pátzcuaro, Michoacán, to discuss ways and means of setting up units to work with the Indians. One of the resolutions passed was to establish national institutes in each country. In 1948 Mexico's National Indian Institute was created. The coordinating body was the Inter-American Indian Institute, formed as an immediate result of the Pátzcuaro conference.

In Mexico the founding director was Dr. Alfonso Caso, discoverer of the riches in Tomb 7, Monte Albán. The first pilot unit was guided by Mexico's great social anthropologist, Dr. Gonzalo Aguirre Beltrán. I read his books as they appeared. His first was a demographic study of Mexico, and a new one was published yearly. His most outstanding quality as a man of science is that he sees each person as an individual and works accordingly. I had visited the INI pilot unit at San Cristóbal de Las Casas, Chiapas, and was most impressed with what I saw.

Perhaps the most important factor was that, administratively, an anthropologist was in charge, with doctors, teachers, agronomists, plumbers, masons, carpenters, and puppeteers working under him, studying the cultures with which they were involved — not attempting to impose a foreign culture. In the medical center young Indians, as they became bilingual, learned to be lay health workers, or *promotores de la salud*. As they developed, they were encouraged to continue studying to become teachers.

Most exciting of all was to observe the Indians holding a dialog with the puppets, which were dressed exactly as they were, speaking their language, discussing such themes as latrines, a new school, a connecting road, a new seed corn, new ways to contour land, and so forth. As the audience responded, a cultural exchange ensued, and in the next presentation the suggestions offered previously continued to be evaluated until the Indians and the puppets were in agreement on methods of work.

From this pilot unit, others had been established. There were too few of them. I knew we were collaborating with one where the dam was being built, and I hoped I would never have to go there, for it was hotter than hell. But that was exactly what Julio de la Fuente wanted of me!

He asked if I would go to their unit at Temazcal, where the dam was being built, to teach their doctors how to teach for health, and to begin the program for health workers.

"No, thank you," I replied. "It is too hot there. I can't stand heat. I don't like to teach doctors. They are a bunch of compartmentalized stuffed shirts who listen only to fellow doctors."

He questioned my judgment of the INI doctors; later I was to discover his attitude had been valid. He insisted that I go for three months. I told him that I worked for the upper part of the watershed, not the lower part, so I could not go. He smiled as he said, "I'll speak to the director of the whole watershed, the low and the high, and I'll get you on loan to us." I did not like that idea at all and promptly put it out of my head.

When I arrived at the Teachers' Institute, I had been the target of suspicion as the *gringa*, on a state level. Now, in the last days of the conference, I was to feel it again on a national level. At the table near me were two men from the federal Office of Education. One was an expert on the school farming unit, and the other, on teaching techniques. I had listened to both of them speak, but neither one had attended my classes.

Now the one with a strong Madrid accent was saying, in a voice loud enough for me to hear, "So now the United States of America sends its spies disguised as public health anthropologist-teachers."

I stared straight at the Spaniard. "Were you thinking of me? You are a Spanish republican refugee, are you not? Or are you really a Franco fascist disguised as a republican?"

He sputtered, "What do you know of Spain?"

I replied with a question, "What front were you on?"

"And what do you know about fronts?" he countered.

I shocked him when I stated, "I was on the Madrid front in 1937 during the battle of Jarama."

He questioned me and questioned me. And the more he did, the more sheepish he became.

Four days earlier I had tried to make Eva less antagonistic, and I ended up four days later on very much the same note with a Spanish republican refugee.

By this time I had gone to many Teachers' Institutes. My teaching program had jelled, with few changes, in accordance with the geography and culture of the group with which I was working. There were nine school zones in my district, which meant 27 teachers' meetings a year. Most of the zones had to be reached by mule, some by train or jeep. When a new airstrip was finally built, it was marvelous.

I had learned that the pilot of our Cessna liked chocolate cake. When a trip was scheduled to an area where there was a new strip, the captain got chocolate cakes, baked as bribes to take me by plane. For example, Zacatepec, the main town of the Mixe area, was a hard, five-day mule trip, 10 to 12 hours daily. Since a one-day mule trip was equivalent to ten minutes by air, it could take only fifty minutes to Zacatepec by air, as contrasted with five days by land. Not that the strip was at Zacatepec, for that town had to have a fence around it to keep the people from falling off into deep ravines. The strip was on a small level spot near a town originally called Chisme (Gossip). Since the villagers didn't like that name, it was changed to Matamoros. From Matamoros to Zacatepec was only a ten-hour mule ride.

Soon I would have to go to a Teachers' Institute in Zacatepec. I could not do enough for Captain Silva. I baked cakes for him, and I begged my chief to persuade the captain to take us with him. Finally he agreed, and now we had only to wait for a clear morning to get through the clouds hanging over that area.

Early one morning, the weather reports were good for the Mixe area. The sky was cloudless. Quickly we got together, rolled the plane out of the hangar, and were off. The plane could hold four: the pilot; David, who would remain a few weeks in the Sierra to teach sports in the various villages; the federal school inspector for that area; and myself. David and the pilot pointed out the narrow trails over which we had ridden on previous trips, and I was glad not to be there now. It was magnificent seeing this highest part of the watershed from a plane. But fifty minutes later, as we descended and I caught a glimpse of that little strip on a shaved-off hilltop, deep ravines around it, I just closed my eyes. I did not want to see it. Our pilot was anxious to get out before the clouds closed him in, and they were moving in and dropping rapidly.

Across a ravine lay the small village of Matamoros. It was typical of Mixe villages, the huts hanging on cliffsides, the trail going round and round, up and up. It was on the slopes of the divide on the Gulf Coast side of Oaxaca, and warm enough for coffee trees, which grew under the banana trees.

Four mules were waiting for us. The teacher from that town joined us for the short ten-hour ride to Zacatepec. The trails were steep, but I had become accustomed now to swaying along with the mule. I was thirsty. They told me five hours, halfway over, there was water. They did not tell me, however, that the water bubbled up very slowly in one little spot and that I should try to get to it before the mule drank. I was not fast enough. The mule drank her fill, and I had to wait for more water to appear.

Zacatepec was different from any Mixe village I had visited. It appeared as if two mountain tops had been welded together. I mentioned it to David, and he told me that in a sense I was right. There had been a deep ravine in the center, separating the two parts of Zacatepec. The village authorities decided that anyone old enough to pass that way should drop in baskets of refuse, rocks, sand, and just about anything. It had taken years and years, but now the top was level and provided a site for the basketball court, the town square and, around it, the municipal offices, the state representatives' offices and the school with classes through the sixth grade.

As we passed the municipal building, I noticed young boys being tested for music. They had reached the age of 10, when they began their service to the community. Those who had a good ear for music would train for the band. The men past 35 who had been in the band, the *ancianos*, were doing the testing. Music was so important to the Mixes that it was no wonder the state band in the city of Oaxaca had so many Mixe members.

We dismounted from our mules and walked across to the schoolhouse. Again I saw the wall painting that had caught my attention in other schools in the Mixe area. From beyond a great mountain fire, faces were peering through the flames from a deep cave with many people in it. "There must be a story to that," I remarked to David. He told me legend had it that whenever any group — the Zapotecas or Mixtecas, even the Spaniards — threatened to conquer the Mixes, they went into a cave and set fire to the forest. According to the Mixes, they had never been conquered. I liked the Mixes, and it was mutual. They were independent, could not brook conquerors; and when I heard what sounded like a Dutch word in their language, I would really identify with the Mixes. *Meisje* in Dutch means a young girl about 16, and in Mixe it means a young boy of about the same age.

We were up so high that the clouds were below us. The sun shone brightly on the town square. Most of the teachers had arrived, and there were *abrazos* all around. Here were Nacho, Lupita and Flora from Totontepec, with whom I had slept on school tables at my first Institute in the Mixe zone. Many of the teachers had since slept in the long corridors of my home when they came into Oaxaca city. One wedding had taken place in my living room. No longer did I feel like an outsider.

Most formally, I was introduced to the *cacique*, Luis Rodríguez. He recalled the occasion of our first meeting in Oaxaca, when he had told me not to be afraid to come to the Sierra. He also remembered my reply, "I'm not afraid of the Sierra. I'm only afraid of rats and slippery adobe mud, not of men." What a contradiction he was: strong boss, but tender with any youngster who tested well in music. He was always present at those times. The teachers feared him. He resisted all modern ideas that threatened his tight control over the area.

This was my third meeting in the Mixe area for that school year. We reviewed and augmented the teaching in previous sessions. Reports were given on the efficacy of the school program in the eradication of malaria and *mal del pinto*. Most exciting was to watch the teachers do demonstration jobs in teaching for health through the school program right through the sixth grade. I sat back and glowed. They were better than I had been. They had become versed in the global method of education.

The town square rarely had more than fifty people walking across it, except when a basketball game was in progress. When I walked out of the room where all the women teachers slept, the square was jammed. I could not believe my eyes. Obviously, it was *tianguis*, or market day. *Tianguis* had been official market day, usually held weekly, in Indian villages from the time the Indians began living in communities, long before the Spaniards arrived. One always expected *tianguis* to be crowded with people from all nearby towns, but I never expected to see crowds from far away.

On straw mats the Tehuanas had spread out their smoked dried fish, wrapped in banana leaves; salt fish lay in piles. I knew the women by their long skirts ruffled at the bottom, short colorful *huipiles*, and the gold coins that hung around their necks and in their ears. Nearby were Yalaltecas and other women from the Rinconada (A Corner in the Mountains). The Yalalteca wore a long, white *huipil* with a brightly colored tassel at the neck. Those from the Cajón villages wore a white skirt about ten yards wide, a snowy white homespun *huipil*, skirt and blouse held together with a wide, shocking pink, 12-inch belt made of raw silk dyed with the juice of the cochineal, an insect.

I wondered how the Zapoteca-speaking people were communicating with the Mixe, but Spanish interpreters abounded. Many were bilingual. It was like Diego Rivera's mural of a *tianguis* in the National Palace, Mexico City. The *zócalo* was jammed with prospective buyers and with people sitting on straw mats, their orderly piles of goods before them. By one o'clock in the afternoon, the square was practically empty.

Some had walked six days, some less, to reach Zacatepec. The Tehuanas and women vendors from other areas filled the *tianguis*. One day it was Zacatepec that had its market; the next day, perhaps less than a day's walking distance away, another village would have its *tianguis*. For example, on the six-day walk back to the Isthmus of Tehuantepec, the Tehuana might cover five different markets in as many towns.

To find a quiet place, I entered the church. I was feverish, and every part of my body ached. Perhaps the idols could help me, I thought, remembering Anita Brenner's book, *Idols Behind Altars*. I had to get through that day, and hoped I would feel less horrible by the next morning, when I had a ten-hour mule ride ahead of me to Matamoros where the plane was to pick me up. Fortunately, the federal inspector and David were carrying the load that day. At sundown we had the closing ceremony, the flag lowered to the singing of the Mexican national anthem. Many teachers planned to get off at four in the morning to return to their schools.

A *topil*, a guide, was sent to accompany me to Matamoros the next day, he on foot and I on mule. He spoke a bit of Spanish, less than I did. Not that we communicated. I was breaking out all over with a pimply rash. It took all my strength of character to stay on the mule. When we reached the water hole, I simply let the mule drink first, and then I lay down with my mouth over the sandy hole where the water oozed out into a hollow. When we got to Matamoros, someone blew up my air mattress, and I fell upon it.

Half-awake, half-asleep, feverish, I wondered in the deep night what the cat was doing in my bed. I awakened, and it was a big rat nibbling at my hand. How I prayed to get out, to have the plane pick me up at once! I decided to wait on the strip. The village teacher helped me ride to it on a mule. I could hardly walk.

Two days and nights I sat on the strip, listening to the plane trying to get through the clouds, then flying away. I kept a fire going against insects and animals. If the plane did not pick me up, it would be two days down the slopes on foot, one day in a dugout canoe down a swift river to the Isthmus highway, then a bus to Tehuantepec and another to Oaxaca.

Finally a plane did land, but it was not ours. It was a single-motor plane that came to pick up bags of raw coffee beans. I pleaded with the pilot to take me instead of coffee beans. He asked who would pay. I explained that the Papaloapan Commission would. I actually hung on the wing so that he could not easily leave without me.

Then he asked, "Are you an archaeologist?"

My reply was, "I look like a ruin, I know, but I'm a cross between an anthropologist and a public health worker."

Back in Oaxaca, the doctor confirmed my suspicions. I had chicken pox.

My desk, as I have said, was in the office with that of our radio operator. I enjoyed hearing our pilot calling in, listening to the orders coming through for our head engineer. When there were no voices, soft music played. Only three of us worked in this side room off the other offices: David, with whom I traveled; the radio operator; and me. When I was at my desk, it meant that I had a report to write, which I dreaded. If only Spanish were my language! But first I had to write it out in English, then translate it to the best of my ability. After that, one of the secretaries would feel sorry for me and put it into proper Spanish.

Suddenly, while I was deep in concentration, I heard, "Señora de Vries is to report to Temazcal for three months." The operator typed it, an original for my boss and a copy for me. I was furious. I had forgotten that Julio de la Fuente of the INI had promised to have me transferred. Everyone talked about Temazcal (Steam Bath) as being hotter than hell. It was where the dam was being built, below sea level. And what about my good life with my daughter? My home, Oaxaca, to come back to? Fortunately, it was a weekend. The boss was away and would not return until Monday. That meant I would have to do some female conniving. I would assume that he did not want me to go, that the arrangements had been made over his head. I would raise the question: For whom did I work, to whom was I responsible? If worst came to worst, I would resign. I would not go to Temazcal for three months. Of that I was sure.

I was very fond of our boss, Mr. Jiménez, who was to lose his life in service to the Papaloapan Basin. Dressed in the most feminine fashion I could manage, I requested an interview with him Monday.

I asked about his wife and four children, in the correct Mexican manner. He asked about my daughter in the States and the little one who lived with me. One does not rush a Mexican; one first observes the courtesies. When he asked if I had a problem, I replied by asking him why he no longer wanted me in the Upper Papaloapan. (I had asked the radio operator to hold the wire until I was able to talk with engineer Jiménez.)

Then I informed him of the orders directing me to report that day to the main office in Ciudad Alemán for assignment to Temazcal. Thank heavens, he took the head-of-the-house position and said, "No one asked me about this. You belong to the Upper Papaloapan, not to the Lower." Immediately he radio-phoned our main boss, Raúl Sandoval, and after much discussion a compromise was reached: I was to go for one week every month to represent the Papaloapan Commission at Nuevo Paso Nacional, where the INI unit was beginning. There I was to teach the health workers, beginning with the doctors. Julio de la Fuente had won, even if it was to be only one week a month that I had to endure the heat. My good housekeeper, Celia, would take care of Toby as she did when I went to the Mixe area, often away longer than a week.

As it was already late, I would be taken to my destination in our Cessna. Otherwise it meant twelve hours to Mexico City by bus, then ten hours in another bus to Ciudad Alemán. By plane it would take a bit more than an hour. If one can love a small plane with a beautiful butterfly painted on it, I certainly did. It was so much more comfortable than an ornery mule. On occasion, though, when the airport at Oaxaca was fogged in, the pilot would ask if there were any cars coming down the highway. Waiting until I told him none was visible, down we would swoop onto the highway near Oaxaca, landing on the first level, unoccupied stretch of road past Etla. Quickly we would hop out and push the plane off the road. Often the jeep would be waiting for us, when the captain had called in to report that we were unable to enter the airport. Those landings did bother me, for there was always the possibility of a fast bus rushing at us head-on.

But Ciudad Alemán had a port for bimotor planes, and if all was clear, it should be a smooth trip. The next day was as clear as a bell, even the Mixe area unclouded. We would fly directly over the Santo Domingo River. I checked to see that I had an adequate supply of insect repellant for the bugs that loved me so much, as well as more than sufficient salt tablets and aspirin.

In no time we were flying over San Pablo Guelatao, then Ixtlán. Our new road made a deep red cut through the mountains, but there it ended. Later we would fly over the part that was being built from Ciudad Alemán. One day the two would meet.

The Victory

We were over the highest part of the divide, and Veracruz lay ahead of us. Dropping over Valle Nacional, we saw the seven cuts we had made in the land so that the Papaloapan could flow to the sea instead of flooding the area. They were like shiny silver ribbons. The Santo Domingo was rushing to join the Río Tonto. In the V, where the rivers joined to become the Papaloapan, lay the town of Tuxtepec. Below us, under construction, loomed a factory that was to make paper from the wood on the slopes of the divide. Ahead of us lay Ciudad Alemán. We asked for permission to land and for a jeep to pick us up at the airport. We had made it in fifty minutes.

Over roads cut through the jungle, now bordered by sugar cane or bananas, we drove to our main office. Ciudad Alemán, according to plans, would one day be a great industrial city. Now it was just one barrack after another but, at the same time, the heart and soul of the program. Streets were well laid out. Flowering shrubs were everywhere. The guest house was a dream. As there were no visiting ambassadors or other dignitaries, I could have a room in the guest house. I had never had it so good at any previous point in my work with the Papaloapan Commission. The swimming pool was just outside my window. The room was screened, and it had a bathroom. Enjoy it while you can, I thought. I knew it would be only for that day and night, because I had to be briefed by the directors of education and medical services. Neither one of them was in accord with an anthropological approach to working with the Mazatecas, the 20,000 Indians who would have to leave their homes and the graves of their ancestors.

First I walked to the office of the director of education for my briefing on the training of teachers. He was not in agreement with the National Indian Institute, which held that the Mazateca must first be taught to read and write in his own language, be encouraged to learn of his past, become more secure, and so be somewhat cushioned against the trauma of confronting the 20th century. And the fact that an anthropologist was in charge did not sit too well with him either. Nevertheless, he was a tremendous force in Mexican education. I respected him and listened to him.

In my meetings with the medical director, I merely listened. We were miles apart in philosophy. His approach was exclusively curative medicine, and mine was preventive. Mine, in public health, was slower, but seemed to me more worthwhile, on the premise that it is much more intelligent to help people help themselves to eliminate and to control the diseases that could ravage their own bodies.

My work touched both directors, so each one felt I was responsible to him, as did my engineer boss, too. That was easy to handle; all I had to do was write a report with carbon copies, the original for my boss, copies to the education and health departments.

I knew it would be a pleasurable learning experience to work under the direction of Dr. Romano, who was in charge of the INI-Papaloapan Commission coordinating center. Fortunately, there was general agreement that I was the logical person to represent the Commission in view of my public health background, heavily seasoned with anthropology. The Commission's engineers wanted to speed up the transfer of the remaining 20,000 Indians out of the area to be flooded. The INI wanted them better prepared for the move. I agreed with the INI. I could not see the great rush. Even though sand had been moved out of the actual dam site, and some of the land was already under water, it would be at least another year before the gates were closed.

After briefings on the problems facing both the INI and the Commission in their cooperative work in Nuevo Paso Nacional, I knew enough to know how little I really knew. I trusted that Dr. Romano would help me further. The next morning, the early heat already quite unbearable, Margarito, the education department's driver, was ready with his jeep to take me to the dam.

Dust whirled from the dirt-gravel road. Big trucks, little trucks, cement mixers, caterpillars rumbled back and forth. Set into the side of the road were neatly laid-out villages and a schoolhouse clearly lettered C.P. The schoolhouse was low, open to the breeze — the rare one that might pass that way — with a basketball court facing it. The villages bore the names of those that were already under water, the first to be moved. Sugar cane and bananas were the crops, for it was the same type of soil. This had been part of the overall planning: sugar to sugar, coffee to coffee. When the waters crept up to the foothills where coffee was grown under banana trees, those coffee planters would be moved to similar foothills, but in the state of Veracruz. One of the problems was that the people of Veracruz did not want them, for so many had *mal del pinto*.

All along the road were C.P. signs. It reminded me of the time I wrote to friends in the States saying I was working with the C.P. and wondered later why there had been no replies. When some of them came to Mexico, I realized that McCarthyism had indeed left its mark. They had thought I was involved with the Communist Party. To us C.P. meant Comisión del Papaloapan. Now another large C.P. sign appeared on a bridge crossing a lush jungle river. We were in the state of Oaxaca and had left the state of Veracruz. Soon we would come to Nuevo Paso Nacional, a name meaning "a new national step." There the INI unit was located, and a half-mile farther on would be the big dam and Temazcal, the boom town springing up around the dam works. I sat on the edge of my seat, eager to see the dam.

Our dam! The big dam! How we of the Papaloapan Commission loved to talk about our work, and especially about our dam! When the hydroelectric plant was finished, it would provide adequate power to three states: Puebla, Veracruz, and Oaxaca. We resented the fact that foreigners were working on the hydroelectric plant, though what I kept forgetting — and so did the other two Hollanders — was that we, too, were foreigners. One of the Hollanders had helped plan the dike road along the Papaloapan River to protect the villages of Tlacotalpan and Cosamaloapan. Previously the traffic had been by river boat;

now all traffic moved along on a road built as a dike. The other Dutchman, from the Dutch East Indies, was an expert on planting in lowland tropics and was now working in Valle Nacional. On the day that the village of San Pablo Guelatao held a surprise ceremony for me, naming me honorary mayor of the town and presenting me with a gold-tipped wand. I had really become one of the men and women who were so proud to be part of the achievements of the C.P.

I talked Margarito into taking me all the way up to the top of the massive dam before he delivered me to Dr. Romano. Four years before, men who could operate bulldozers, caterpillars, and other big equipment had to be brought in from all over the Republic. Now it was the Mazatecas who were adding the finishing touches. During the jungle-clearing phase, the Indians could not believe what was told them through interpreters. They had never seen those monsters of machines, lifting earth, digging, mixing cement. Now, not only did the Indians speak Spanish, but they also knew how to operate the machines.

At our feet, where the Río Tonto was diverted, it ran shrieking, whirling, cascading through a narrow cut, furious at being controlled. At the end of the dam, directly on top, stood a building that looked like an ancient pyramid. Inside, the walls were covered with an exciting painting depicting the history of the Mazatecas, the past, the floods, and the potential future of Mexico. This mural had been executed under the supervision of Diego Rivera. On what was to be a lake stood empty houses and a lonesome church. The scene was sad, but the mural took the edge off the sadness as one glimpsed the future.

Driving down from the dam, we were in Temazcal. It looked like a boom town, with temporary buildings, shacks, houses made of corrugated tin; pigs, chickens and children running everywhere. But shining through the clouds of dust rose the modern school, primary through high school. The other building, very modern and screened, was the hospital. Both had been built by the C.P.

As we dropped toward Nuevo Paso Nacional, it grew hotter

and hotter. Already I had taken a man's handkerchief, wet it and wrapped it around my neck, hoping that the process of evaporation over my carotid artery might keep me more comfortable.

In Nuevo Paso Nacional the streets were lined with trees. Although temporary, the buildings were in good taste. A small medical building stood at the entrance to town. Farther along on a rise appeared the INI Center. We had arrived.

Dr. Romano greeted me warmly. In the offices of the Center there was hardly a blank space on the wall. Maps and dynamic charts of villages showed where the rate of malaria was decreasing, as were *mal del pinto* and hookworm. New schools were being built in new villages, and old villages in the lake area were being abandoned. The anthropologist showed me around the village, and I was impressed. In the school, children were busy printing, first in Mazateca and then in Spanish. The Frenet method of teaching was followed. Upon inquiry I learned that one of the Spanish republican refugees of 1940, a Frenet disciple, believed firmly that learning was made easier and more meaningful through printing. When he landed in Veracruz, instead of going on to Mexico City he remained in a small town, San Andrés Tuxtla, and established a school using that method. Today Mexico is dotted with Frenet schools.

Proudly, children were learning their own legends and history, as told by the old story-tellers. These accounts, as well as modern history, had been mimeographed in both languages, Mazateca and Spanish, and all were taken home to the families. Their cultural background, thus fortified, was retained by the people as they moved into the mestizo culture.

Near the school was the theater, an audio-visual center. Not that theater was held there often, but it was a base. It functioned, in fact, as a workshop. Posters were being made to help in educating the Mazatecas in certain areas, according to specific needs. For example, the day I walked in, posters concerning hookworm were being produced. Aside from other assets, these posters were valid culturally. The Mazateca woman was dressed exactly according to custom in the lower part of the Mazateca region: the birds embroidered round and round her *huipil* seemed poised for flight. If they had placed the birds in the center, the Mazateca would know immediately that the poster was wrong and that this was the *huipil* worn in the mountains by the Mazatecas of Huautla de Jiménez, an area that was not to be inundated. The poster showed a schoolchild pointing to the sandals on her feet with one hand — signifying that no hookworm could work its way through the sole — while with the other she held sandals out to her mother. The lettering was in Mazateca and Spanish. That some of the best teaching in the home could be done through the student was now especially confirmed for us.

Marco Antonio Montero, a young man in his late twenties, was already known for his direction of Arthur Miller's plays in Mexico City. Dr. Gonzalo Aguirre Beltrán, who always had the knack of getting people he wanted to drop what they were doing and work for him, was behind Marco's trip to San Cristóbal de Las Casas, where the first INI demonstration unit had been established to work with the Chamula Indians. With the Chamulas, Marco had developed the use of the puppet theater. Naturally, when the important work in the Papaloapan Basin began, he transferred to the unit at Nuevo Paso Nacional. Puppets hung on the walls, puppets were being made, puppets were being dressed exactly as they should have been. I saw the snakelike spirochetes that caused *mal del pinto*. There were puppets that looked like bats in the antiencephalitis play, portraying the danger of the bat's bite. Puppets, puppets all over the place.

From there the plays went out by jeep to the river, and up the river by boat to the villagers who were to move out. The puppets discussed everything, such as, "Have you got your land grant given by the King of Spain during the early colonial period?" A Mazateca would ask, "Why?" and the puppet would answer, "So that you can be paid for your lands, of course, and get the same kind of land for your crops." Both Indian and puppet could say things that would not have been said normally. I had discovered this trick in the Upper Papaloapan, and Marco had been using it for years. He was an expert. I planned to learn from him in any spare time I had.

From the theater workshop we walked over to the little house that had been the laboratory for the medical unit, where I was to sleep that week. It was near the river. Across from it was the basketball court and the community dining room. The dining room seemed to cower under the big dam that loomed in the distance. Every time I ate there, I couldn't help hoping that the dam was strong and well built. Despite the nearness of the river, all we got was meat, tough meat at that.

I still had to face the medical staff, and I hoped that Julio de la Fuente had not told the doctors that I had said I would not teach doctors because they were so compartmentalized. Walking down the slope to the medical building, I was aware of the warm greetings given to Dr. Romano, greetings that were returned with equal warmth.

I was introduced to the young doctor in charge, Dr. Ignacio Barragán, who later became director of the School of Rural Medicine at the National Polytechnic Institute in Mexico City. With him were four other young doctors, and a staff that consisted of a laboratory technician and a nurse-midwife. I knew that, being from the newly established "Poly" rather than the more staid National University, they would be less compartmentalized, for Poly students had more sociology, more humanities, and a global education relating to Mexico's needs. Nevertheless, I could not see myself teaching doctors. These were young doctors who might know their medicine, but I doubted that they knew anything of teaching skills or how to break up their knowledge into words understandable to the people with whom they worked.

In their eyes I could read what they were thinking. I was a

foreigner and not a doctor. Therefore, it seemed much more logical to invite them to listen to me teach the teachers. I suggested to them that, since they knew much more than I, perhaps they would be good enough to criticize my teaching for health when we met at supper each night. I could sense the expansion of their young egos. Dr. Romano said nothing, but I could see he approved of my idea.

With an anthropologist in charge, it meant that the medical work was being coordinated with the school, the puppet brigade, and other projects. The doctors took turns going by boat and then by mule to the home areas of the Mazatecas who were to be moved out. Their objective was to help them become as free of disease as possible. When they invited me to go with them on one of their trips, I said I would be delighted to travel by boat, but no more than that. I wanted relief from a mule for at least a few weeks. The mule and I never did really take to each other.

I began my all-day, four-day teaching stint with the teachers, the students and the medical staff, following the same pattern I had worked out for other zones where I taught. First, I summarized the systems of the body and how they operated. Then I demonstrated how to explain, how to dramatize, so that these systems would come to life, and how to integrate this knowledge through all phases of the school program. Germs, the good ones and the bad ones, I explained with emphasis here on the spirochete that causes *mal del pinto*. Then I went on to the intestinal worms, and the bugs that bite and leave their victims with an unwelcome gift. And I did not forget first-aid and home nursing. As I spoke, sweat ran down my face. Every day I wet a long, soft towel and wrapped it around my neck. I have never felt such humid heat, or such biting insects. By the end of the week I was covered with welts and swellings.

Before supper I would walk to the river. It looked so placid on the surface, but I had been told how dangerous it was. Its name was Río Tonto, meaning foolish river. Finally I stepped in, but kept close to the bank. That water at least was cool.

Even after the sun had set, it was hot in Nuevo Paso Nacional. When we sat around the dining room tables — the medical staff, the teaching staff, the anthropologist, and Marco of the puppets — I kept the wet towel on my neck while we shared our knowledge and experiences, giving and taking until we all felt we had learned from one another.

My week was up, and I promised to return the next month — not that I had become accustomed to the heat, but I did love working in the INI unit with Dr. Romano and his staff. However, all I wanted at that moment was to get a lift to Oaxaca in one of our planes, either the bimotor of Ciudad Alemán or our own Cessna. I was in an agony of prickly heat and swollen bites, and near heat prostration.

At Ciudad Alemán I made my verbal report to both the medical and educational directors. I was out of luck, for there was no plane to fly me home, and I had to wait for the bus to take me out. I decided to go by the southern route, inasmuch as I had not traveled it before. It was a short ride from Ciudad Alemán to Veracruz, only a few hours. At Alvarado we stopped to wait for the ferry, then crossed the mighty Papaloapan where it enters the sea. As I bought fried fish roe at a stand, I watched children dancing *la bamba*, each with a full glass of water poised on his head, and never a drop spilled.

The ferry struggled against the strong current to avoid being swept to sea, as had happened several times in the past. Gradually we began climbing out of the desperate heat and rode alongside a lovely long lake. The surrounding hills were covered with mounds and pyramids, marking a large Totonaca site. Totonacas still live there. I had read that the lake was formed when six volcanoes blew their tops. I made up my mind then and there that someday I would vacation at Lake Catemaco. Dropping again, we came to the narrow Isthmus of Tehuantepec.

The bus was to continue south along the Gulf of Mexico, so I had to change buses for the trip west to Tehuantepec. As I waited in Acayucan for a bus to take me across the Isthmus, I sat opposite the jail and observed the bargaining process as prisoners at the bars tried to sell their handmade goods, chiefly bags and hammocks. Lord, it was hot!

There was a new four-lane highway to Tehuantepec, and within two hours we were there. From Tehuantepec, it was only six more hours to Oaxaca, but I decided to spend the night there, in order to witness the Tehuana scenes that Miguel Covarrúbias described so well in his book, *Mexico South*. The Zapoteca women of the Isthmus are outstandingly different from those of the Valley of Oaxaca and the mountain areas. In the Valley and in the mountains, the Zapotecas don't think too much of the Isthmus women who, in their opinion, wear the pants in the family. To see the women vendors in the market at six in the morning, it certainly looked like it. All the commerce was run by them, while the men worked in the fields. I had seen Tehuanas at Zacatepec, where they arrived after five or six days of tough, uphill mountain climbing. On the market square they sat relaxed, sure of themselves, selling their dried fish. Great women, I thought.

Six hours later I was back in Oaxaca — home. It had taken longer this way, but it had been more interesting. Despite the heat, I looked forward to returning to Nuevo Paso Nacional — but please, by plane?

At least I would have a little more than two weeks at home. The next Teacher's Institute was to be held in Tamazulapan, in the Mixe area. It was only a two-day mule trip, and not too much climbing. I even looked forward to being on a cold mountain-top after the heat of Nuevo Paso Nacional. I simply could not take the heat, and was not too surprised that I wasn't feeling well. I blamed it on the heat, as I continued working and getting ready for the Tamazulapan meeting.

The first day on the mule was not too bad, but on the second day dusk fell quickly, and the mule and I both shivered. I was cold and could not control the chills. Fortunately, both David

The Victory

and the mule knew the way. All I recall is being lifted off the mule and placed on school tables pushed together to make a bed. Later my fever rose so high that I became irrational. One teacher had an Arelen medication with her, and another had penicillin. Each one gave me a hypo. How confusing to the enemies in my body that must have been! One was against malaria, and the other — who knows what it was for! My chills and fever did subside, but I was too weak to teach.

While I lay on the tables, a young priest who had been assigned to the Mixes came to call on me. I wondered if it were because he wanted to give me the last rites, and quickly I said, "I am not a Catholic!"

He laughed and replied, "No. I only want to know if you can get the Papaloapan Commission to match the 1,000 pesos we have raised."

"What do you want it for? That's what they will ask me," I managed to tell him.

He explained that the primary school wanted to establish a preprimary and nursery school. I assured him I would try to influence my boss to match the funds.

He was one of the many priests I met in the mountains, helping me to unlearn the bias against the Catholic clergy my family had given me as a child. He himself was a victim of bias. He was a dark-skinned Mexican Indian; and since the bishop preferred light-skinned priests from Europe, he had been sent to the hills, along with many others of his kind. Most of them became my friends. We were working on the same wave lengths, they for the Catholic Church and I for the Commission.

But now that I was lucid, how was I to get out? Runners had been sent to notify our office to order the jeep to the terminal point of our road. Slowly, with David's help, I was able to make it down the slopes to the spot where we hoped the jeep would be waiting. It was not there. David stole some corn from the fields, and we ate roasted ears to sustain us. My chills were beginning again.

What a relief, finally, to see the jeep come around the last curve to where the road ended! Two hours later I was in my own bed, and sick. Obviously I had malaria — chills and fever daily. Horrible, horrible! And I would have to expect recurrences, all because a mosquito had bitten me two weeks before at Nuevo Paso Nacional, a mosquito who had not read the C.P. sign saying that the area had been sprayed with DDT.

If only we had worked by the same rules as the Commission for the Eradication of Malaria. Their workers had to take preventive pills twice a week. If they got malaria, they were fired. Why hadn't anyone told me of those preventive pills? Although I was back in the office within 15 days, I was to take pills for three months to prevent the recurrences. With whom was I angry, myself or the mosquito?

Eating hot liver at home and cold liver sandwiches at the office, I tried to restore a bit of iron to my blood stream, as I struggled with reports. Working with engineers of all kinds — road, civil, sanitary, and so forth, as well as agronomists and architects, whose achievements could be readily measured by miles of roads built, numbers of small dams constructed, trees planted, schools erected, and so on, my reports were unsatisfactory. Raúl Sandoval, that wonderful young man whose vision and hard work inspired us all to give of ourselves until it ached, wanted photos. The Commission bought me a Brownie 2A, the only camera I thought I could handle. I did not particularly like to take photos, but I had to take them for a photo mural of my work. Every year there was a photo exhibition of the works of the Papaloapan Commission.

Mr. Sandoval understood as I explained that real results could be measured only over a period of time, as mortality and morbidity rates dropped. He had seen the photos I took of the new nursing station at Valerio Trujano: health workers learning to bandage; babies being weighed on a fish scale; puppet shows presented; babies, placed on a low wooden frame and not the dirt floor, getting drops in their eyes immediately after delivery. When he saw those he said, "You are not a photographer." I agreed. He decided that the Commission's official photographer should follow me about and take photos. Carlos Leal was a marvelous photographer, and I was eager to see his photos. Not that Carlos especially liked going to some of the areas to which I traveled.

One day I sat in the office awaiting instructions and hoping I would not see another mule for a long time. Suddenly, over the radio-phone, I heard excited voices and crackling. It sounded like, "The plane is crashing!" My first concern was for Captain Silva and our Cessna. The announcements continued, "The plane is burning!"

Those aboard were Raúl Sandoval, our executive director; the pilot; and Carlos Leal, the photographer. All were burned to death. We wept for them all.

With the loss of our beloved Raúl Sandoval, we could not help but feel that Mexico had lost part of her future. He was about 35 years old, intelligent, erudite, an excellent engineer, a fine organizer. He knew every nook and cranny of the watershed. The Indians loved him; his staff loved him. When he was graduated from the National University, he went to work in Michoacán on the test watershed area in Uruapan. There Lázaro Cárdenas was planning a complete watershed control project, global in concept. Sandoval and many others in the Papaloapan Commission had worked with Cárdenas. He strengthened their idealism and helped direct it toward positive work. The greatest of the young engineers was Raúl Sandoval, and now he was dead.

We were numb. Whom would the President appoint in his place? We waited as we listened to the reports of the Indians from the hills who were walking down to the funeral rites in Ciudad Alemán, where the ashes of all three were to be buried. The next day we hung around the radio-phone listening, listening and sorrowing.

The immediate director of our Upper Papaloapan office was

encouraged to continue his position. His name was W. Jiménez, the engineer who shortly afterward died of a heart attack on the road we were building across the divide, the most difficult section. Again, the bottom dropped out from under us, even though we liked the engineer who came to take his place, Anaur Abdalla, who was transferred from the Lower Papaloapan office. He, too, was a member of the Commission's young group of dedicated workers.

I had had one case of chicken pox, two bouts with malaria, and one split muscle in my abdomen. Therefore, I had merely closed my eyes when the mule went around sharp turns on a narrow ledge, or when the plane felt as if it would surely crash in landing — only somewhat frightened, taking things good-humoredly. Now, suddenly, I saw accidents and illness everywhere I went. I wondered if I were becoming psychotic. In traveling over the new road being constructed to meet the one from the Veracruz side of the divide, I saw great sections of road that looked as if they would slide down with the first rain. Worrying about the bite of the black fly and ensuing blindness, I found I was avoiding going in that direction. What if I should contract *mal del pinto*? Could I stand another attack of malaria? My hernia had reappeared, and another bias muscle had split. I felt like a hypochondriac, but mainly I was scared. At the same time, who wanted to forego the honor and pleasure of working with the staff and the people of the Papaloapan watershed? Not I. I would wait for better health and the new executive director.

And then came the new man, appointed by the President to take over where Raúl Sandoval had left off. Listening to him once, twice, observing the changing attitudes, I decided I wanted to get out. From greatness we had fallen to pettiness. I spoke to Mr. Abdalla about resigning.

"You can't," he said.

"Why not?" I asked.

He explained that a federal employee could be fired, but could not resign; it simply was not done. Instead, I would be given indefinite leave, indefinite sick leave. A strange custom, but still it feels good to know that I am on leave from the Papaloapan Commission and can move on to the Río Balsas Commission if I can ever stand the sight of a mule again.

Less and less money was available. True, most of the major works had been finished, such as the big dam, the 20,000 Mazatecas moved out of the lake area, the connecting road from Oaxaca to Veracruz nearly completed. The hydroelectric plant was in operation. Whole areas and landscapes had been changed. Most significant of all, the people within the watershed, Indian and mestizo, had been treated with as much interest as a new hydroelectric plant. Never before in Mexico had such a tremendous undertaking as the control and utilization of the mighty Papaloapan River been executed.

There is a time to stay with a job, and a time to leave it. That was my time to leave. Physically, in particular, it was time to leave. In the past I had felt bright enough from the neck up, but now I was weak all over. I felt every one of my 52 years. Then the splitting muscle finally gave way, resulting in a strangulated hernia. That meant immediate hospitalization. I felt lucky merely to be alive.

Toby was finishing primary school and getting ready for high school. What next? The best immediate thing was to take in house guests to make ends meet; also, to rent the back part of a store that sold arts and crafts and begin to sell some of my own collection from the mountains.

In late 1956 an anthropology congress on a national level was held in Oaxaca. While attending the meetings, Marco Antonio Montero, the puppet master who had become theater director at the University of Veracruz, told me that Dr. Gonzalo Aguirre Beltrán, now president of the University, wanted to see me. I admired him greatly. To me he was and is Mexico's greatest anthropologist, the man who gave a unique humanistic slant to Mexican anthropology. I rushed off to look for him.

When we met, his first question was, "What are you doing?"

I replied, "Nothing."

"Whom are you teaching?" he persisted.

"No one at this point," I told him. "Because of my health, I can't work as I did."

"But you must teach," he said, and told me of developments in the University of Veracruz. A school of anthropology had been established, as well as schools of history, philosophy, and some others. He asked me to join his staff, and suggested that I visit Jalapa to see the setup for myself and then decide.

As soon as I was able, I took the bus to Jalapa and explored the plant of the University of Veracruz, as well as school facilities for Toby. I already knew that it would be a marvelous learning experience to work under Dr. Beltrán.

"What specifically do you want me to do?" I asked him, and he told me: 1) teach anthropology and public health to fourth-year anthropology students; 2) teach the members of the graduating class in medicine, anthropology and public health before they go off to do their social service; and 3) establish a school for foreign students, first as a summer session, then trying for an all-year program.

With my experience, the first two would be no problem; but a school for foreign students was something entirely new to me. But I learned how to handle it in the following five years at the University of Veracruz.

On May 10, 1962, while I was working in Jalapa, Veracruz, President Adolfo López Mateos signed the decree making me a Mexican citizen! All the fears of the FBI seemed to lift off my shoulders. Suddenly I felt free. I was home.